A Tropical Fish
Yearns for Snow

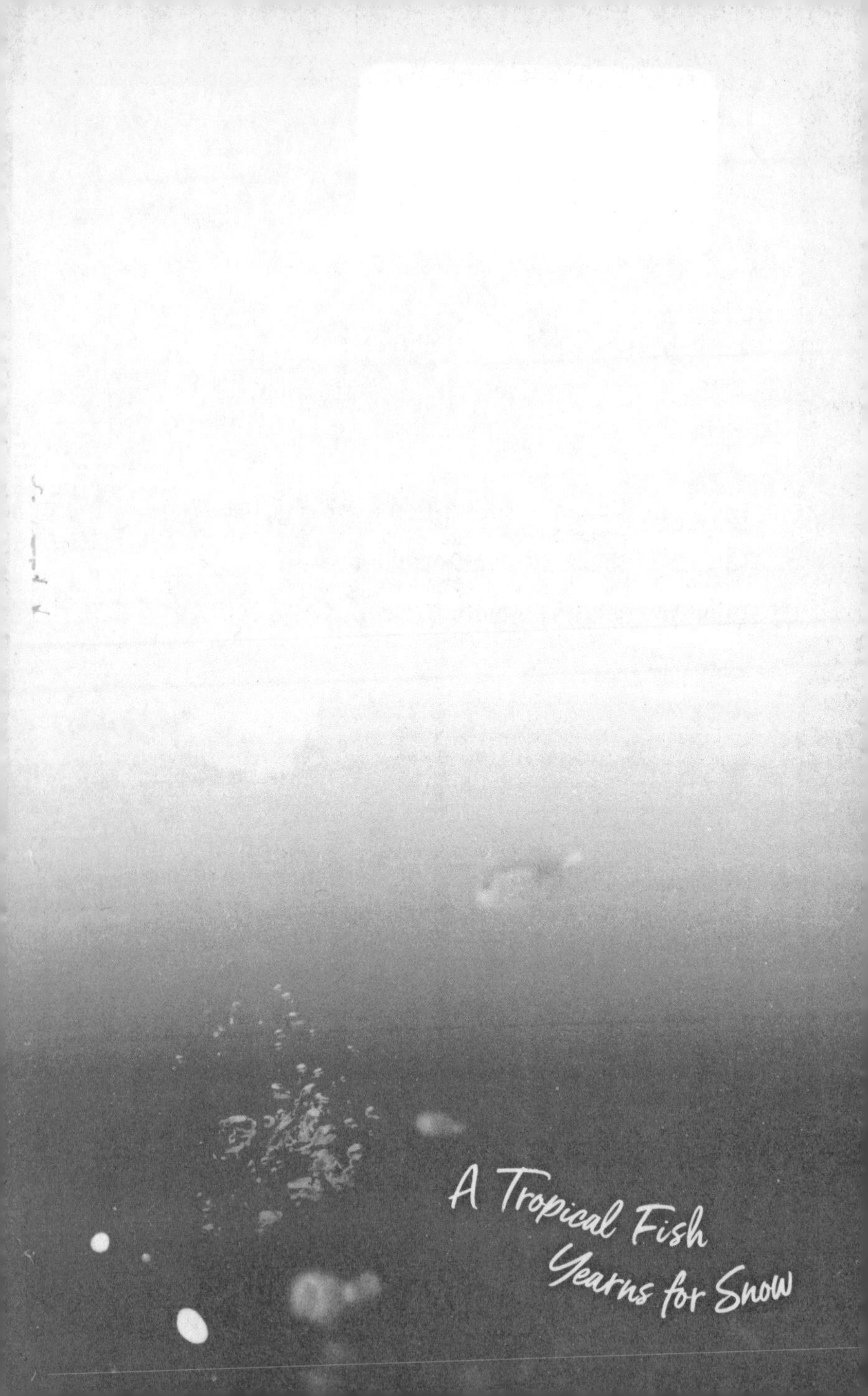
A Tropical Fish
Yearns for Snow

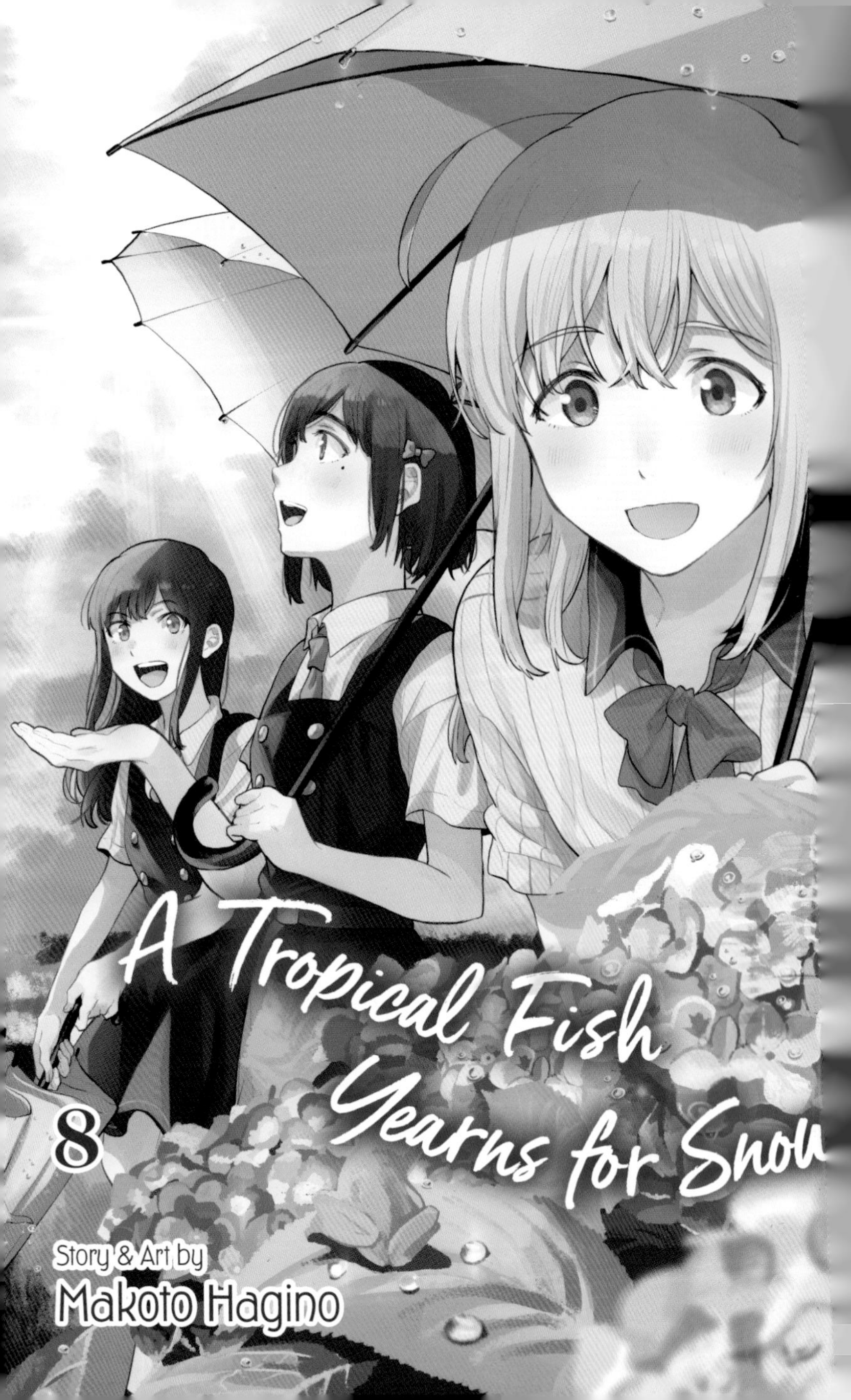
A Tropical Fish Yearns for Snow
8
Story & Art by
Makoto Hagino

The Story So Far

Konatsu transfers to Nanahama High School from the city and meets Koyuki, the only member of the Aquarium Club. The two girls naturally take a liking to each other because they're both lonely, so Konatsu ends up joining the club. Konatsu and Koyuki begin to spend more time together, but this leads to a painful misunderstanding. Konatsu confronts Koyuki with the feelings in her heart, and they reaffirm their bond with each other. Meanwhile, Konatsu still misses her father, but she comes to terms with the realization that loneliness doesn't always fade with time and decides she's ready to face the future. Circumstances are slowly changing for both girls...

...cters

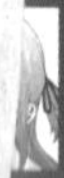

Konatsu Amano

A second-year student who transferred to ...ma High School as a first- ...he had trouble adapting to ...w surroundings until she met ... and joined the Aquarium Club.

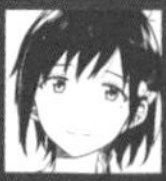

Koyuki Honami

A third-year student and president of the Aquarium Club. Everyone puts her on a pedestal, but she has gradually been breaking out of her shell.

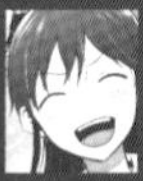

Kaede Hirose

Konatsu's classmate. Due to her perky personality, she has many friends. She's close friends with both Konatsu and Koyuki.

Tank 28: Konatsu Amano Can't Prevent It

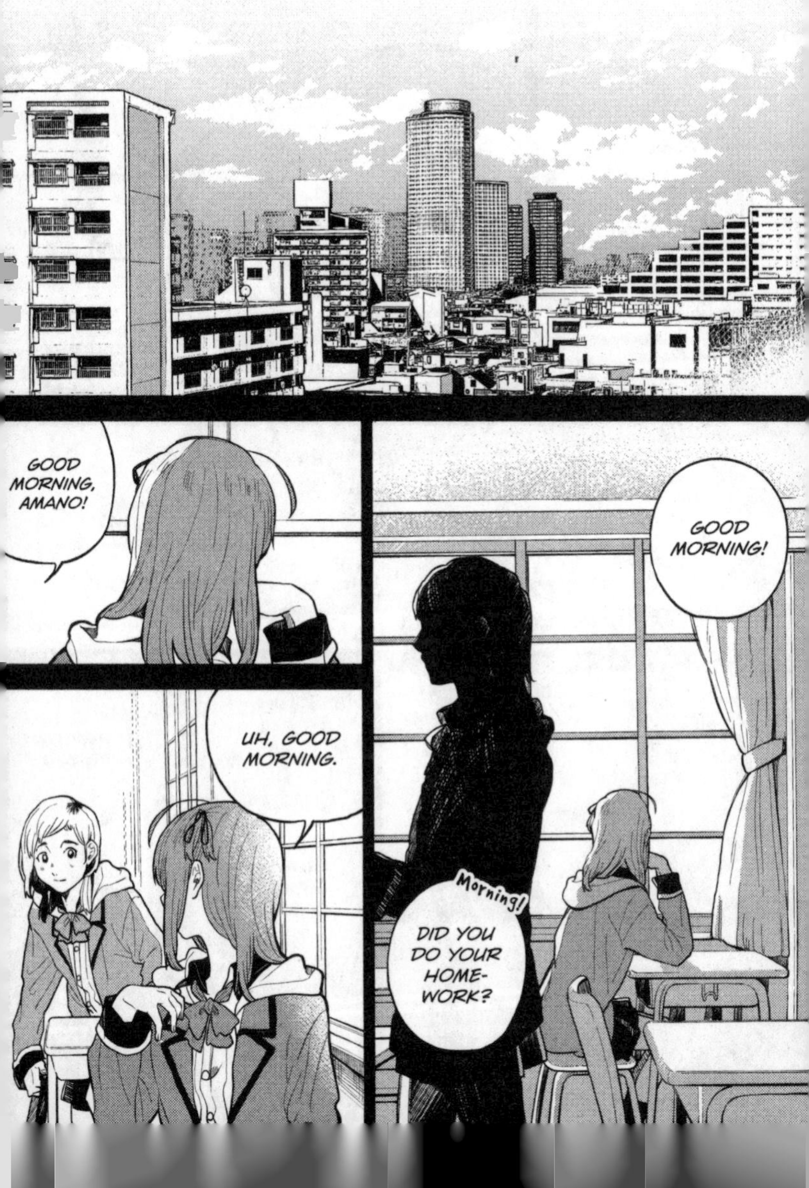
GOOD MORNING!
Morning!
DID YOU DO YOUR HOME-WORK?
GOOD MORNING, AMANO!
UH, GOOD MORNING.

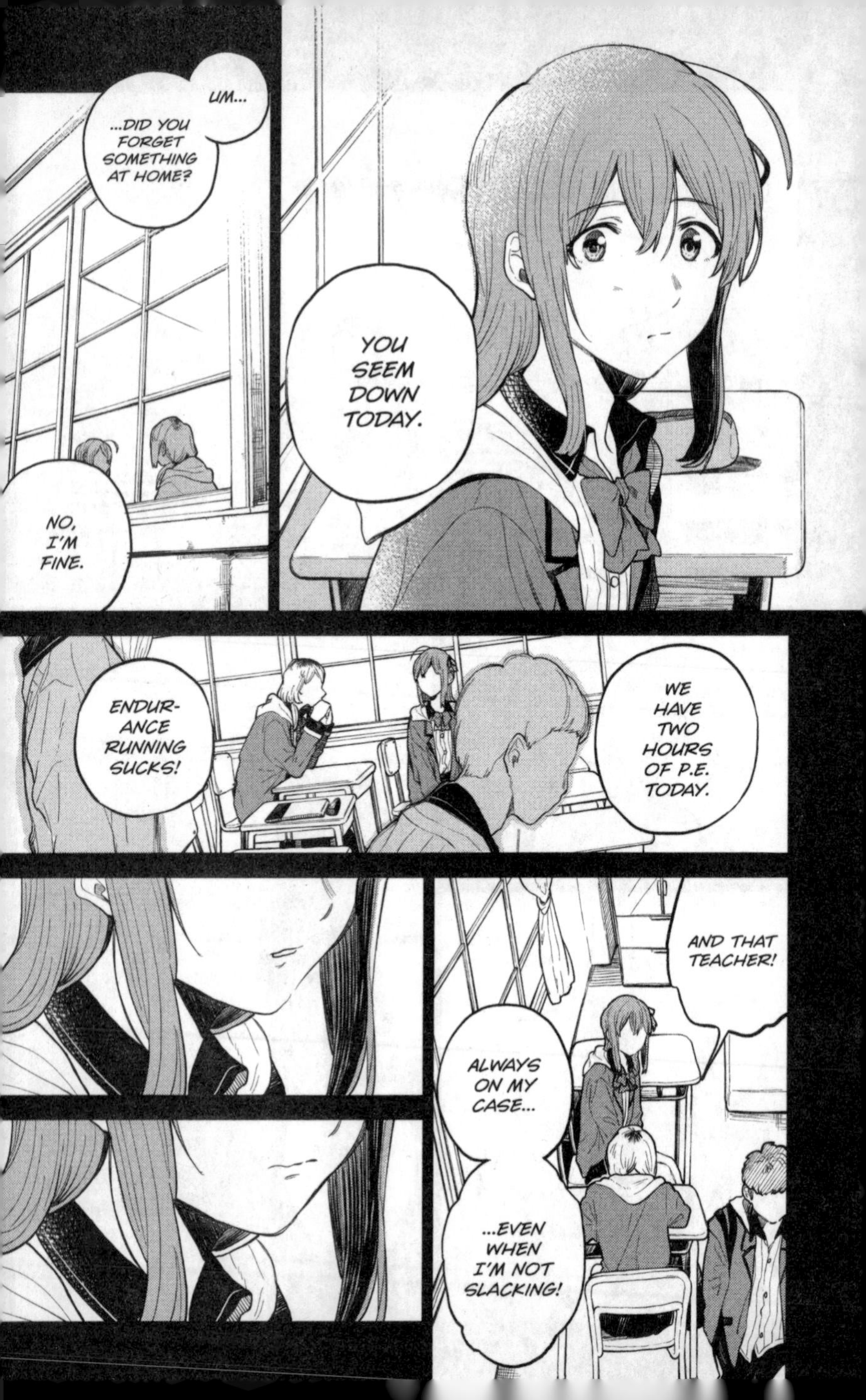
YOU SEEM DOWN TODAY.
UM...
...DID YOU FORGET SOMETHING AT HOME?
NO, I'M FINE.
WE HAVE TWO HOURS OF P.E. TODAY.
ENDURANCE RUNNING SUCKS!
AND THAT TEACHER!
ALWAYS ON MY CASE...
...EVEN WHEN I'M NOT SLACKING!

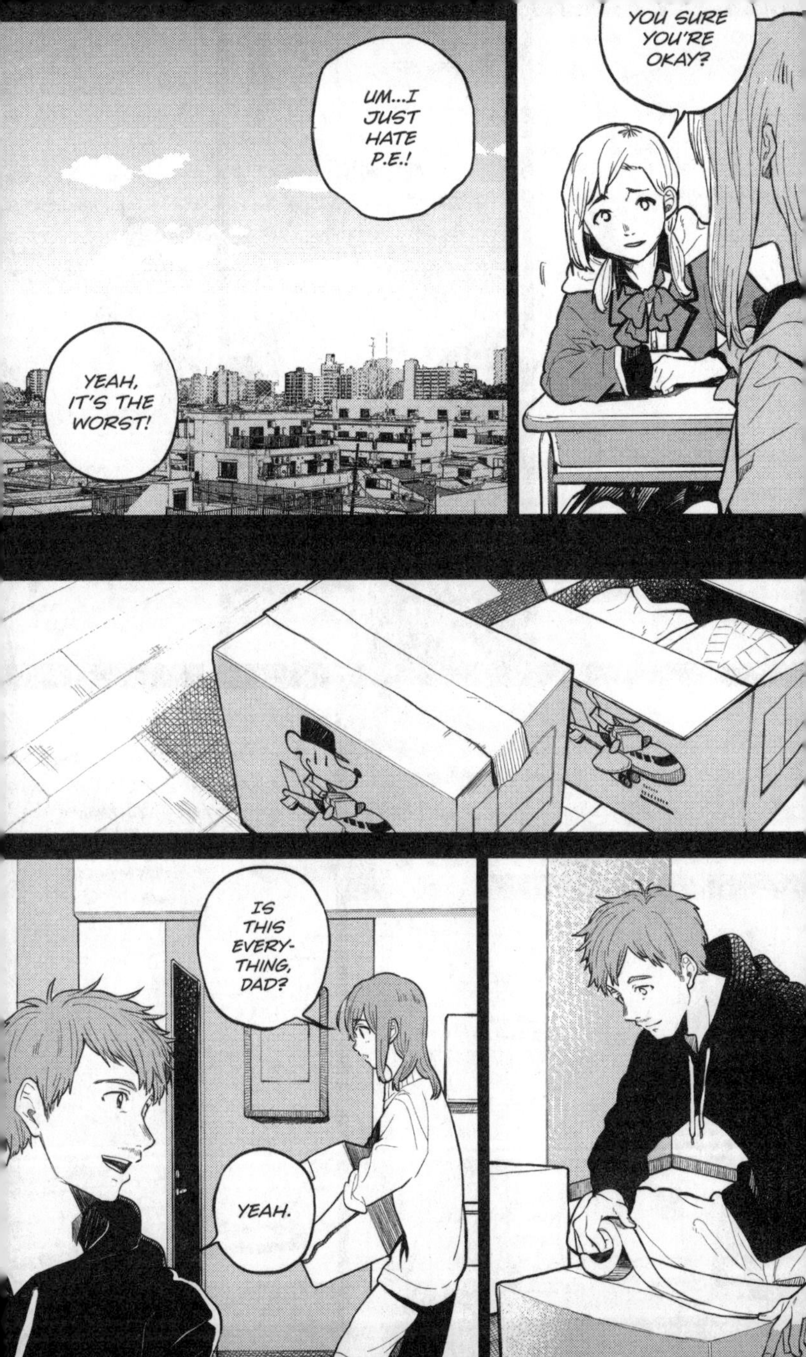
YOU SURE YOU'RE OKAY?
UM...I JUST HATE P.E.!
YEAH, IT'S THE WORST!
IS THIS EVERY-THING, DAD?
YEAH.

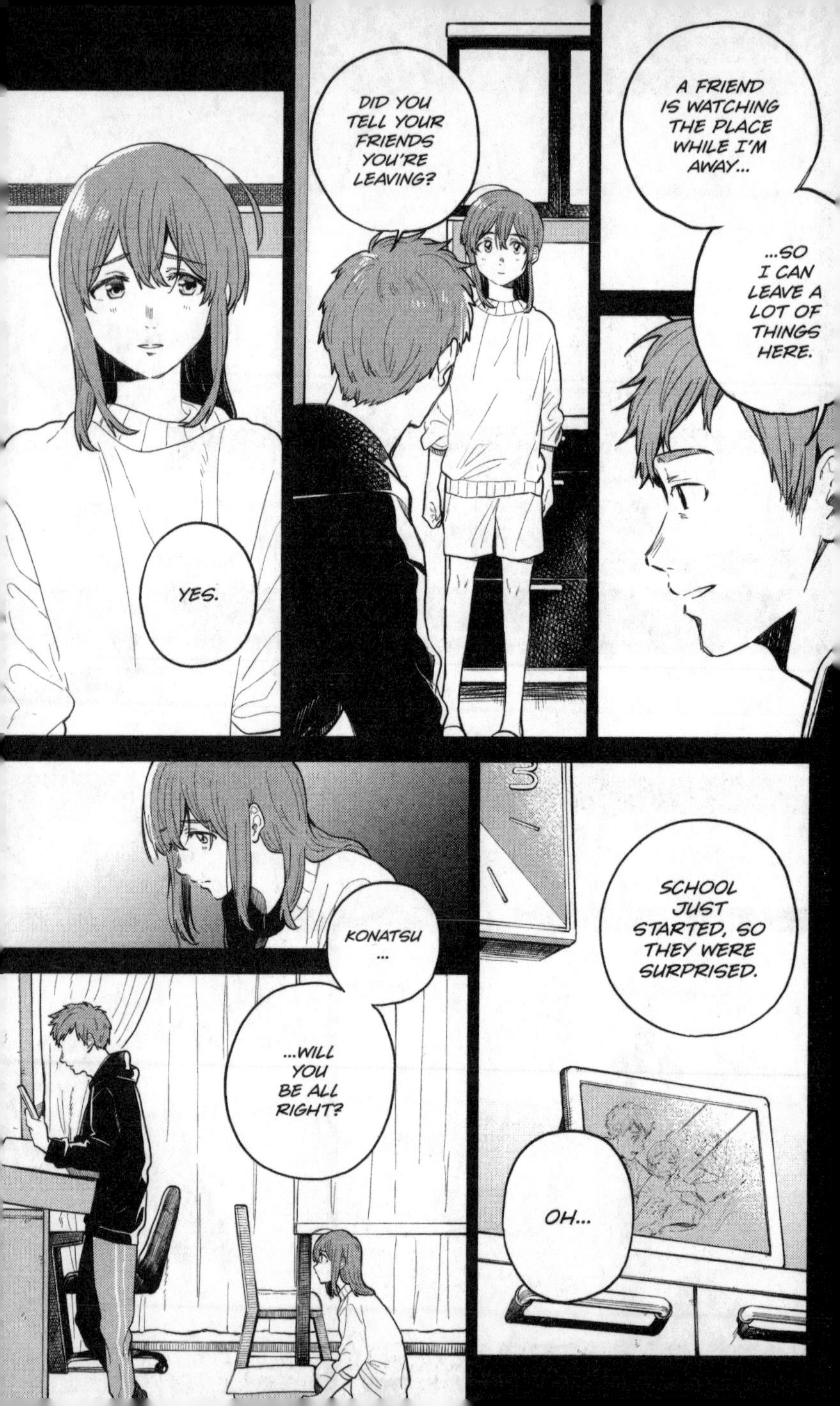
A FRIEND IS WATCHING THE PLACE WHILE I'M AWAY...
...SO I CAN LEAVE A LOT OF THINGS HERE.
DID YOU TELL YOUR FRIENDS YOU'RE LEAVING?
YES.
SCHOOL JUST STARTED, SO THEY WERE SURPRISED.
OH...
KONATSU...
...WILL YOU BE ALL RIGHT?

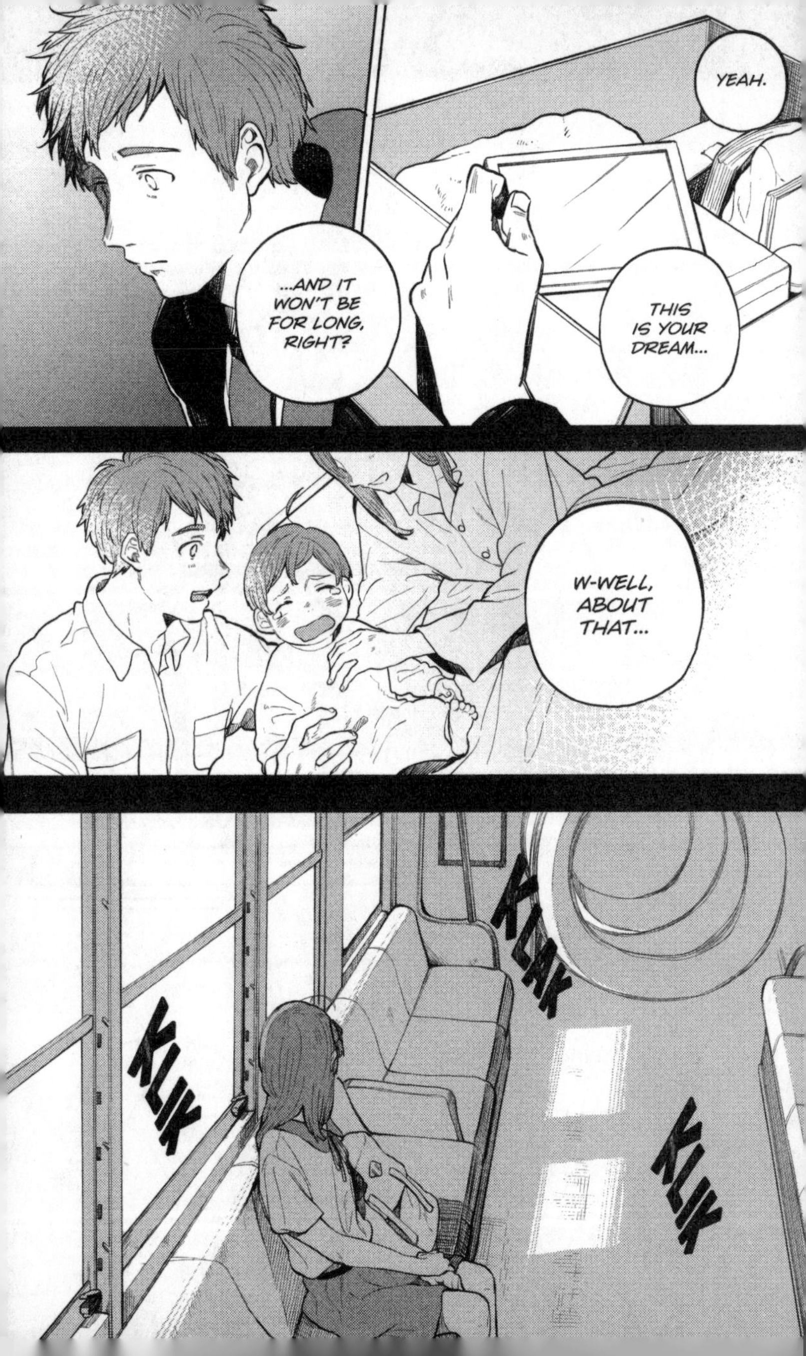
YEAH.
THIS IS YOUR DREAM...
...AND IT WON'T BE FOR LONG, RIGHT?
W-WELL, ABOUT THAT...
KLAK
KLIK
KLIK

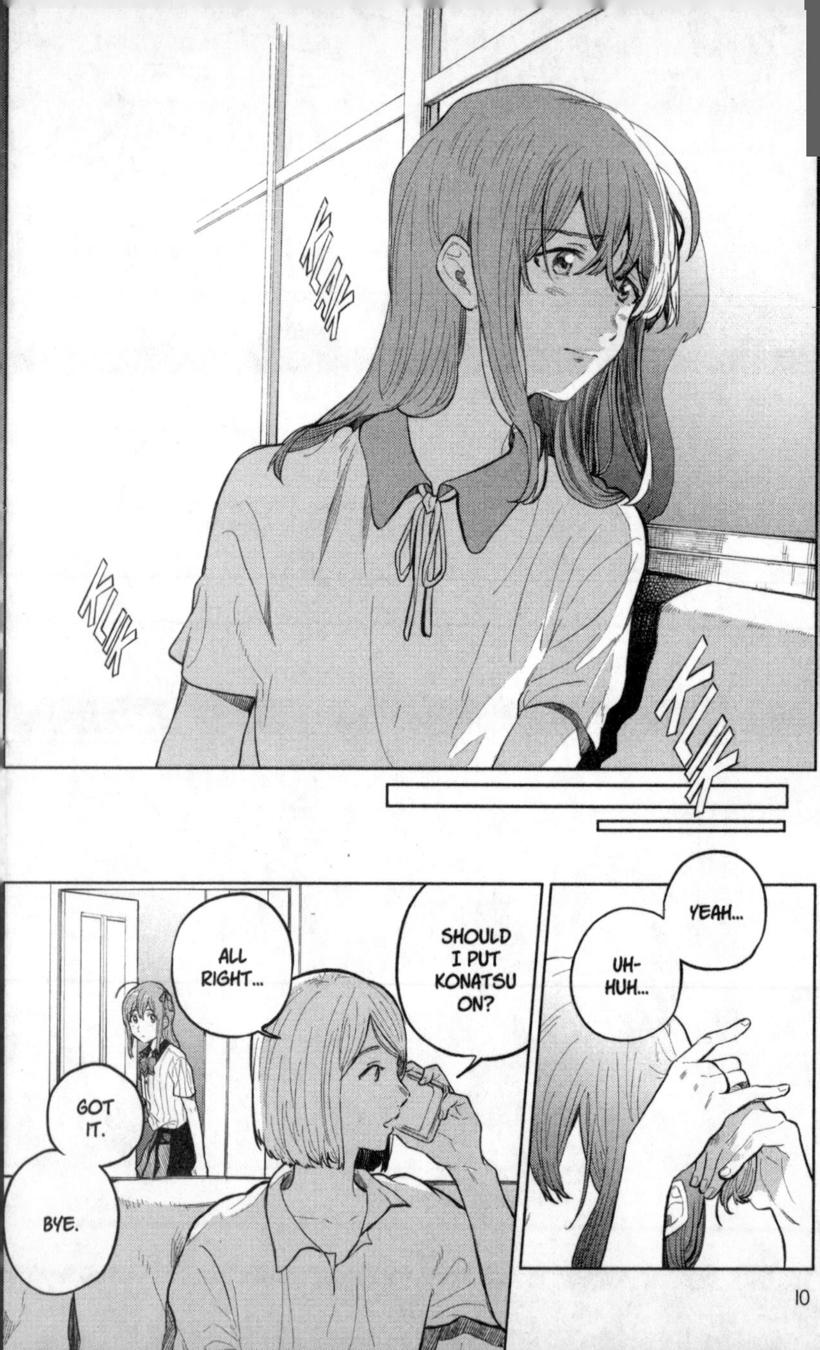
KLAK
KLIK
KLIK
YEAH...
UH-HUH...
SHOULD I PUT KONATSU ON?
ALL RIGHT...
GOT IT.
BYE.

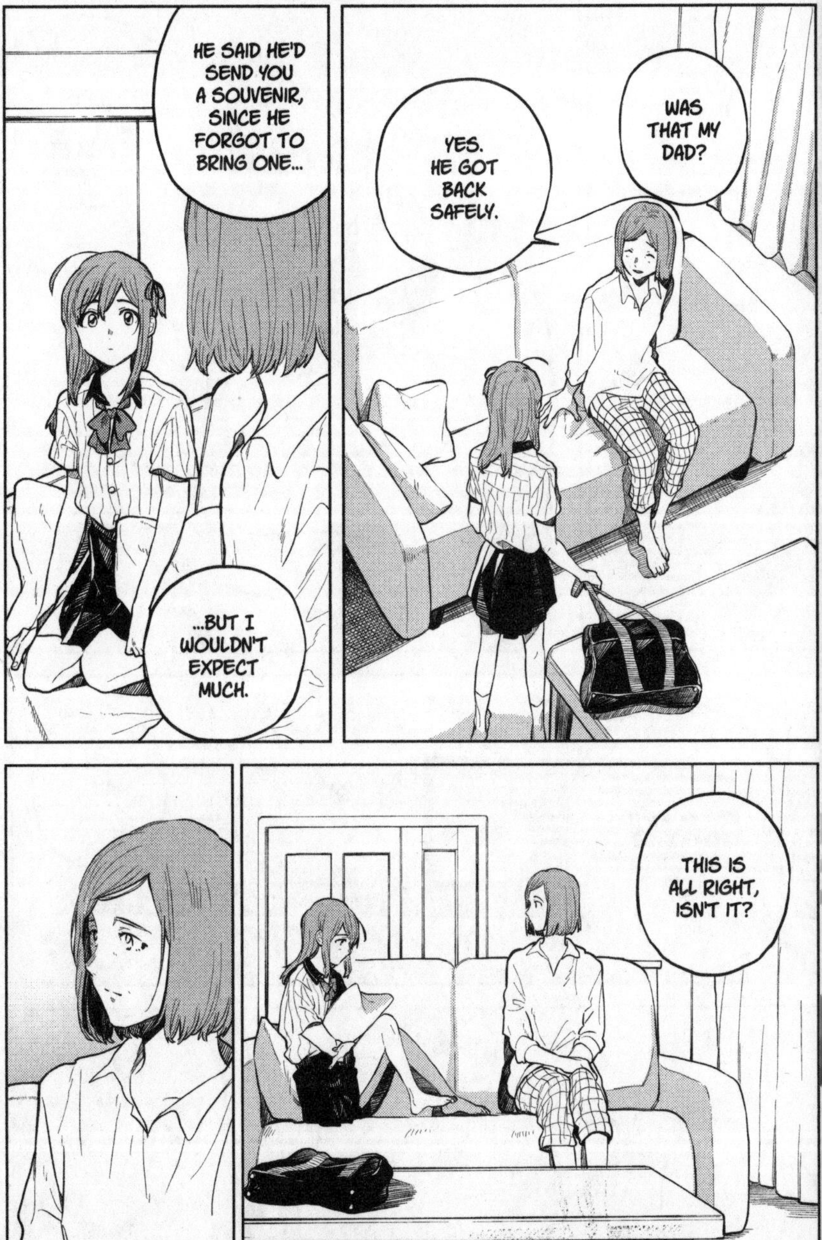
WAS THAT MY DAD?
YES. HE GOT BACK SAFELY.
HE SAID HE'D SEND YOU A SOUVENIR, SINCE HE FORGOT TO BRING ONE...
...BUT I WOULDN'T EXPECT MUCH.
THIS IS ALL RIGHT, ISN'T IT?

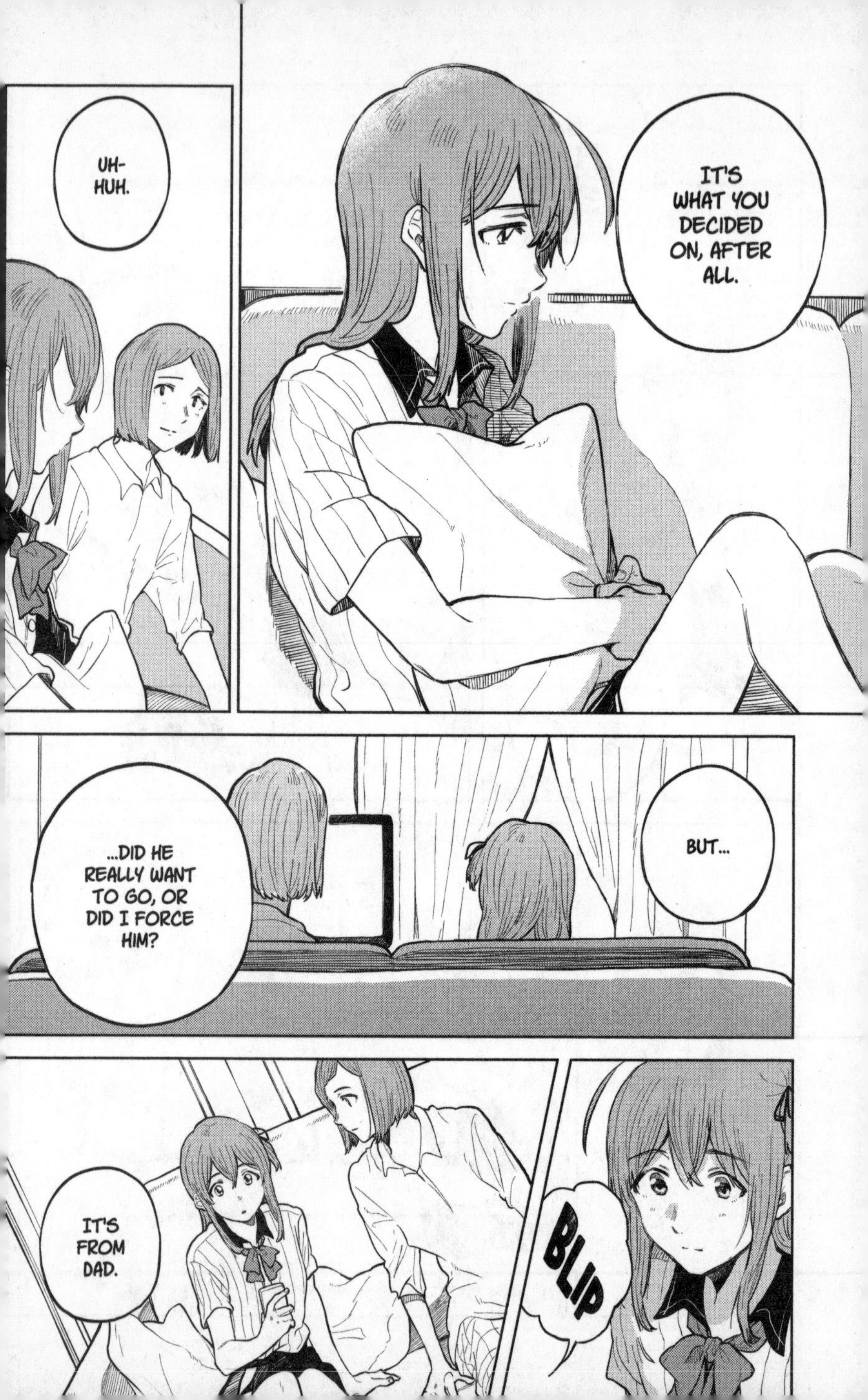
IT'S WHAT YOU DECIDED ON, AFTER ALL.
UH-HUH.
BUT...
...DID HE REALLY WANT TO GO, OR DID I FORCE HIM?
BLIP
IT'S FROM DAD.

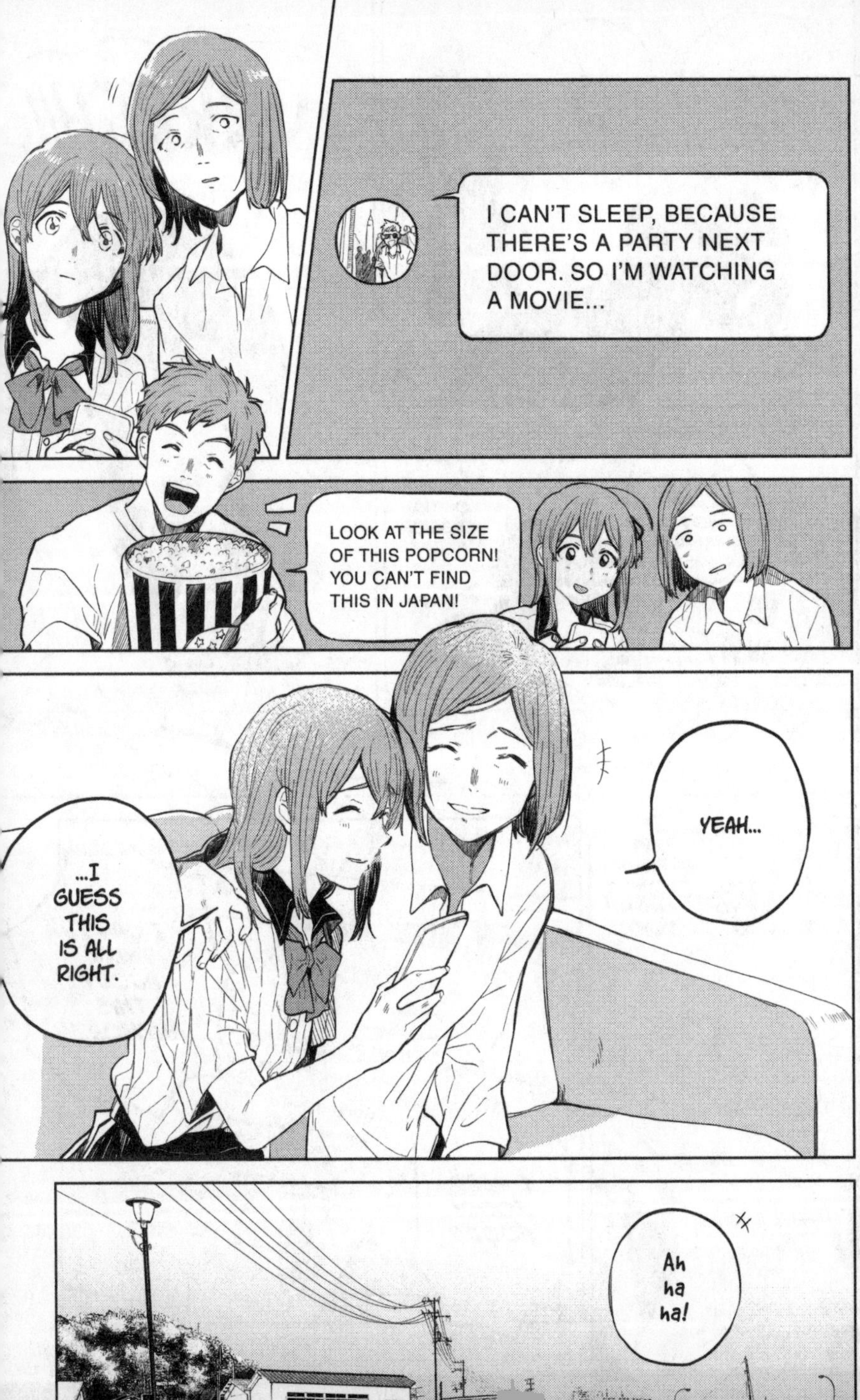
I CAN'T SLEEP, BECAUSE THERE'S A PARTY NEXT DOOR. SO I'M WATCHING A MOVIE...
LOOK AT THE SIZE OF THIS POPCORN! YOU CAN'T FIND THIS IN JAPAN!
YEAH...
...I GUESS THIS IS ALL RIGHT.
Ah ha ha!

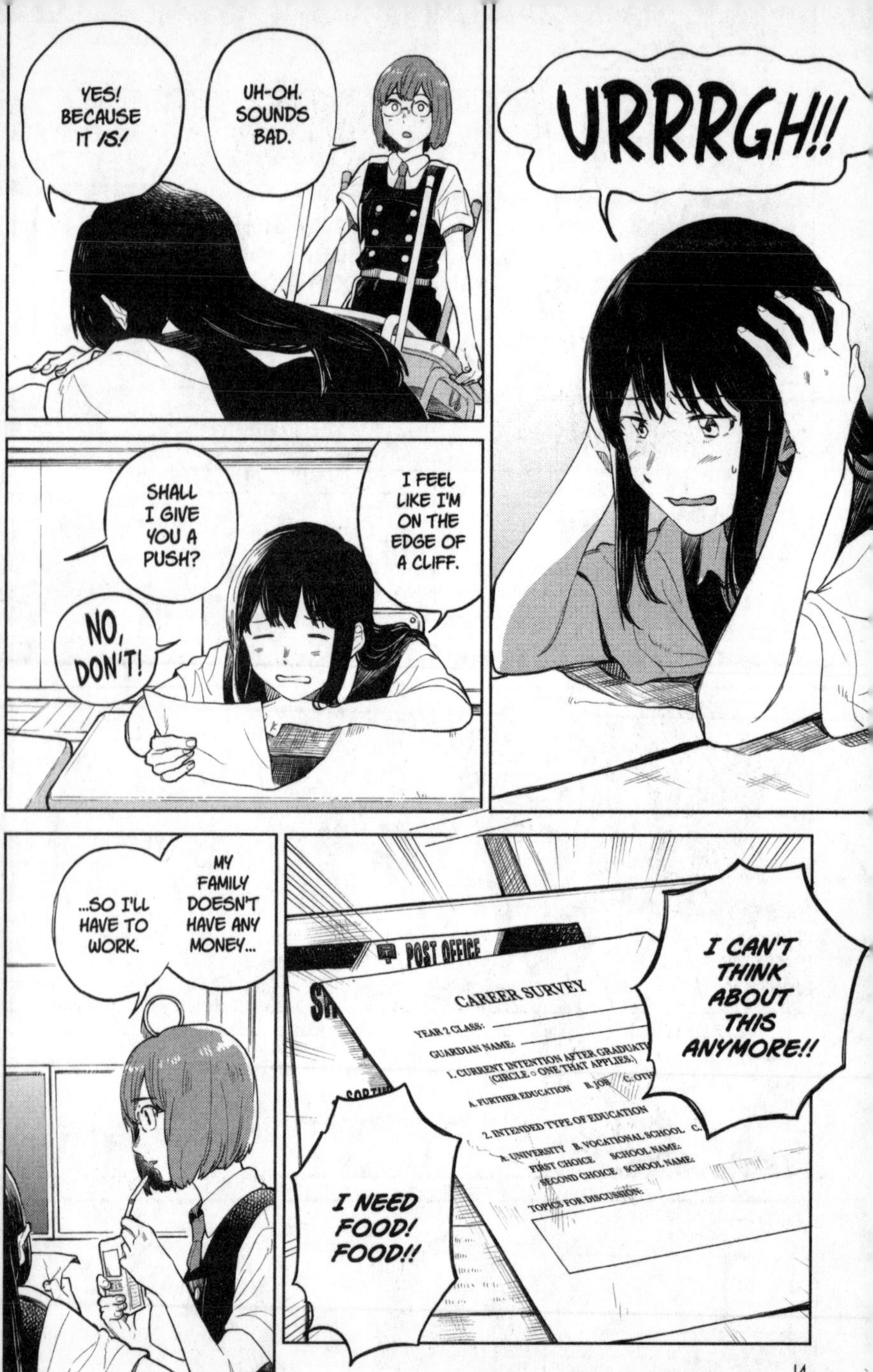
URRRGH!!
UH-OH. SOUNDS BAD.
YES! BECAUSE IT IS!
I FEEL LIKE I'M ON THE EDGE OF A CLIFF.
SHALL I GIVE YOU A PUSH?
NO, DON'T!
I CAN'T THINK ABOUT THIS ANYMORE!!
POST OFFICE
CAREER SURVEY
YEAR 2 CLASS:
GUARDIAN NAME:
(CIRCLE ○ ONE THAT APPLIES.)
A. FURTHER EDUCATION B. JOB
2. INTENDED TYPE OF EDUCATION
A. UNIVERSITY B. VOCATIONAL SCHOOL
FIRST CHOICE SCHOOL NAME:
SECOND CHOICE SCHOOL NAME:
TOPICS FOR DISCUSSION:
I NEED FOOD! FOOD!!
MY FAMILY DOESN'T HAVE ANY MONEY...
...SO I'LL HAVE TO WORK.

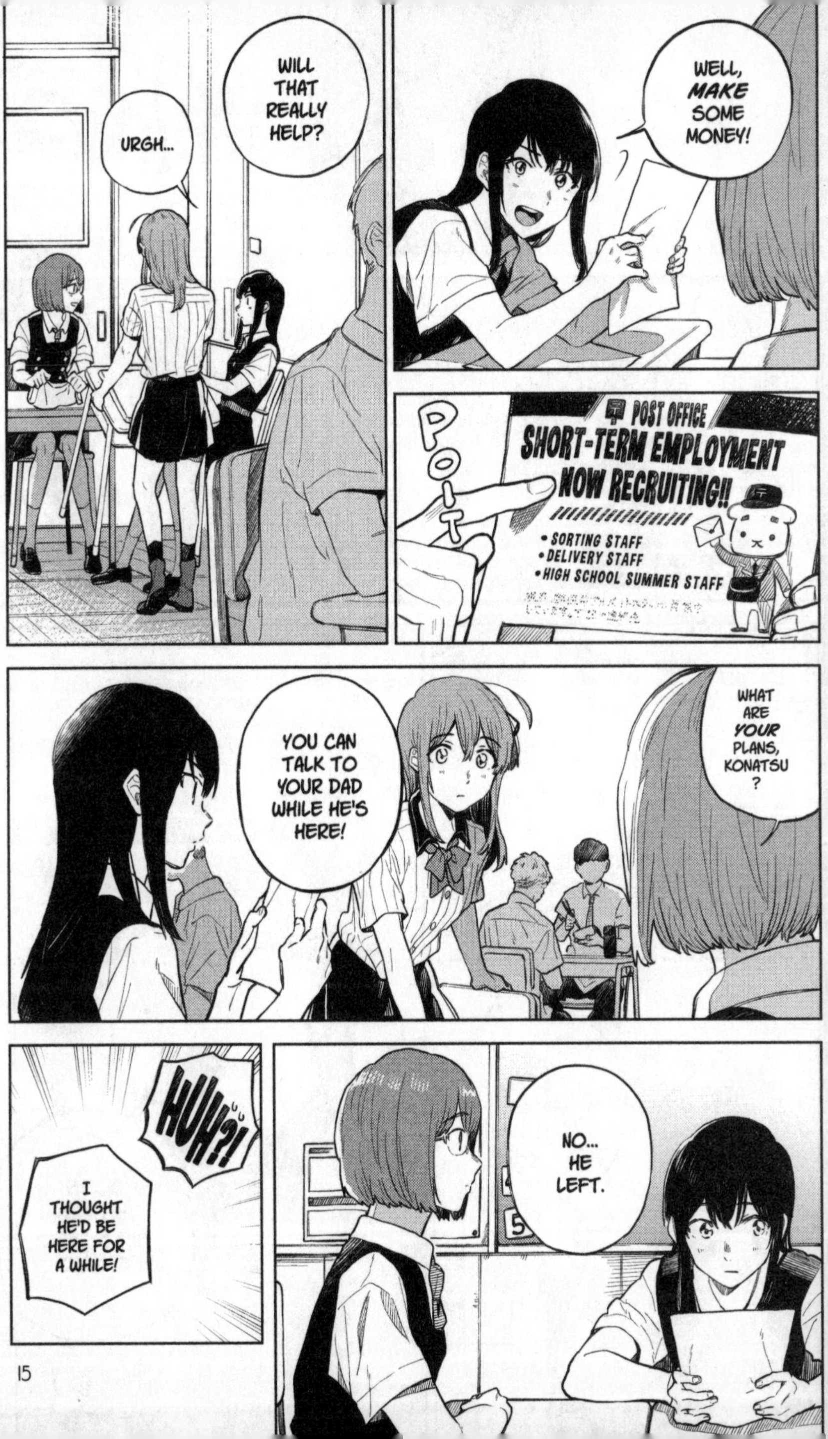
WELL, *MAKE* SOME MONEY!
POIT
POST OFFICE
SHORT-TERM EMPLOYMENT
NOW RECRUITING!!
• SORTING STAFF
• DELIVERY STAFF
• HIGH SCHOOL SUMMER STAFF
WILL THAT REALLY HELP?
URGH...
WHAT ARE *YOUR* PLANS, KONATSU?
YOU CAN TALK TO YOUR DAD WHILE HE'S HERE!
NO... HE LEFT.
HUH?!
I THOUGHT HE'D BE HERE FOR A WHILE!

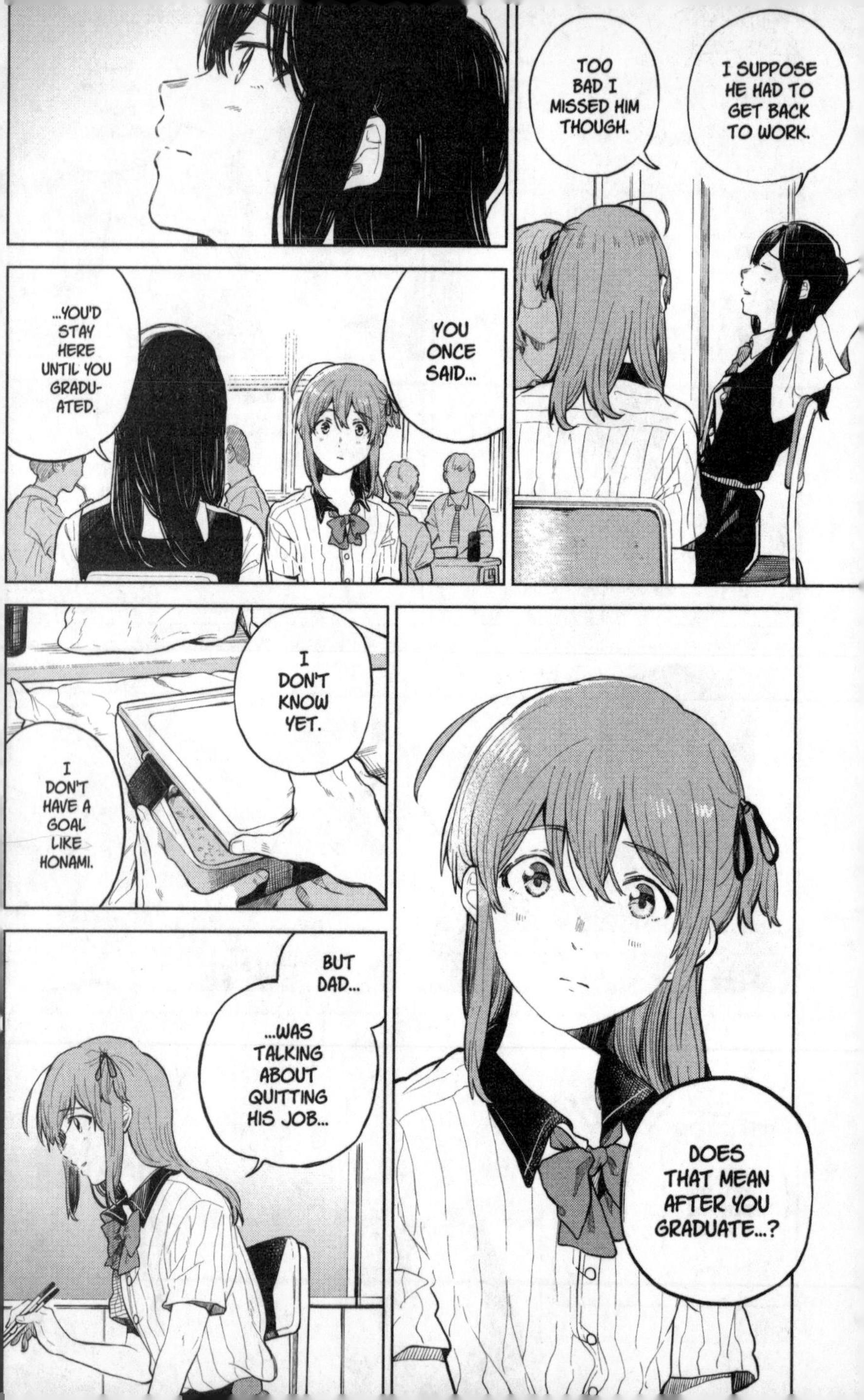
I SUPPOSE HE HAD TO GET BACK TO WORK.
TOO BAD I MISSED HIM THOUGH.
YOU ONCE SAID...
...YOU'D STAY HERE UNTIL YOU GRADU-ATED.
DOES THAT MEAN AFTER YOU GRADUATE...?
I DON'T KNOW YET.
I DON'T HAVE A GOAL LIKE HONAMI.
BUT DAD...
...WAS TALKING ABOUT QUITTING HIS JOB...

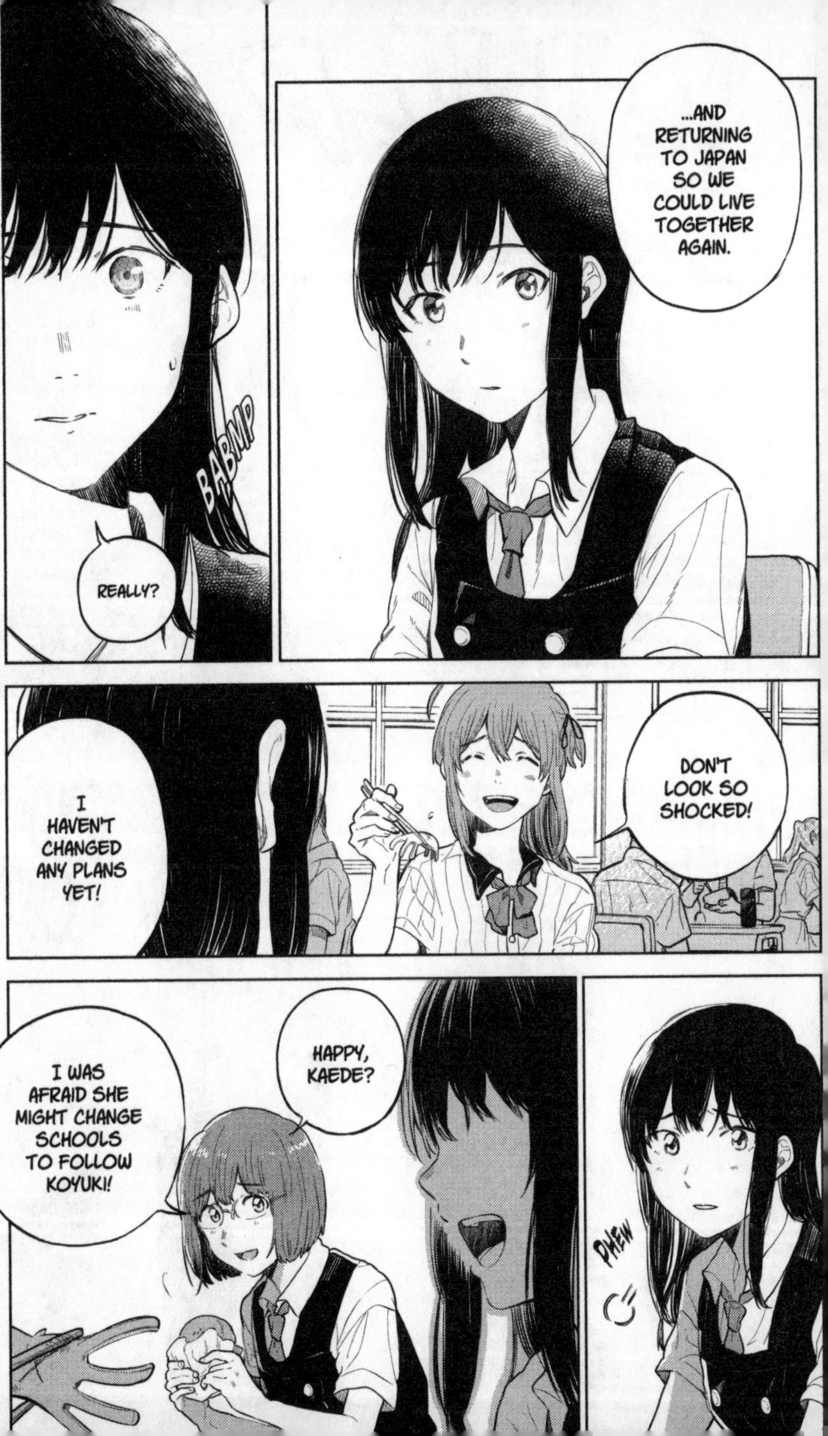

...AND RETURNING TO JAPAN SO WE COULD LIVE TOGETHER AGAIN.
BABMP
REALLY?
DON'T LOOK SO SHOCKED!
I HAVEN'T CHANGED ANY PLANS YET!
PHEW
HAPPY, KAEDE?
I WAS AFRAID SHE MIGHT CHANGE SCHOOLS TO FOLLOW KOYUKI!

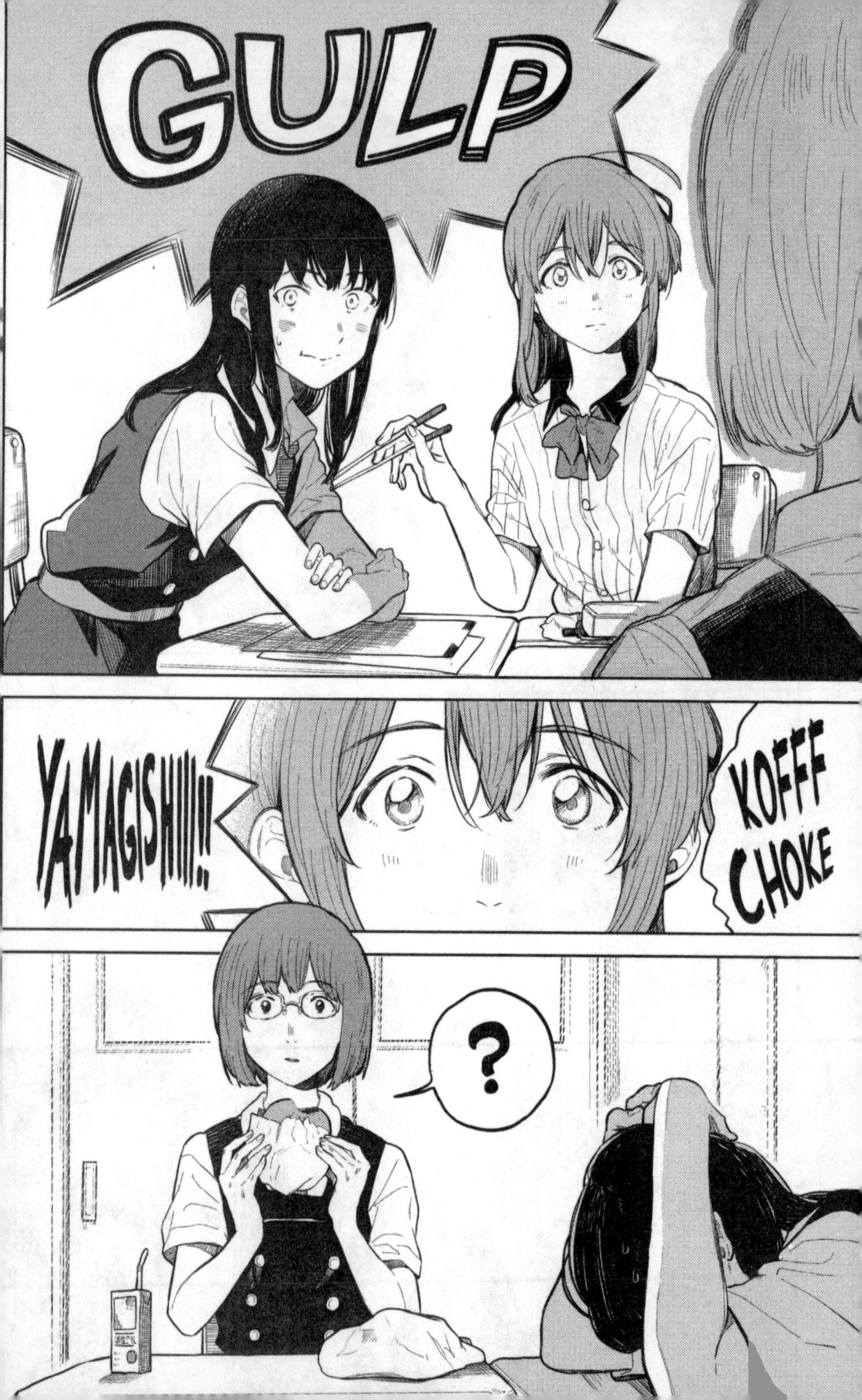
GULP
KOFFF CHOKE
YAMAGISHIIII!!
?

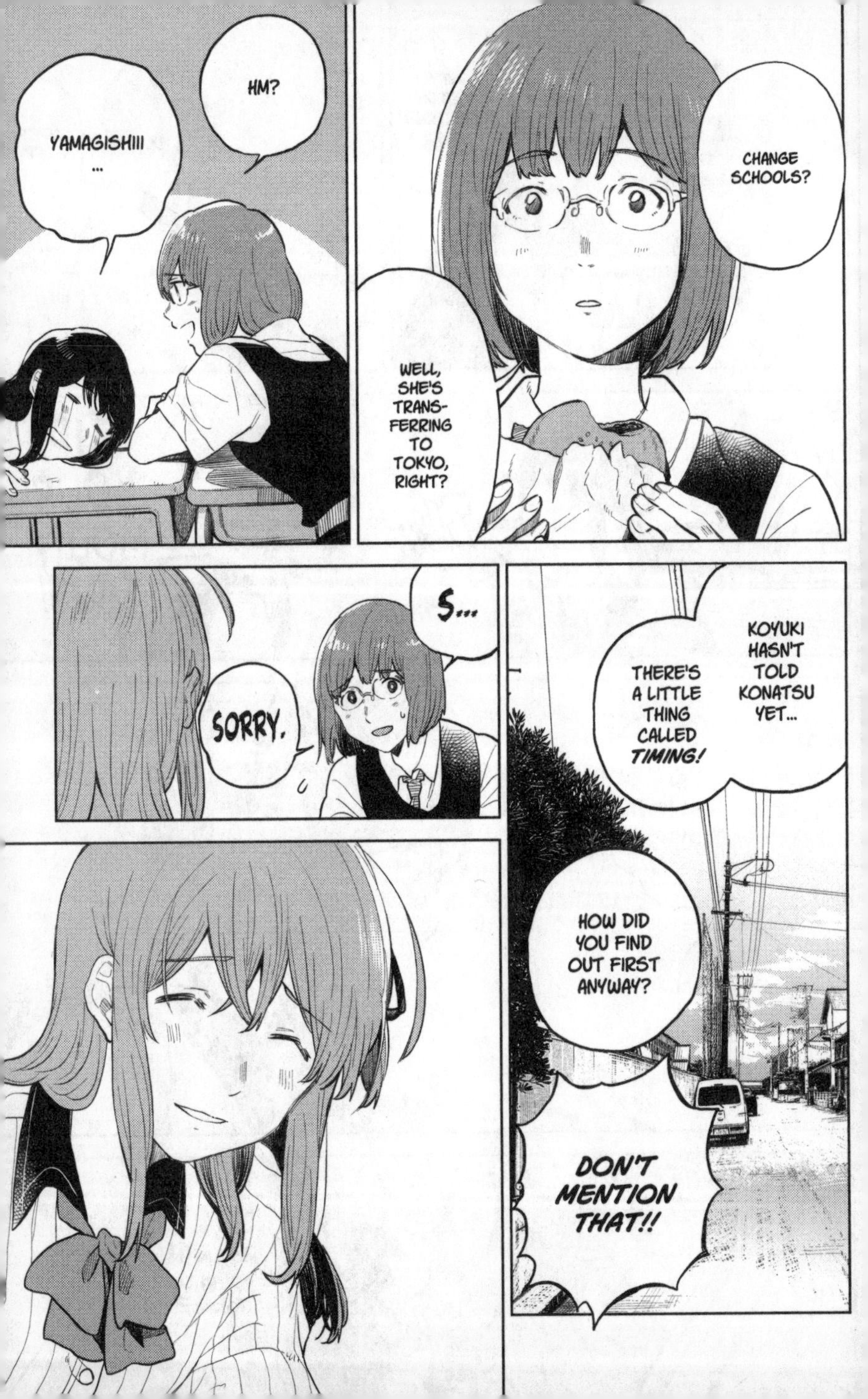
CHANGE SCHOOLS?
WELL, SHE'S TRANS-FERRING TO TOKYO, RIGHT?
HM?
YAMAGISHIII ...
KOYUKI HASN'T TOLD KONATSU YET...
THERE'S A LITTLE THING CALLED *TIMING!*
HOW DID YOU FIND OUT FIRST ANYWAY?
DON'T MENTION THAT!!
S...
SORRY.

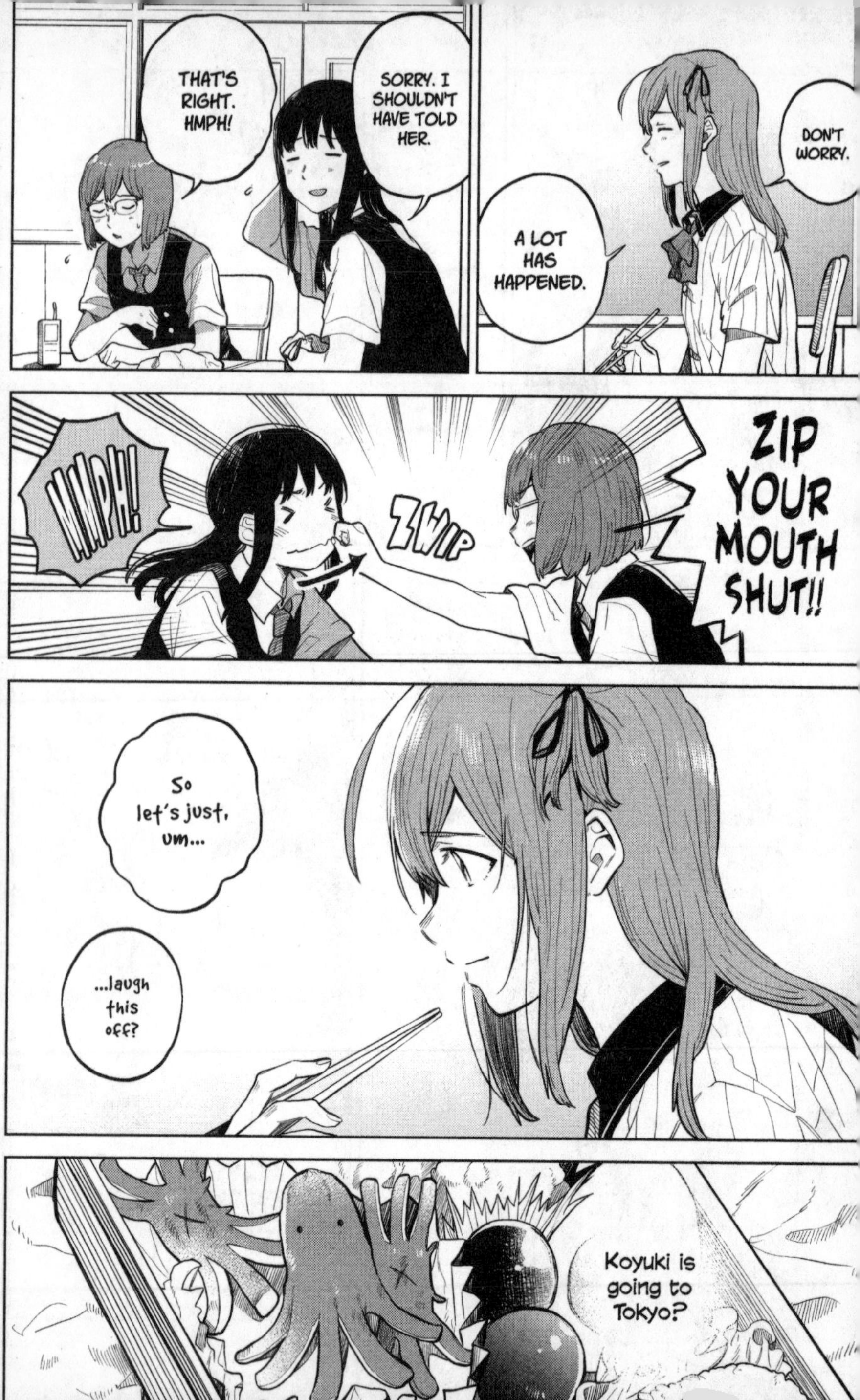
DON'T WORRY.
A LOT HAS HAPPENED.
SORRY. I SHOULDN'T HAVE TOLD HER.
THAT'S RIGHT. HMPH!
ZIP YOUR MOUTH SHUT!!
ZWIP
MMPH!
So let's just, um...
...laugh this off?
Koyuki is going to Tokyo?

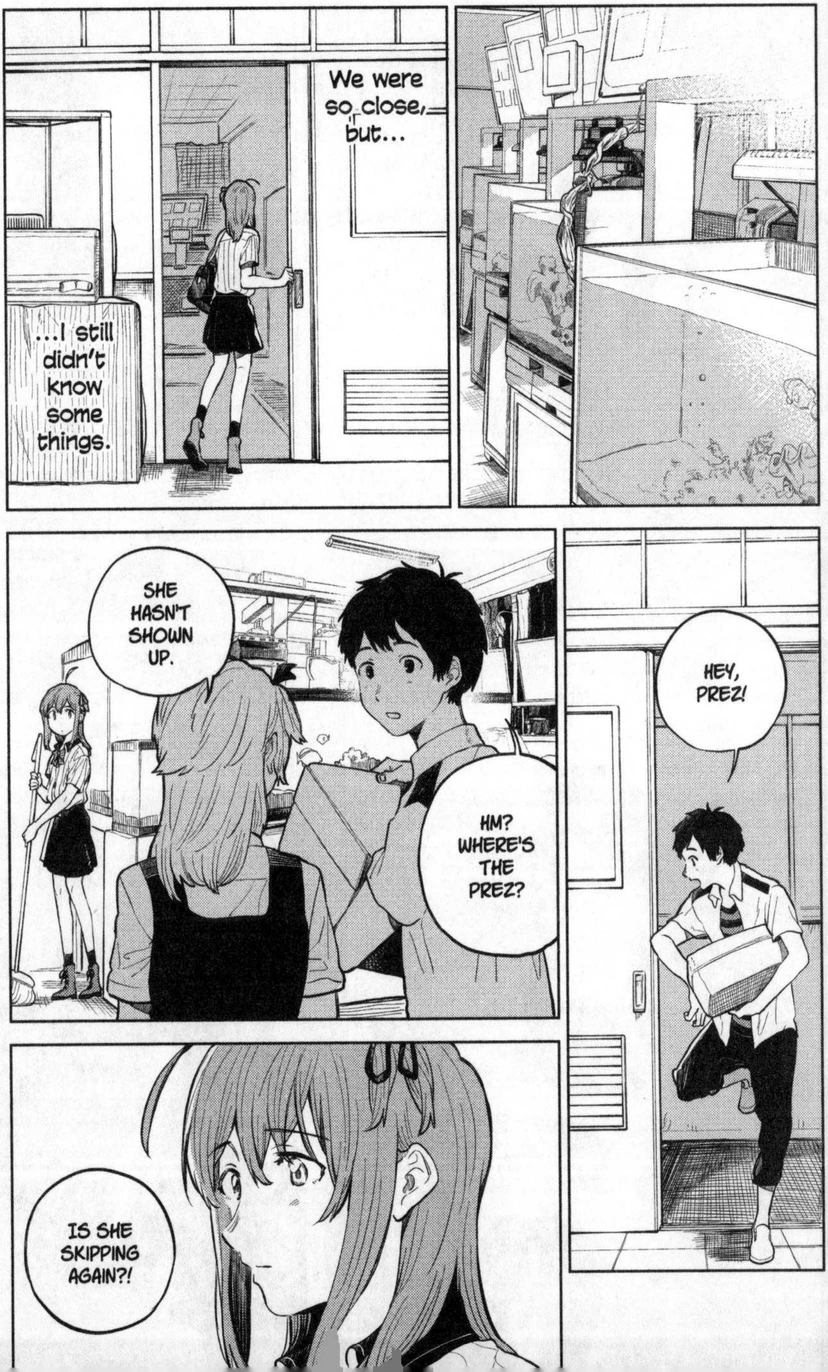
We were so close, but...
...I still didn't know some things.
HEY, PREZ!
HM? WHERE'S THE PREZ?
SHE HASN'T SHOWN UP.
IS SHE SKIPPING AGAIN?!

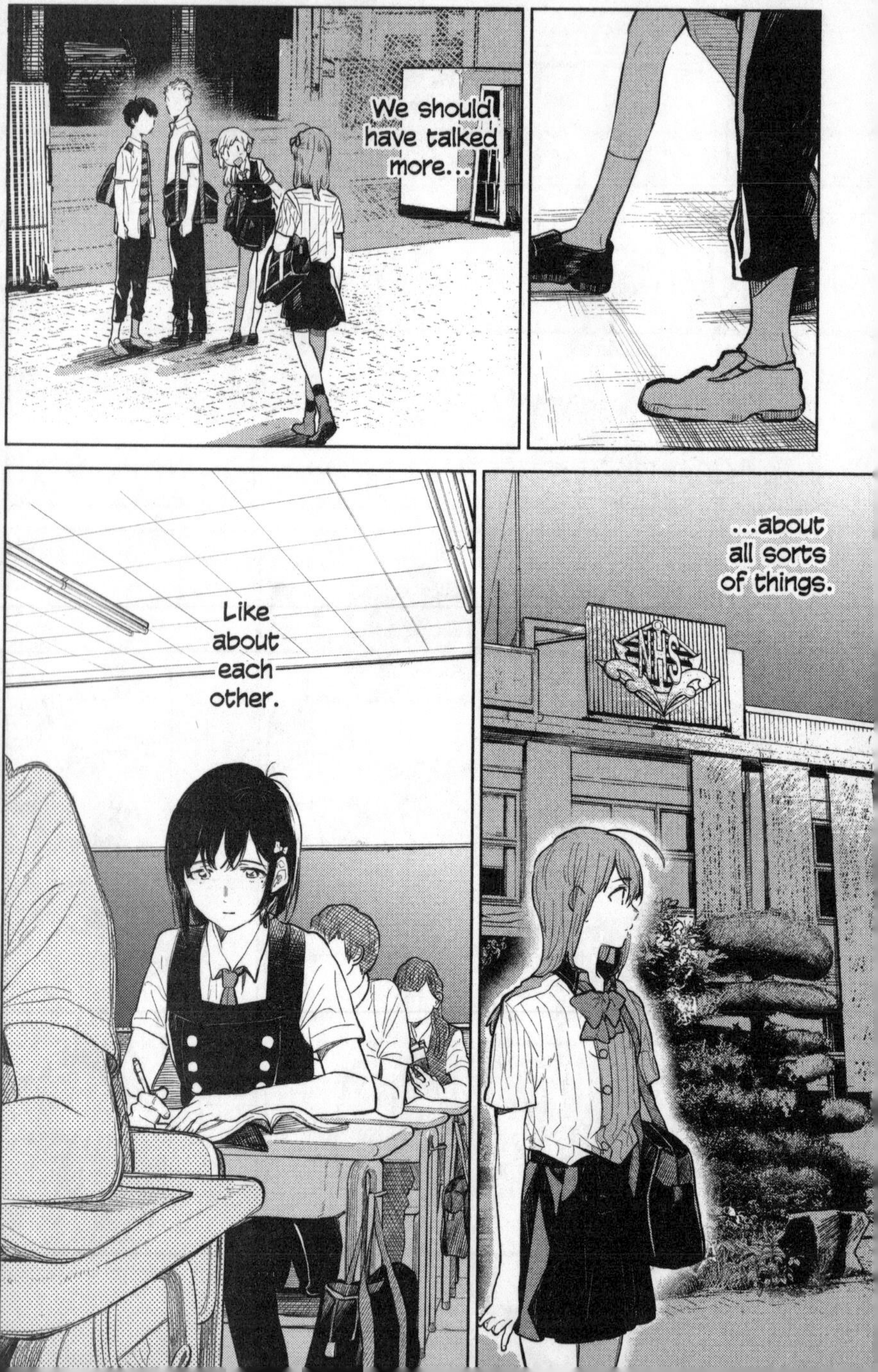
We should have talked more...
...about all sorts of things.
Like about each other.

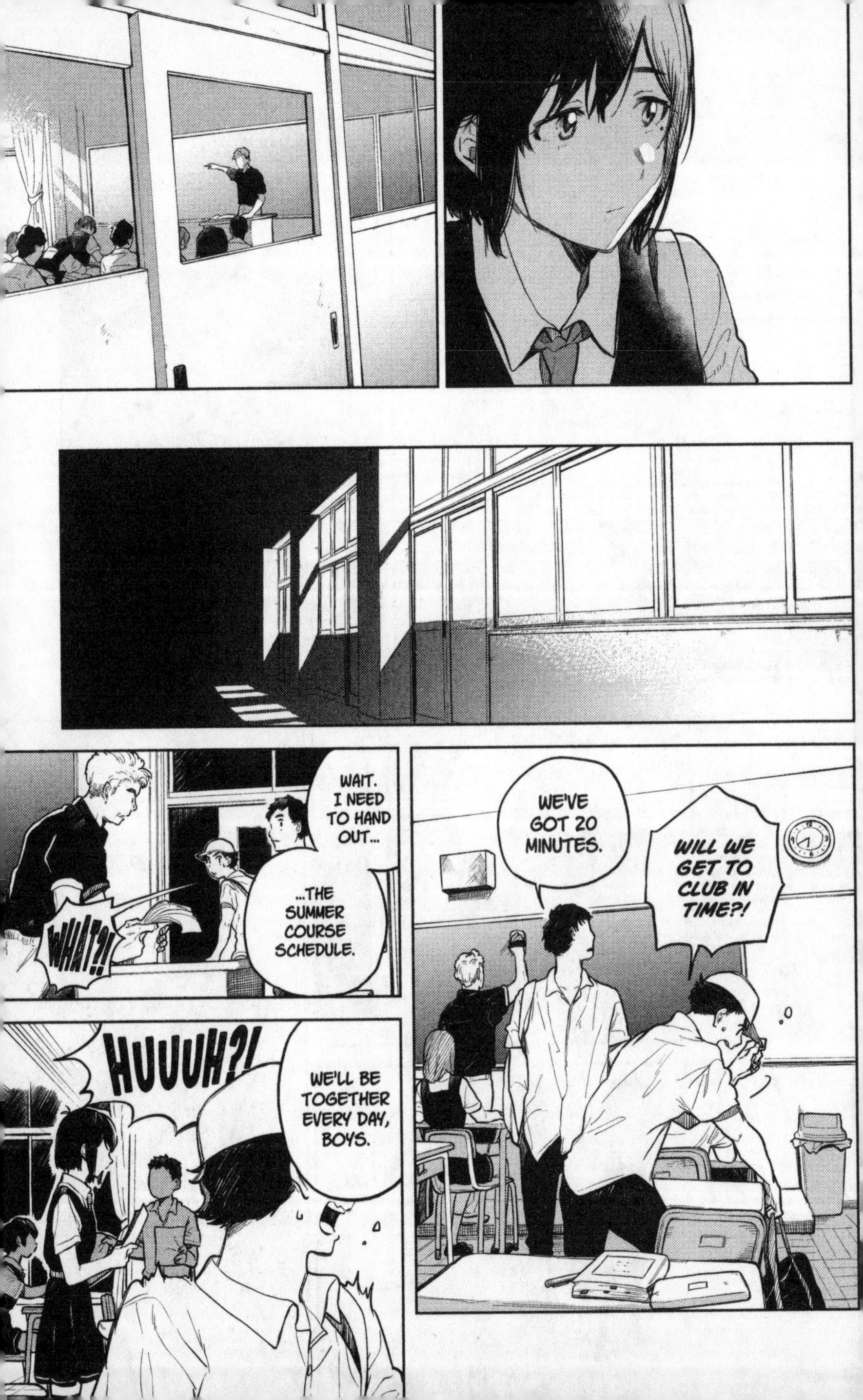
WE'VE GOT 20 MINUTES.
WILL WE GET TO CLUB IN TIME?!
WAIT. I NEED TO HAND OUT...
WHAT?!
...THE SUMMER COURSE SCHEDULE.
HUUUH?!
WE'LL BE TOGETHER EVERY DAY, BOYS.

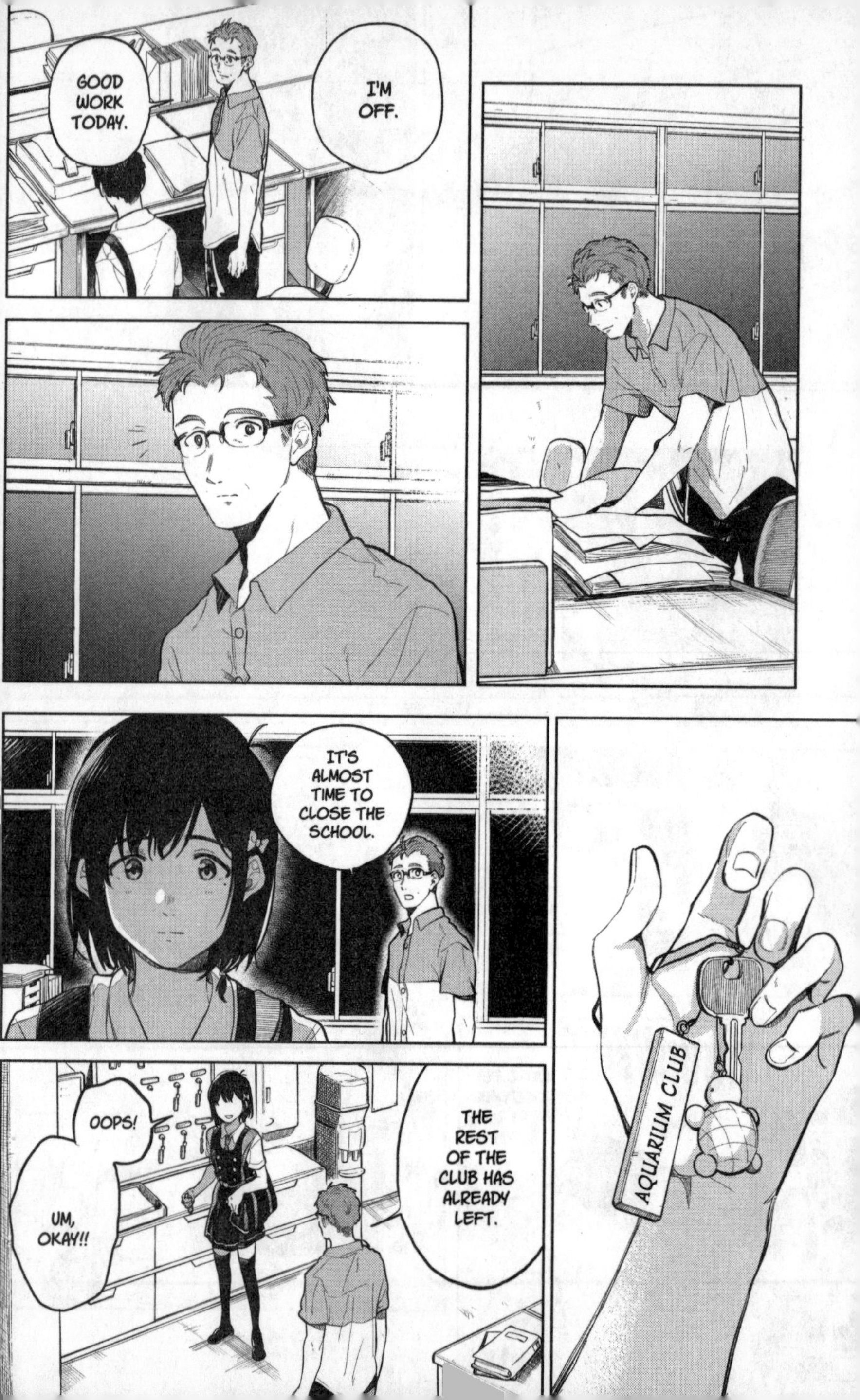
I'M OFF.
GOOD WORK TODAY.
AQUARIUM CLUB
IT'S ALMOST TIME TO CLOSE THE SCHOOL.
THE REST OF THE CLUB HAS ALREADY LEFT.
OOPS!
UM, OKAY!!

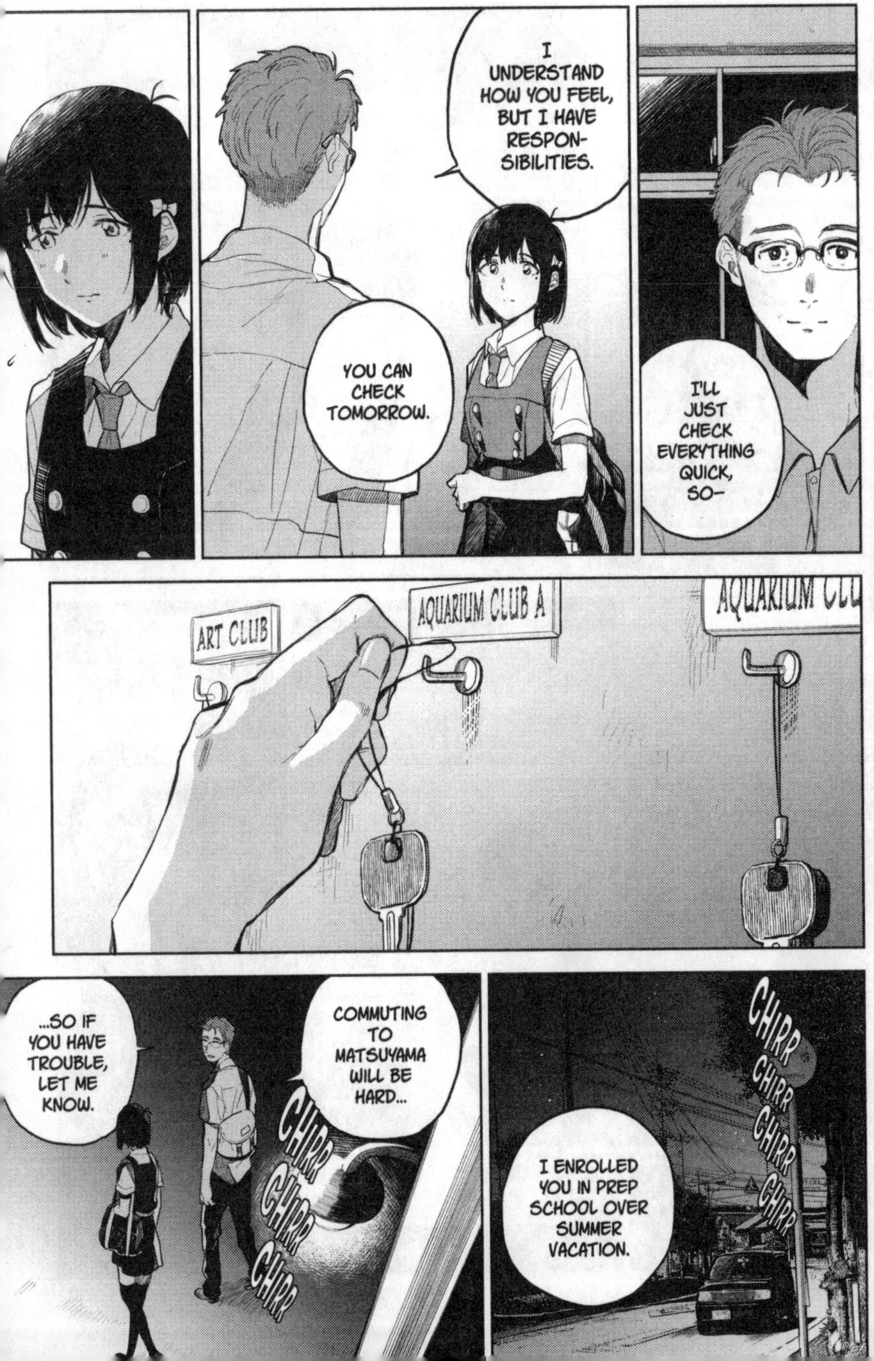
I'LL JUST CHECK EVERYTHING QUICK, SO–
I UNDERSTAND HOW YOU FEEL, BUT I HAVE RESPON-SIBILITIES.
YOU CAN CHECK TOMORROW.
AQUARIUM CLU
AQUARIUM CLUB A
ART CLUB
CHIRR CHIRR CHIRR CHIRR CHIRR
I ENROLLED YOU IN PREP SCHOOL OVER SUMMER VACATION.
COMMUTING TO MATSUYAMA WILL BE HARD...
...SO IF YOU HAVE TROUBLE, LET ME KNOW.
CHIRR CHIRR CHIRR CHIRR

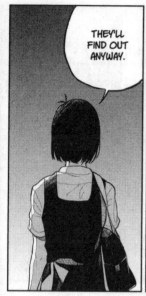

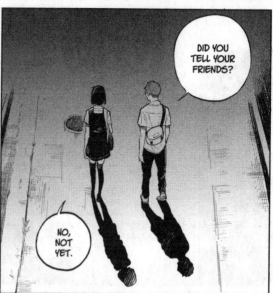

DID YOU TELL YOUR FRIENDS?
NO, NOT YET.
THEY'LL FIND OUT ANYWAY.
"IF YOU LEFT, I'D BE DEVASTATED."

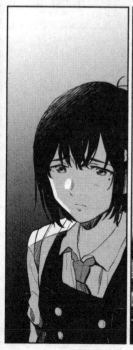

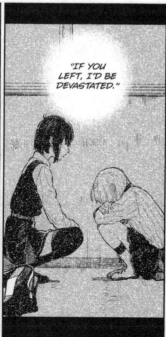

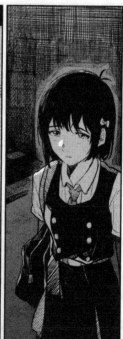

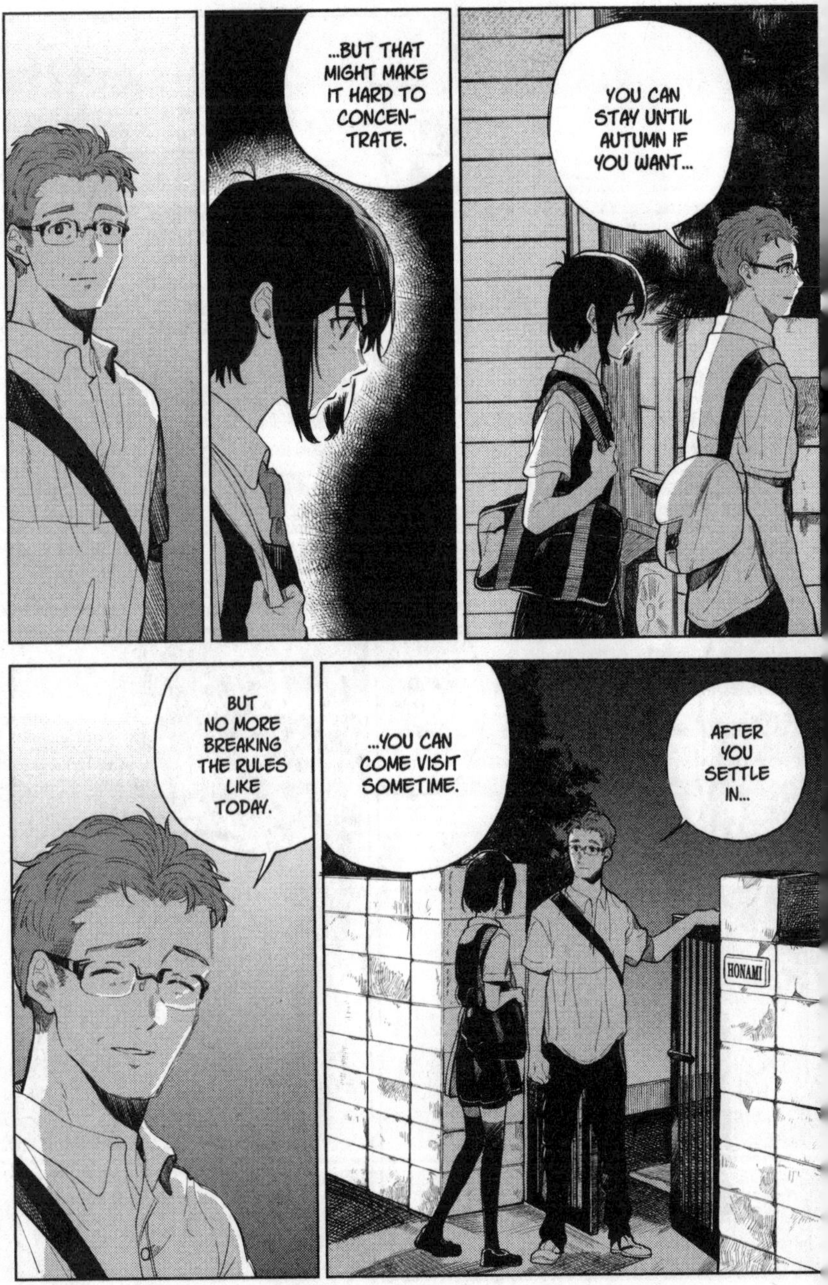
YOU CAN STAY UNTIL AUTUMN IF YOU WANT...
...BUT THAT MIGHT MAKE IT HARD TO CONCENTRATE.
AFTER YOU SETTLE IN...
...YOU CAN COME VISIT SOMETIME.
HONAMI
BUT NO MORE BREAKING THE RULES LIKE TODAY.

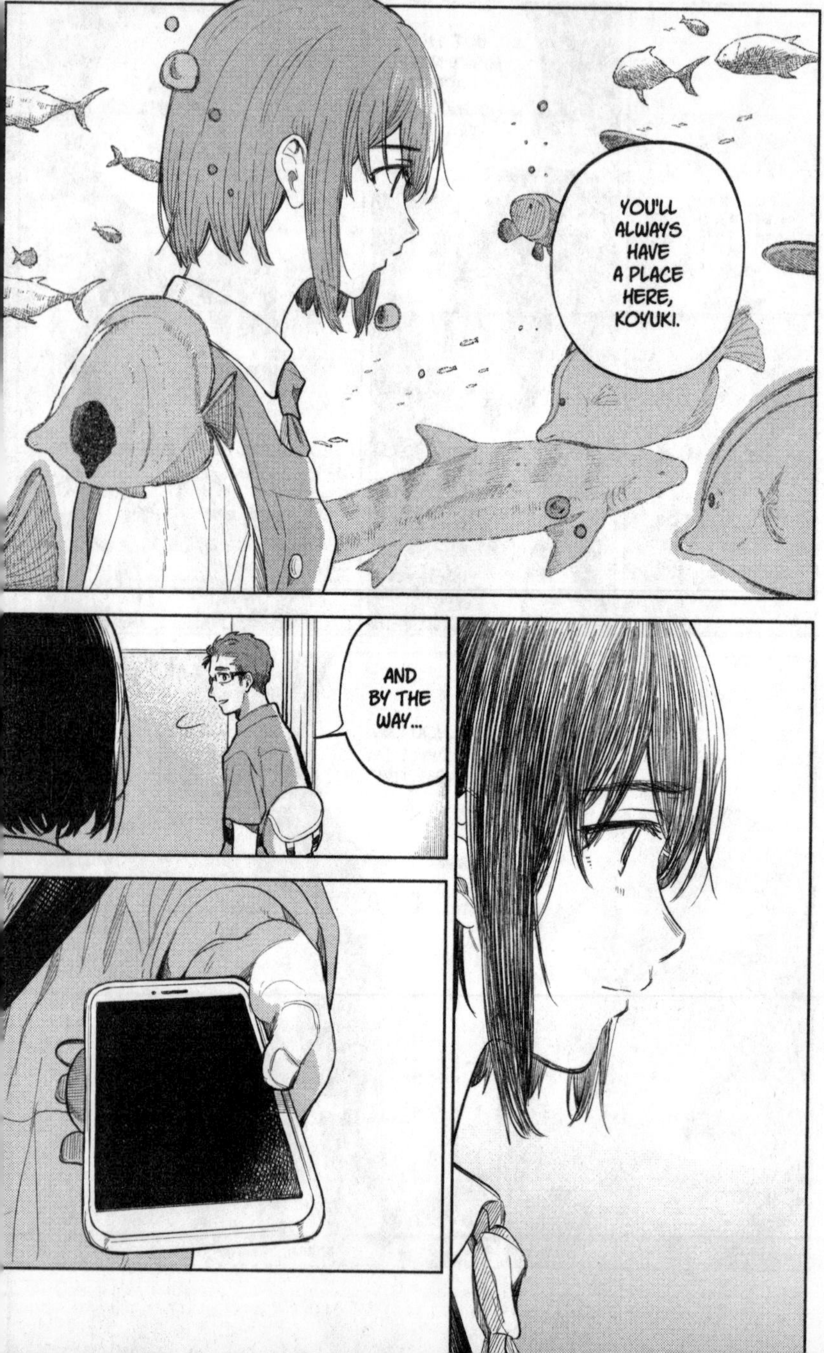
YOU'LL ALWAYS HAVE A PLACE HERE, KOYUKI.
AND BY THE WAY...

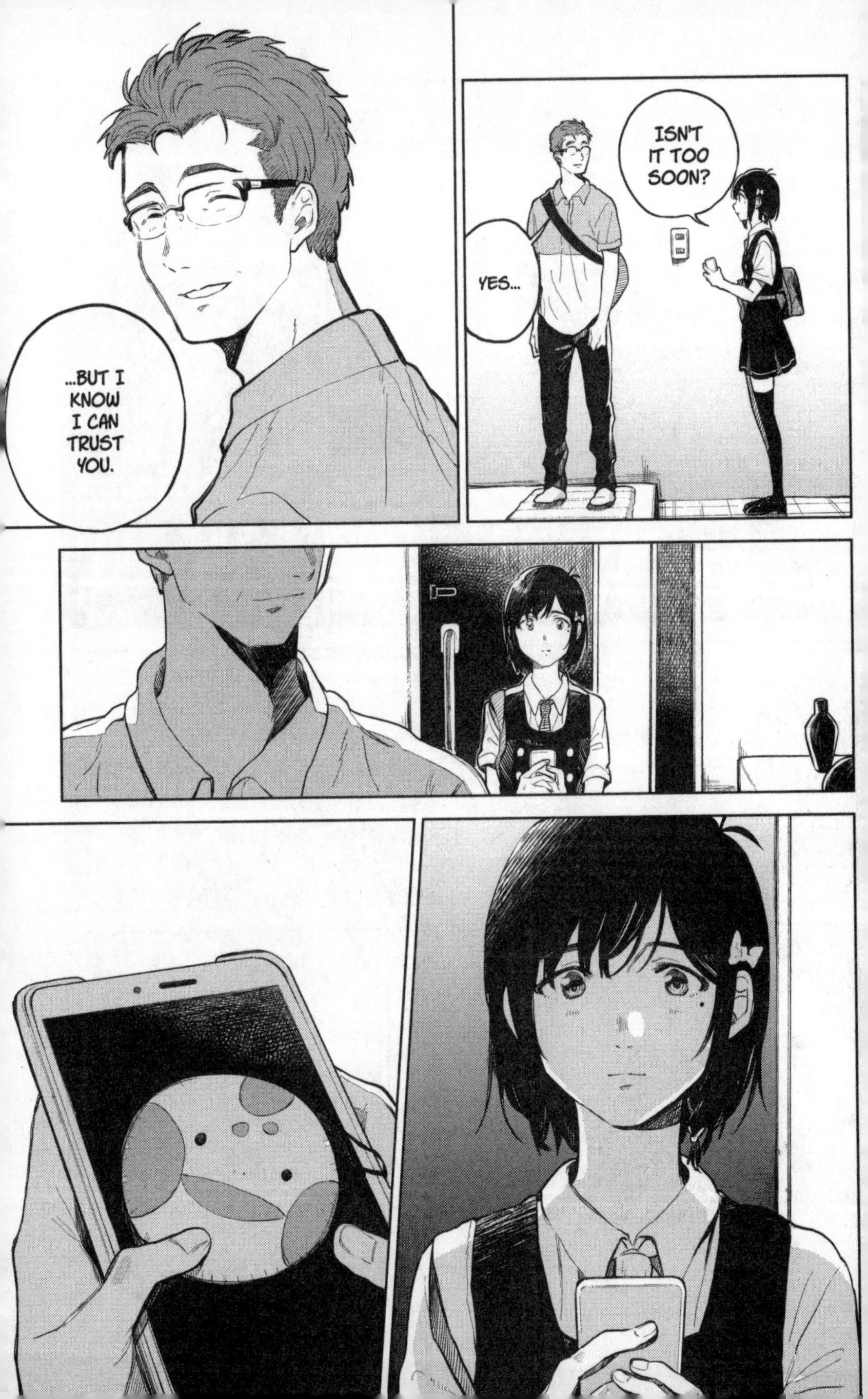
ISN'T IT TOO SOON?
YES...
...BUT I KNOW I CAN TRUST YOU.

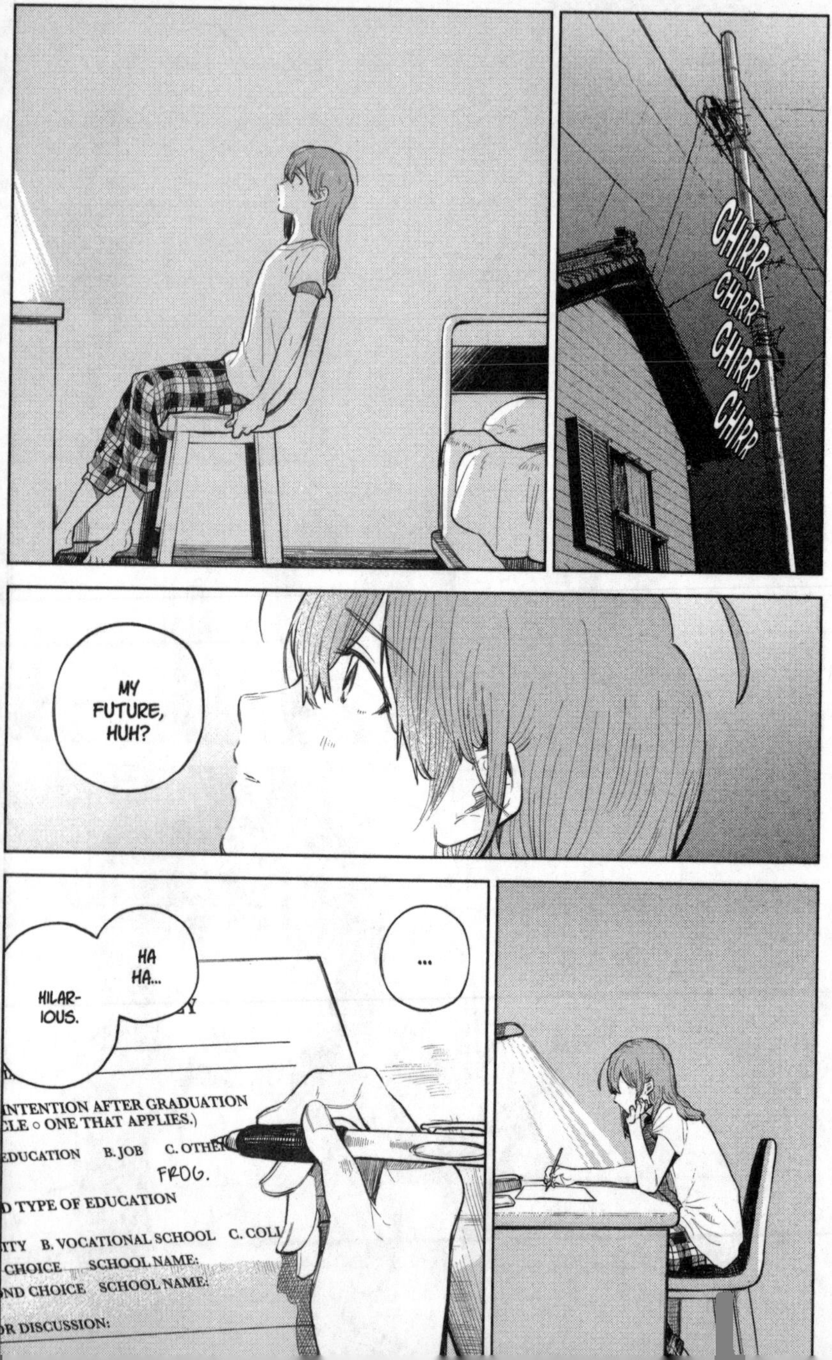
CHIRR
CHIRR
CHIRR
CHIRR
MY FUTURE, HUH?
...
HA HA...
HILAR-IOUS.
INTENTION AFTER GRADUATION
CLE ○ ONE THAT APPLIES.)
EDUCATION B. JOB C. OTHE
FROG.
D TYPE OF EDUCATION
ITY B. VOCATIONAL SCHOOL C. COLL
CHOICE SCHOOL NAME:
ND CHOICE SCHOOL NAME:
OR DISCUSSION:

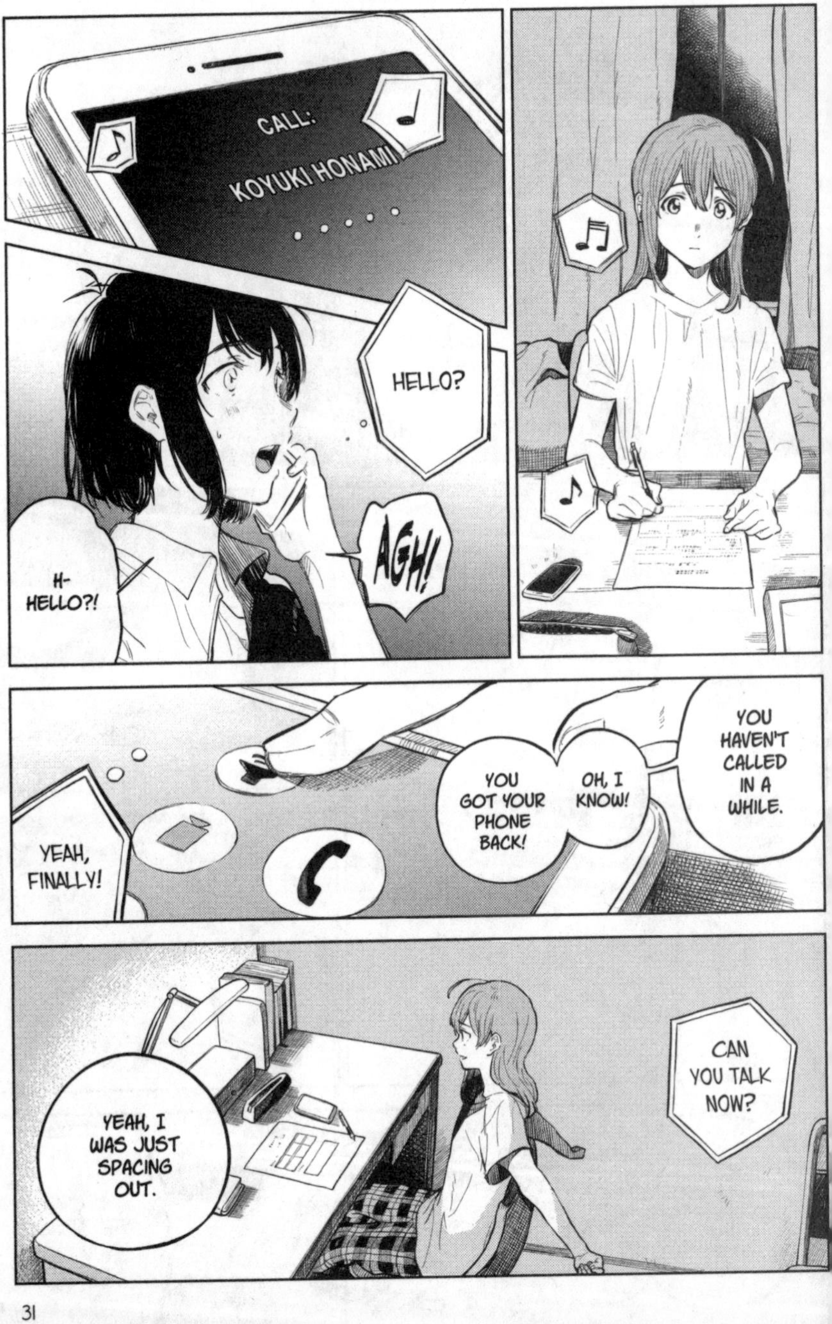
CALL:
KOYUKI HONAMI
HELLO?
AGH!
H-HELLO?!
YOU HAVEN'T CALLED IN A WHILE.
OH, I KNOW!
YOU GOT YOUR PHONE BACK!
YEAH, FINALLY!
CAN YOU TALK NOW?
YEAH, I WAS JUST SPACING OUT.

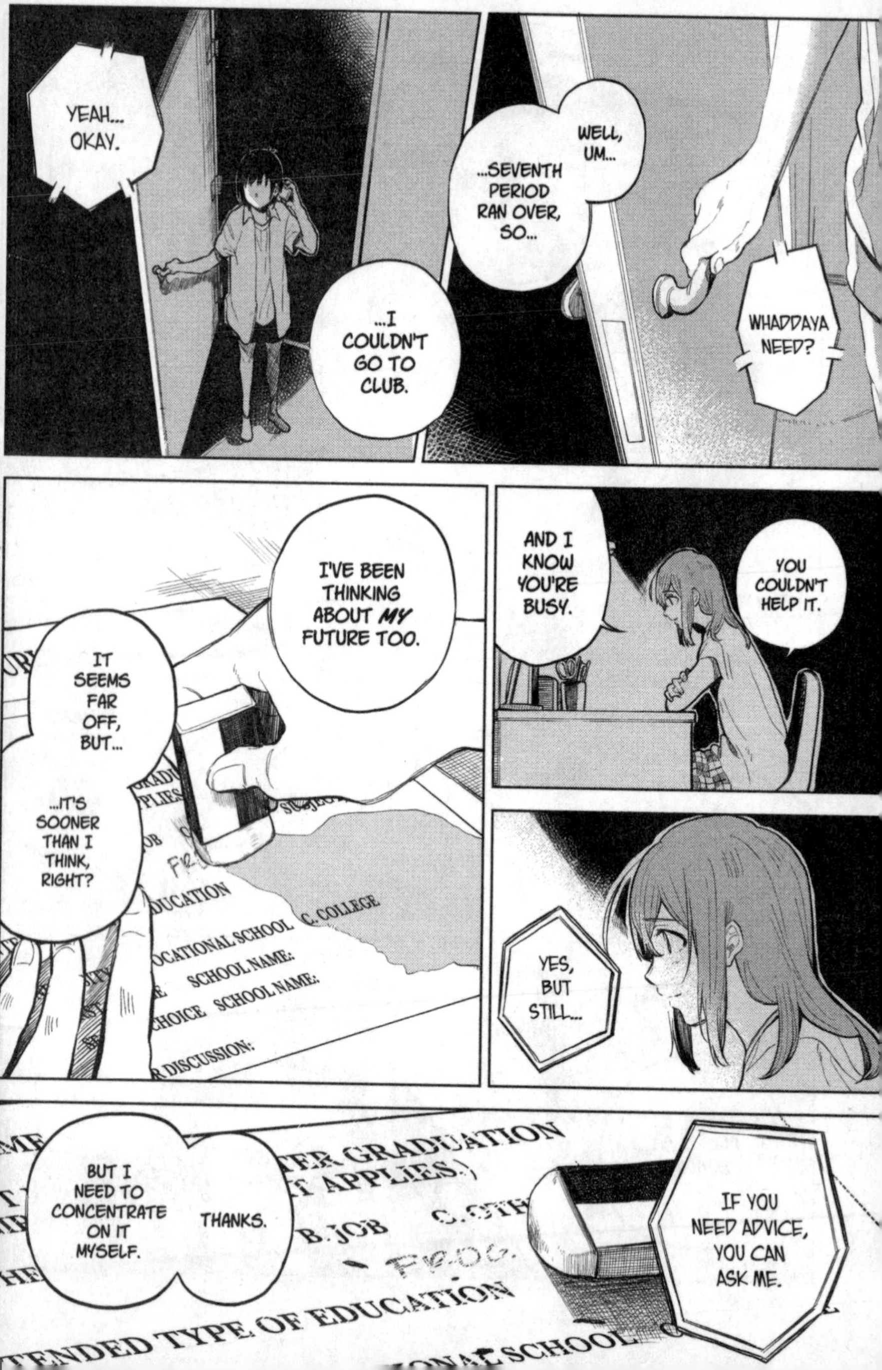
WHADDAYA NEED?
WELL, UM...
...SEVENTH PERIOD RAN OVER, SO...
...I COULDN'T GO TO CLUB.
YEAH... OKAY.
YOU COULDN'T HELP IT.
AND I KNOW YOU'RE BUSY.
YES, BUT STILL...
I'VE BEEN THINKING ABOUT MY FUTURE TOO.
IT SEEMS FAR OFF, BUT...
...IT'S SOONER THAN I THINK, RIGHT?
IF YOU NEED ADVICE, YOU CAN ASK ME.
THANKS.
BUT I NEED TO CONCENTRATE ON IT MYSELF.

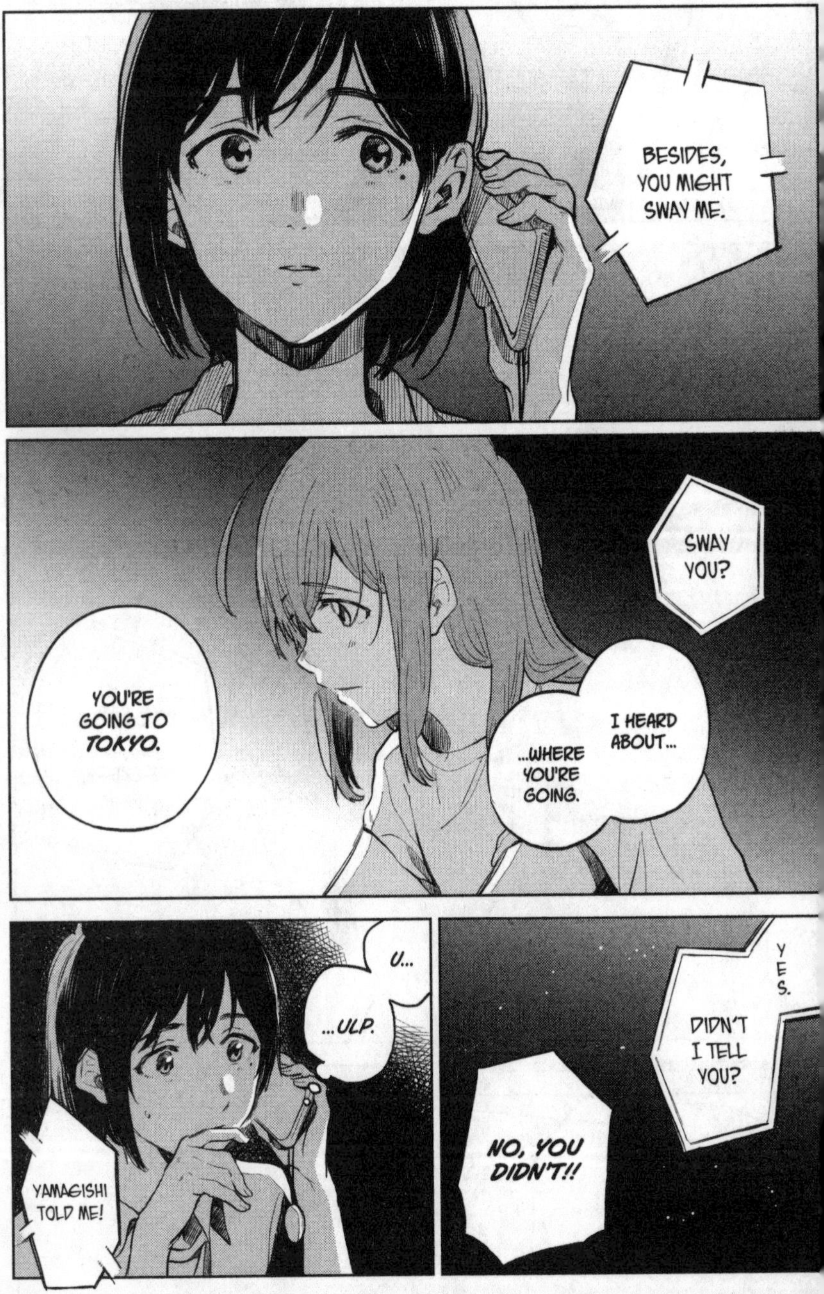
BESIDES, YOU MIGHT SWAY ME.
SWAY YOU?
I HEARD ABOUT...
...WHERE YOU'RE GOING.
YOU'RE GOING TO TOKYO.
YES.
DIDN'T I TELL YOU?
NO, YOU DIDN'T!!
U...
...ULP.
YAMAGISHI TOLD ME!

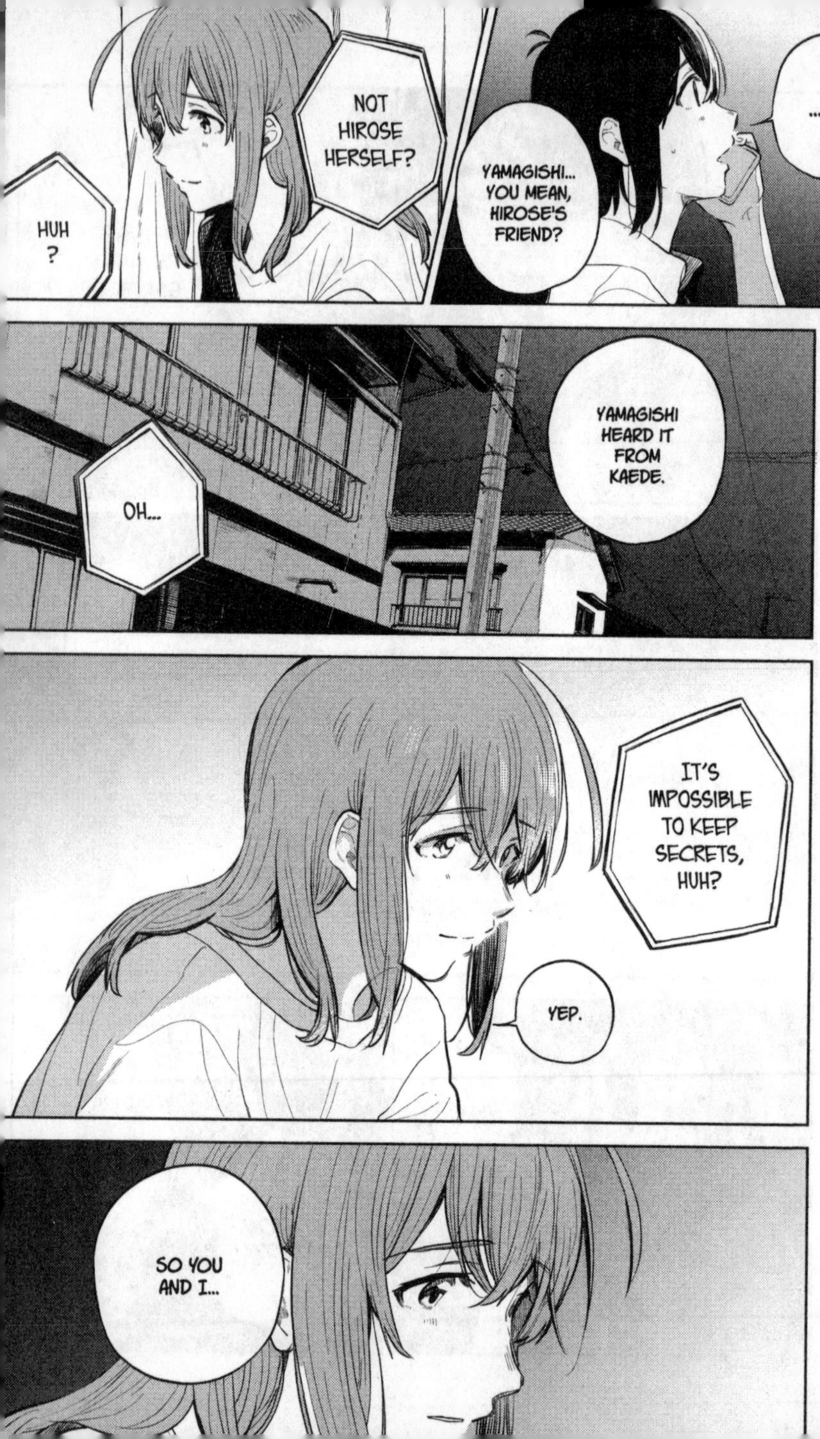
...?
YAMAGISHI... YOU MEAN, HIROSE'S FRIEND?
NOT HIROSE HERSELF?
HUH?
YAMAGISHI HEARD IT FROM KAEDE.
OH...
IT'S IMPOSSIBLE TO KEEP SECRETS, HUH?
YEP.
SO YOU AND I...

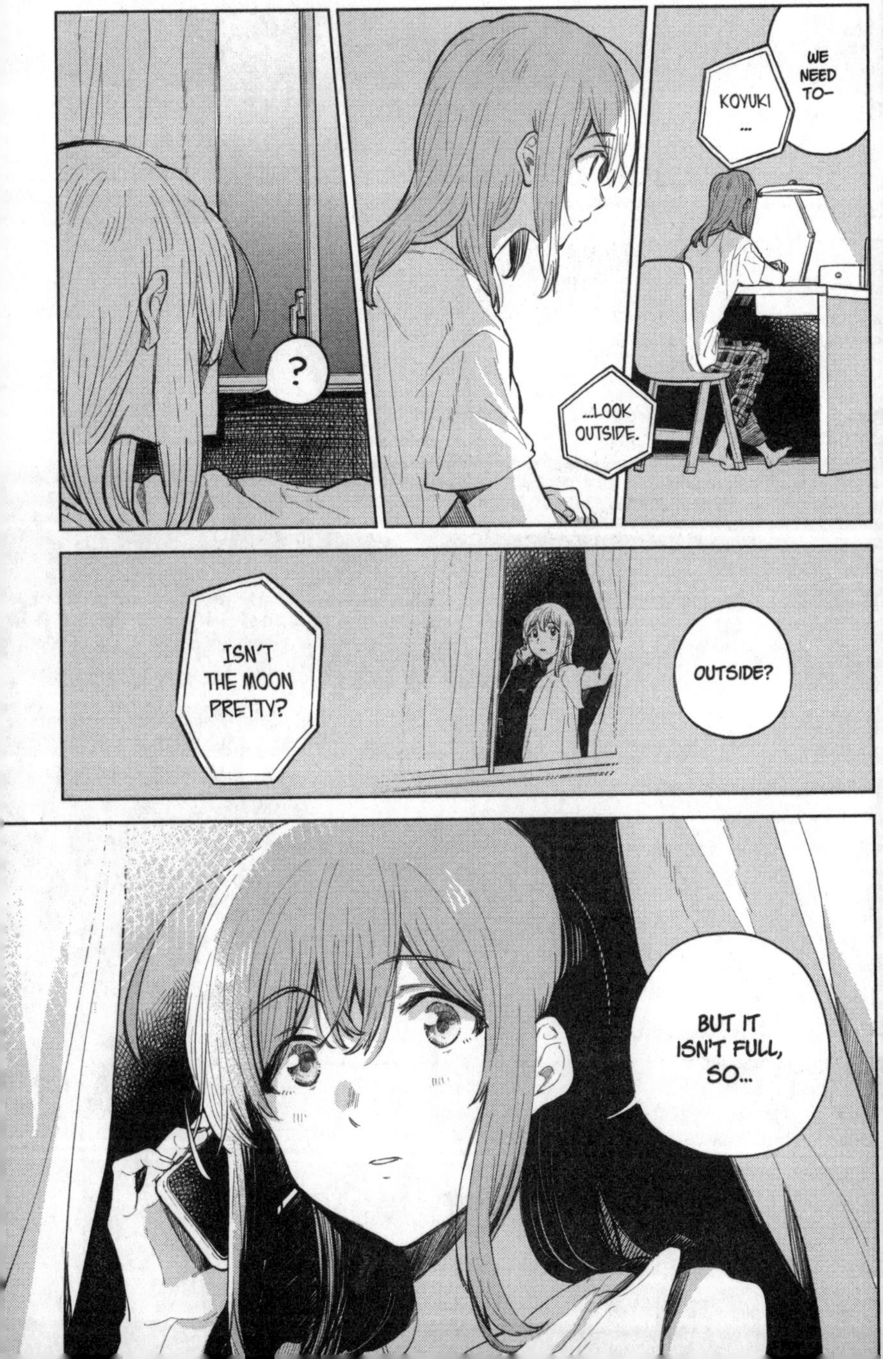
WE NEED TO—
KOYUKI ...
...LOOK OUTSIDE.
?
OUTSIDE?
ISN'T THE MOON PRETTY?
BUT IT ISN'T FULL, SO...

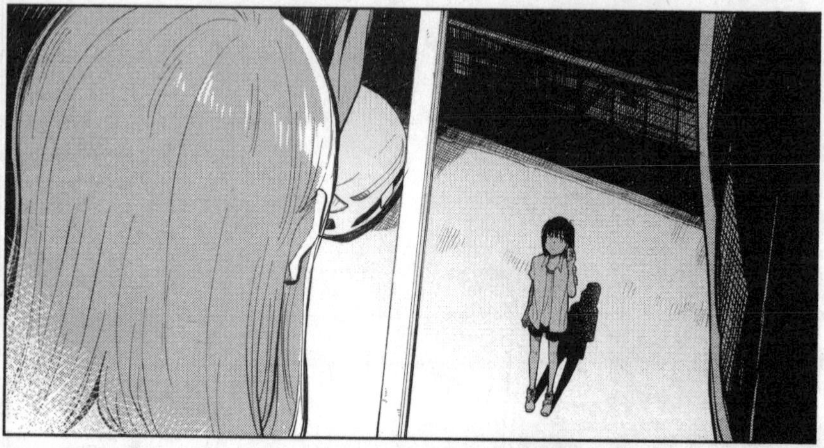
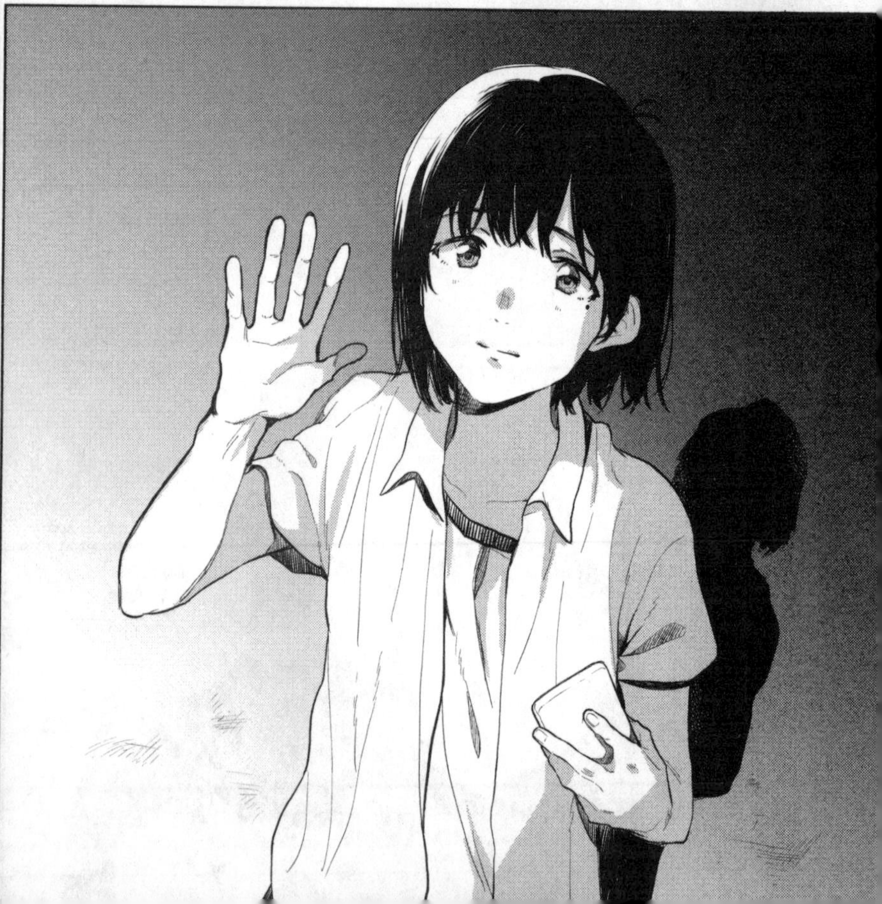

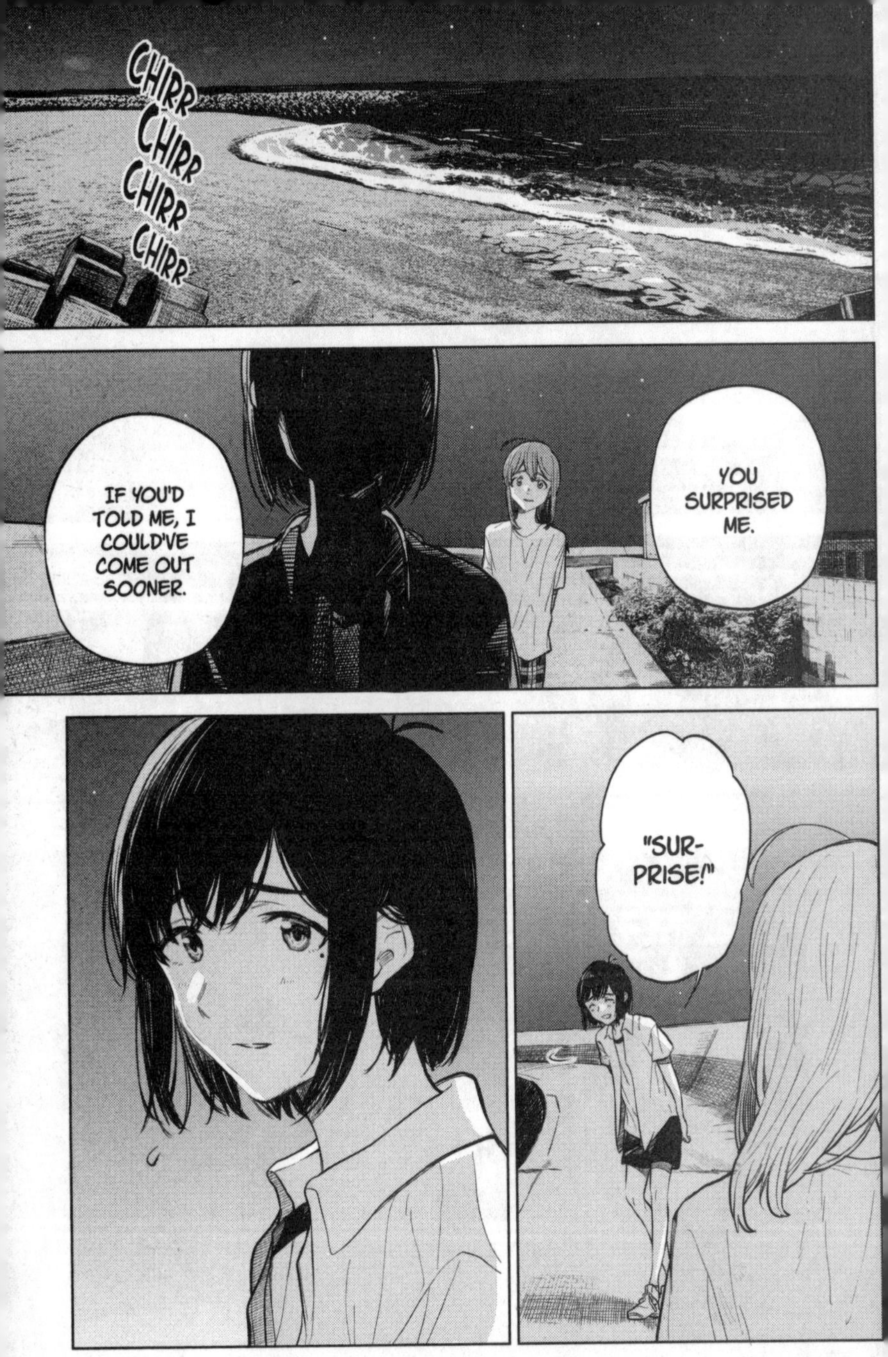
CHIRR CHIRR CHIRR CHIRR
YOU SURPRISED ME.
IF YOU'D TOLD ME, I COULD'VE COME OUT SOONER.
"SUR-PRISE!"

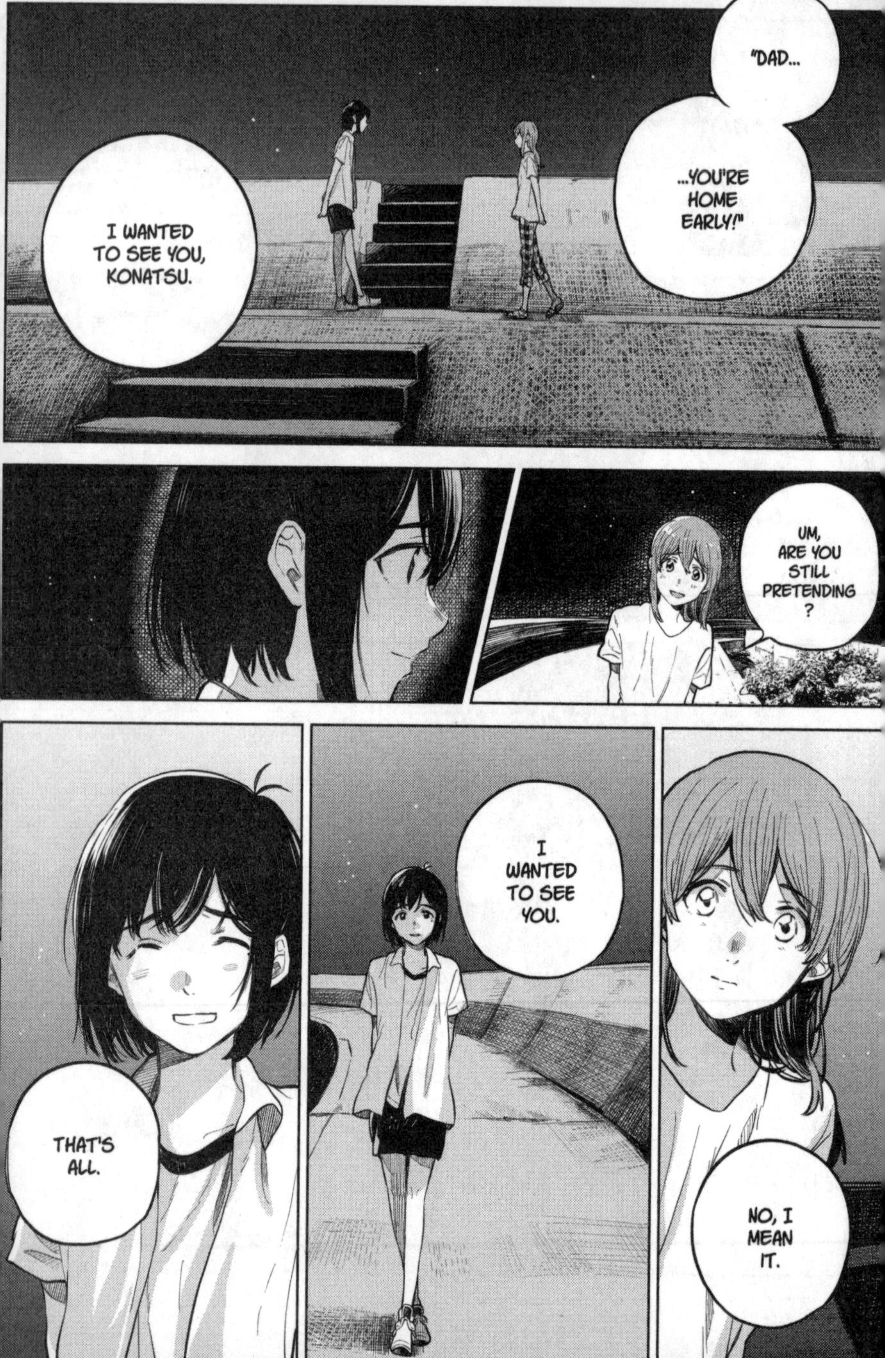
"DAD...
...YOU'RE HOME EARLY!"
I WANTED TO SEE YOU, KONATSU.
UM, ARE YOU STILL PRETENDING?
NO, I MEAN IT.
I WANTED TO SEE YOU.
THAT'S ALL.

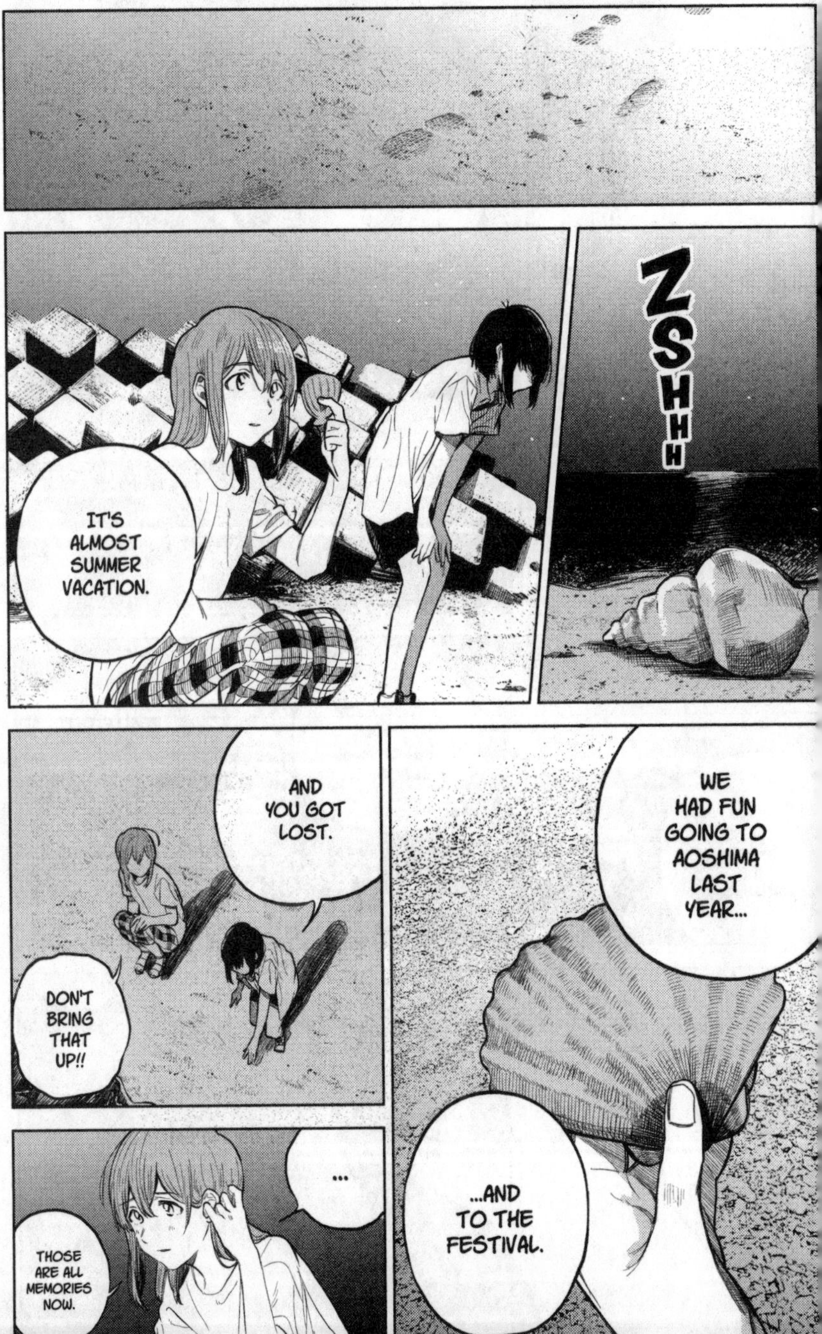
ZSHHH
IT'S ALMOST SUMMER VACATION.
WE HAD FUN GOING TO AOSHIMA LAST YEAR...
...AND TO THE FESTIVAL.
AND YOU GOT LOST.
DON'T BRING THAT UP!!
...
THOSE ARE ALL MEMORIES NOW.

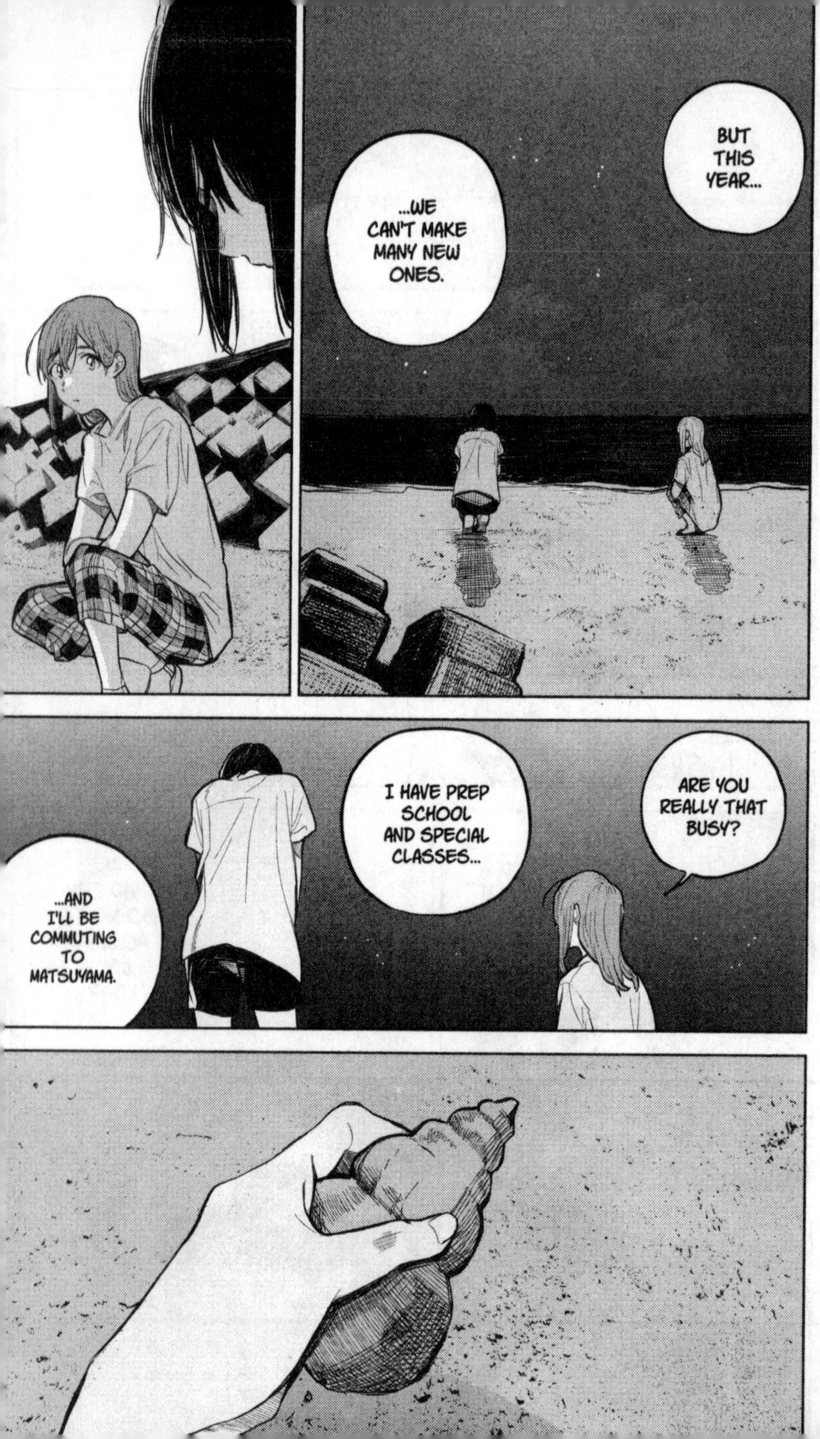
BUT THIS YEAR...
...WE CAN'T MAKE MANY NEW ONES.
ARE YOU REALLY THAT BUSY?
I HAVE PREP SCHOOL AND SPECIAL CLASSES...
...AND I'LL BE COMMUTING TO MATSUYAMA.

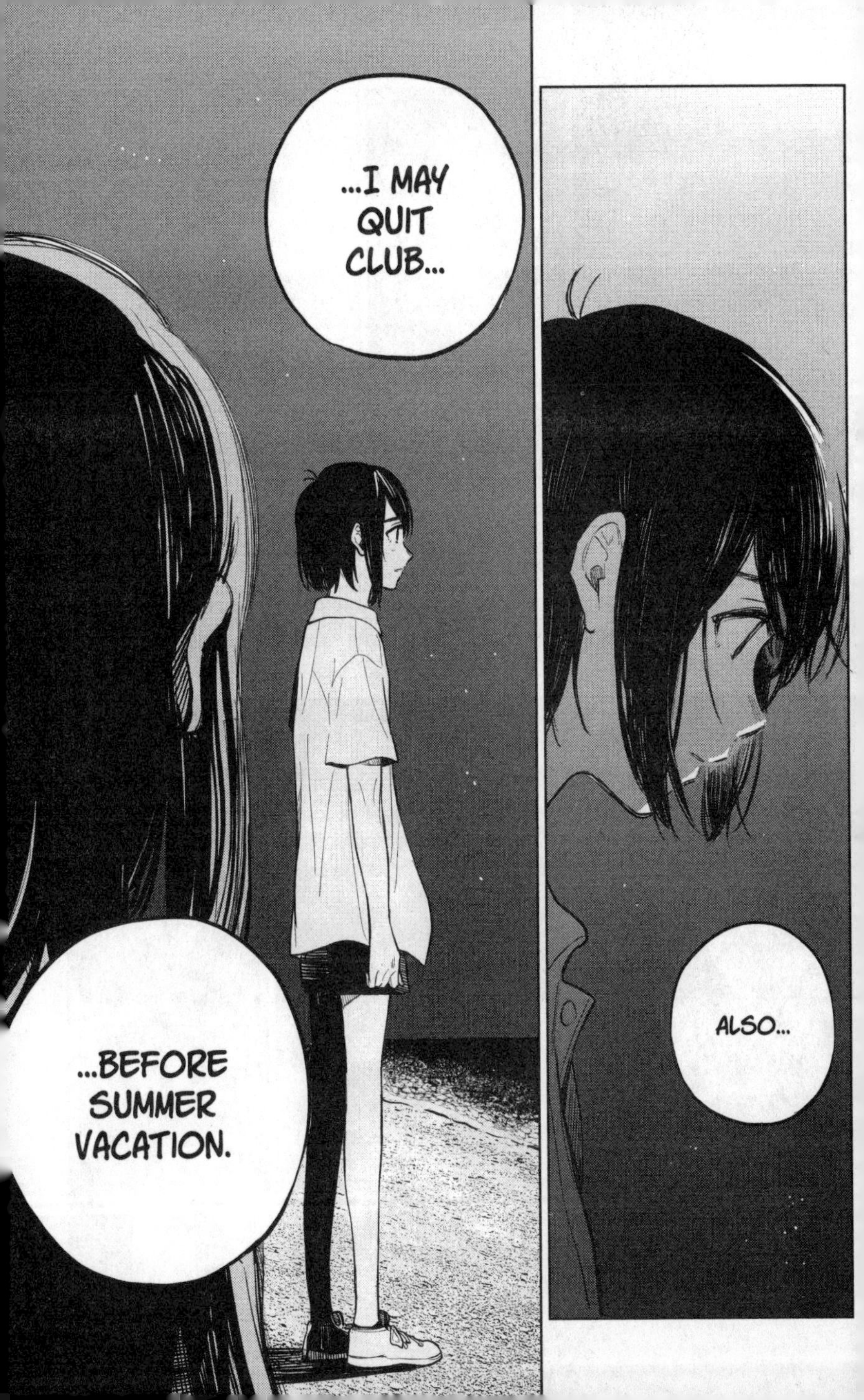
ALSO...
...I MAY QUIT CLUB...
...BEFORE SUMMER VACATION.

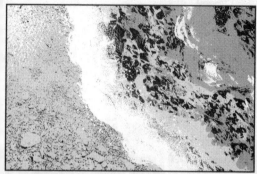

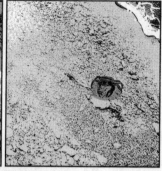

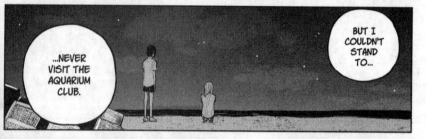

BUT I COULDN'T STAND TO...
...NEVER VISIT THE AQUARIUM CLUB.
SO I'LL STILL POP IN SOME-TIMES.
THIS ISN'T THE END.
BUT...
...I'LL LEAVE THE CLUB IN YOUR CARE.

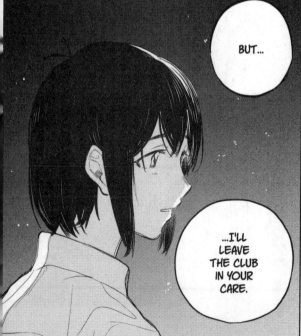

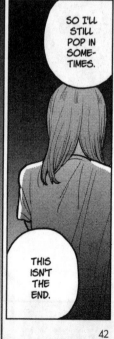

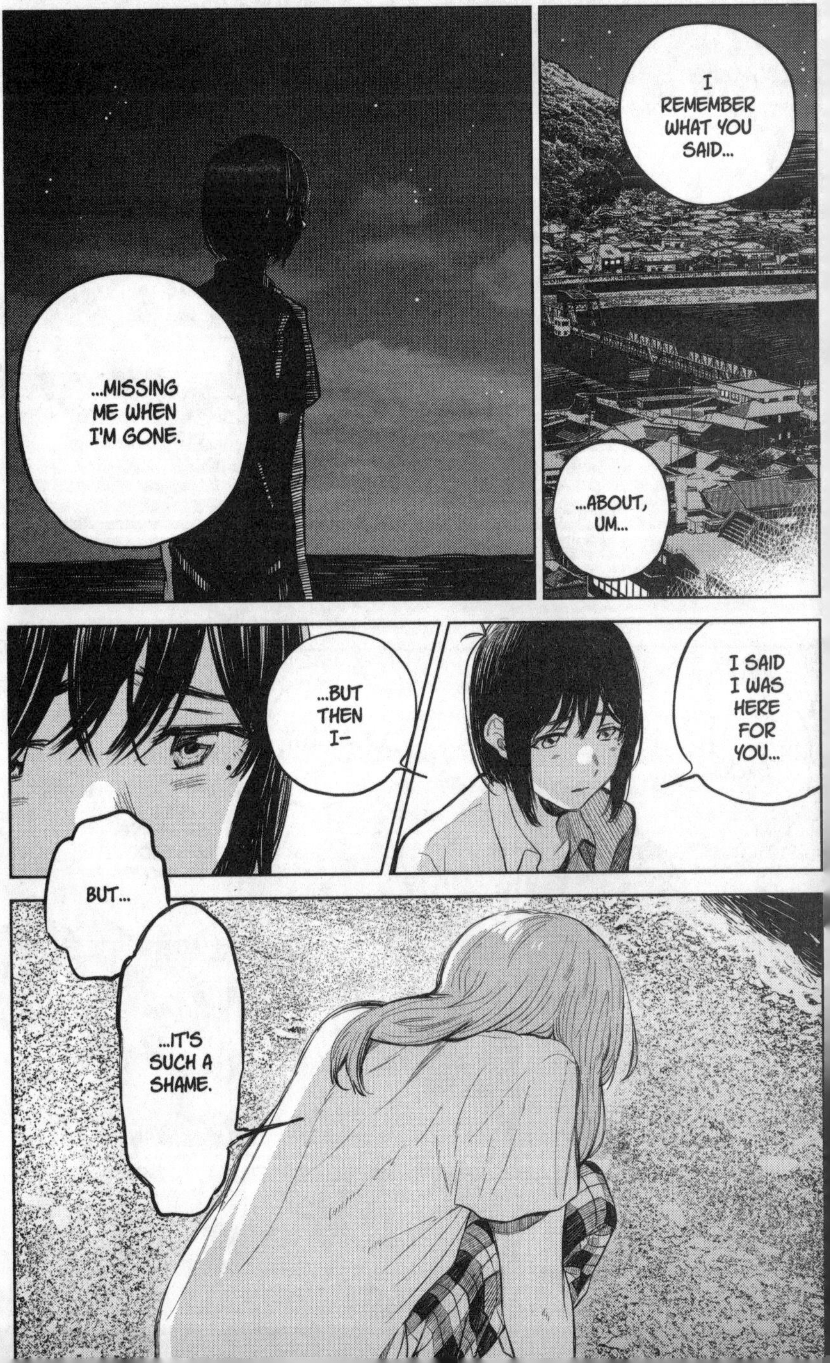
I REMEMBER WHAT YOU SAID...
...ABOUT, UM...
...MISSING ME WHEN I'M GONE.
I SAID I WAS HERE FOR YOU...
...BUT THEN I–
BUT...
...IT'S SUCH A SHAME.

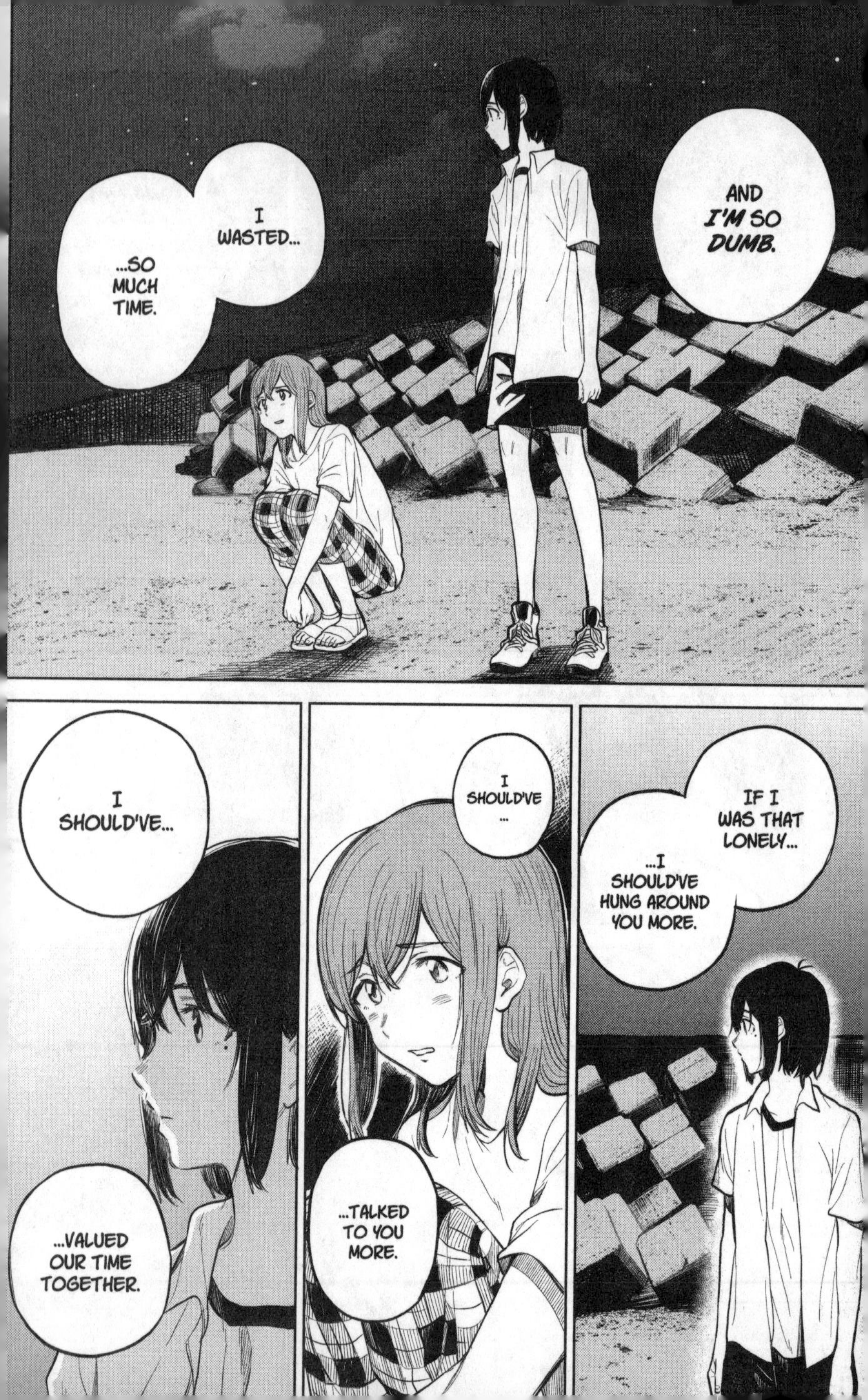
AND I'M SO DUMB.
I WASTED...
...SO MUCH TIME.
IF I WAS THAT LONELY...
...I SHOULD'VE HUNG AROUND YOU MORE.
I SHOULD'VE ...
...TALKED TO YOU MORE.
I SHOULD'VE...
...VALUED OUR TIME TOGETHER.

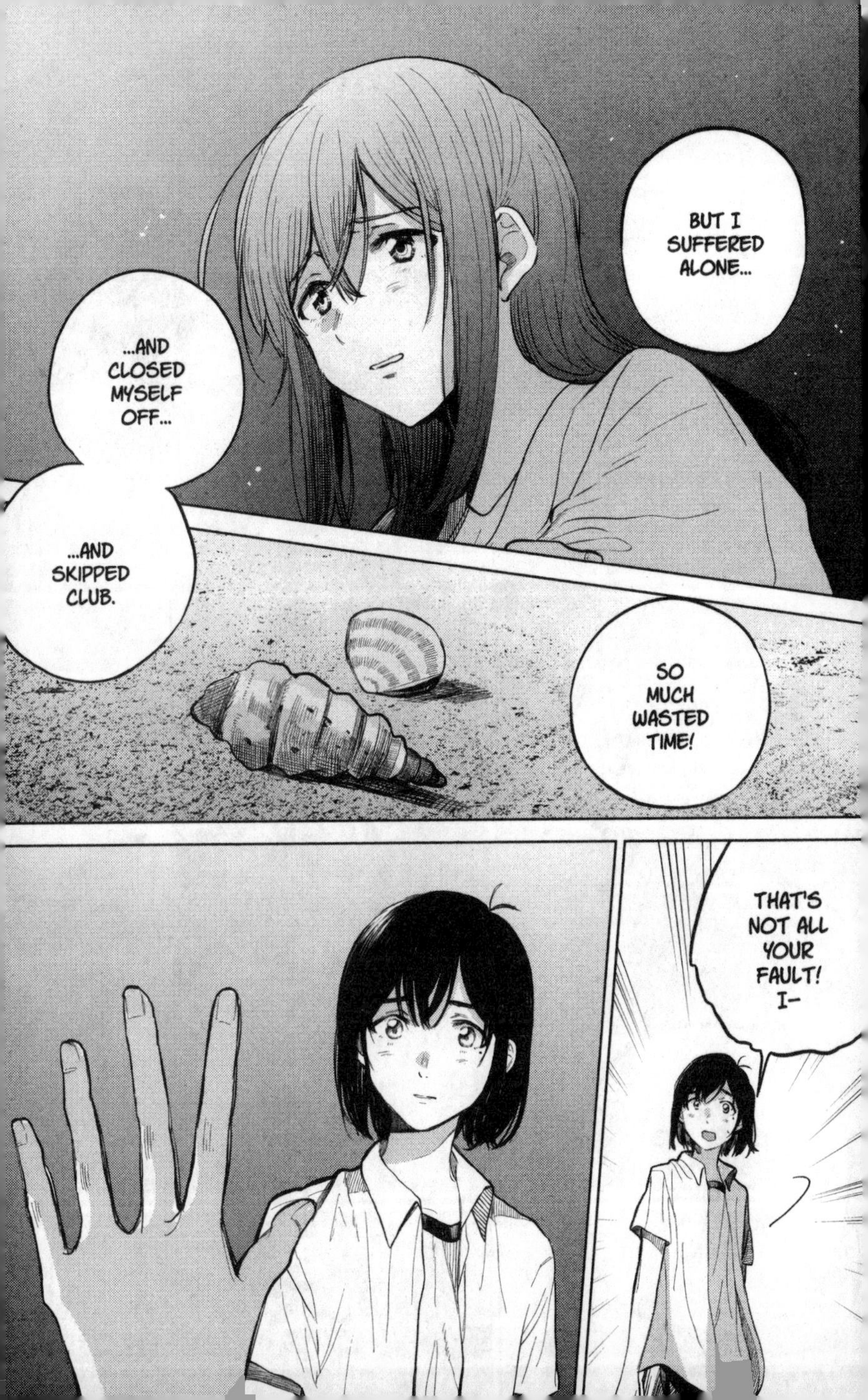
BUT I SUFFERED ALONE...
...AND CLOSED MYSELF OFF...
...AND SKIPPED CLUB.
SO MUCH WASTED TIME!
THAT'S NOT ALL YOUR FAULT! I–

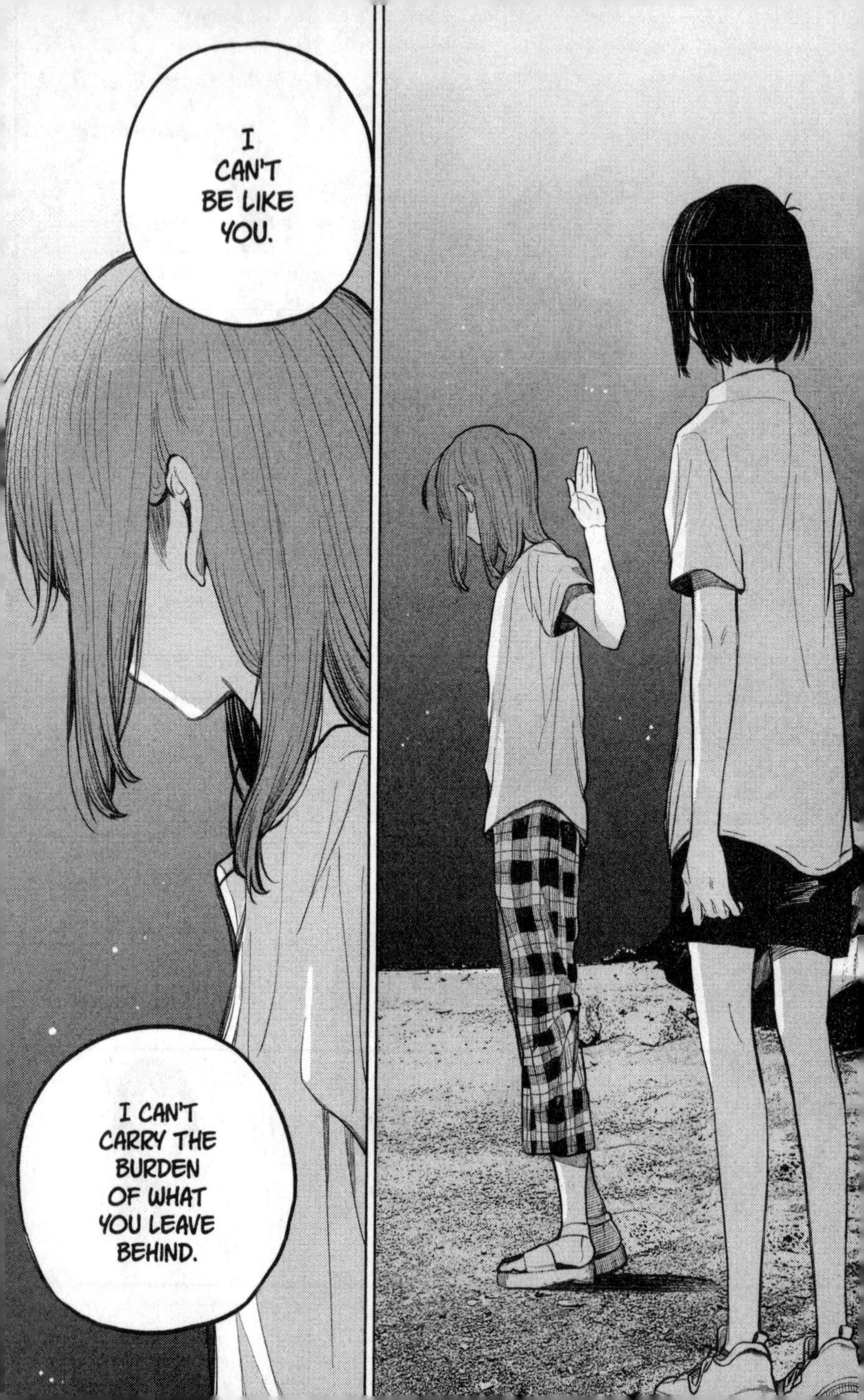
I CAN'T BE LIKE YOU.
I CAN'T CARRY THE BURDEN OF WHAT YOU LEAVE BEHIND.

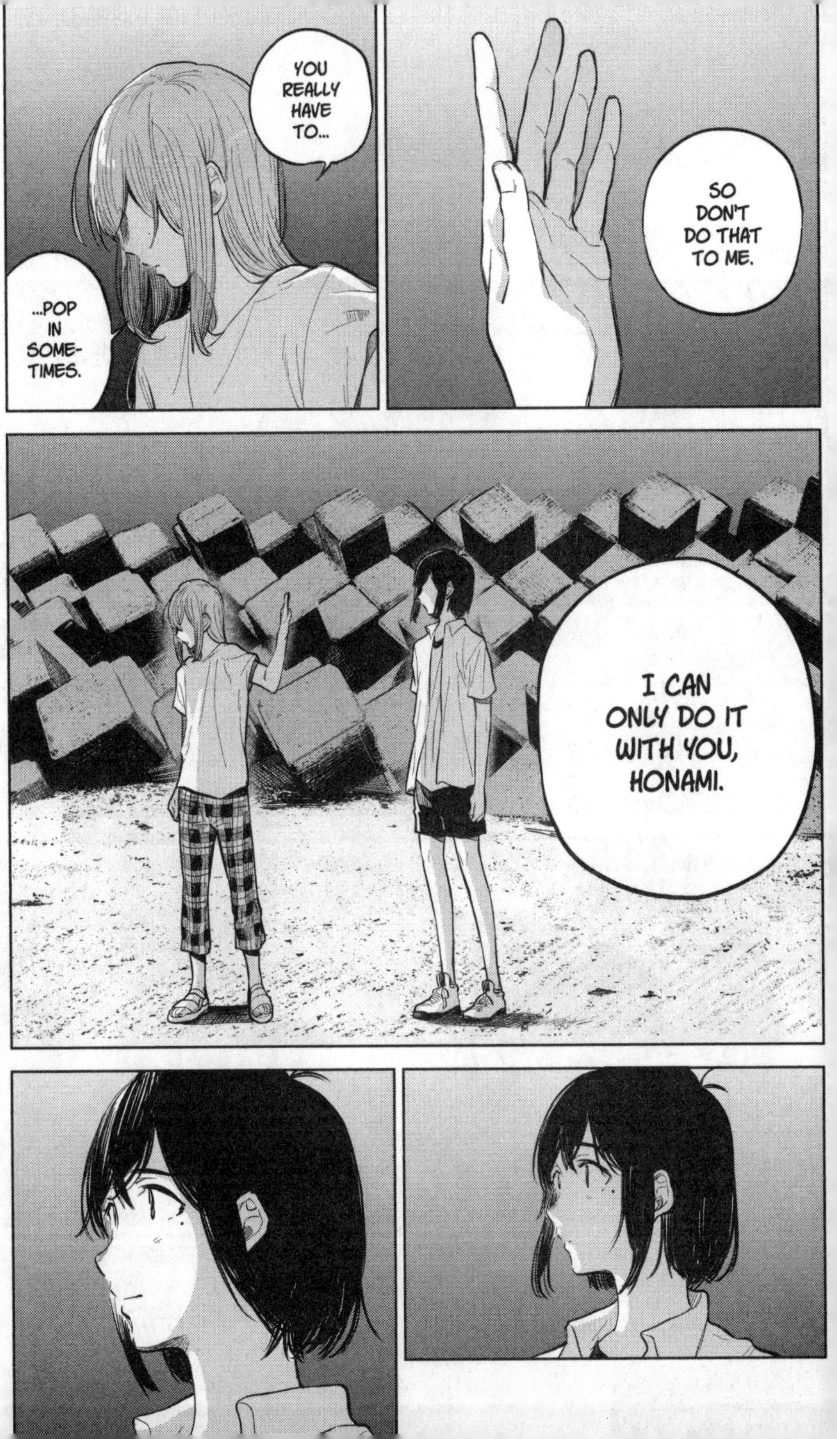
SO DON'T DO THAT TO ME.
YOU REALLY HAVE TO...
...POP IN SOME-TIMES.
I CAN ONLY DO IT WITH YOU, HONAMI.

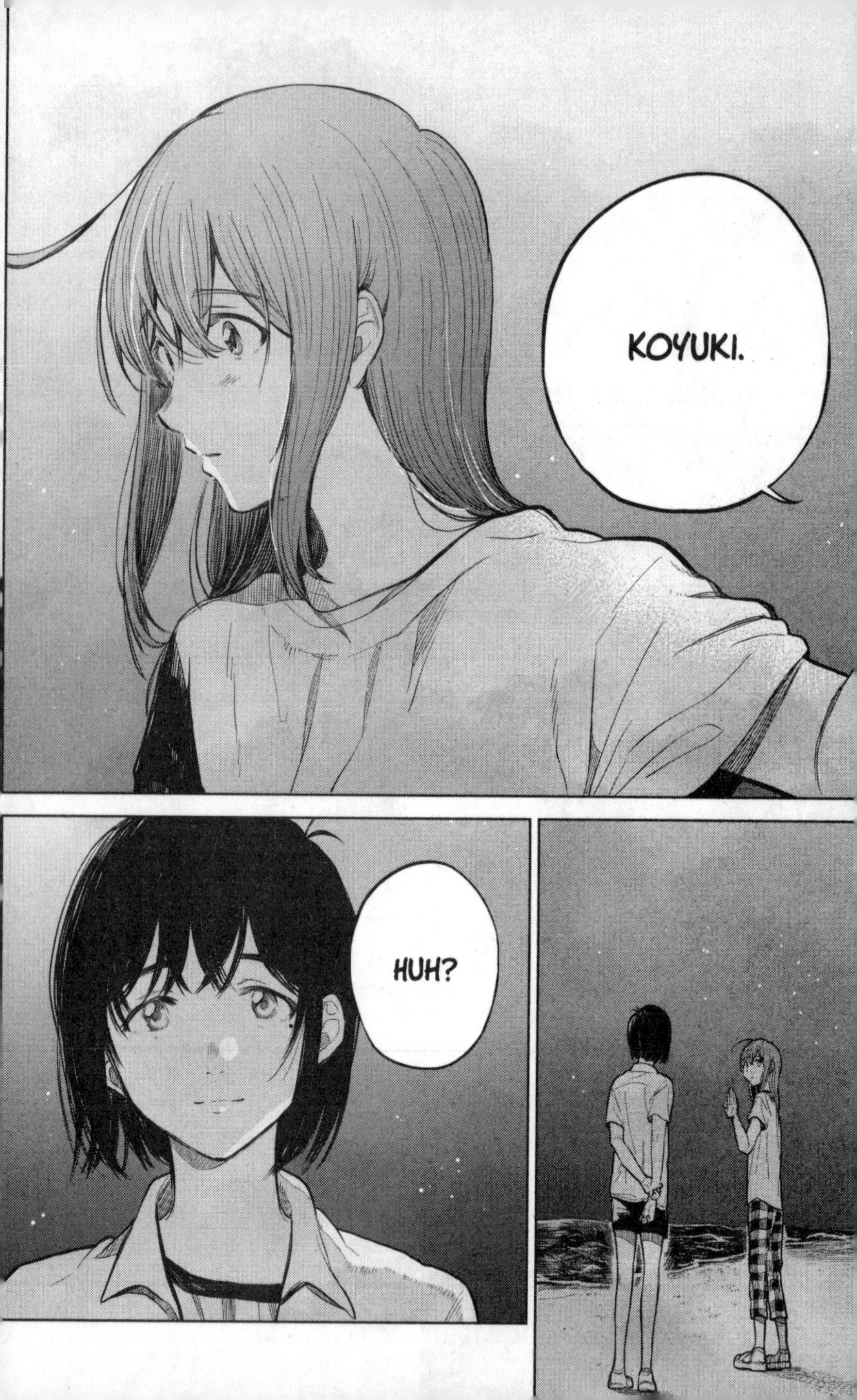
KOYUKI.
HUH?

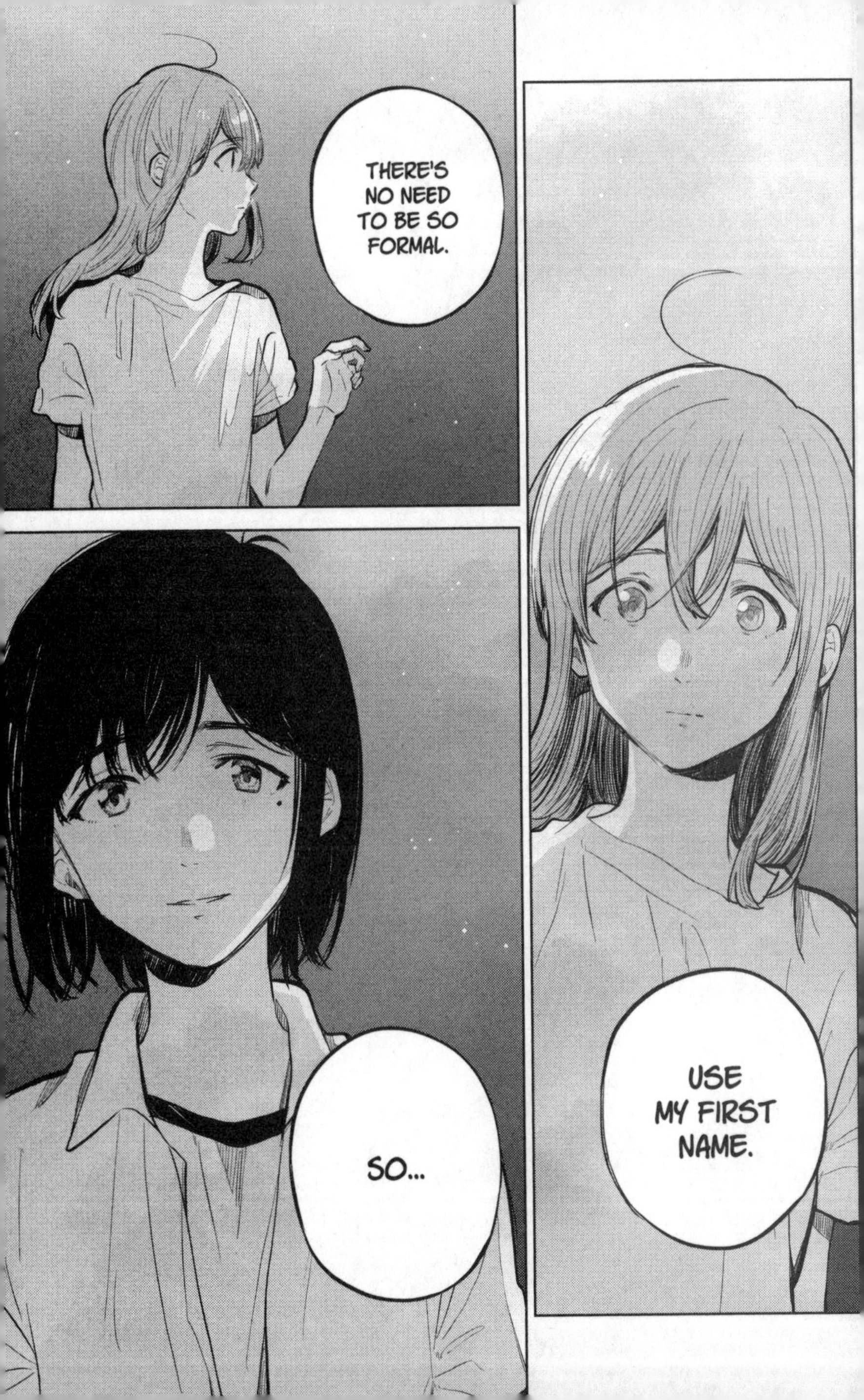
USE MY FIRST NAME.
THERE'S NO NEED TO BE SO FORMAL.
SO...

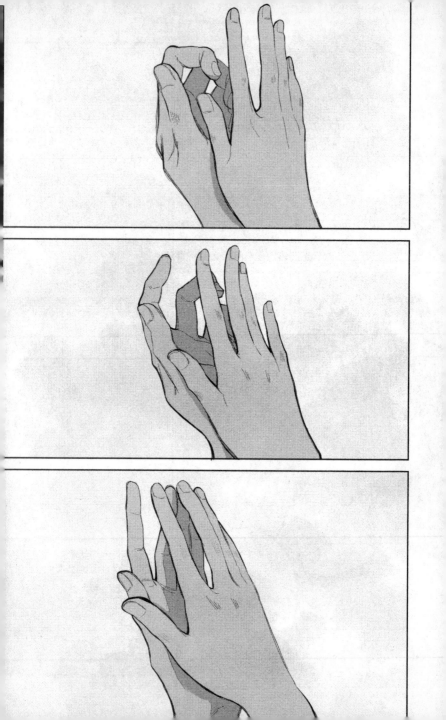

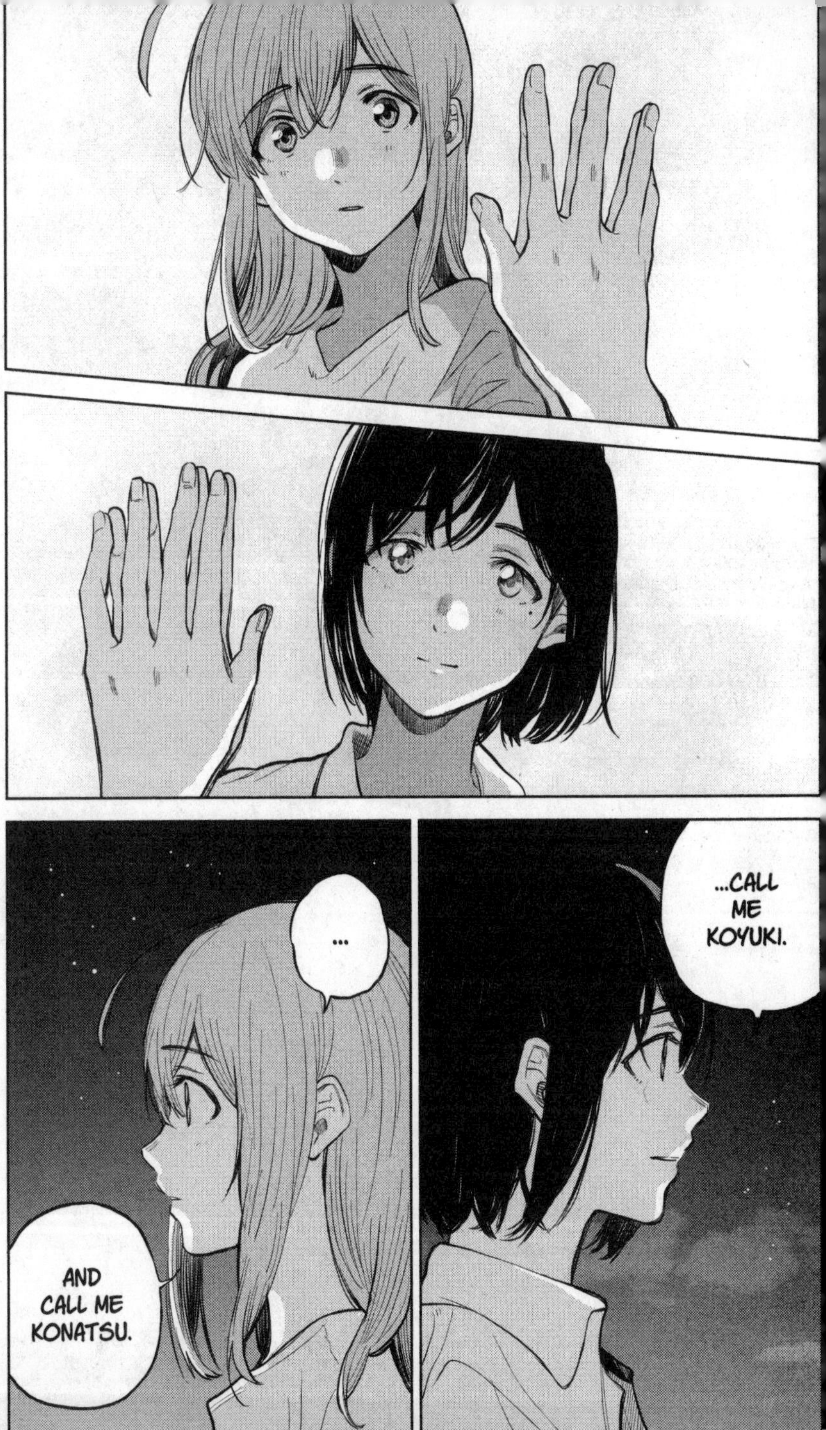
...CALL ME KOYUKI.
...
AND CALL ME KONATSU.

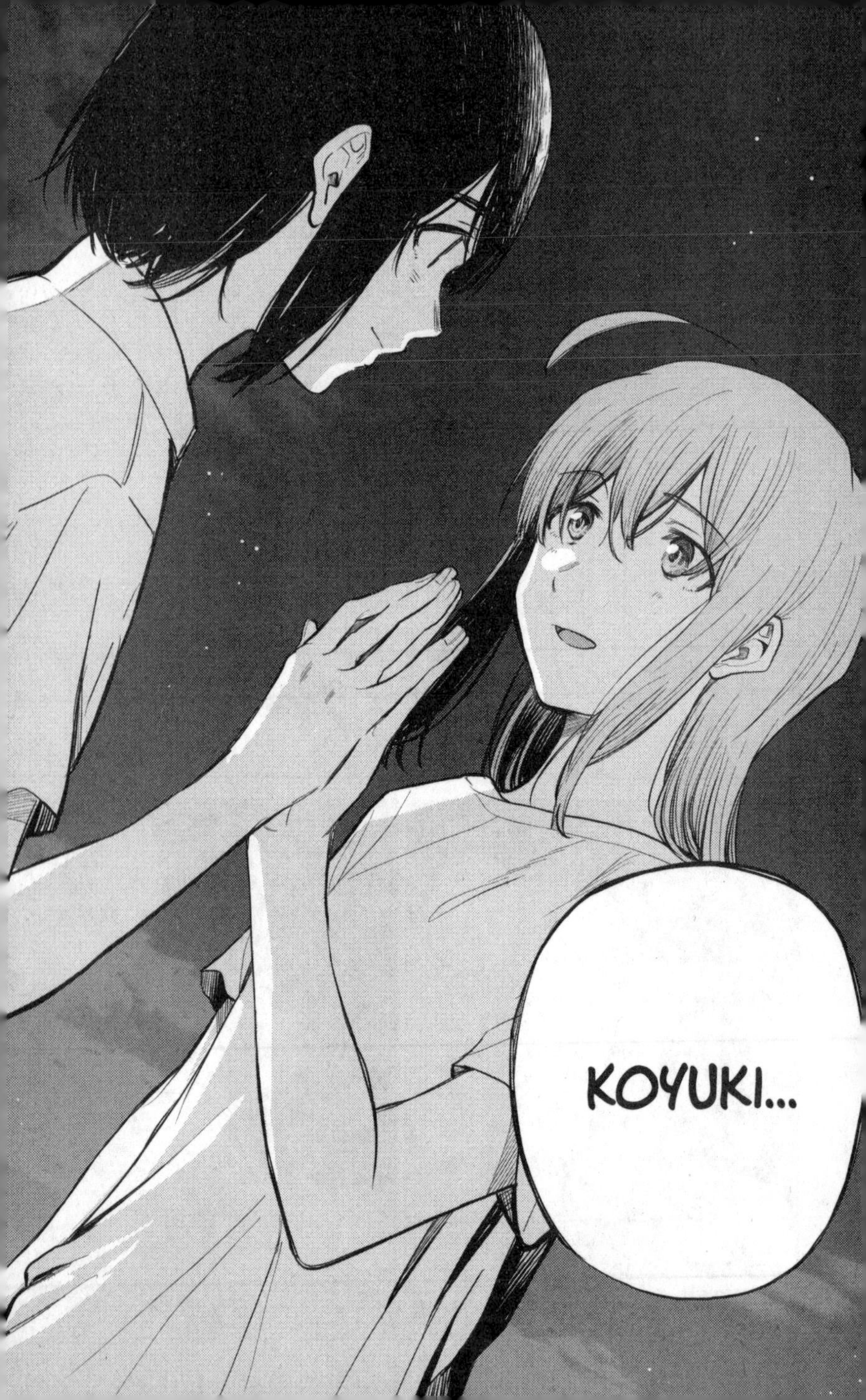
KOYUKI...

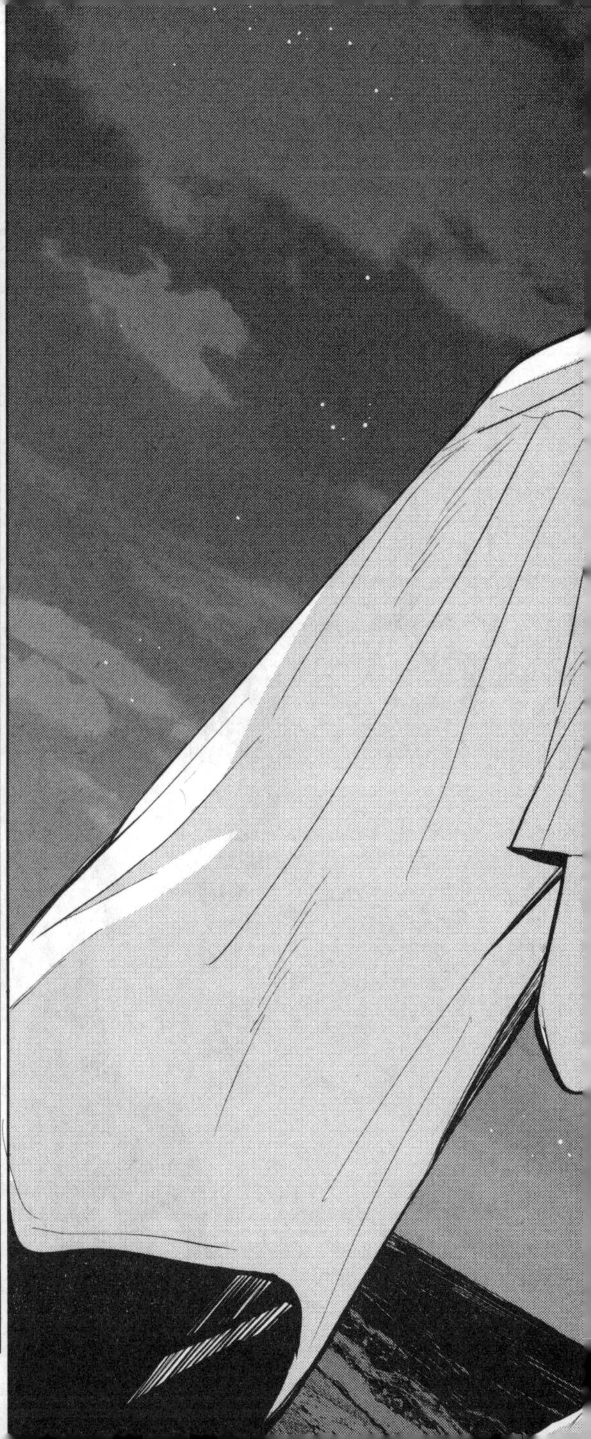

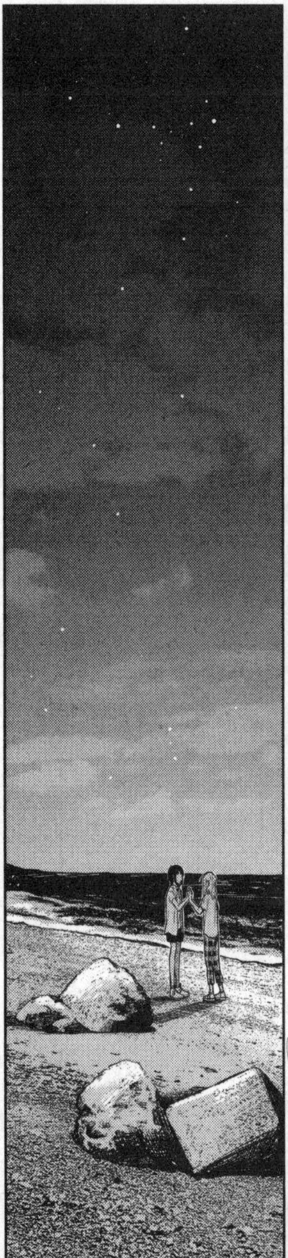

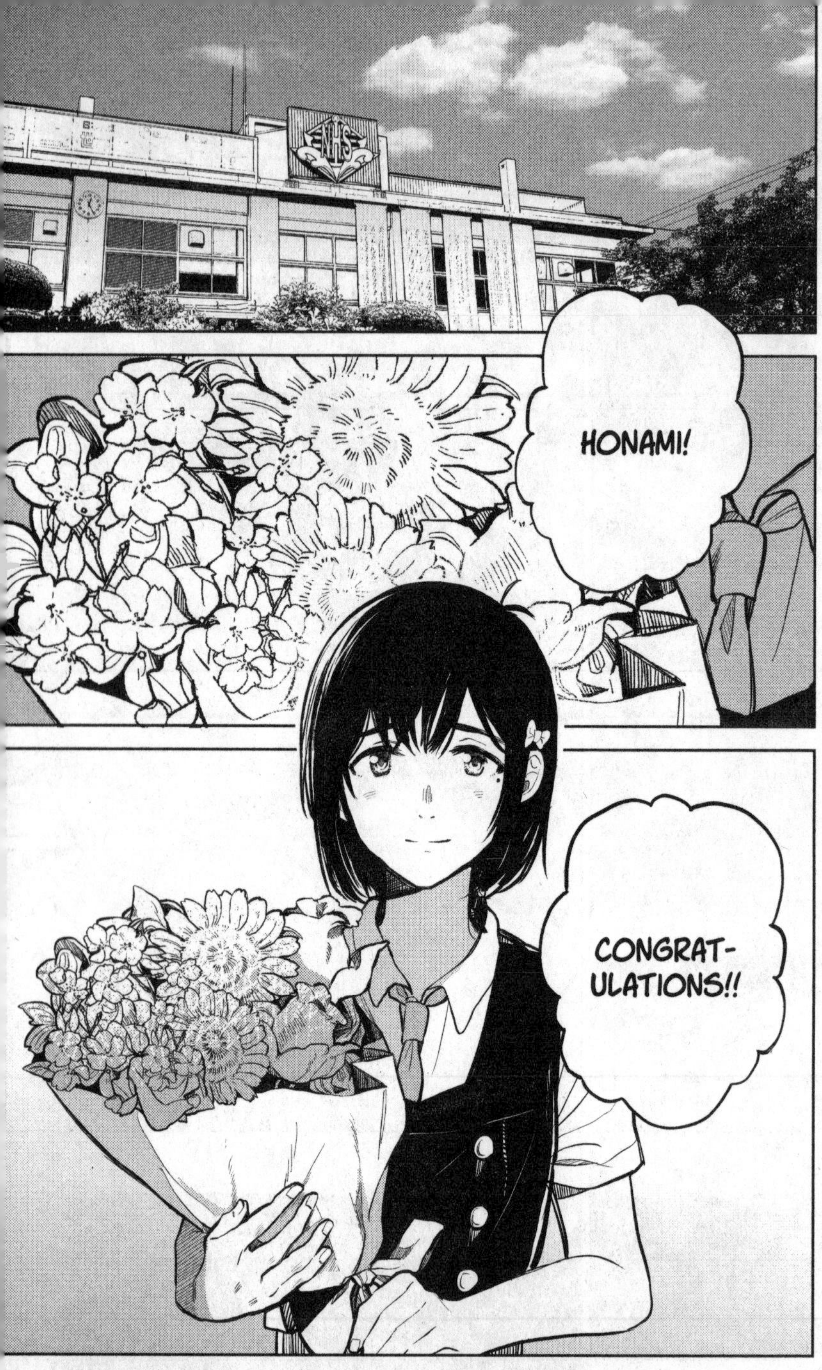
HONAMI!
CONGRAT-ULATIONS!!

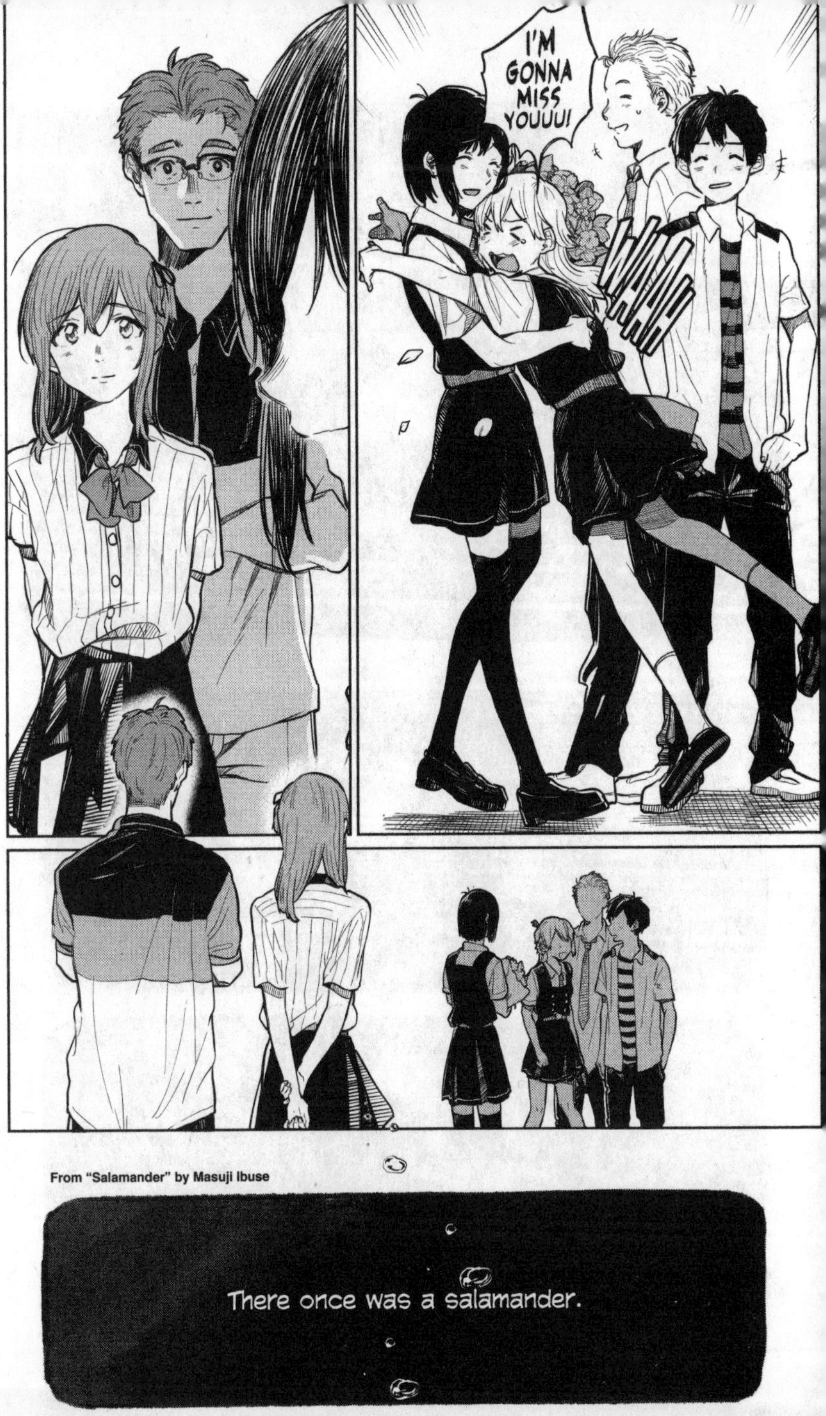
I'M GONNA MISS YOUUU!

From "Salamander" by Masuji Ibuse

There once was a salamander.

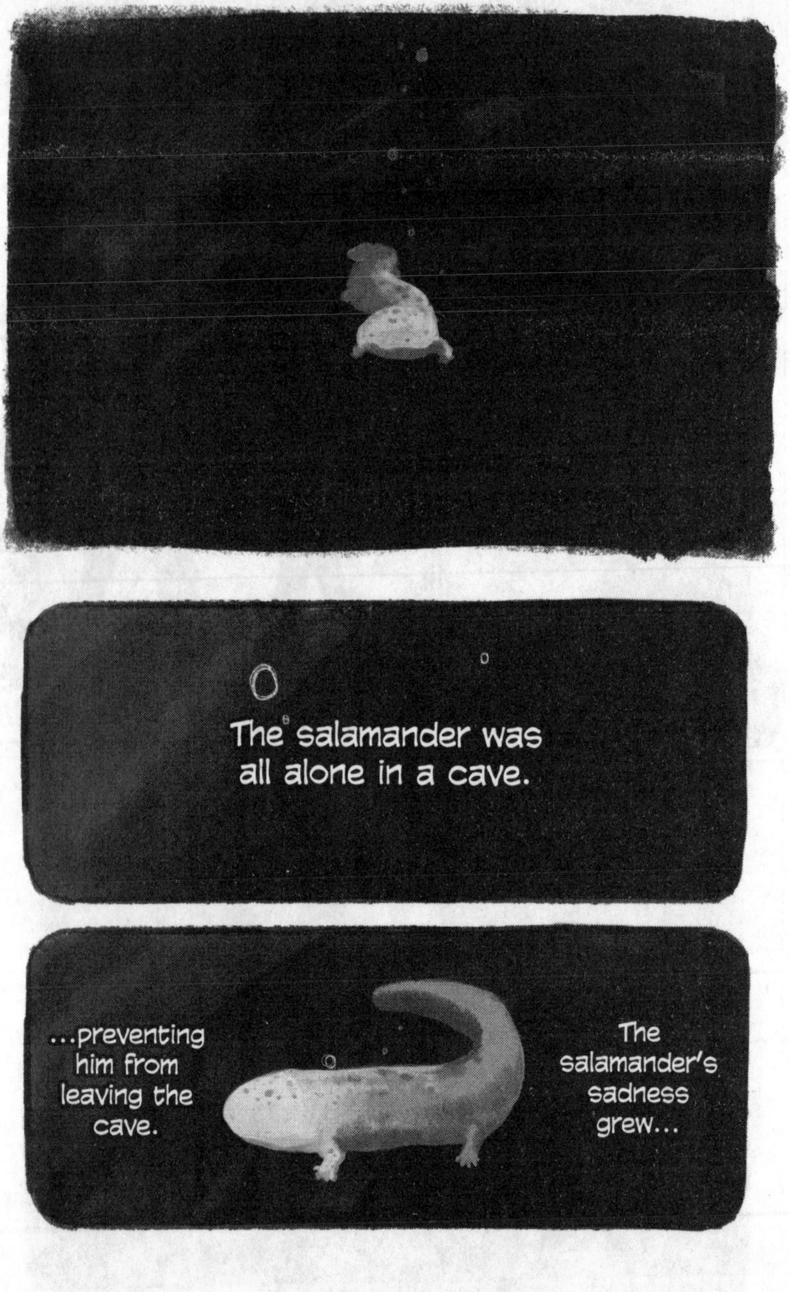
The salamander was all alone in a cave.
The salamander's sadness grew...
...preventing him from leaving the cave.

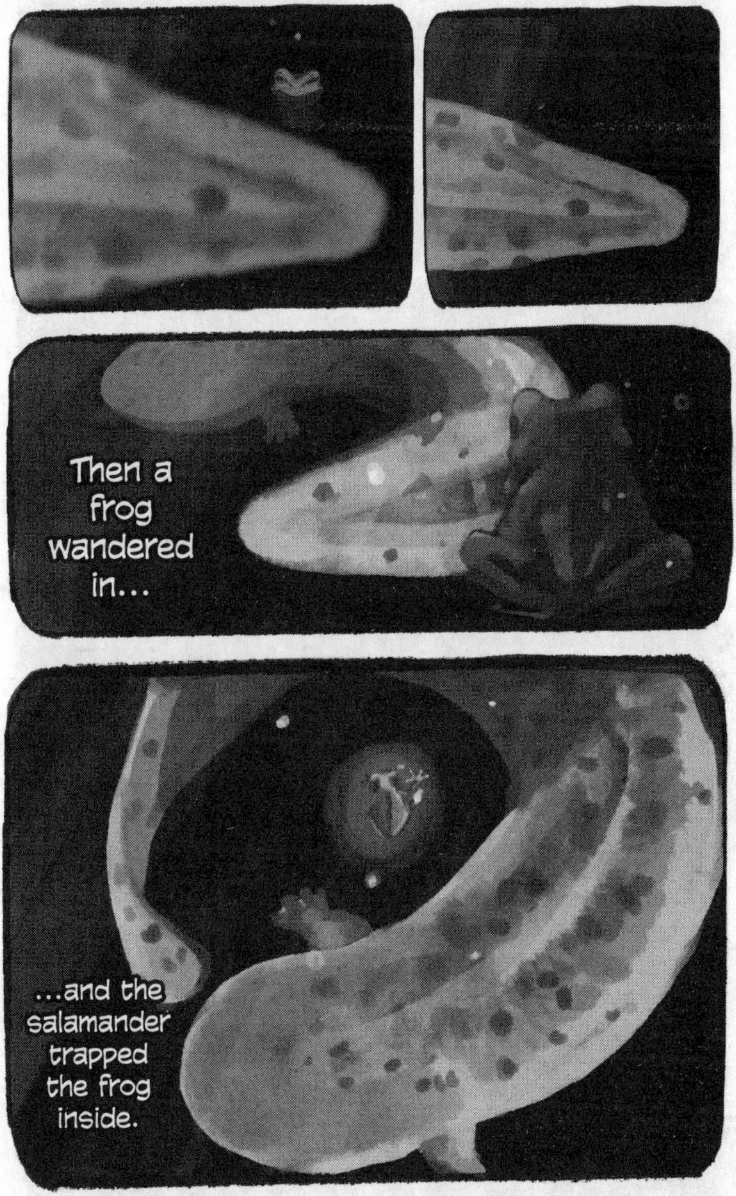
Then a frog wandered in...
...and the salamander trapped the frog inside.

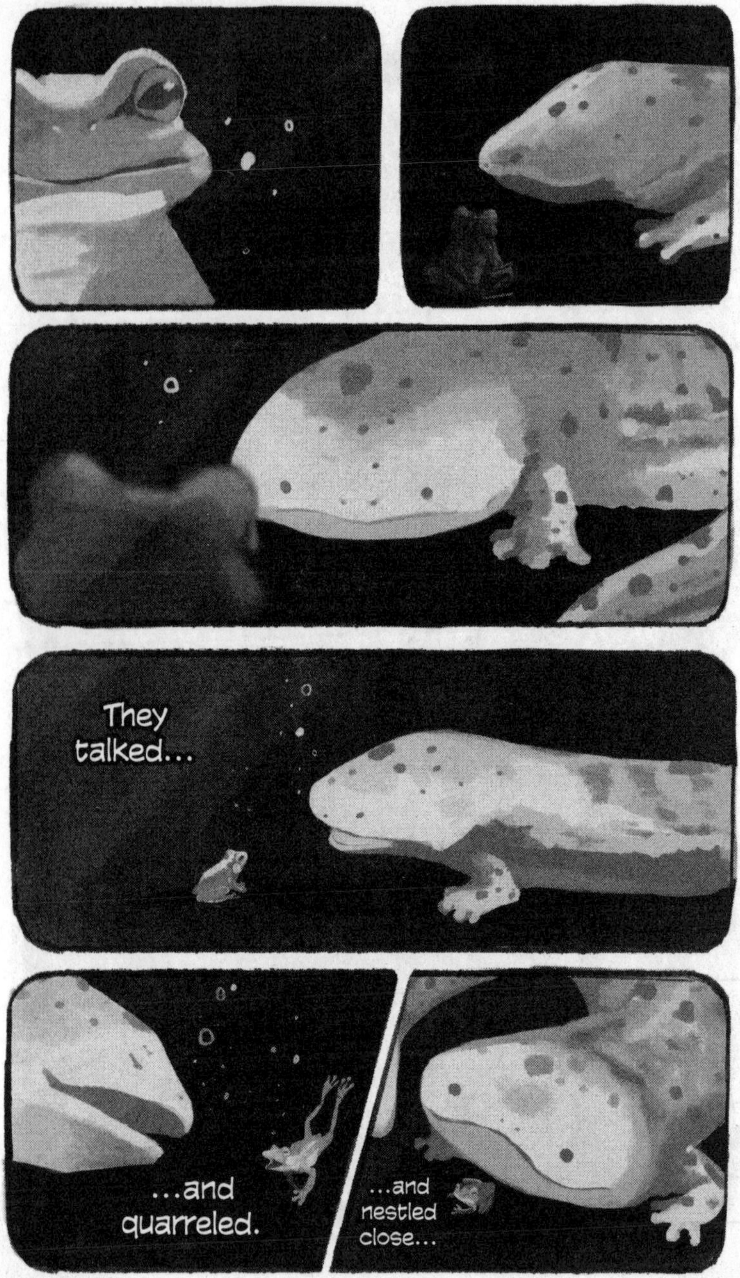
They talked...
...and nestled close...
...and quarreled.

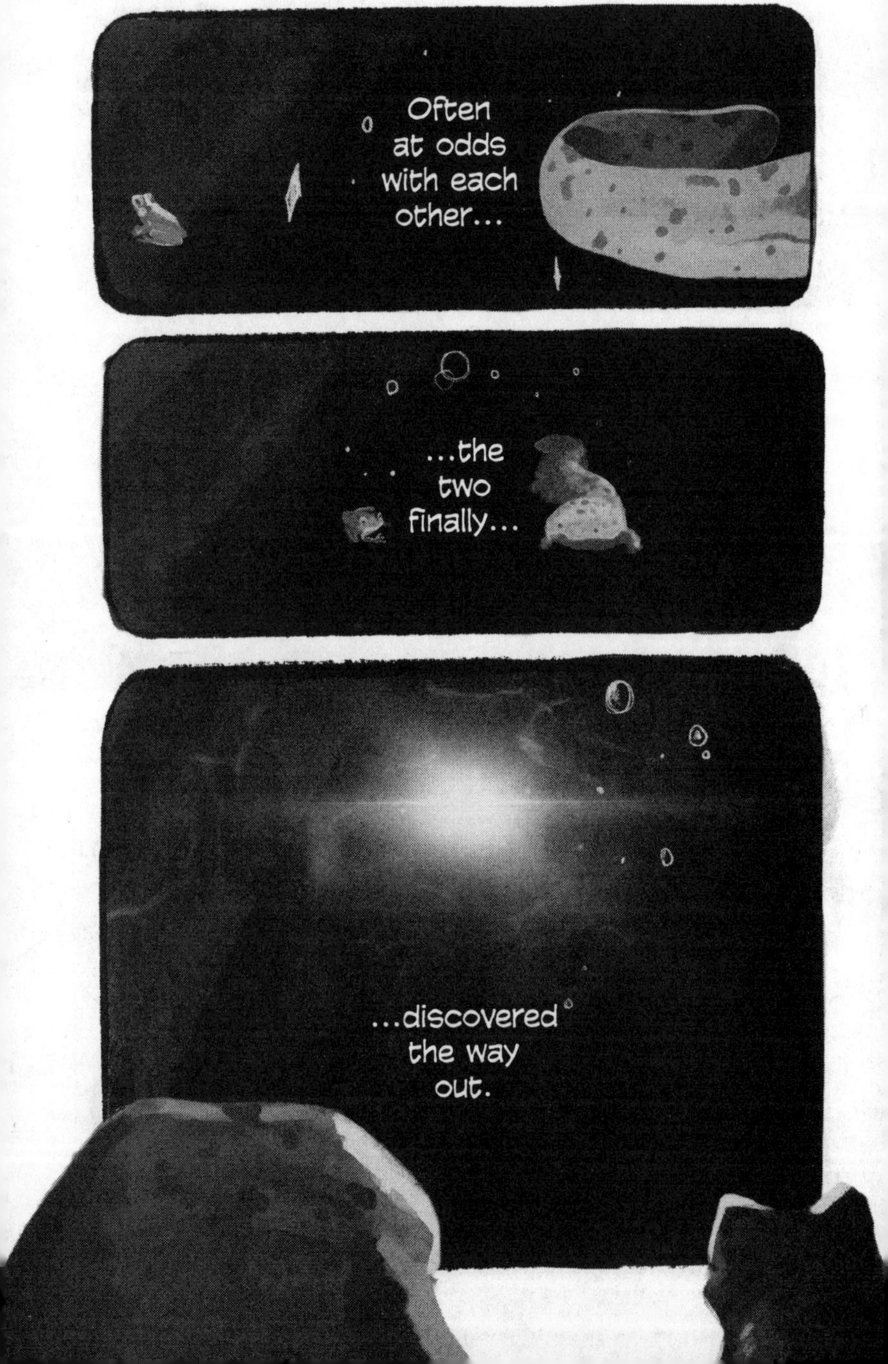
Often at odds with each other...
...the two finally...
...discovered the way out.

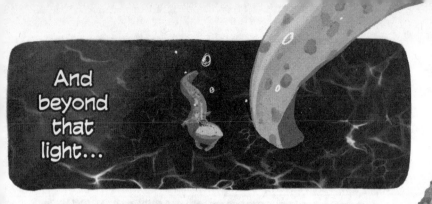

And
beyond
that
light...

...what
did
they
find?

A Tropical Fish
Yearns for Snow

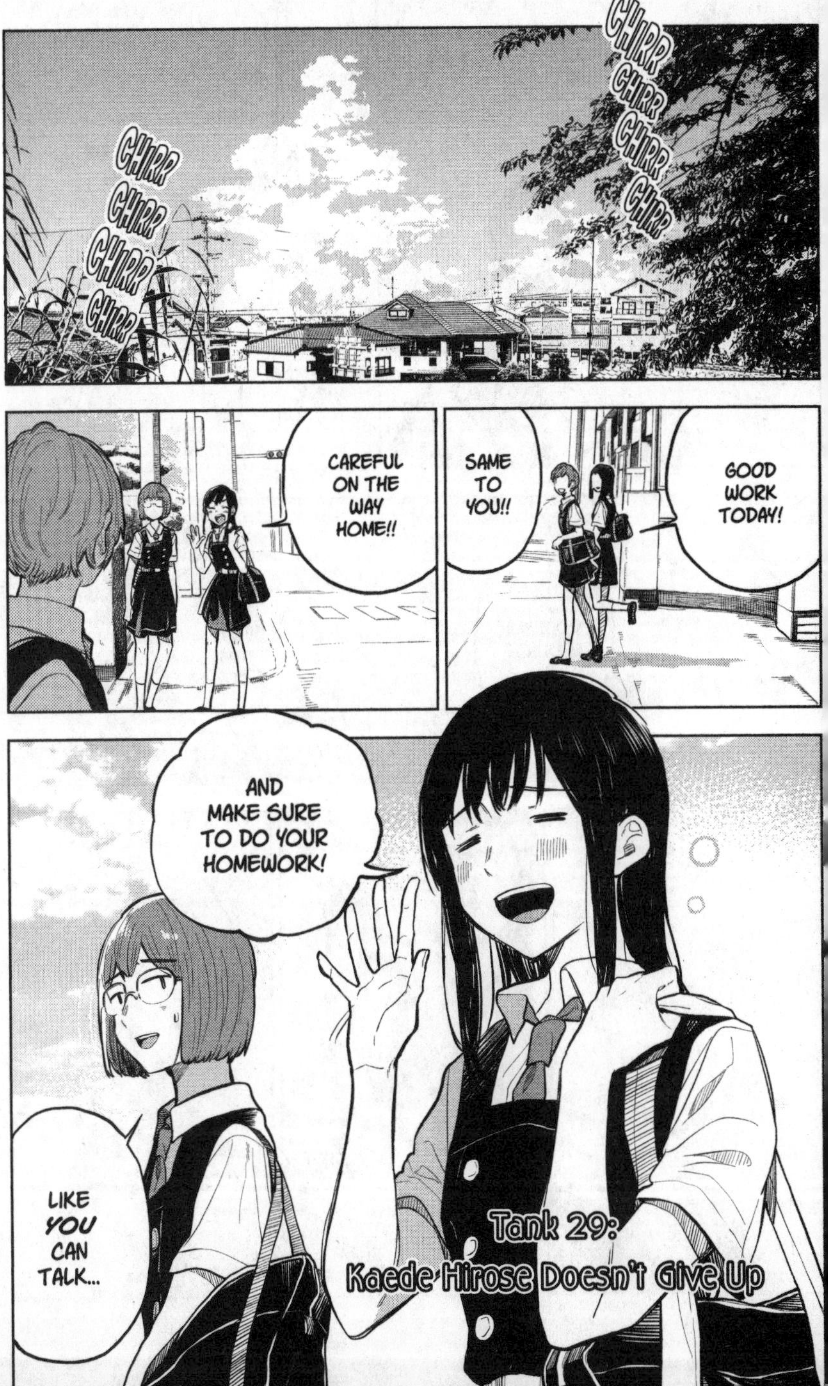
CHIRR CHIRR CHIRR CHIRR
CHIRR CHIRR CHIRR CHIRR
GOOD WORK TODAY!
SAME TO YOU!!
CAREFUL ON THE WAY HOME!!
AND MAKE SURE TO DO YOUR HOMEWORK!
Tank 29:
Kaede Hirose Doesn't Give Up
LIKE YOU CAN TALK...

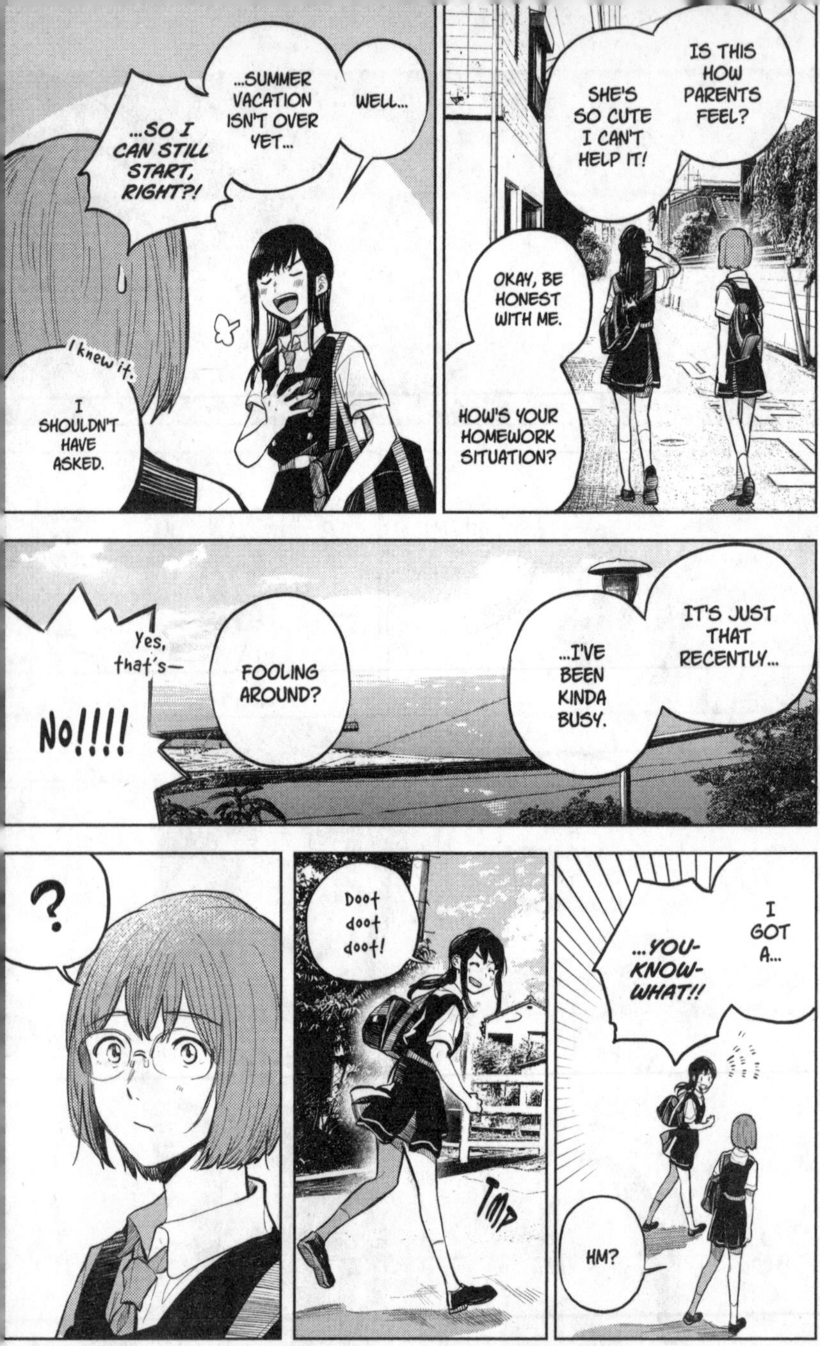
IS THIS HOW PARENTS FEEL?
SHE'S SO CUTE I CAN'T HELP IT!
OKAY, BE HONEST WITH ME.
HOW'S YOUR HOMEWORK SITUATION?
WELL...
...SUMMER VACATION ISN'T OVER YET...
...SO I CAN STILL START, RIGHT?!
I knew it.
I SHOULDN'T HAVE ASKED.
IT'S JUST THAT RECENTLY...
...I'VE BEEN KINDA BUSY.
FOOLING AROUND?
Yes, that's—
NO!!!!
I GOT A...
...YOU-KNOW-WHAT!!
HM?
Doot doot doot!
TMP
?

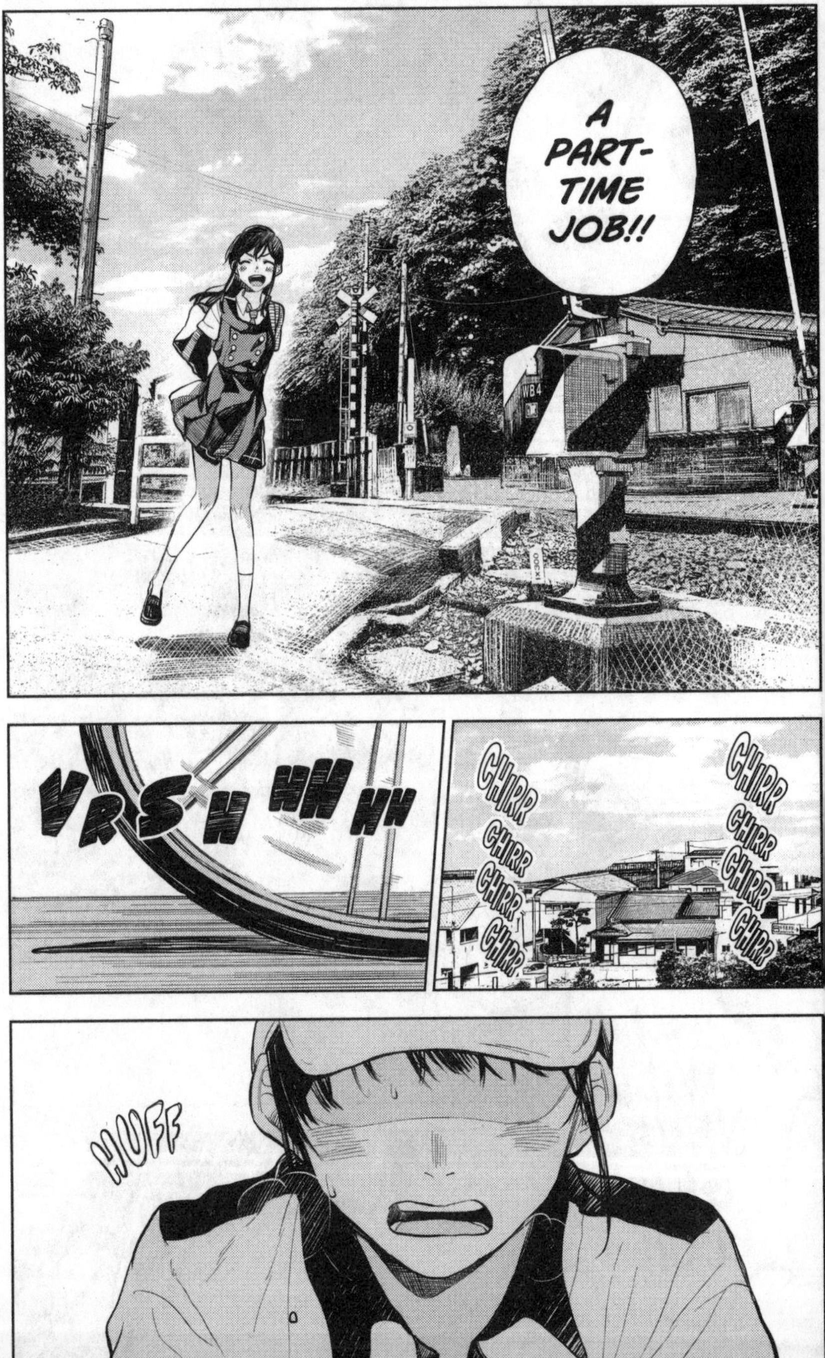
A PART-TIME JOB!!
CHIRR CHIRR CHIRR CHIRR
CHIRR CHIRR CHIRR CHIRR
VRSH HH HH
HUFF

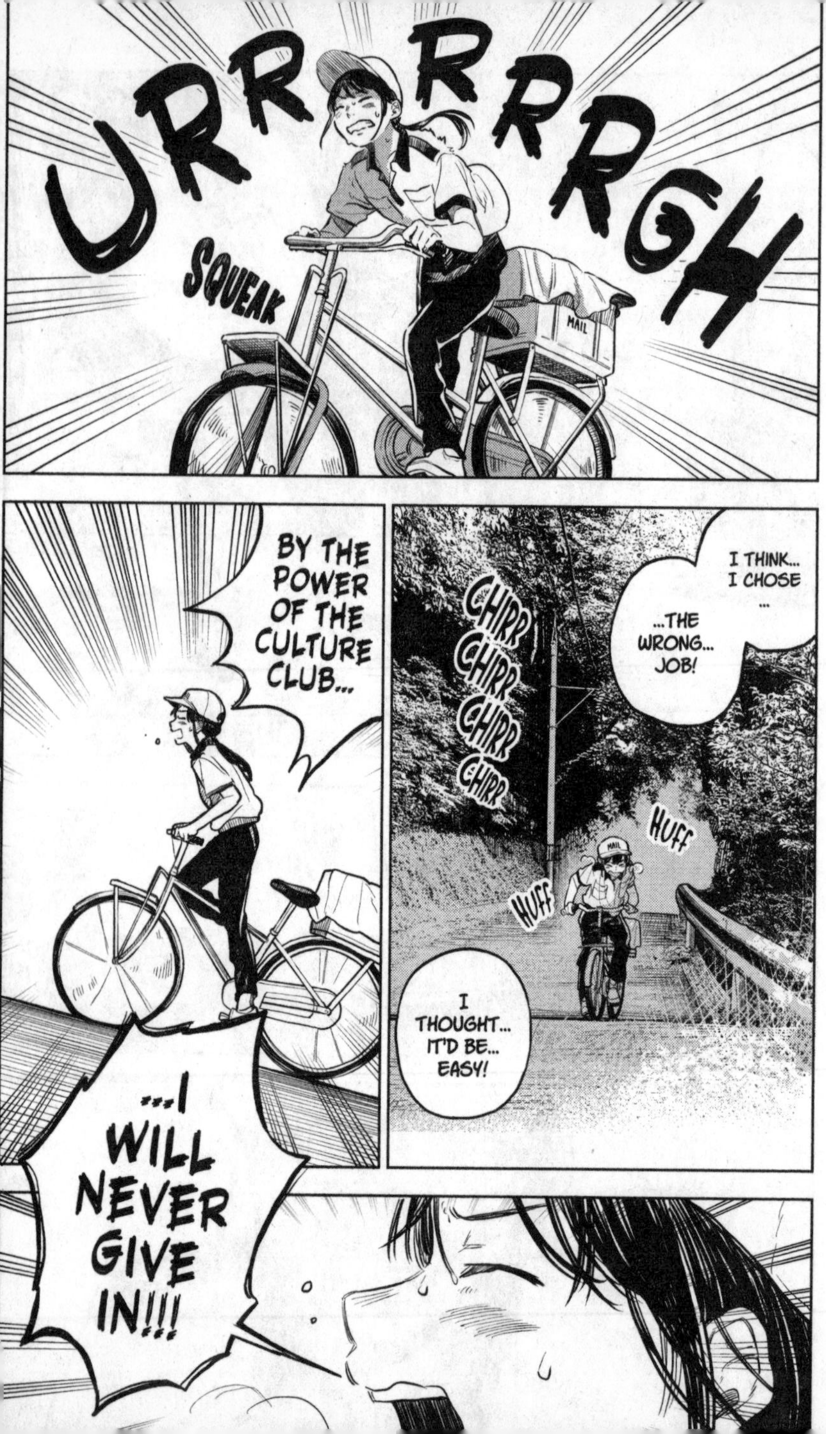
URRRRRRGH
SQUEAK
MAIL
I THINK... I CHOSE ...
...THE WRONG... JOB!
CHIRR CHIRR CHIRR CHIRR
HUFF
HUFF
MAIL
I THOUGHT... IT'D BE... EASY!
BY THE POWER OF THE CULTURE CLUB...
...I WILL NEVER GIVE IN!!!

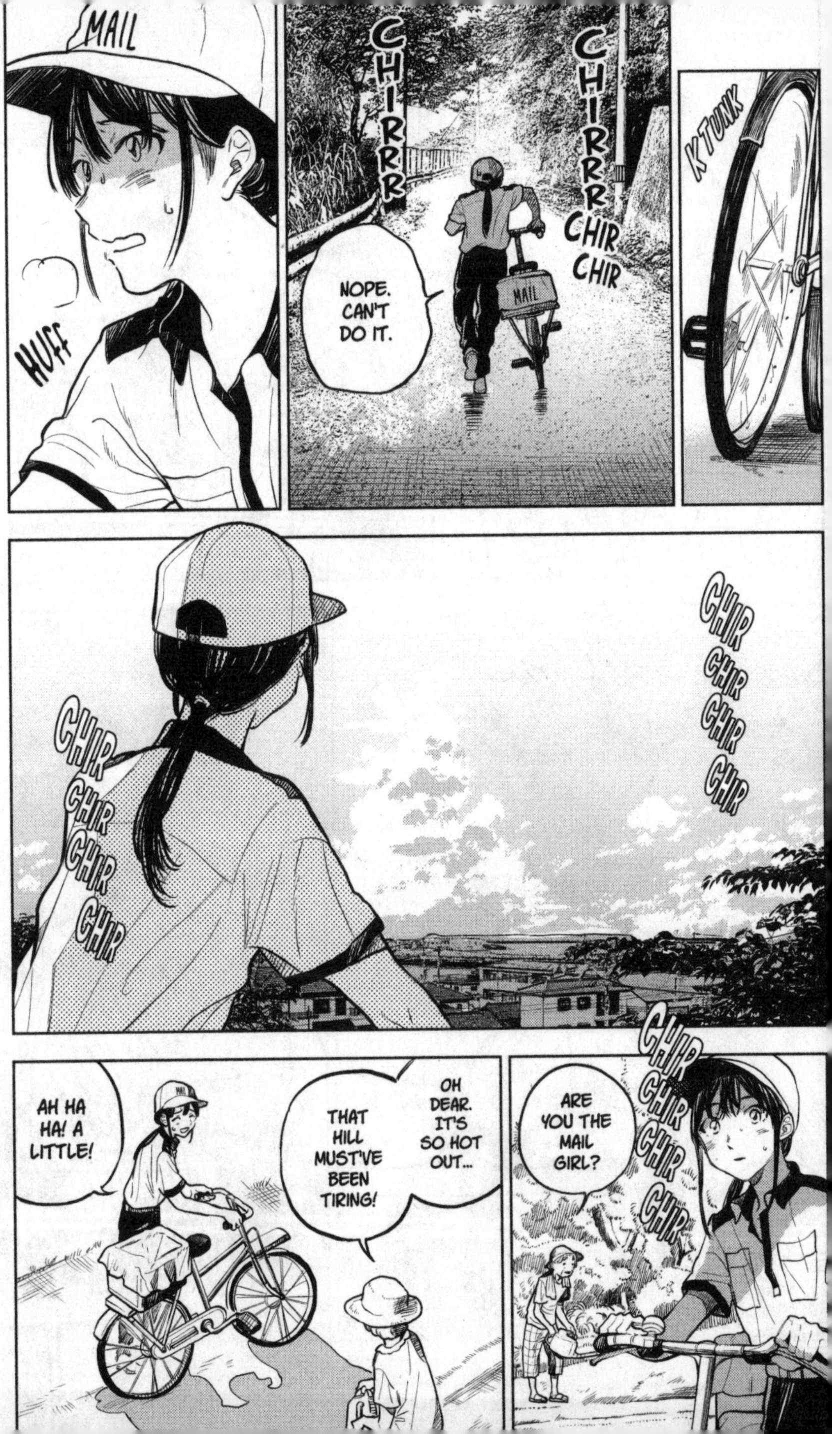
K'TUNK
CHIRRR
CHIRRR
CHIR
CHIR
NOPE. CAN'T DO IT.
MAIL
MAIL
HUFF
CHIR
CHIR
CHIR
CHIR
CHIR
CHIR
CHIR
CHIR
CHIR
CHIR
CHIR
CHIR
ARE YOU THE MAIL GIRL?
OH DEAR. IT'S SO HOT OUT...
THAT HILL MUST'VE BEEN TIRING!
AH HA HA! A LITTLE!

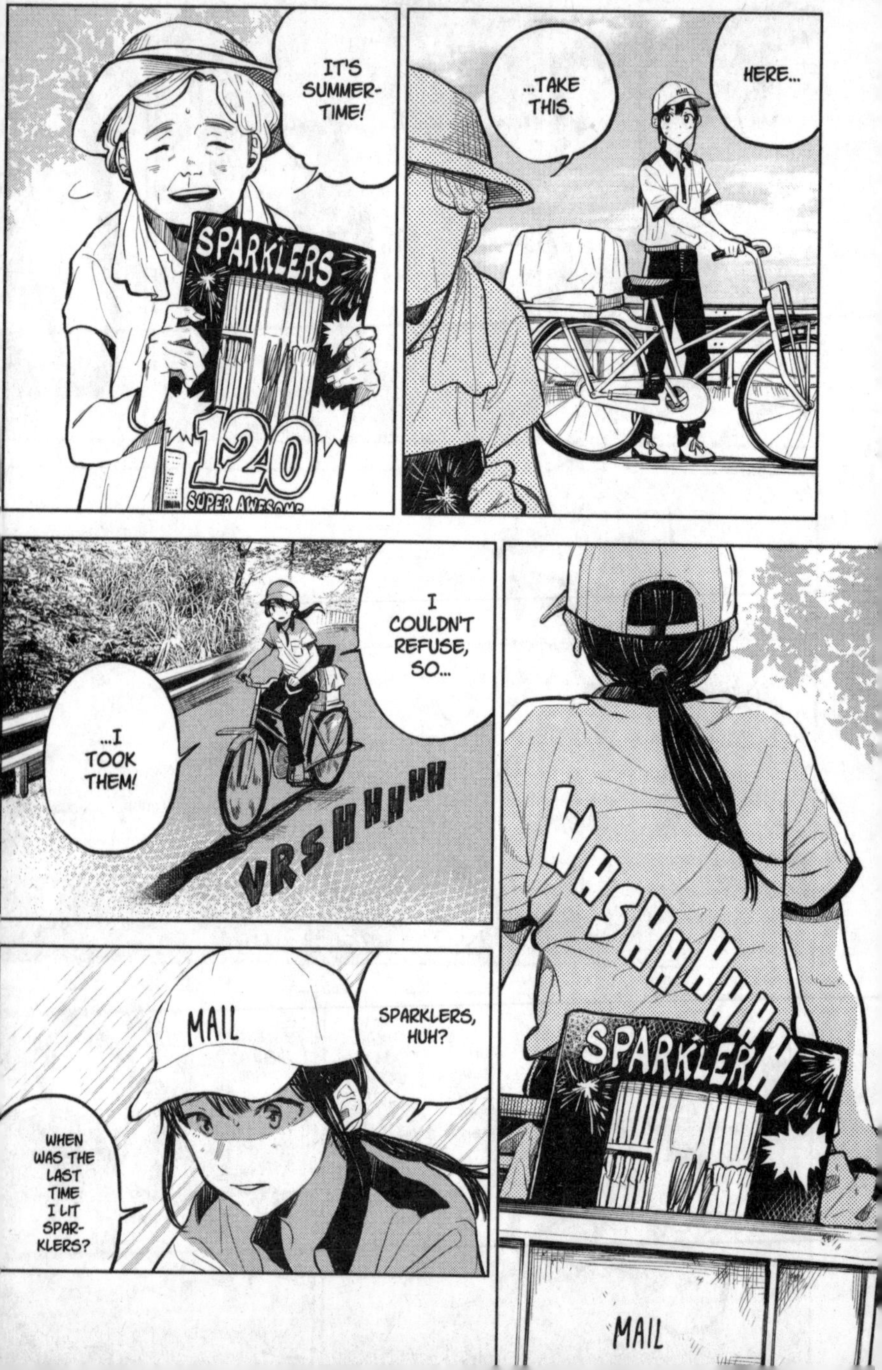
HERE...
...TAKE THIS.
MAIL
IT'S SUMMER-TIME!
SPARKLERS
120
SUPER AWESOME
WHSHHHHHHH
SPARKLER
MAIL
I COULDN'T REFUSE, SO...
...I TOOK THEM!
VRSHHHHH
SPARKLERS, HUH?
MAIL
WHEN WAS THE LAST TIME I LIT SPARKLERS?

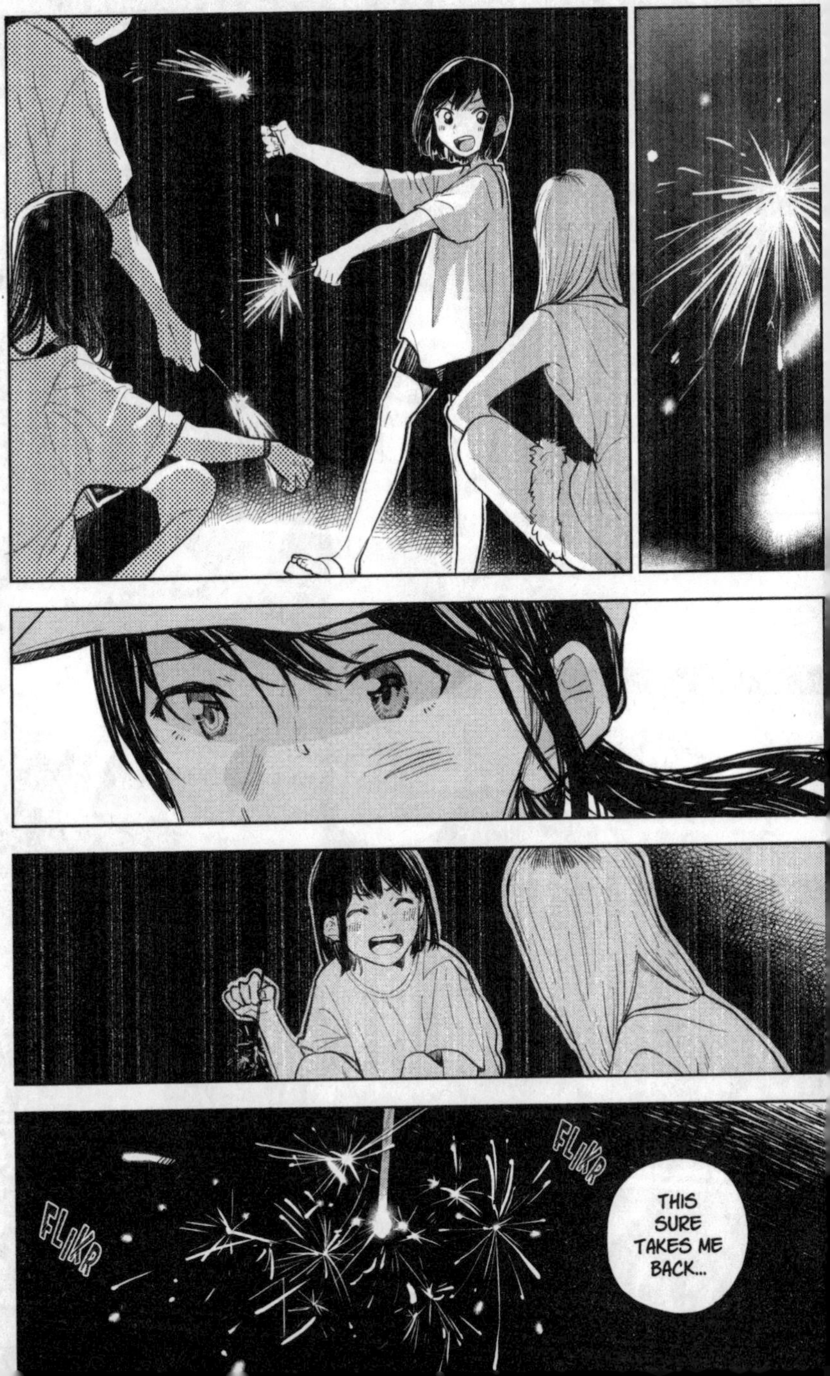
FLIKR
THIS SURE TAKES ME BACK...
FLIKR

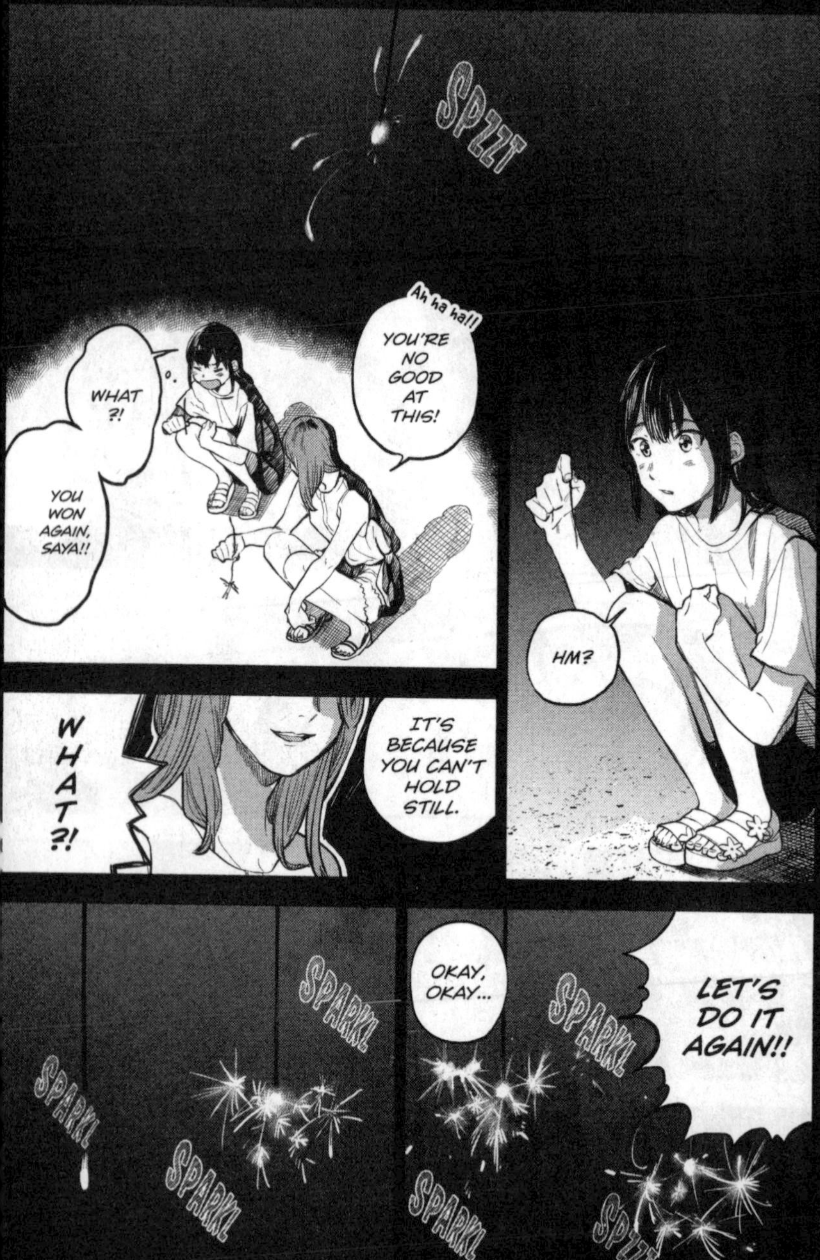
SPZZT
HM?
Ah ha ha!!
YOU'RE NO GOOD AT THIS!
WHAT?!
YOU WON AGAIN, SAYA!!
IT'S BECAUSE YOU CAN'T HOLD STILL.
WHAT?!
LET'S DO IT AGAIN!!
SPARK!
SPZZT
OKAY, OKAY...
SPARK!
SPARK!
SPARK!
SPARK!

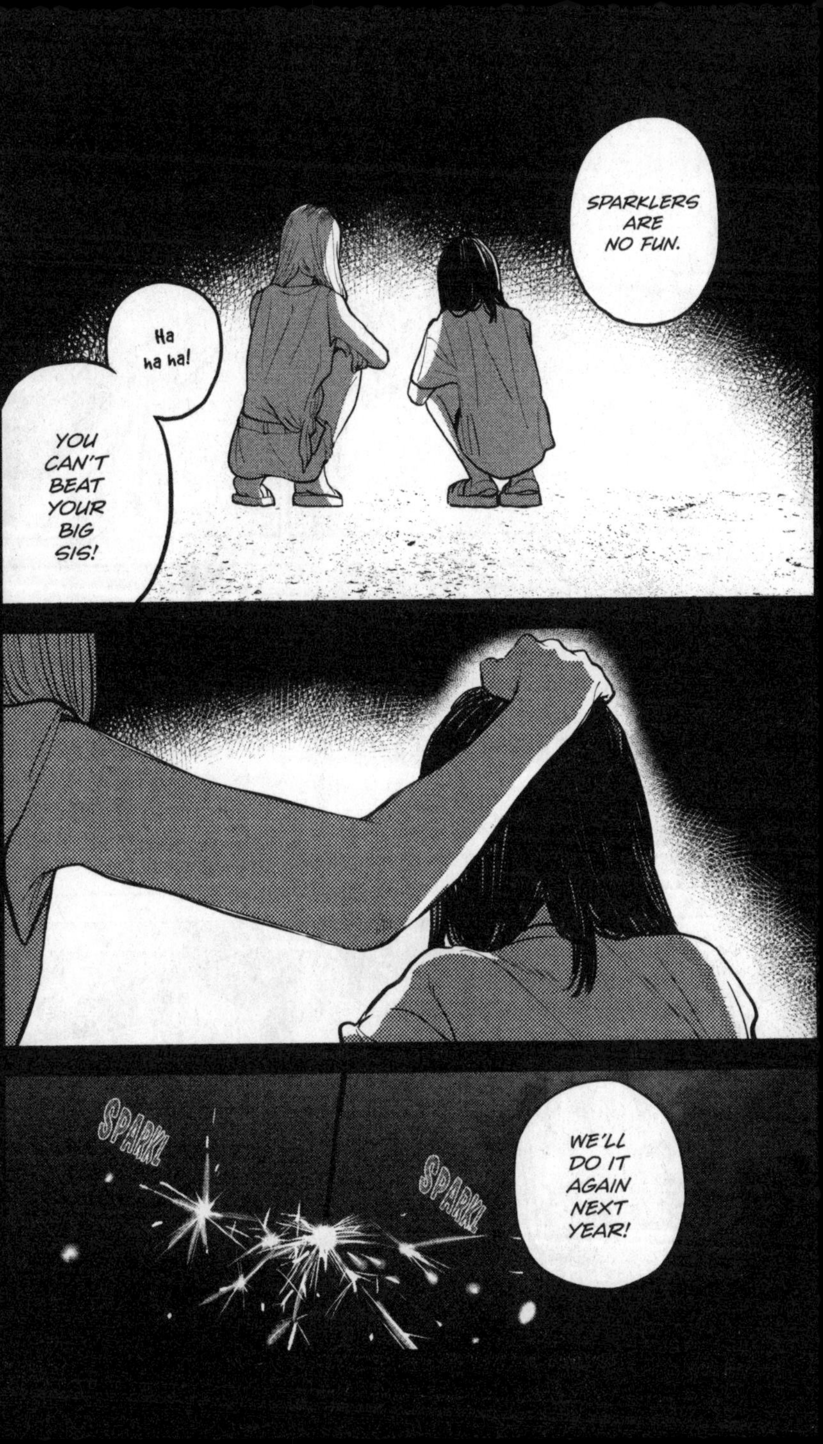
SPARKLERS ARE NO FUN.
Ha ha ha!
YOU CAN'T BEAT YOUR BIG SIS!
SPARK!
SPARK!
WE'LL DO IT AGAIN NEXT YEAR!

KTUNK
CHIRR CHIR CHIR CHIR CHIR
CHIR CHIRRR CHIR CHIR CHIR
CHIR CHIR CHIR CHIR
CHIRR CHIRR CHIRR CHIRR
CHIR CHIR CHIR CHIR
CHIR CHIR CHIR CHIR
That liar...
BMP

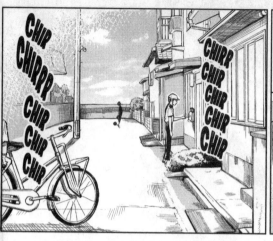

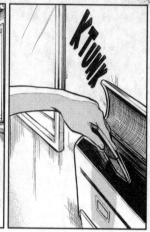

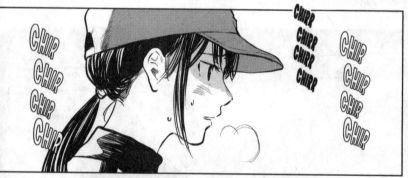

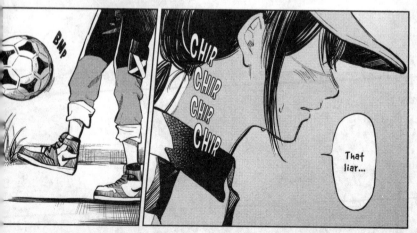

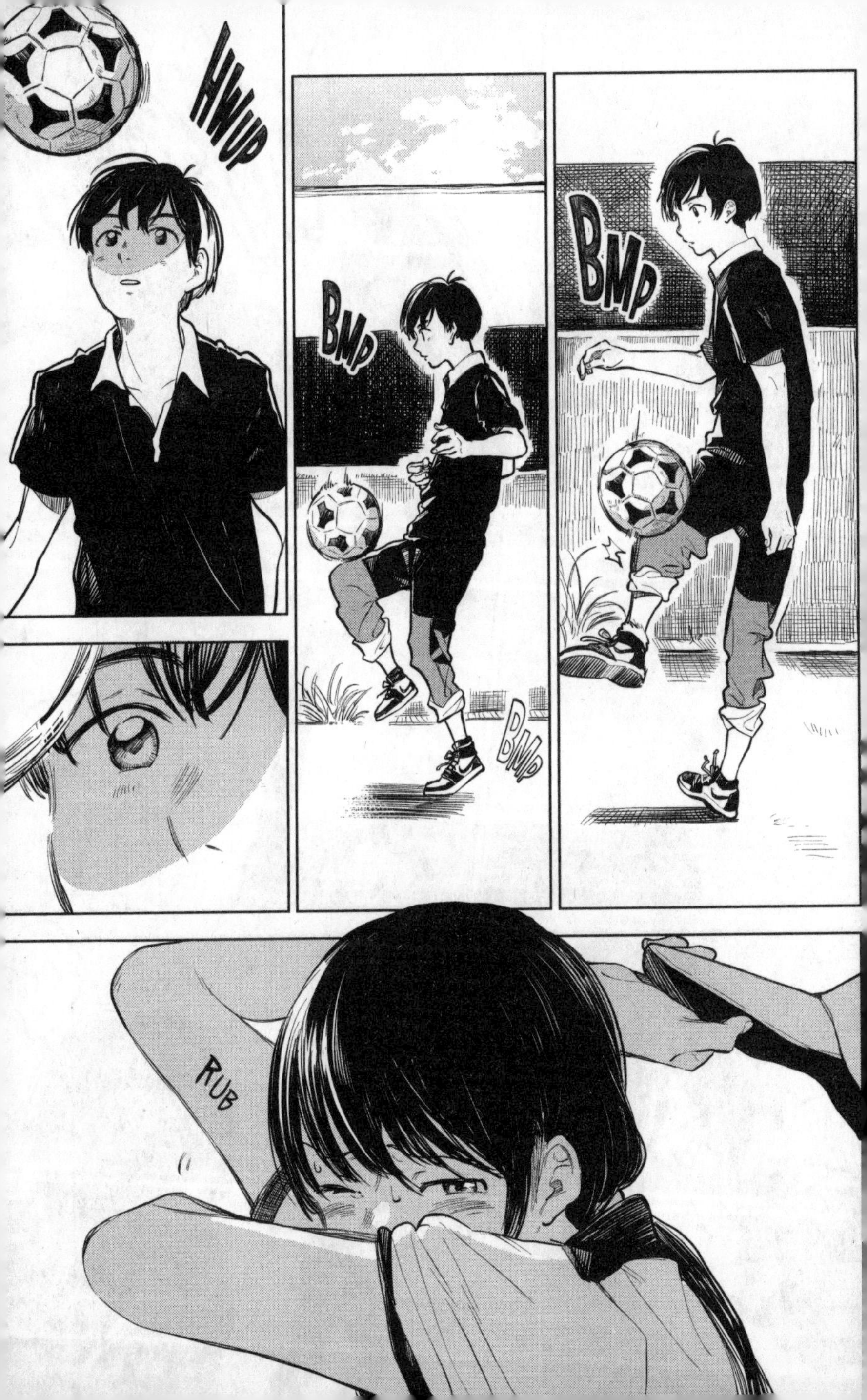
BMP
BMP
BMP
HWUP
RUB

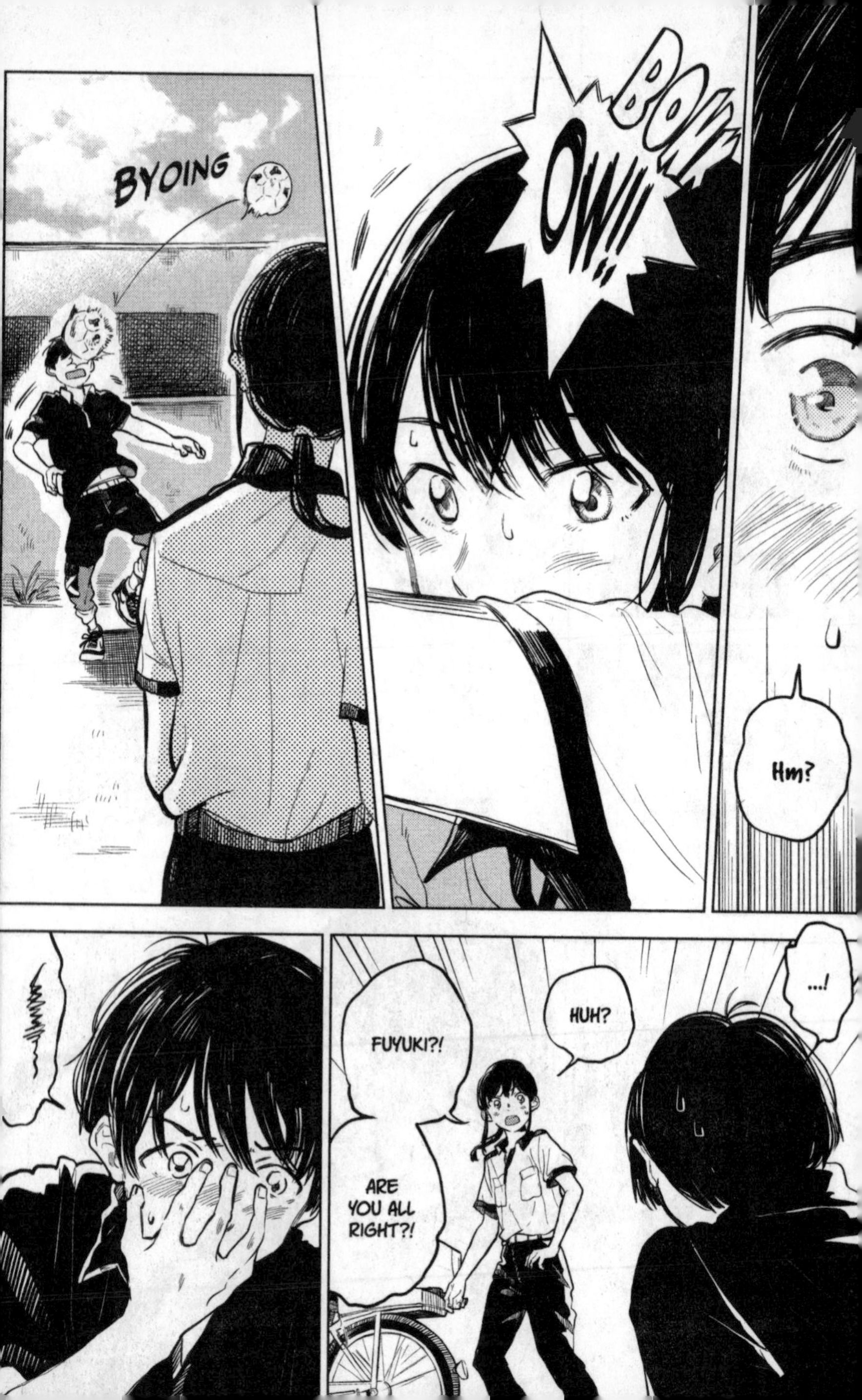
Hm?
BON
OW!!
BYOING
...!
HUH?
FUYUKI?!
ARE YOU ALL RIGHT?!

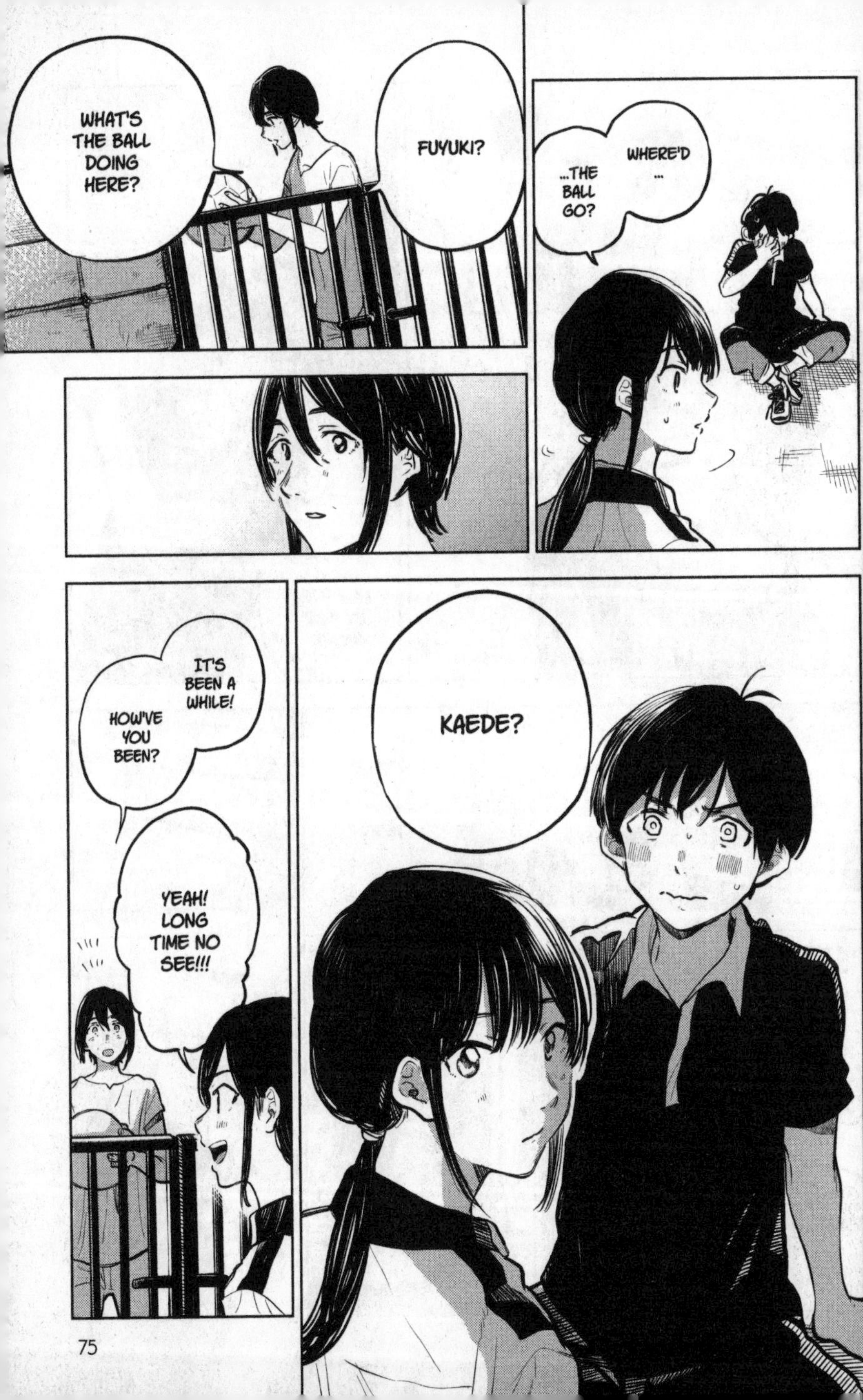
WHERE'D ...
...THE BALL GO?
FUYUKI?
WHAT'S THE BALL DOING HERE?
KAEDE?
IT'S BEEN A WHILE!
HOW'VE YOU BEEN?
YEAH! LONG TIME NO SEE!!!

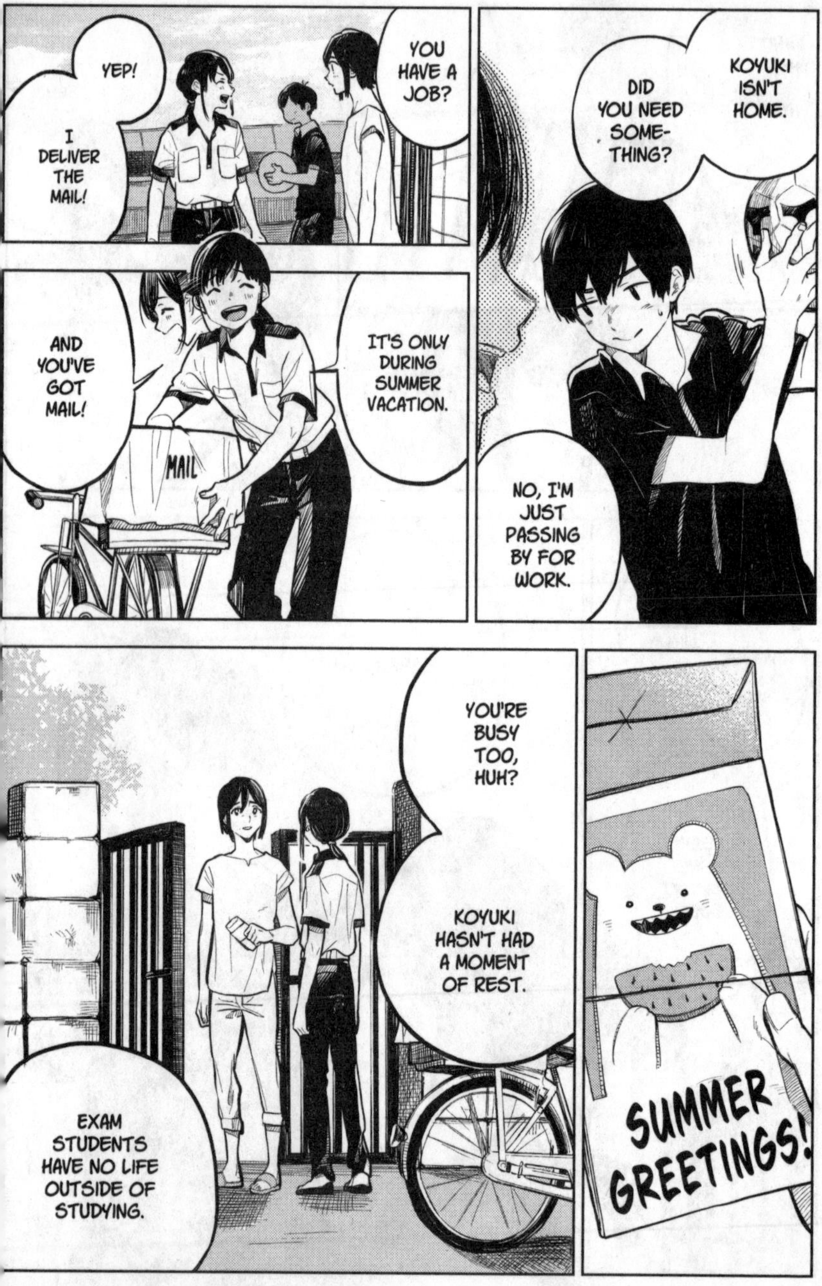
KOYUKI ISN'T HOME.
DID YOU NEED SOME-THING?
NO, I'M JUST PASSING BY FOR WORK.
YOU HAVE A JOB?
YEP!
I DELIVER THE MAIL!
IT'S ONLY DURING SUMMER VACATION.
AND YOU'VE GOT MAIL!
MAIL
SUMMER GREETINGS!
YOU'RE BUSY TOO, HUH?
KOYUKI HASN'T HAD A MOMENT OF REST.
EXAM STUDENTS HAVE NO LIFE OUTSIDE OF STUDYING.

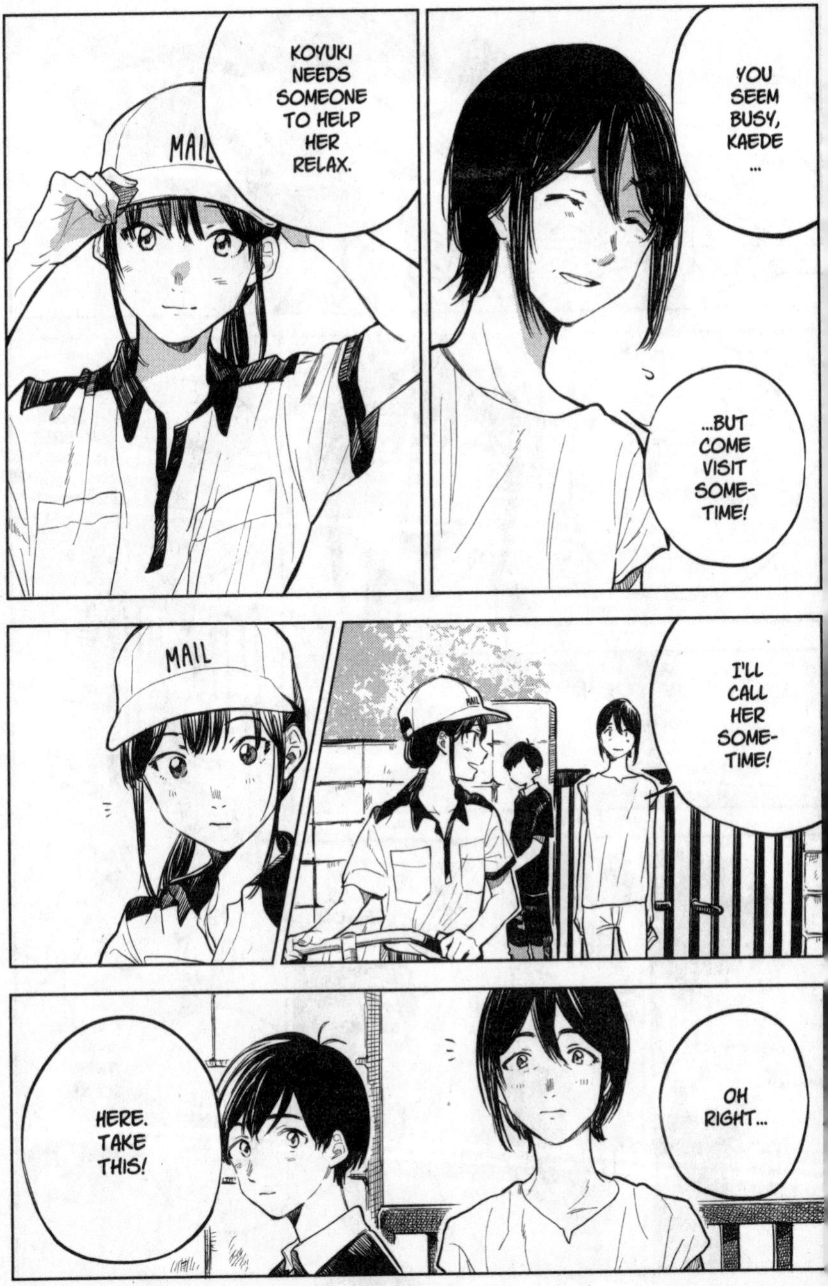
YOU SEEM BUSY, KAEDE ...
...BUT COME VISIT SOME-TIME!
KOYUKI NEEDS SOMEONE TO HELP HER RELAX.
MAIL
I'LL CALL HER SOME-TIME!
MAIL
MAIL
OH RIGHT...
HERE. TAKE THIS!

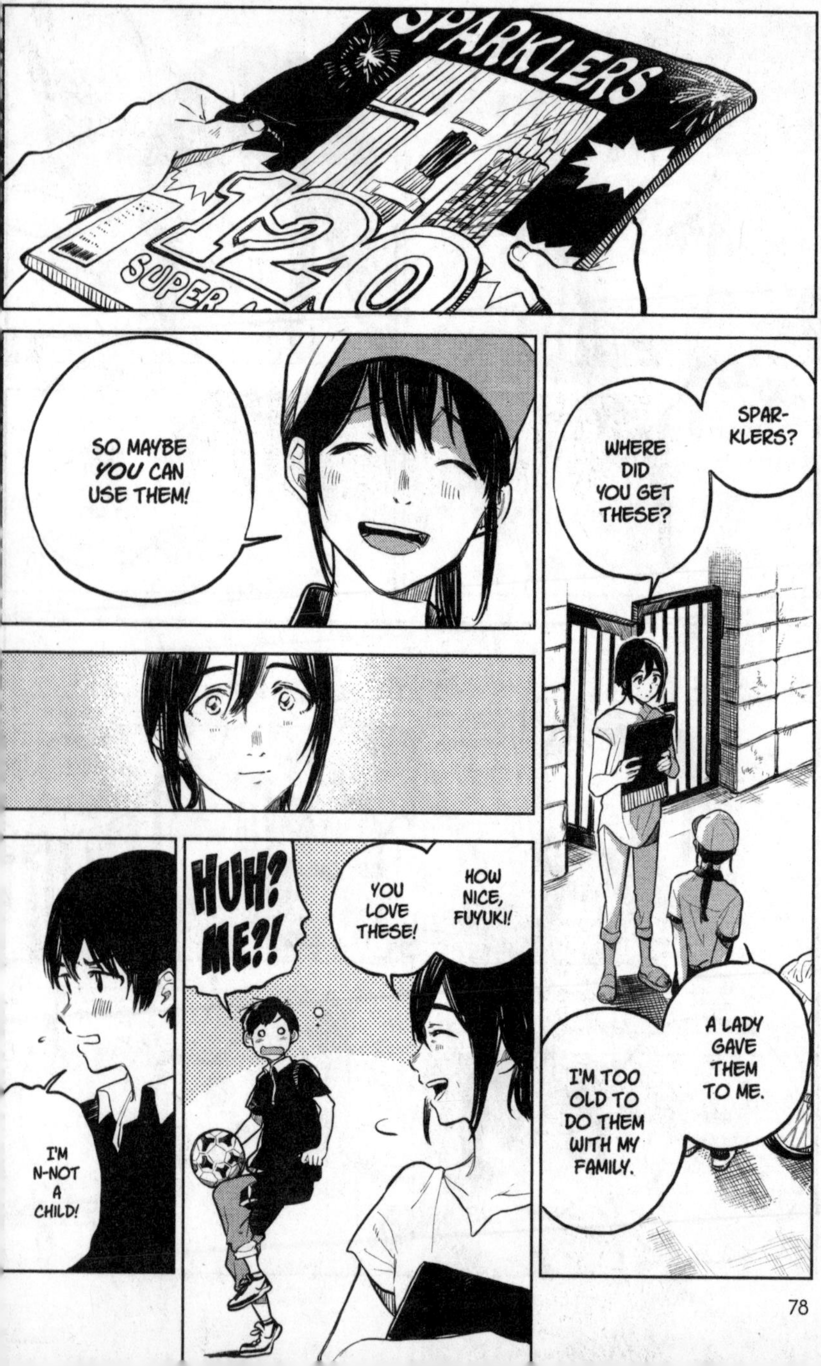
SPARKLERS
120
SUPER
SPAR-KLERS?
WHERE DID YOU GET THESE?
A LADY GAVE THEM TO ME.
I'M TOO OLD TO DO THEM WITH MY FAMILY.
SO MAYBE *YOU* CAN USE THEM!
HOW NICE, FUYUKI!
YOU LOVE THESE!
HUH? ME?!
I'M N-NOT A CHILD!

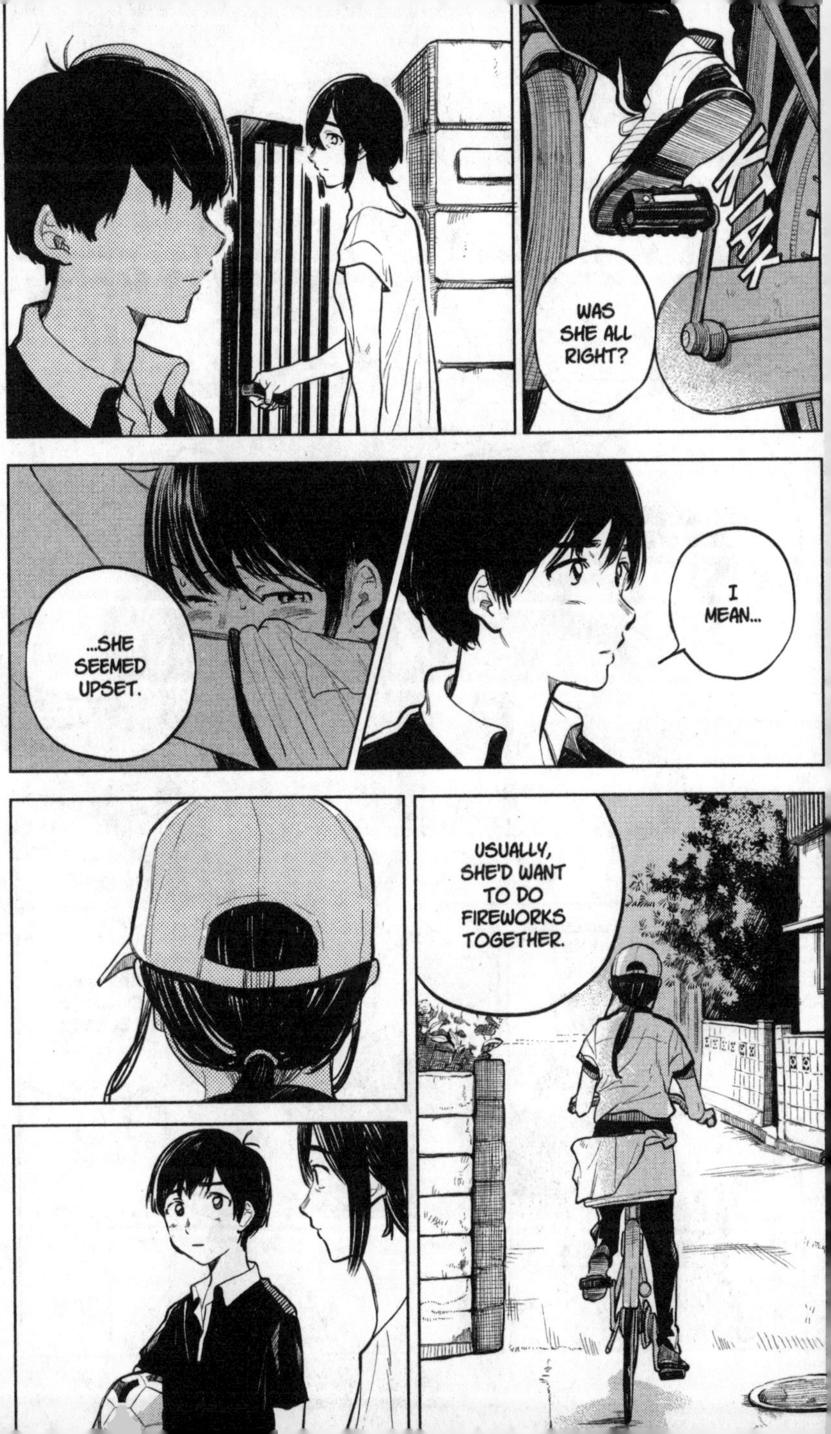
KTAK
WAS SHE ALL RIGHT?
I MEAN...
...SHE SEEMED UPSET.
USUALLY, SHE'D WANT TO DO FIREWORKS TOGETHER.

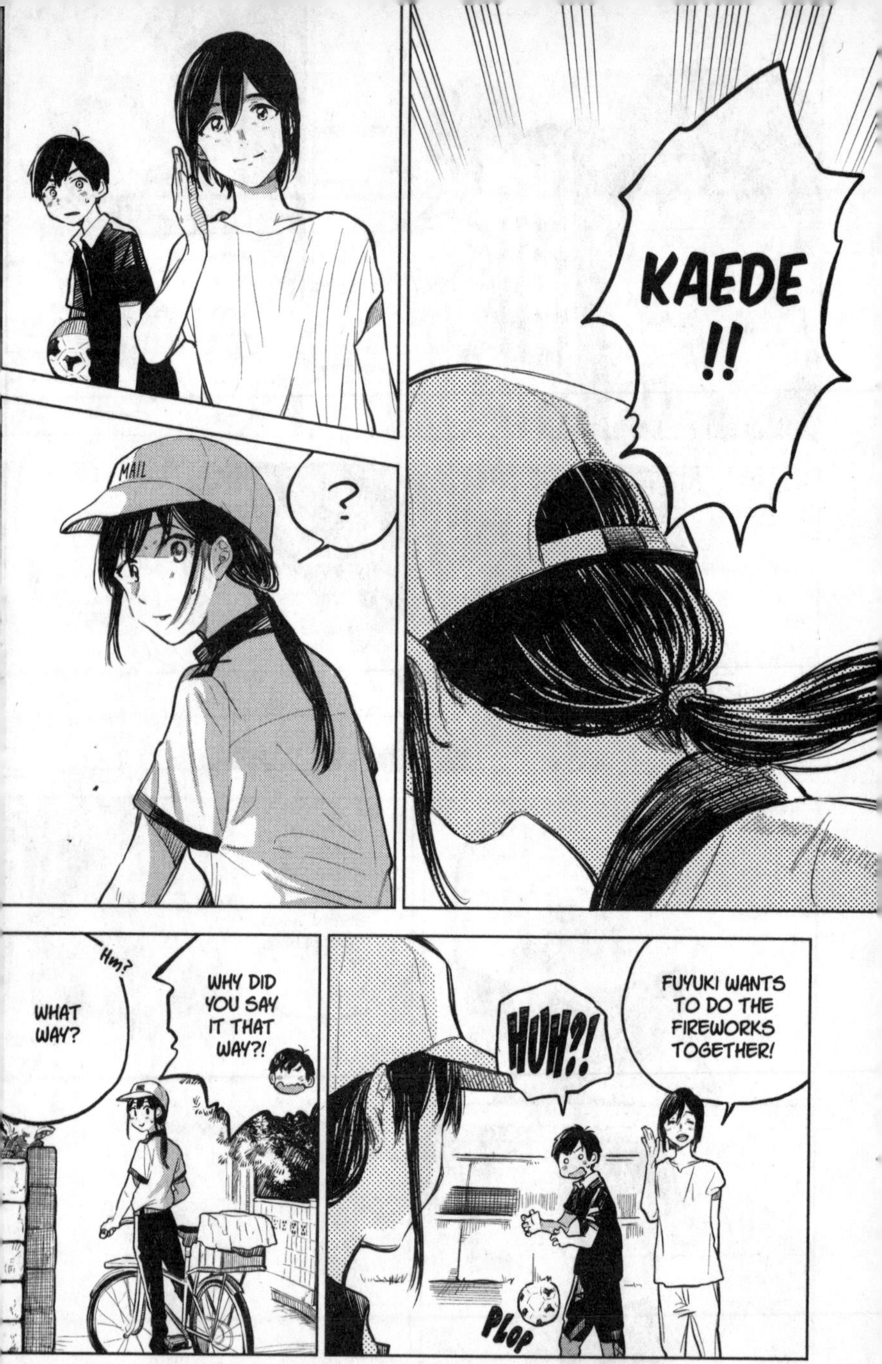
KAEDE !!
?
FUYUKI WANTS TO DO THE FIREWORKS TOGETHER!
HUH?!
PLOP
WHY DID YOU SAY IT THAT WAY?!
Hm?
WHAT WAY?

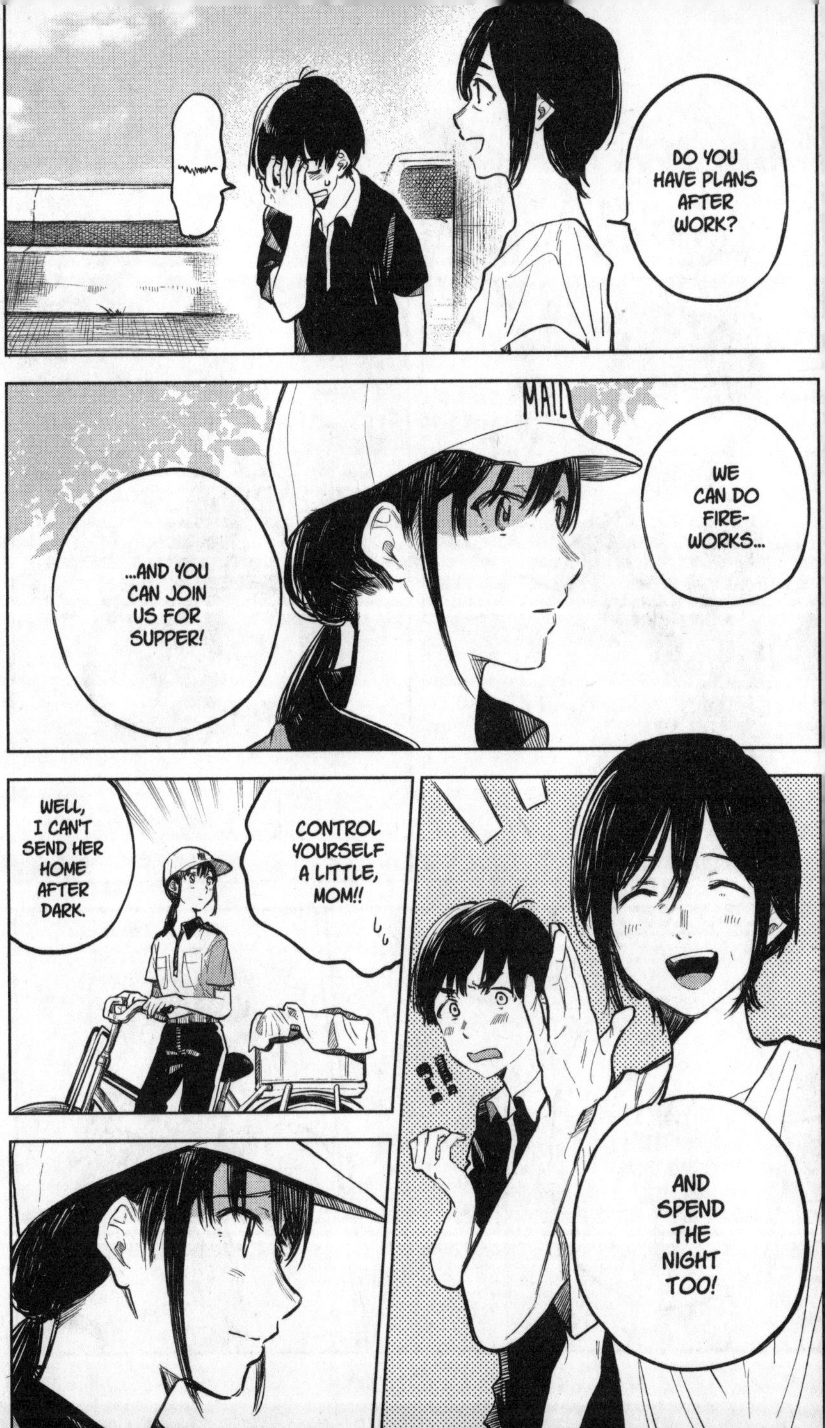
DO YOU HAVE PLANS AFTER WORK?
MAIL
WE CAN DO FIRE-WORKS...
...AND YOU CAN JOIN US FOR SUPPER!
AND SPEND THE NIGHT TOO!
CONTROL YOURSELF A LITTLE, MOM!!
WELL, I CAN'T SEND HER HOME AFTER DARK.

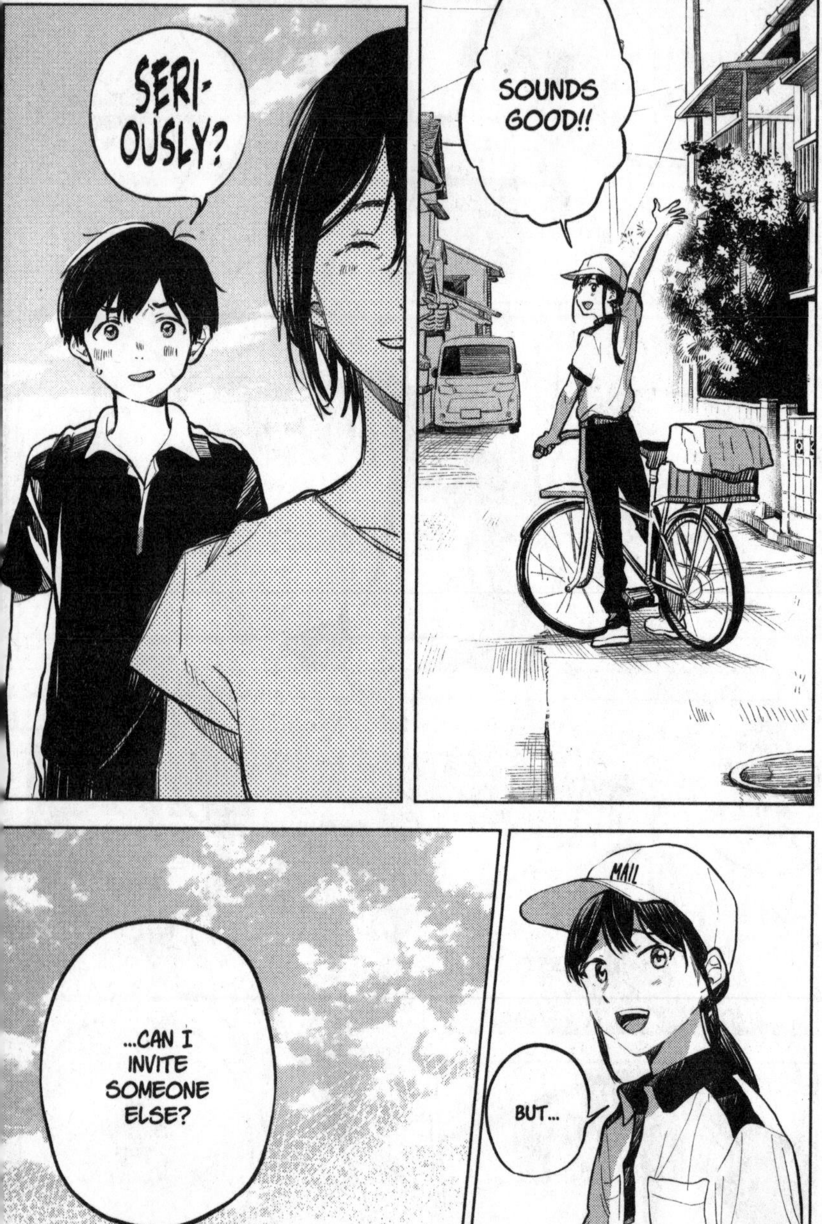
SOUNDS GOOD!!
SERI-OUSLY?
MAIL
BUT...
...CAN I INVITE SOMEONE ELSE?

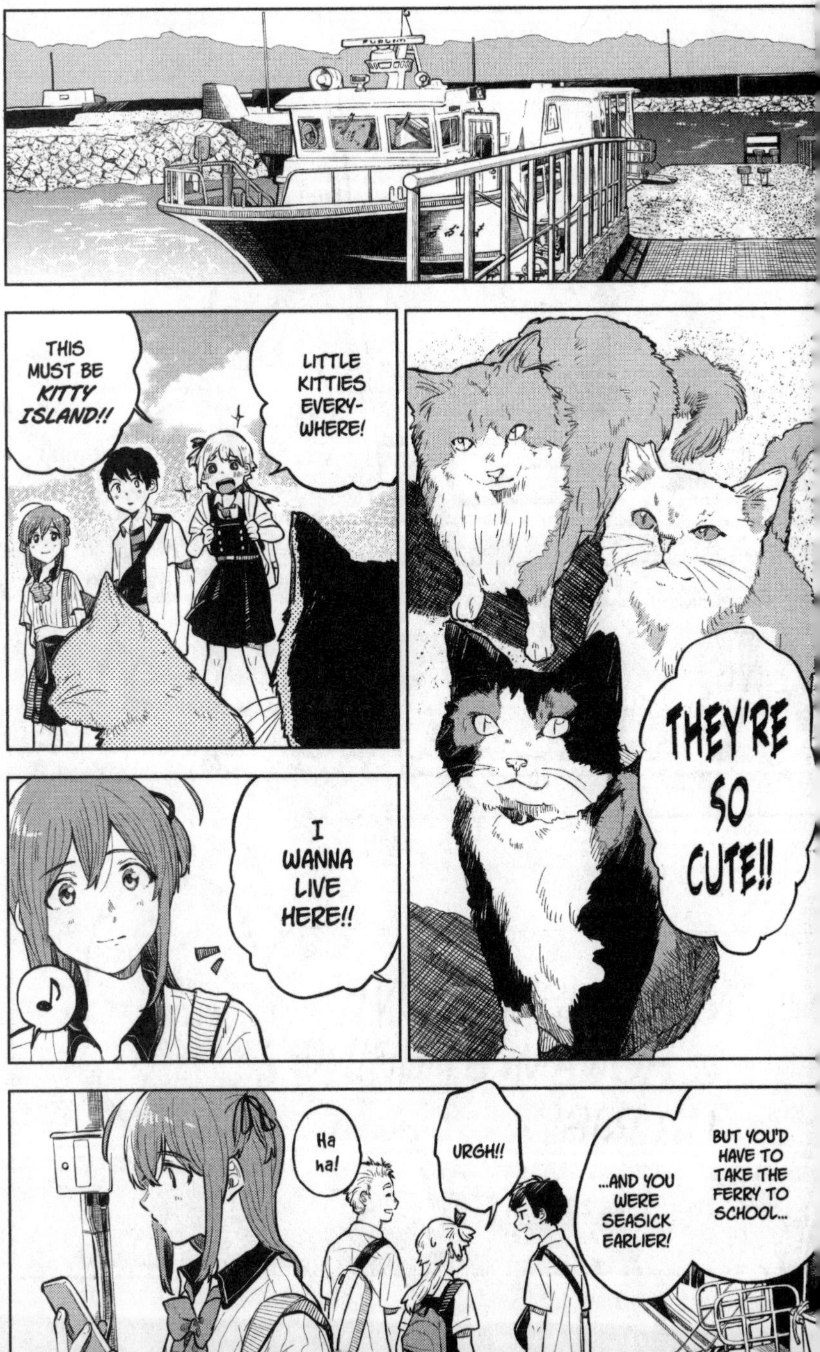
THEY'RE SO CUTE!!
LITTLE KITTIES EVERY-WHERE!
THIS MUST BE *KITTY ISLAND!!*
I WANNA LIVE HERE!!
BUT YOU'D HAVE TO TAKE THE FERRY TO SCHOOL...
...AND YOU WERE SEASICK EARLIER!
URGH!!
Ha ha!

HUH?

WANT A SLEEPOVER @ HONAMI'S? BRING UR PJS!

A SLEEP-OVER?!

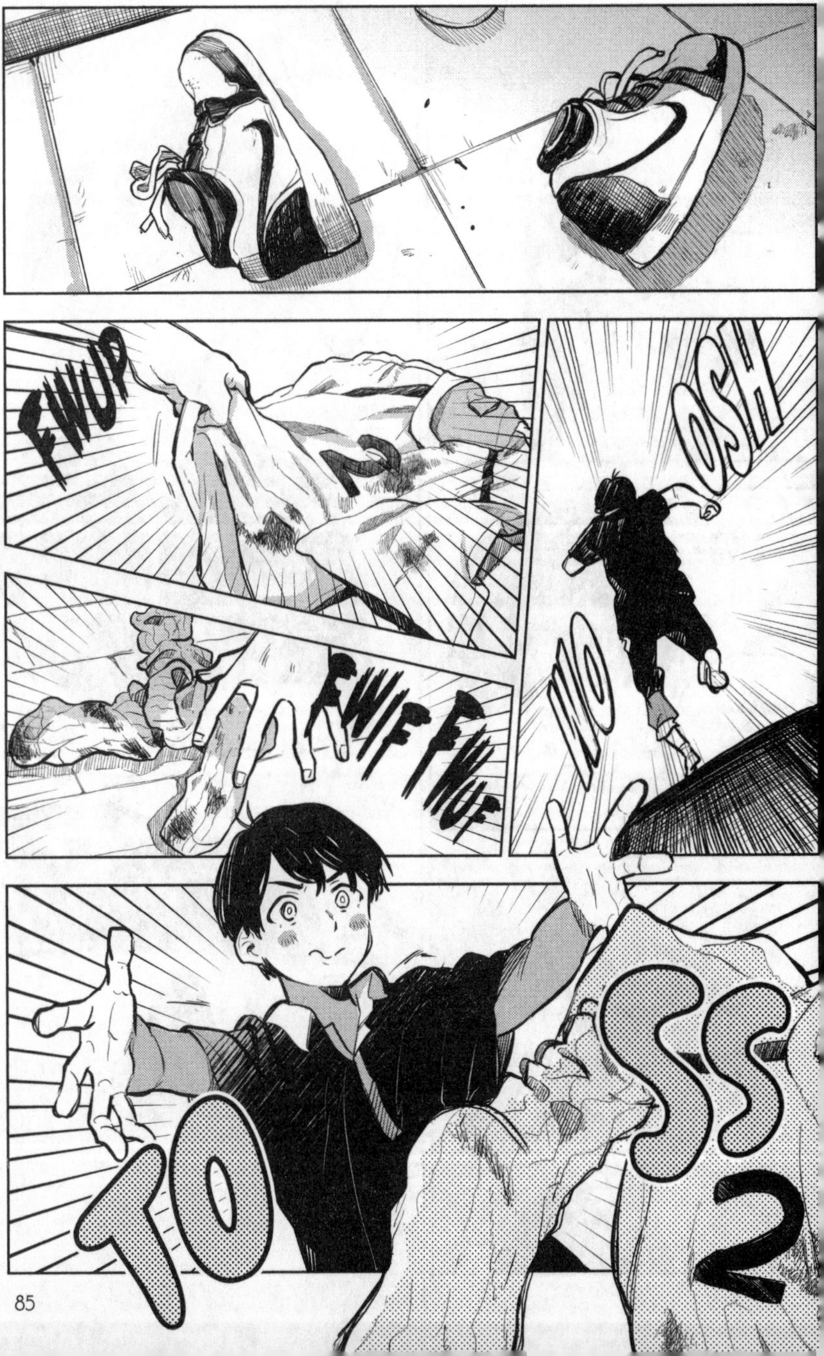
WOOSH
FWUP
FWIF FWUF
TOSS

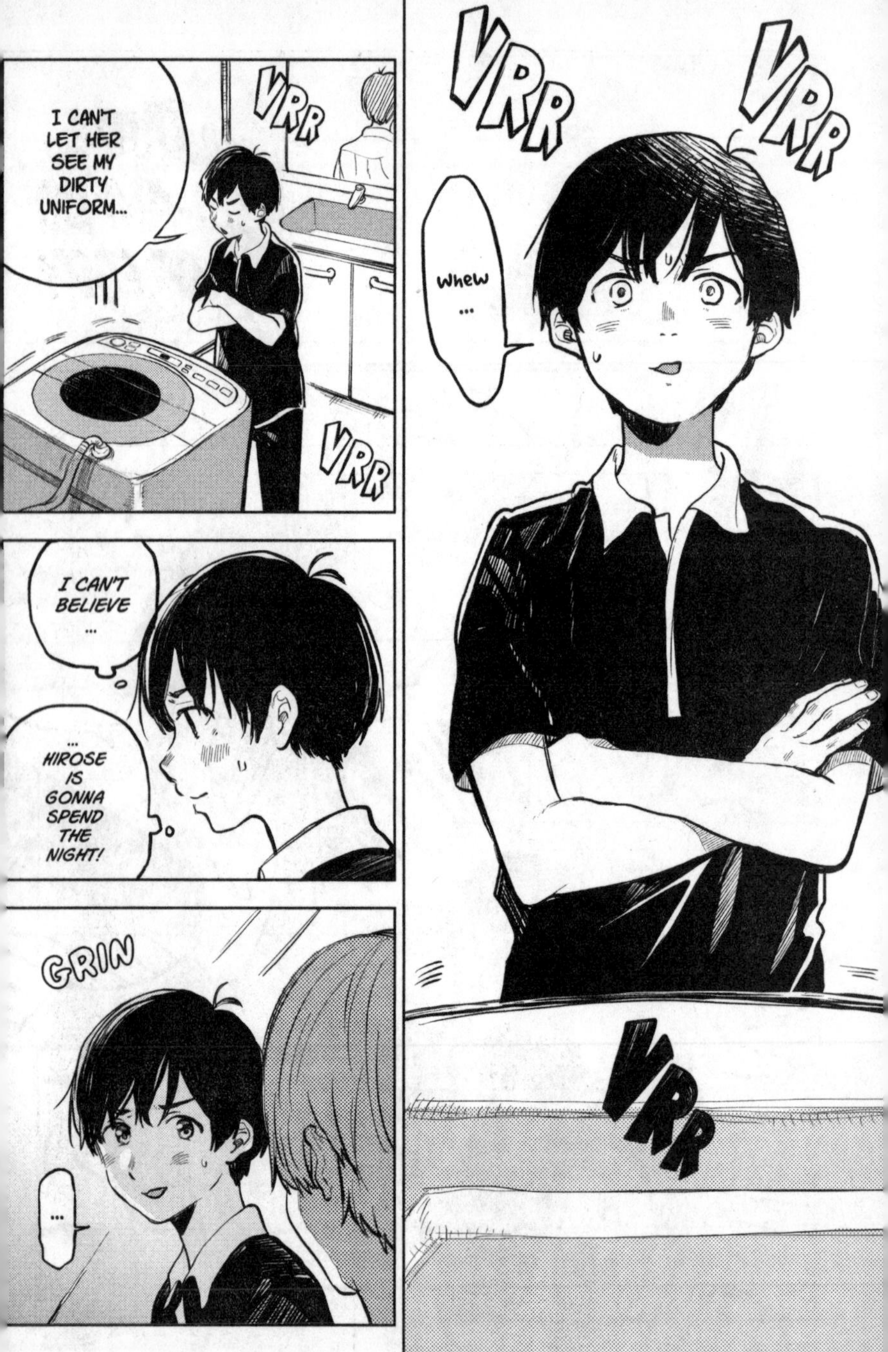
VRR
VRR
Whew ...
VRR
VRR
I CAN'T LET HER SEE MY DIRTY UNIFORM...
VRR
I CAN'T BELIEVE ...
... HIROSE IS GONNA SPEND THE NIGHT!
GRIN
... ...

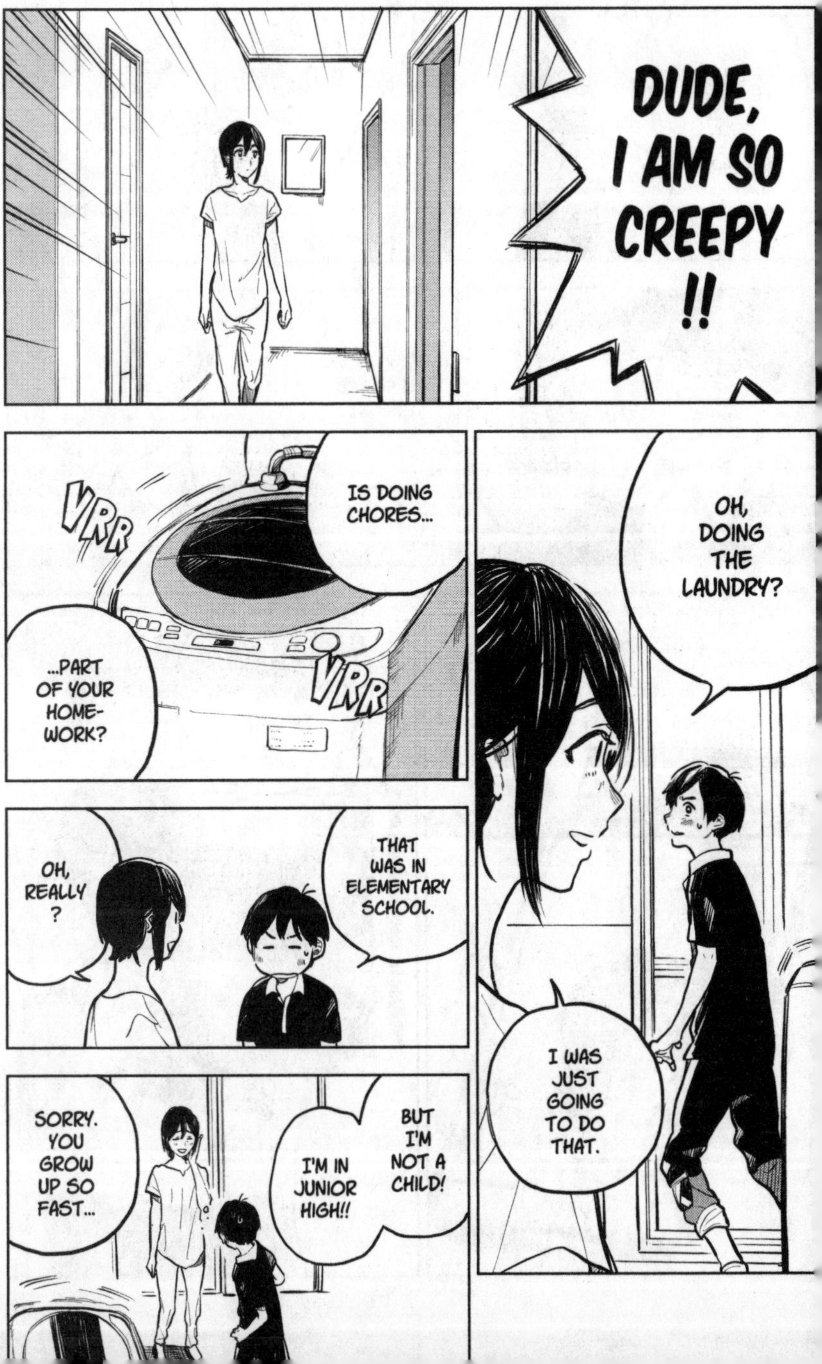
DUDE, I AM SO CREEPY !!
OH, DOING THE LAUNDRY?
I WAS JUST GOING TO DO THAT.
IS DOING CHORES...
VRR
VRR
...PART OF YOUR HOME-WORK?
THAT WAS IN ELEMENTARY SCHOOL.
OH, REALLY?
BUT I'M NOT A CHILD!
I'M IN JUNIOR HIGH!!
SORRY. YOU GROW UP SO FAST...

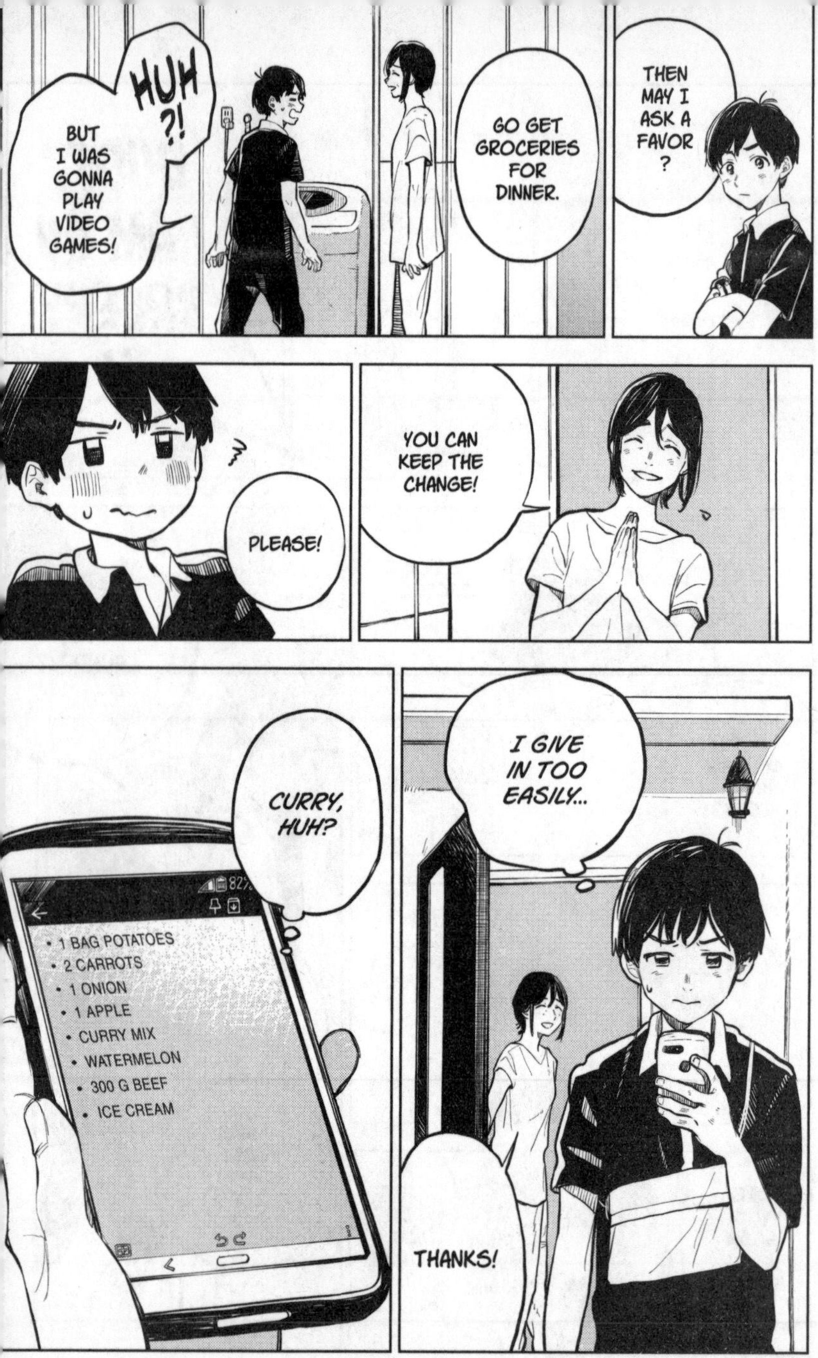
THEN MAY I ASK A FAVOR ?
GO GET GROCERIES FOR DINNER.
HUH ?!
BUT I WAS GONNA PLAY VIDEO GAMES!
YOU CAN KEEP THE CHANGE!
PLEASE!
I GIVE IN TOO EASILY...
THANKS!
CURRY, HUH?
• 1 BAG POTATOES
• 2 CARROTS
• 1 ONION
• 1 APPLE
• CURRY MIX
• WATERMELON
• 300 G BEEF
• ICE CREAM

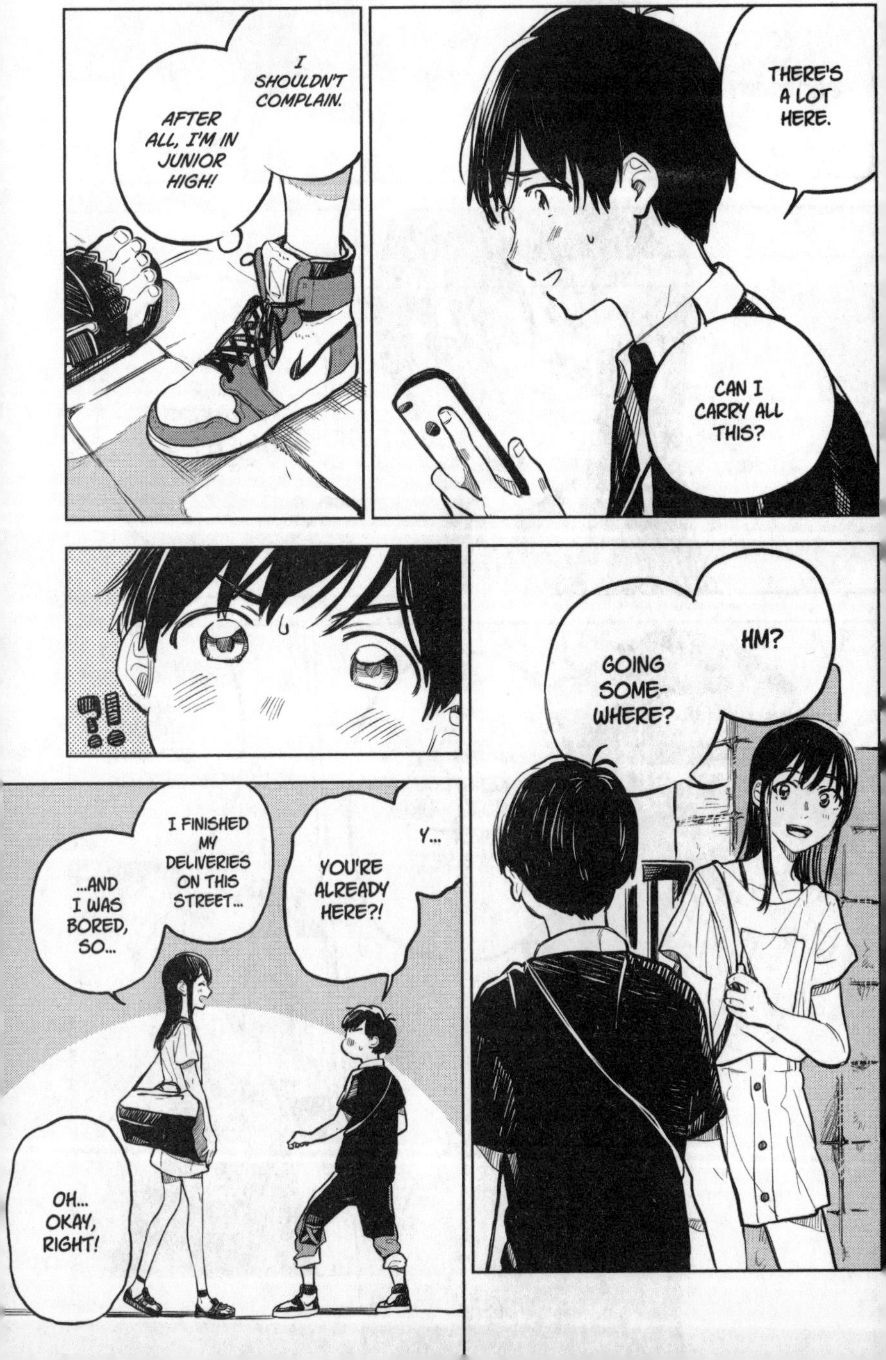
THERE'S A LOT HERE.
CAN I CARRY ALL THIS?
I SHOULDN'T COMPLAIN.
AFTER ALL, I'M IN JUNIOR HIGH!
HM?
GOING SOME-WHERE?
?!
Y...
YOU'RE ALREADY HERE?!
I FINISHED MY DELIVERIES ON THIS STREET...
...AND I WAS BORED, SO...
OH... OKAY, RIGHT!

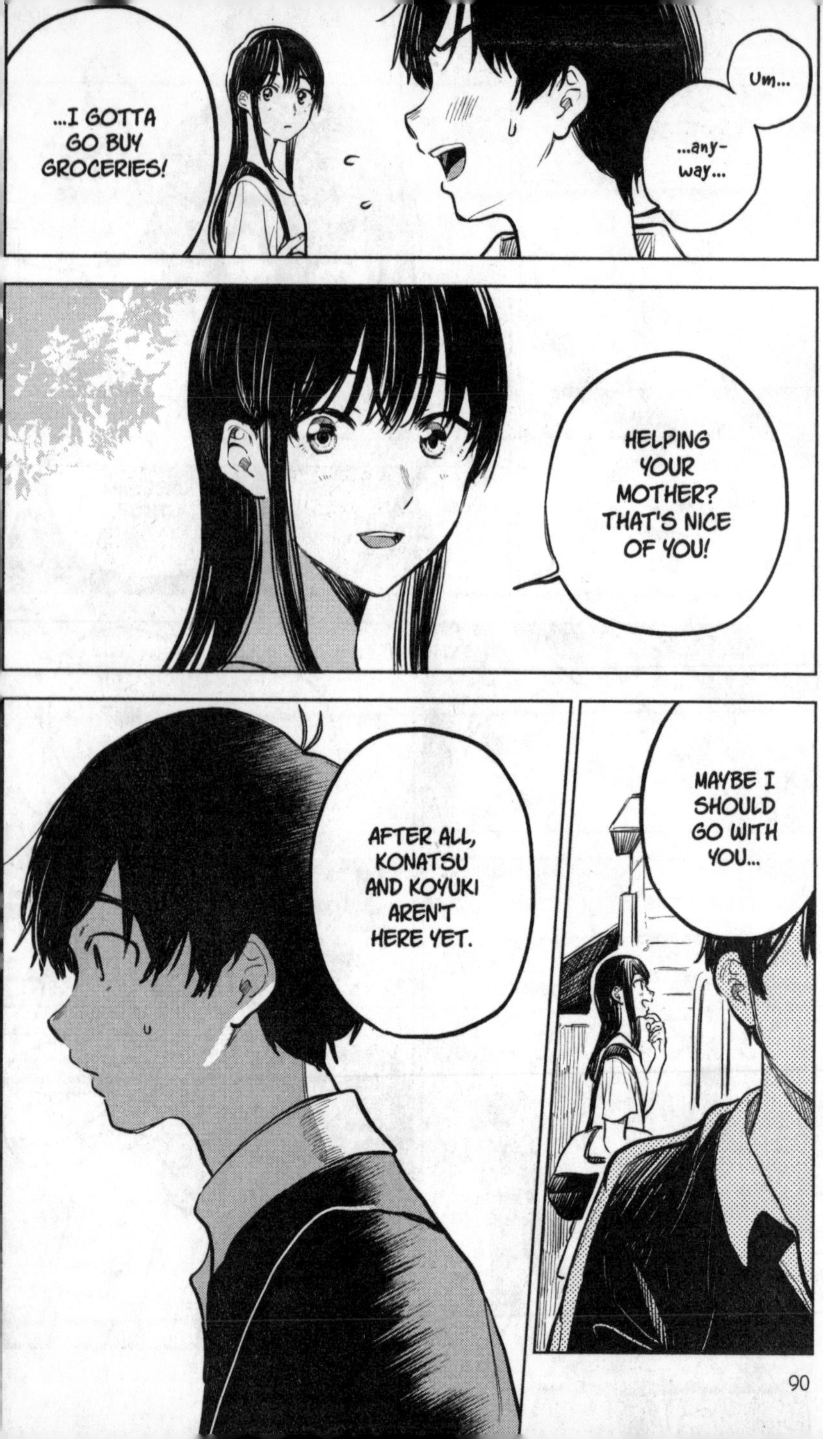
Um...
...any-way...
...I GOTTA GO BUY GROCERIES!
HELPING YOUR MOTHER? THAT'S NICE OF YOU!
MAYBE I SHOULD GO WITH YOU...
AFTER ALL, KONATSU AND KOYUKI AREN'T HERE YET.

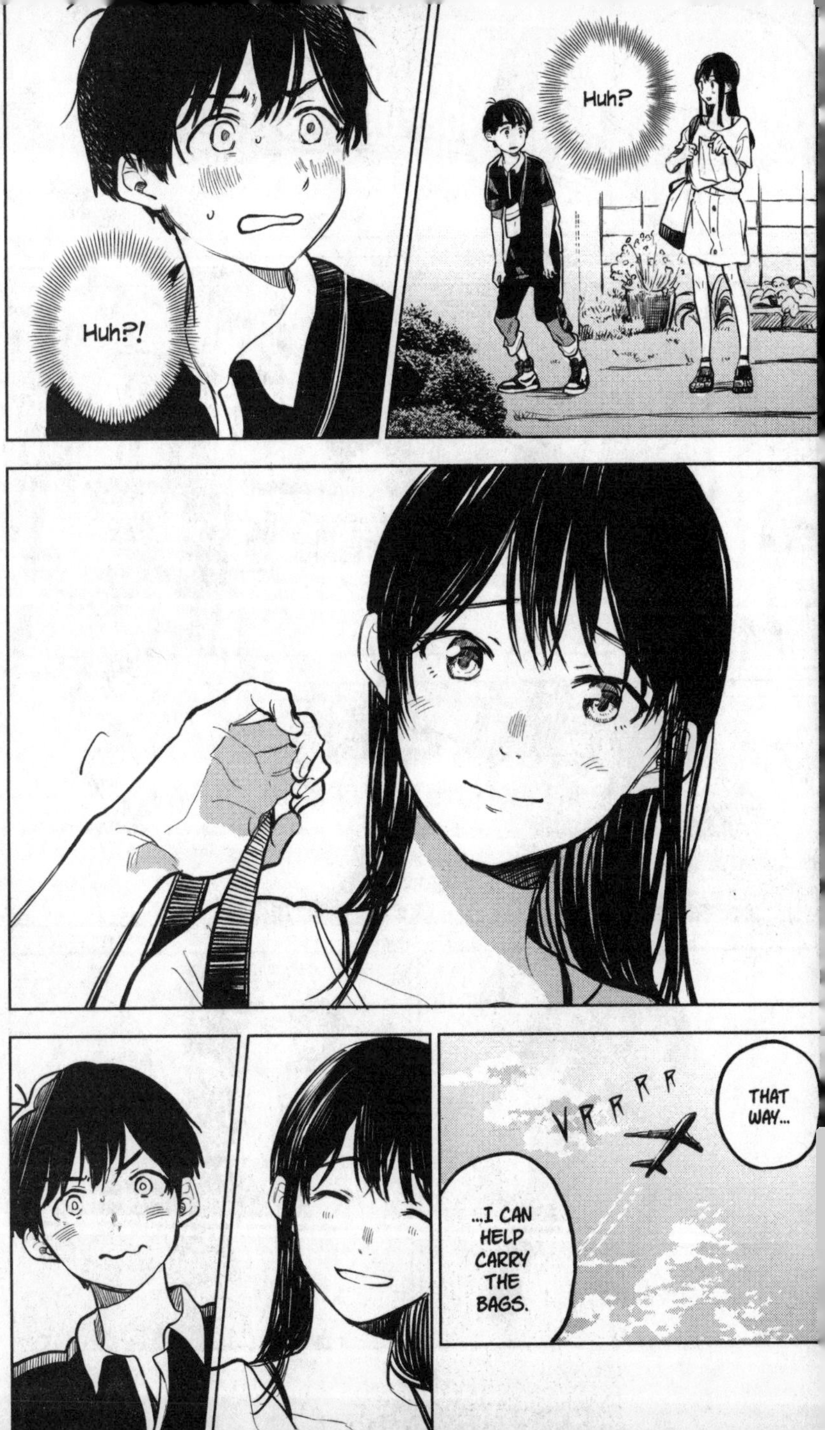
Huh?
Huh?!
THAT WAY...
VRRRR
...I CAN HELP CARRY THE BAGS.

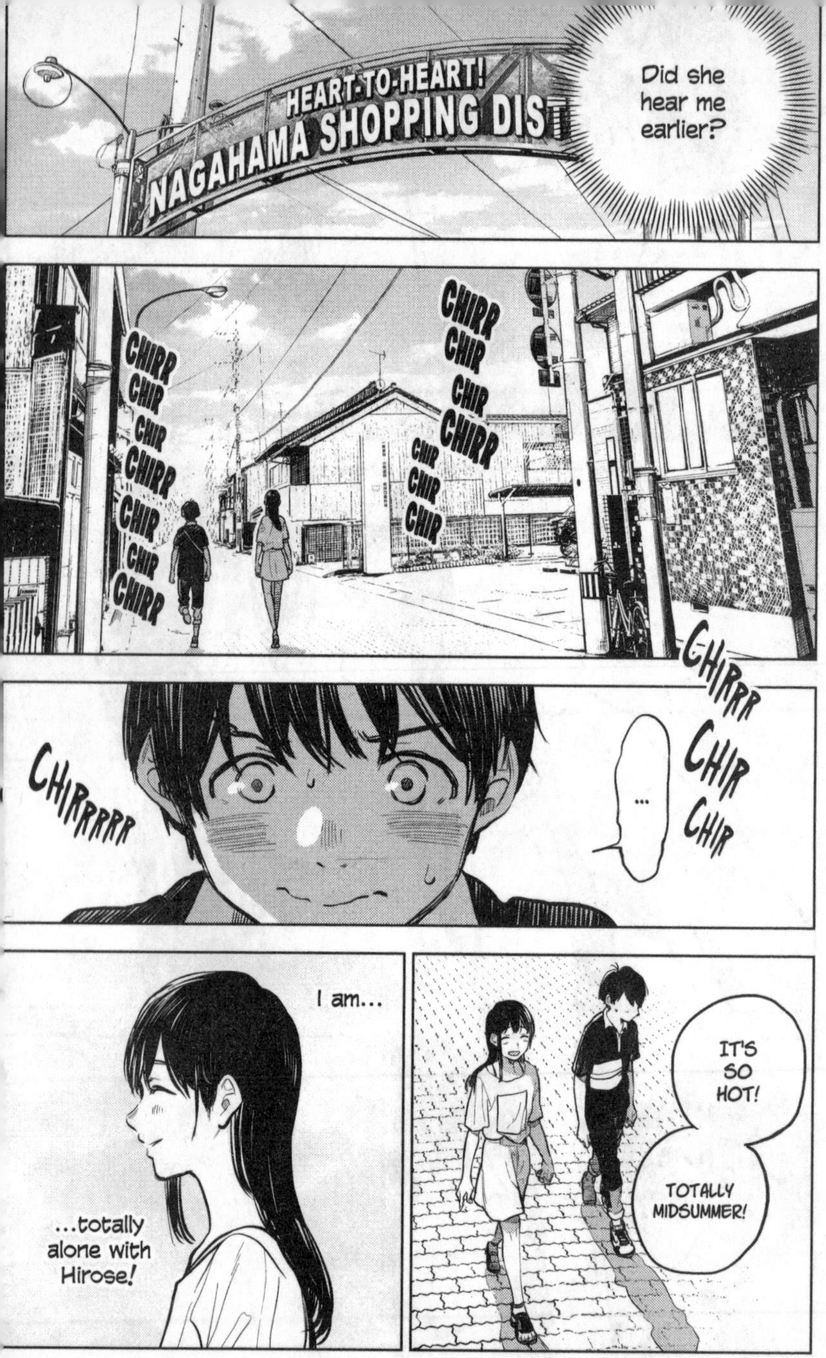
HEART-TO-HEART!
NAGAHAMA SHOPPING DIST
Did she hear me earlier?
CHIRR CHIR CHIR CHIRR
CHIR CHIR CHIR
CHIRR CHIR CHIR CHIRR CHIR CHIR CHIRR
CHIRRR CHIR CHIR
...
CHIRRRRR
IT'S SO HOT!
TOTALLY MIDSUMMER!
I am...
...totally alone with Hirose!

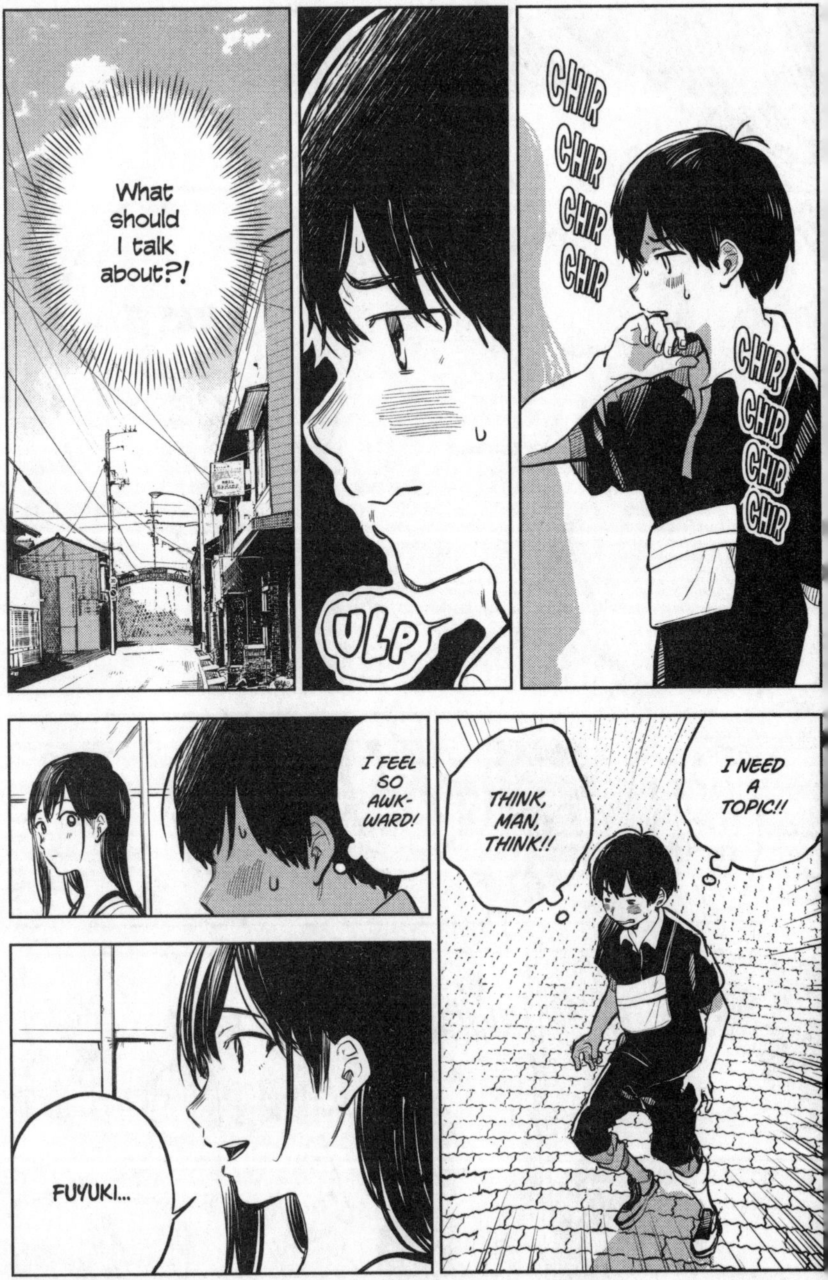
CHIR CHIR CHIR CHIR
CHIR CHIR CHIR CHIR
ULP
What should I talk about?!
I NEED A TOPIC!!
THINK, MAN, THINK!!
I FEEL SO AWK-WARD!
FUYUKI...

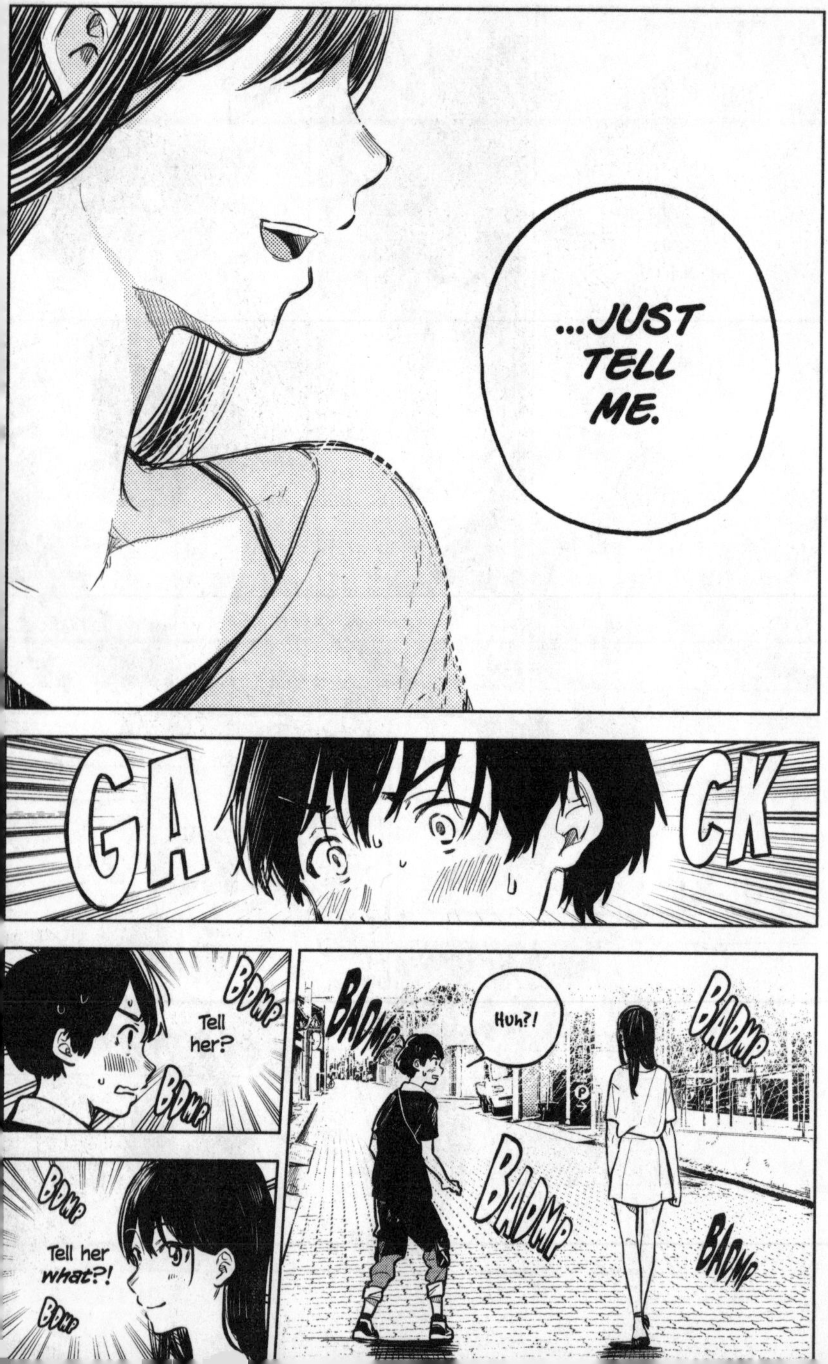
...JUST TELL ME.
GA
CK
BADMP
Huh?!
BADMP
BADMP
BADMP
BDMP
Tell her?
BDMP
BDMP
Tell her what?!
BDMP

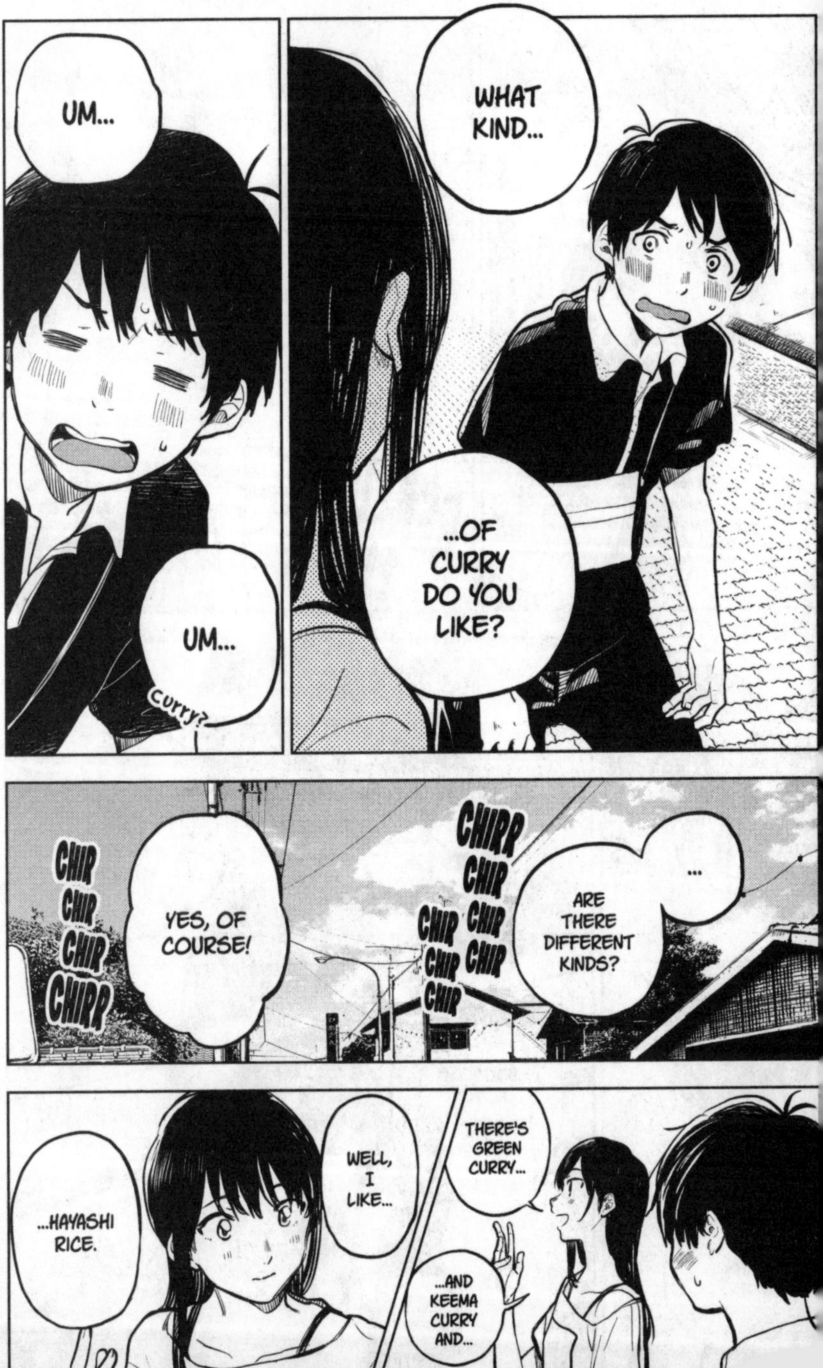
WHAT KIND...
...OF CURRY DO YOU LIKE?
UM...
UM...
Curry?
...
ARE THERE DIFFERENT KINDS?
CHIRR CHIR CHIR CHIR
CHIR CHIR CHIR
YES, OF COURSE!
CHIR CHIR CHIR CHIRR
THERE'S GREEN CURRY...
...AND KEEMA CURRY AND...
WELL, I LIKE...
...HAYASHI RICE.

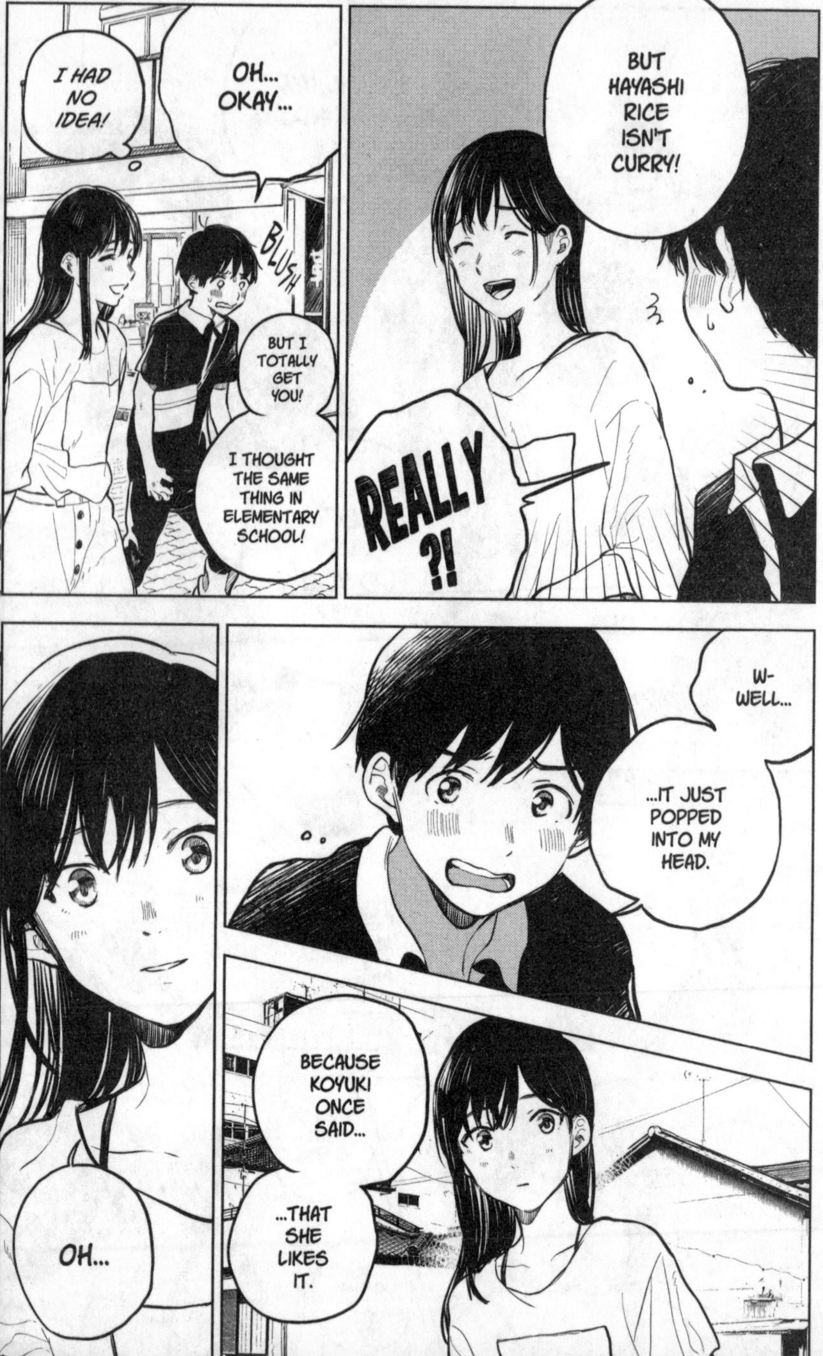
BUT HAYASHI RICE ISN'T CURRY!
REALLY ?!
OH... OKAY...
I HAD NO IDEA!
BLUSH
BUT I TOTALLY GET YOU!
I THOUGHT THE SAME THING IN ELEMENTARY SCHOOL!
W-WELL...
...IT JUST POPPED INTO MY HEAD.
BECAUSE KOYUKI ONCE SAID...
...THAT SHE LIKES IT.
OH...

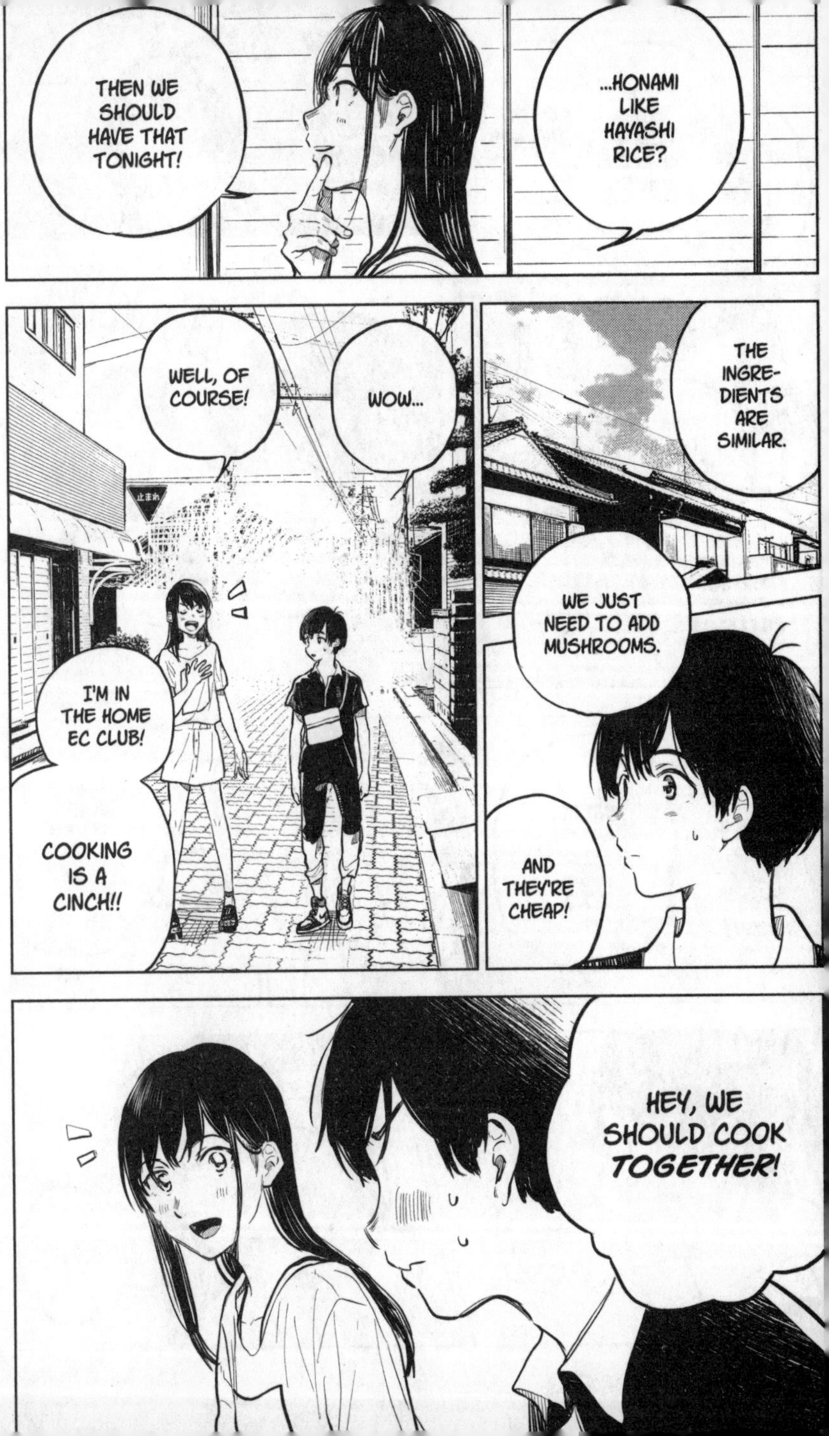
...HONAMI LIKE HAYASHI RICE?
THEN WE SHOULD HAVE THAT TONIGHT!
THE INGRE-DIENTS ARE SIMILAR.
WE JUST NEED TO ADD MUSHROOMS.
AND THEY'RE CHEAP!
WOW...
WELL, OF COURSE!
I'M IN THE HOME EC CLUB!
COOKING IS A CINCH!!
HEY, WE SHOULD COOK *TOGETHER*!

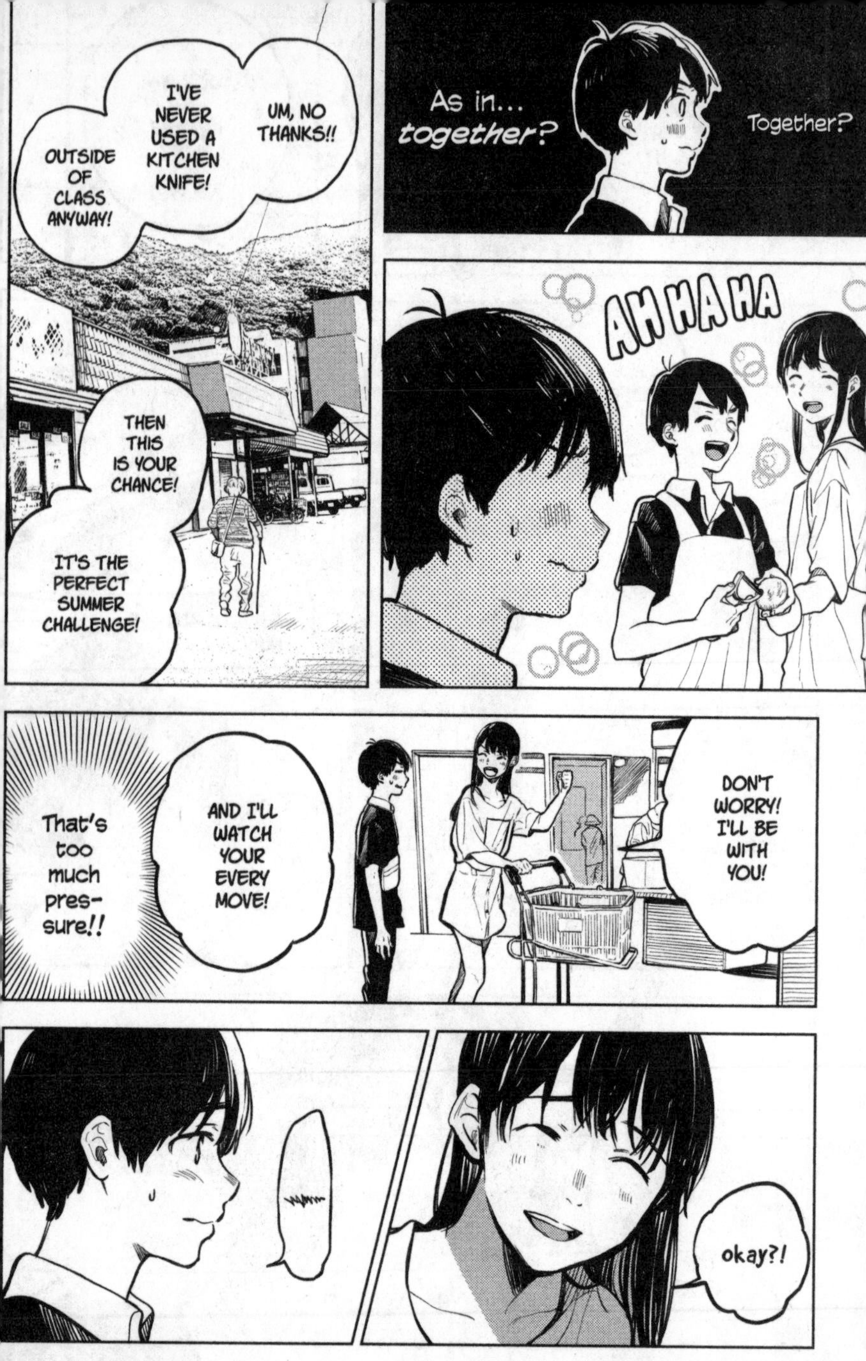
Together?
As in... together?
AH HA HA
UM, NO THANKS!!
I'VE NEVER USED A KITCHEN KNIFE!
OUTSIDE OF CLASS ANYWAY!
THEN THIS IS YOUR CHANCE!
IT'S THE PERFECT SUMMER CHALLENGE!
DON'T WORRY! I'LL BE WITH YOU!
AND I'LL WATCH YOUR EVERY MOVE!
That's too much pres-sure!!
okay?!

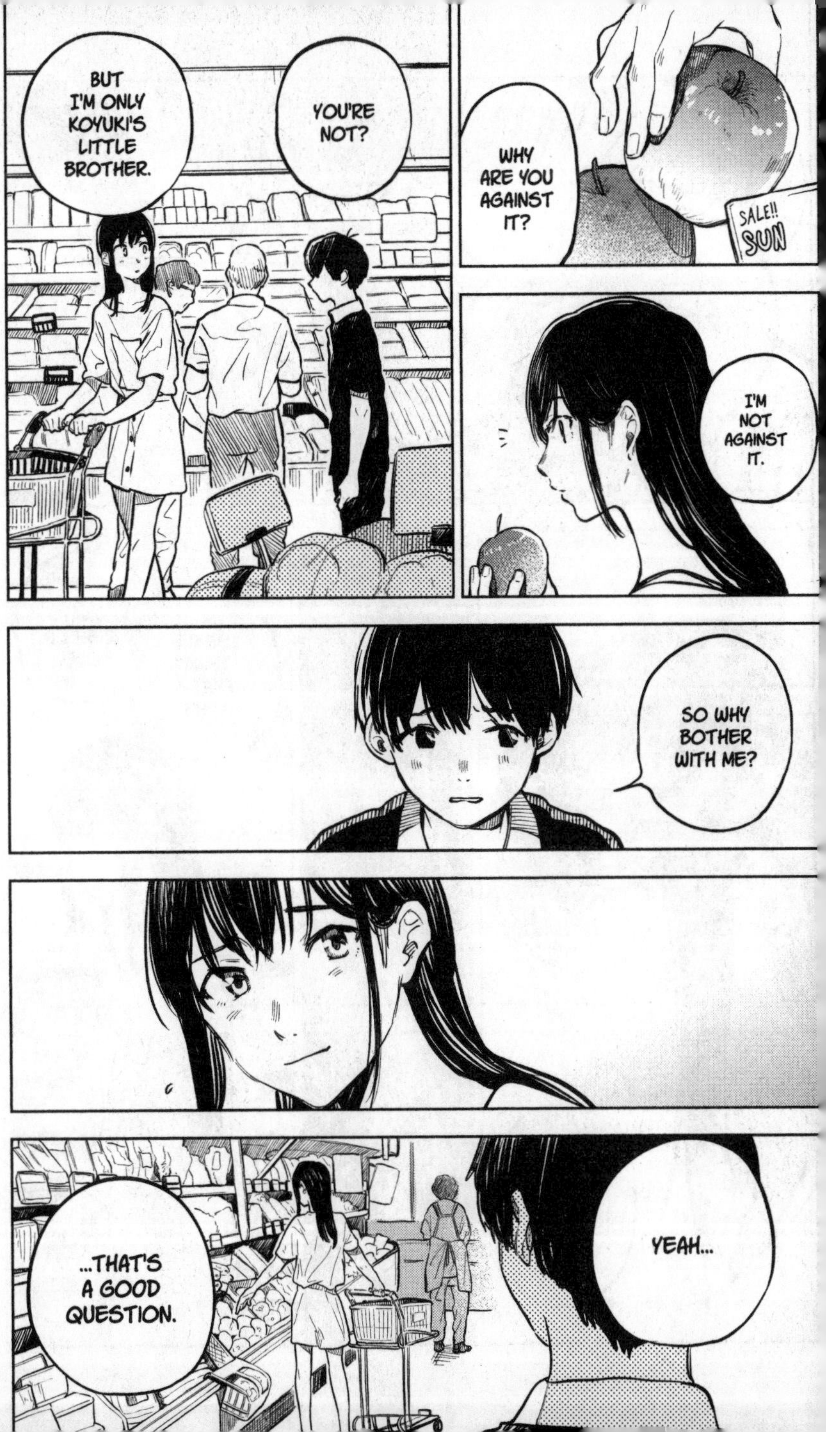
SALE!! SUN
WHY ARE YOU AGAINST IT?
I'M NOT AGAINST IT.
YOU'RE NOT?
BUT I'M ONLY KOYUKI'S LITTLE BROTHER.
SO WHY BOTHER WITH ME?
YEAH...
...THAT'S A GOOD QUESTION.

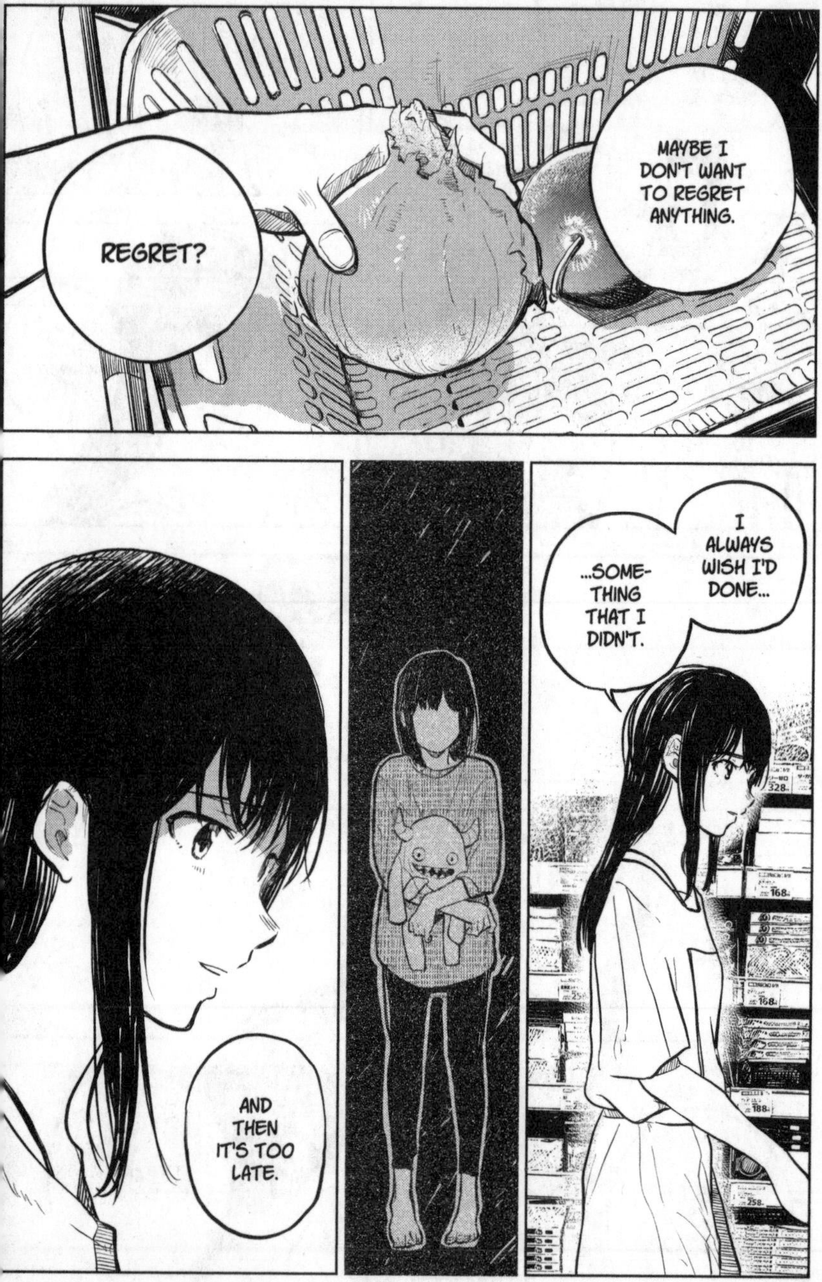
MAYBE I DON'T WANT TO REGRET ANYTHING.
REGRET?
I ALWAYS WISH I'D DONE...
...SOME-THING THAT I DIDN'T.
AND THEN IT'S TOO LATE.

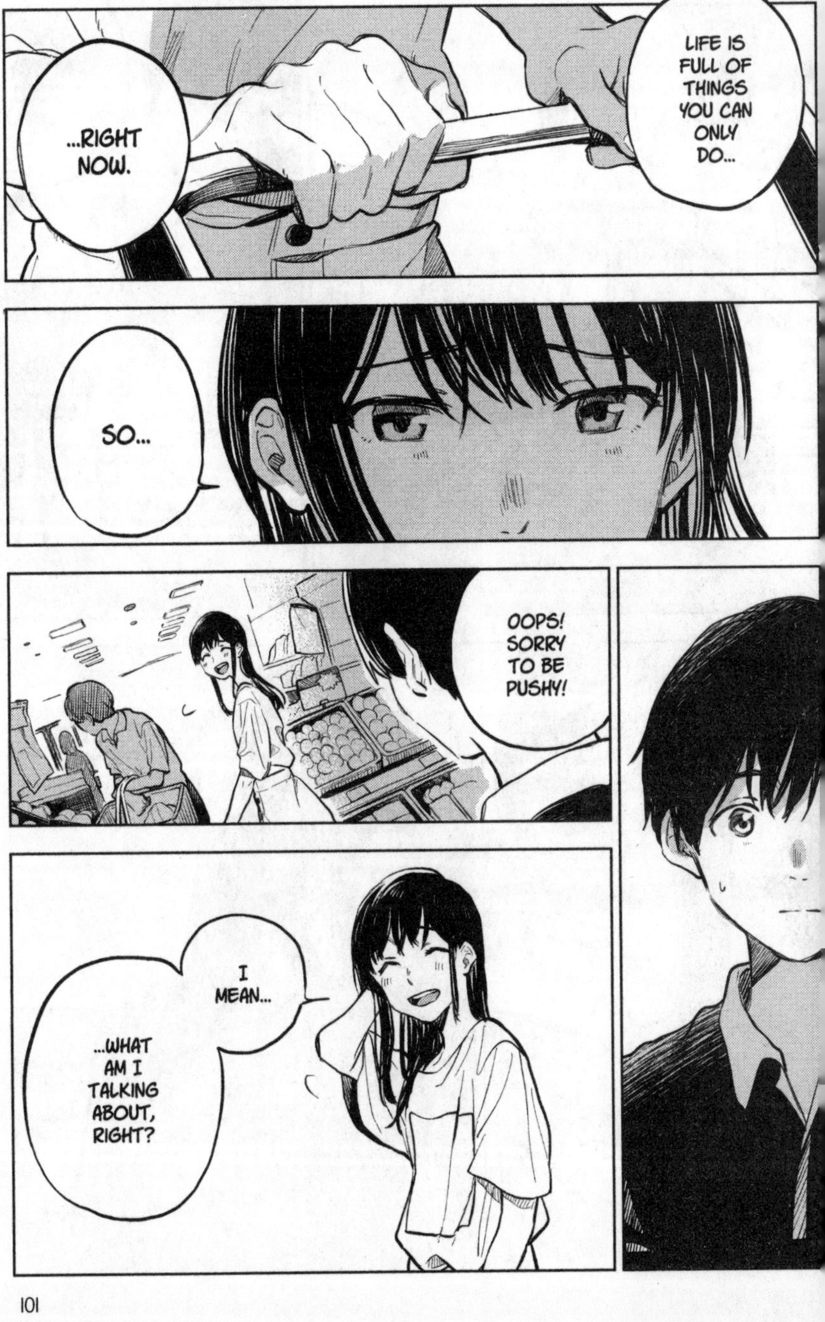
LIFE IS FULL OF THINGS YOU CAN ONLY DO...
...RIGHT NOW.
SO...
OOPS! SORRY TO BE PUSHY!
I MEAN...
...WHAT AM I TALKING ABOUT, RIGHT?

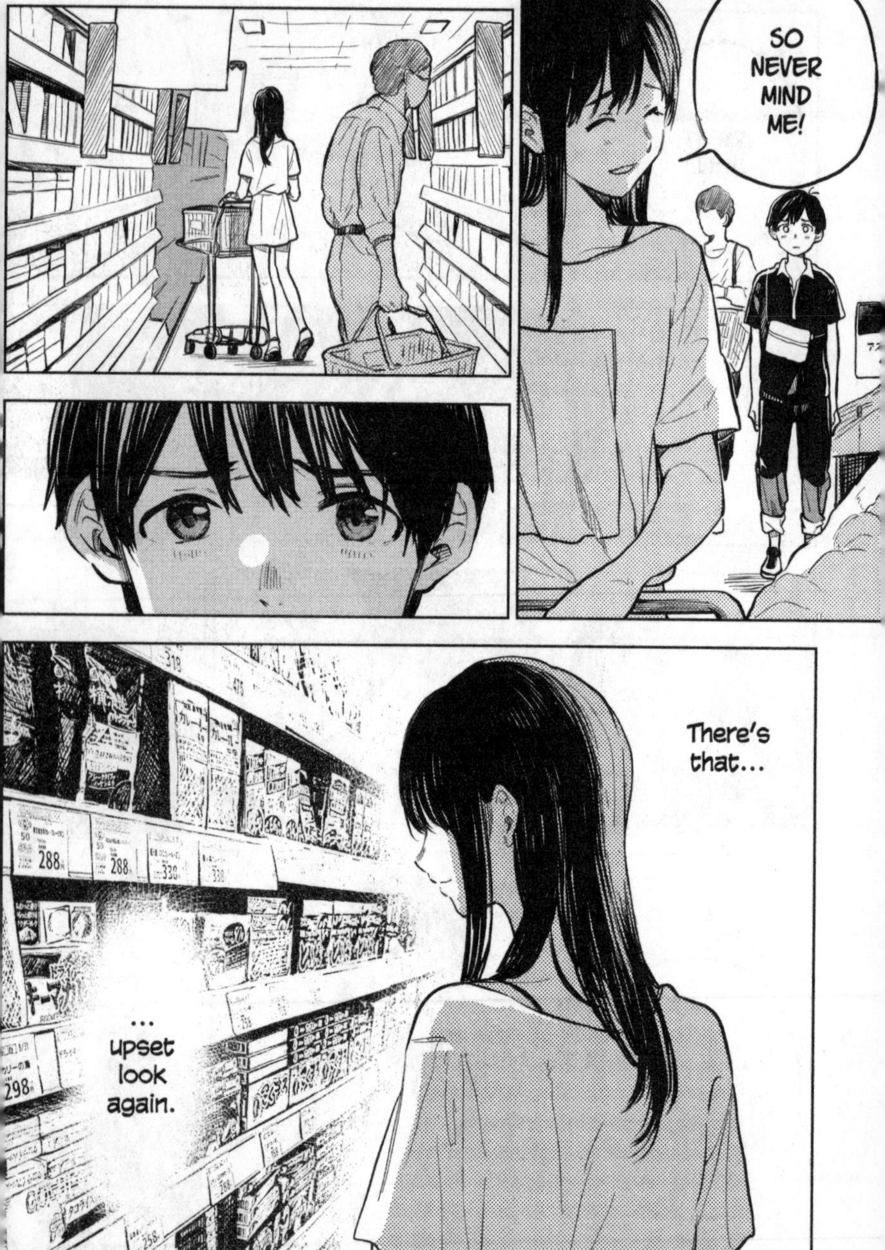
SO NEVER MIND ME!
There's that...
... upset look again.

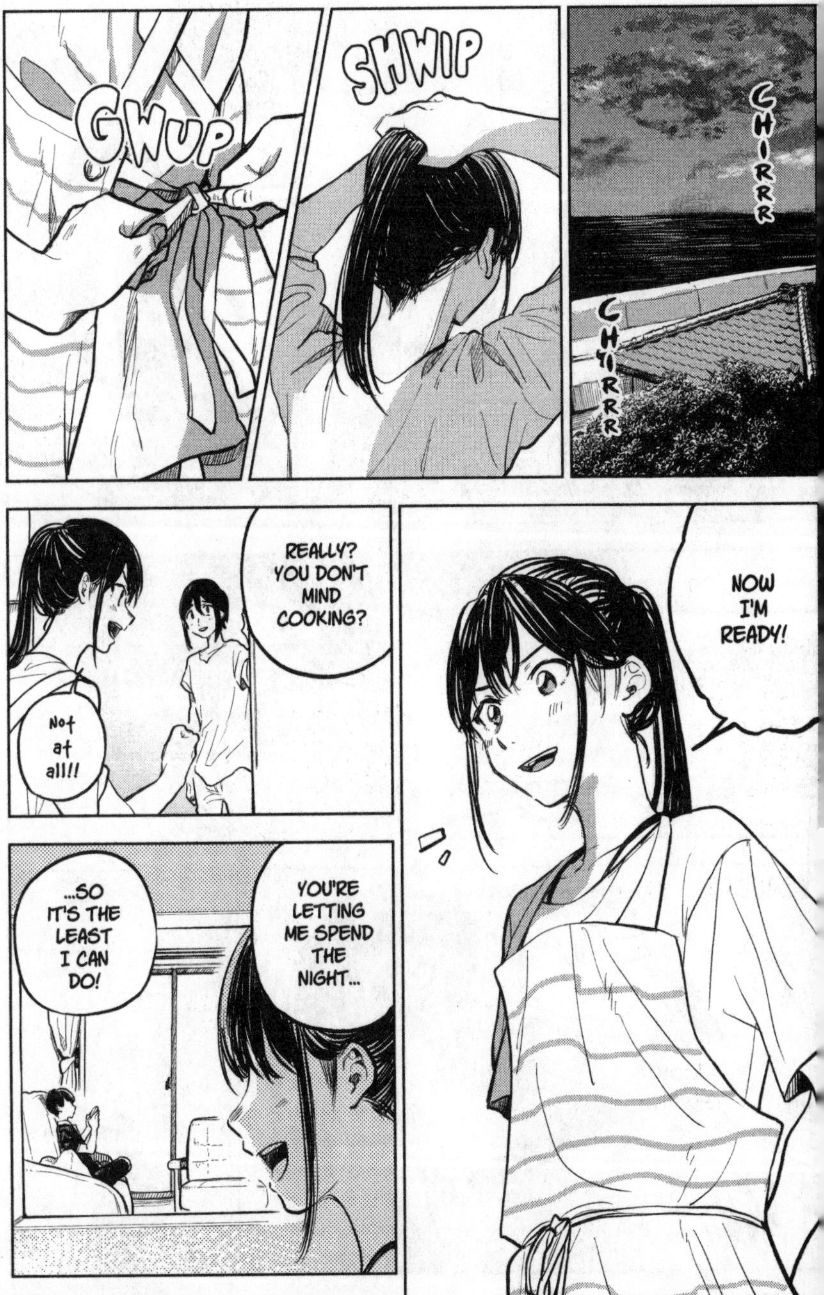
CHIRRR
CHIRRR
SHWIP
GWUP
NOW I'M READY!
REALLY? YOU DON'T MIND COOKING?
Not at all!!
YOU'RE LETTING ME SPEND THE NIGHT...
...SO IT'S THE LEAST I CAN DO!

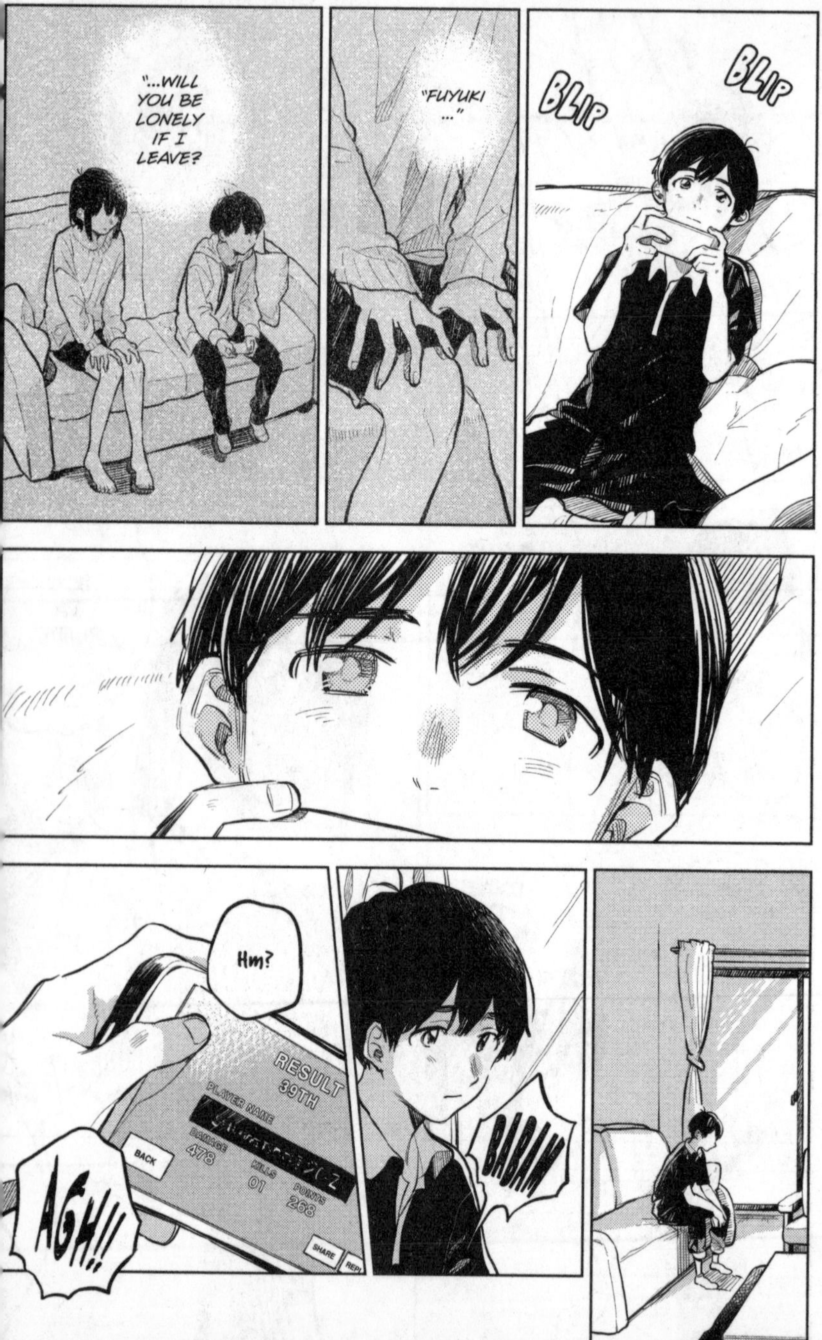
BLIP
BLIP
"FUYUKI ..."
"...WILL YOU BE LONELY IF I LEAVE?
BABAM
Hm?
RESULT
39TH
PLAYER NAME
DAMAGE
478
KILLS
01
POINTS
268
BACK
SHARE
AGH!!

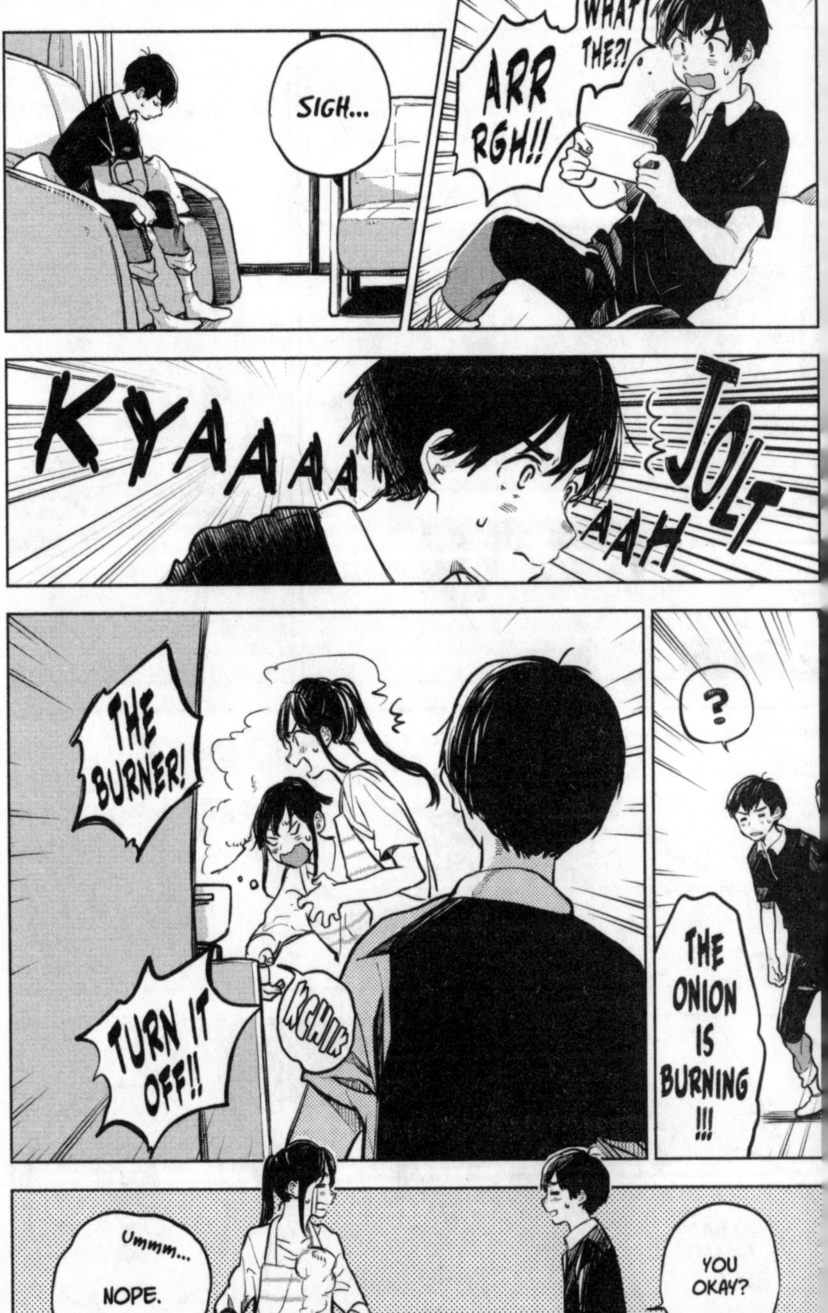
WHAT THE?!
ARR RGH!!
SIGH...
JOLT
KYAAAAA
AAH
?
THE ONION IS BURNING!!!
THE BURNER!
KCHIK
TURN IT OFF!!
YOU OKAY?
Ummm... NOPE.

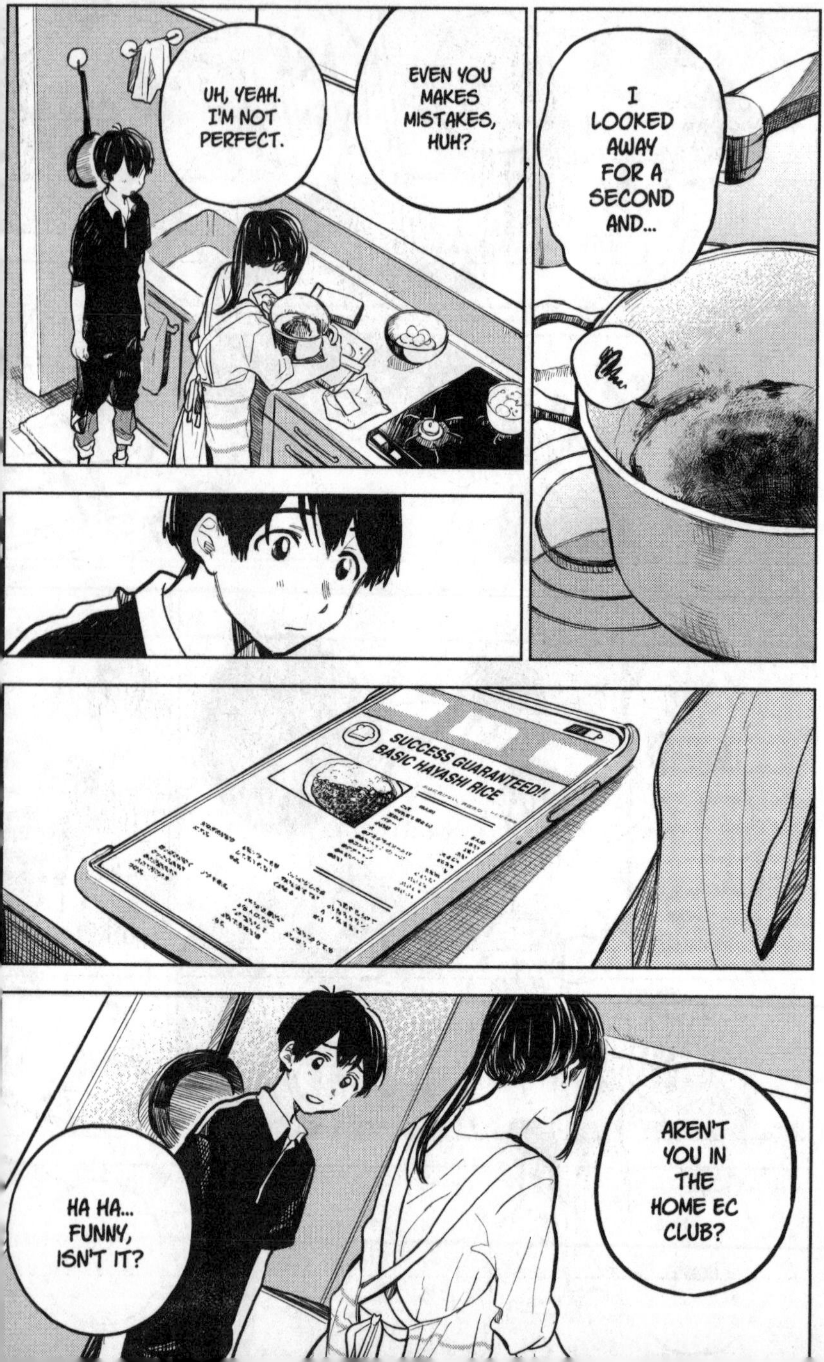
I LOOKED AWAY FOR A SECOND AND...
EVEN YOU MAKES MISTAKES, HUH?
UH, YEAH. I'M NOT PERFECT.
SUCCESS GUARANTEED!! BASIC HAYASHI RICE
AREN'T YOU IN THE HOME EC CLUB?
HA HA... FUNNY, ISN'T IT?

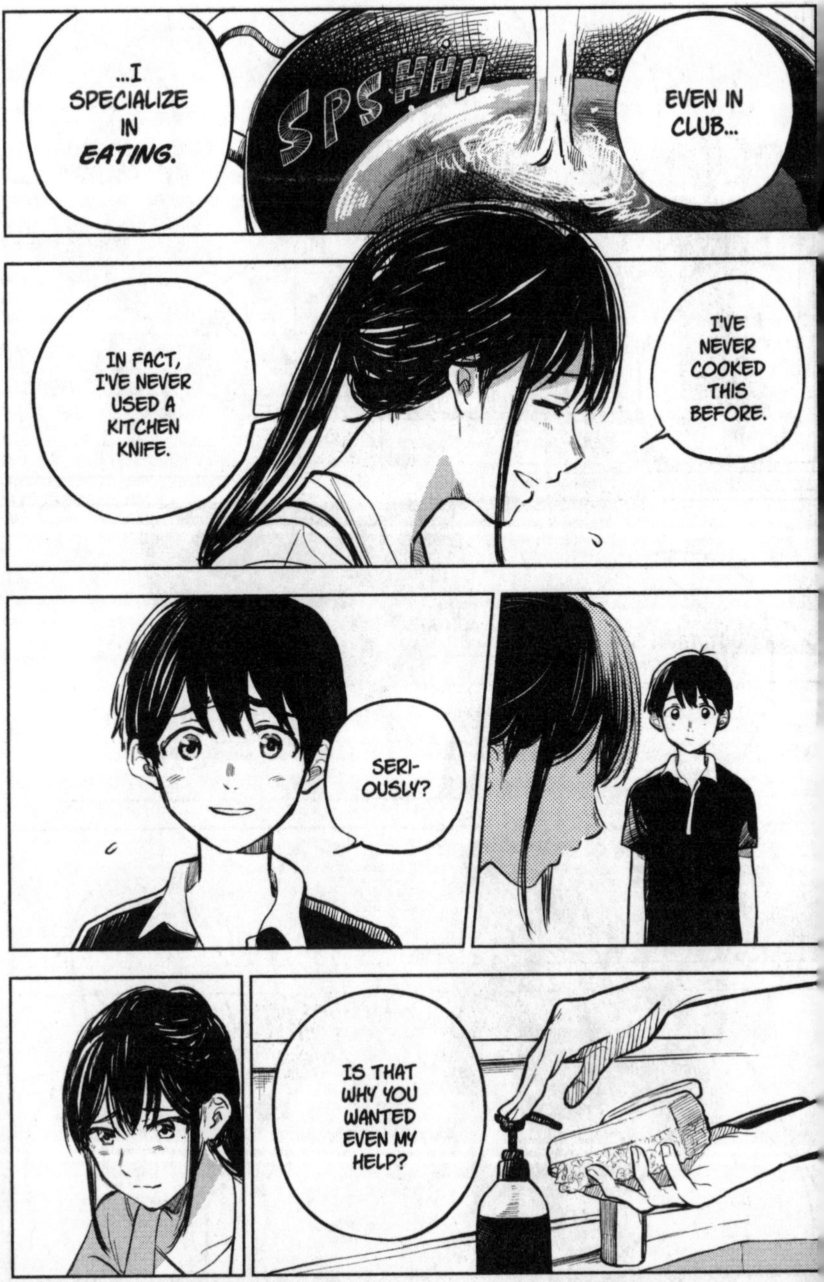
EVEN IN CLUB...
SPSHHH
...I SPECIALIZE IN EATING.
I'VE NEVER COOKED THIS BEFORE.
IN FACT, I'VE NEVER USED A KITCHEN KNIFE.
SERI-OUSLY?
IS THAT WHY YOU WANTED EVEN MY HELP?

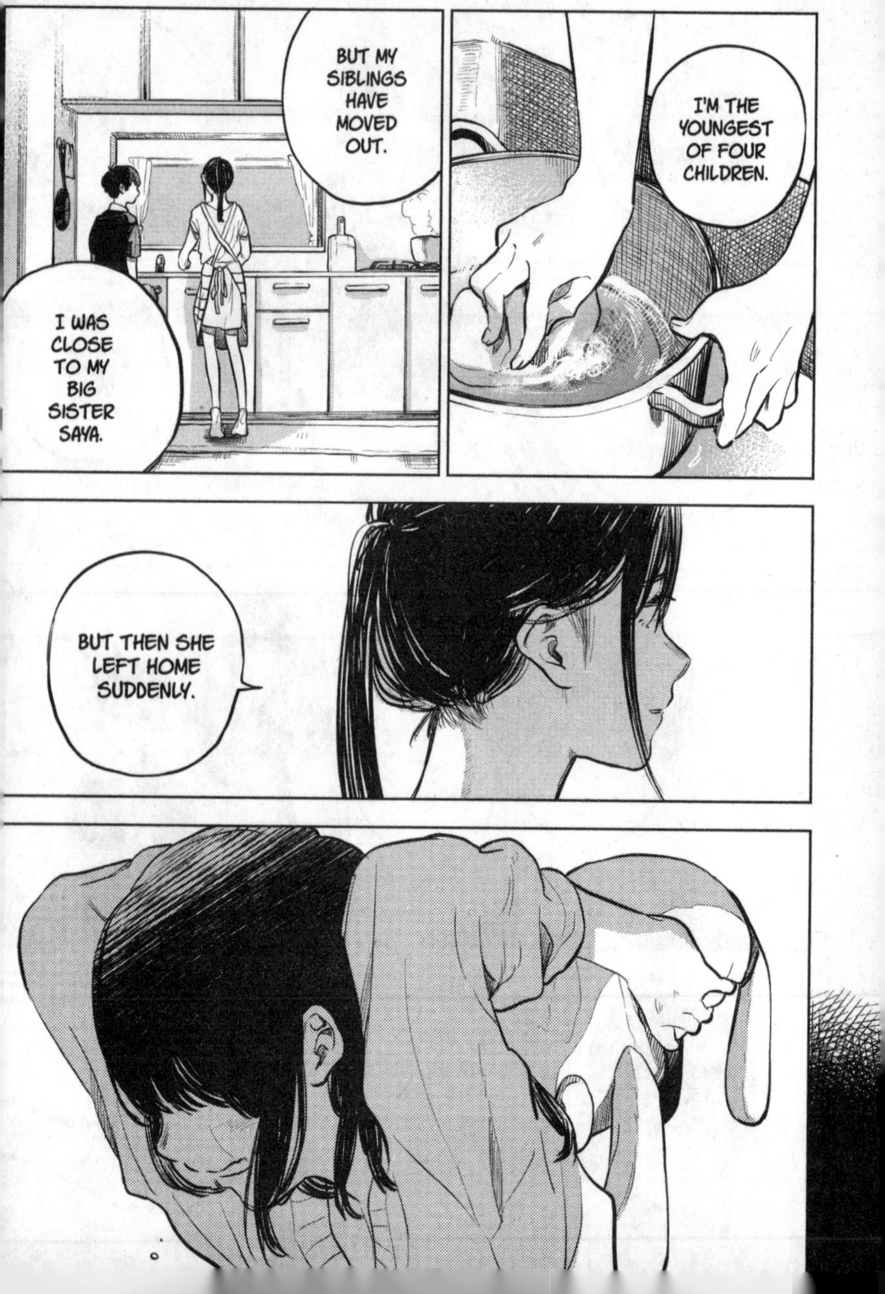
I'M THE YOUNGEST OF FOUR CHILDREN.
BUT MY SIBLINGS HAVE MOVED OUT.
I WAS CLOSE TO MY BIG SISTER SAYA.
BUT THEN SHE LEFT HOME SUDDENLY.

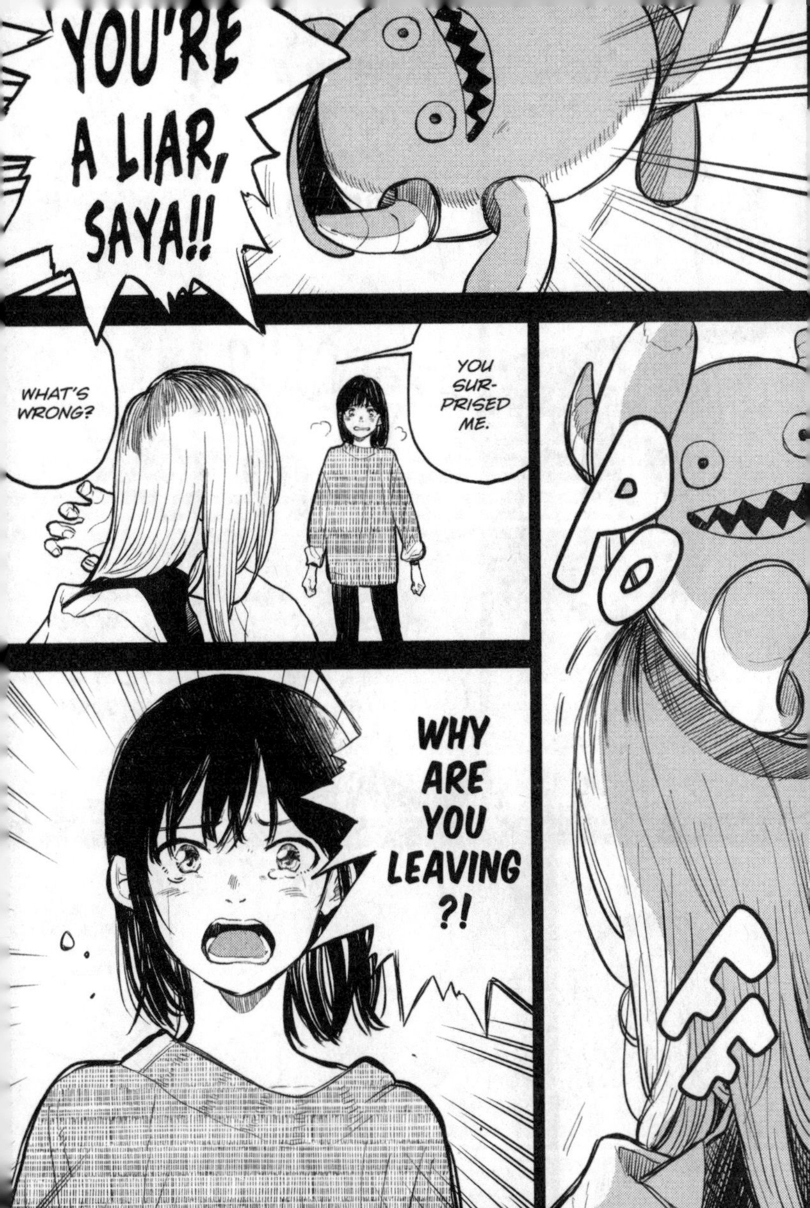
YOU'RE A LIAR, SAYA!!
POFF
YOU SUR-PRISED ME.
WHAT'S WRONG?
WHY ARE YOU LEAVING?!

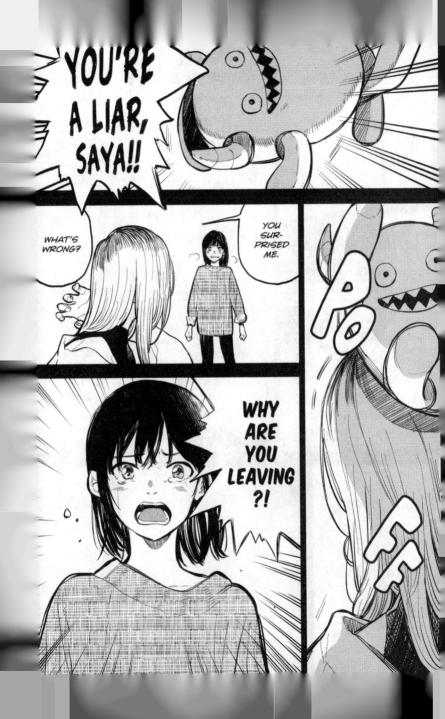

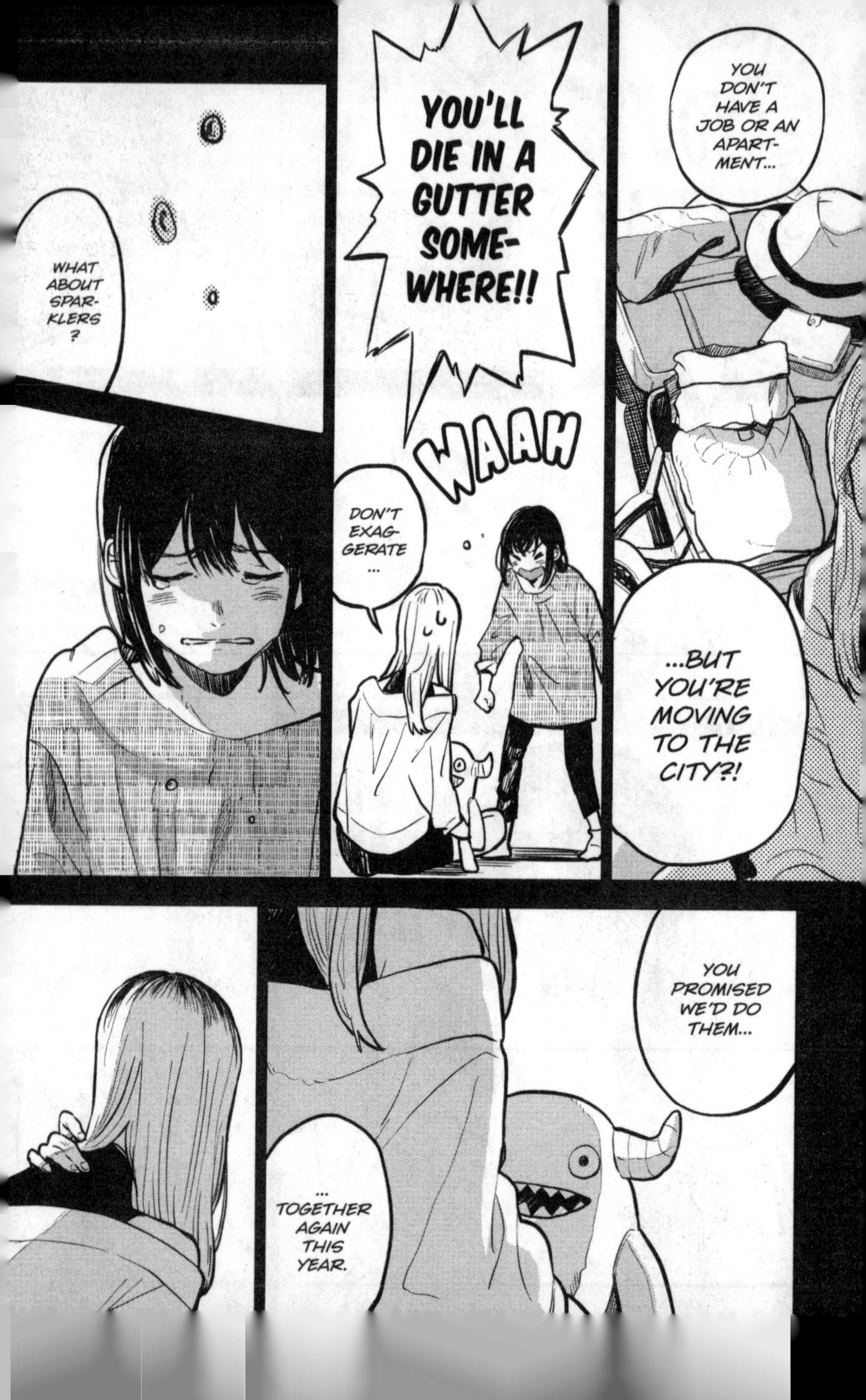
YOU DON'T HAVE A JOB OR AN APART-MENT...
...BUT YOU'RE MOVING TO THE CITY?!
YOU'LL DIE IN A GUTTER SOME-WHERE!!
WAAH
DON'T EXAG-GERATE ...
WHAT ABOUT SPAR-KLERS ?
YOU PROMISED WE'D DO THEM...
... TOGETHER AGAIN THIS YEAR.

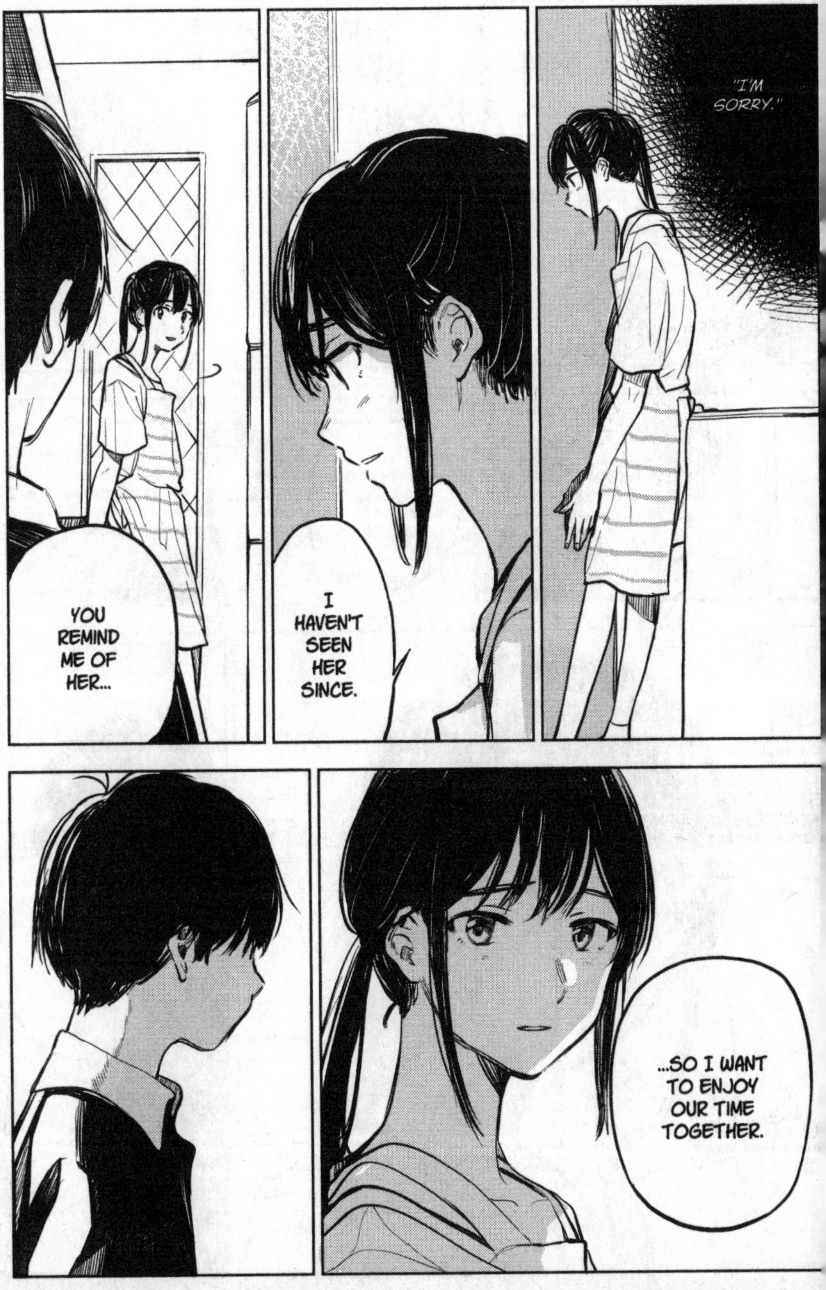
"I'M SORRY."
I HAVEN'T SEEN HER SINCE.
YOU REMIND ME OF HER...
...SO I WANT TO ENJOY OUR TIME TOGETHER.

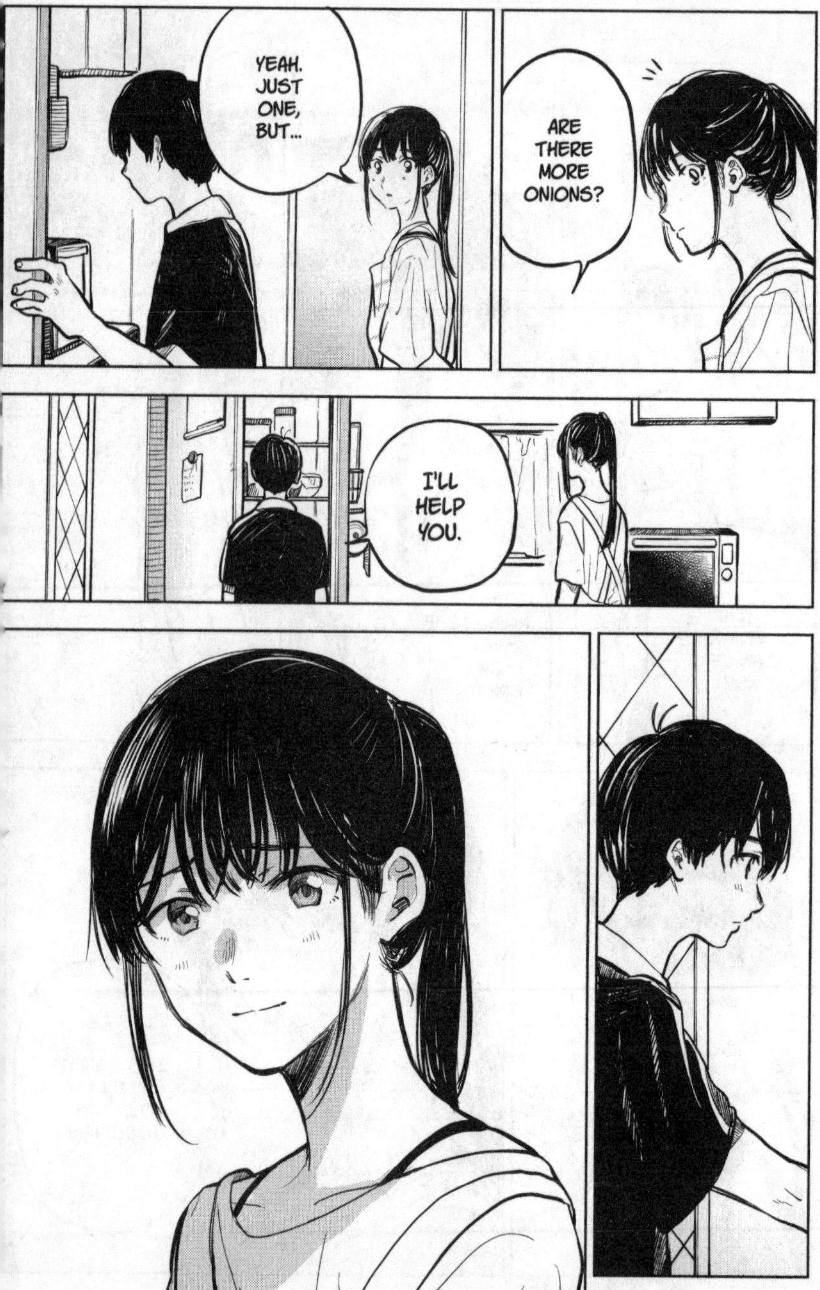
ARE THERE MORE ONIONS?
YEAH. JUST ONE, BUT...
I'LL HELP YOU.

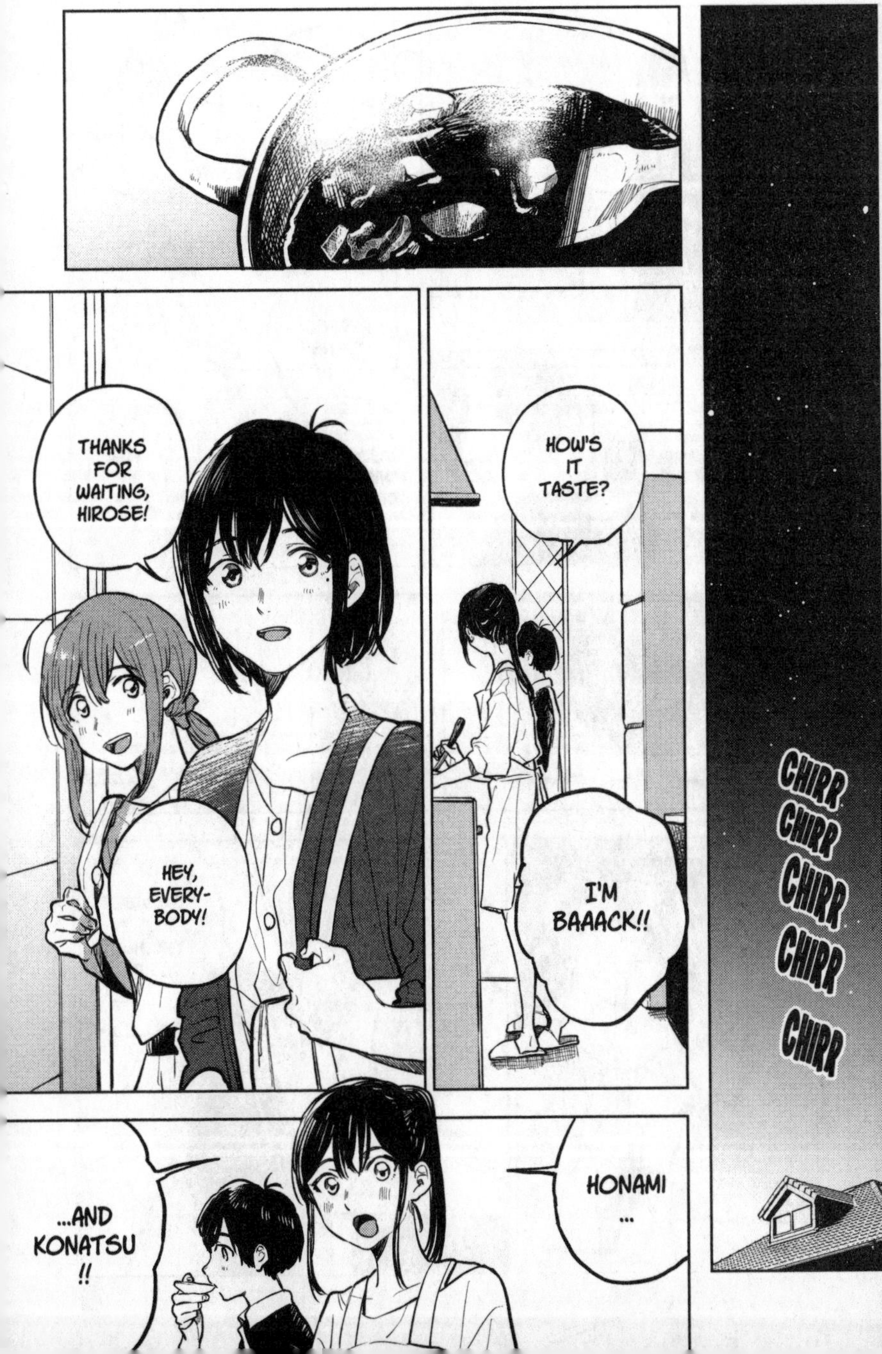
CHIRR
CHIRR
CHIRR
CHIRR
CHIRR
HOW'S IT TASTE?
I'M BAAACK!!
THANKS FOR WAITING, HIROSE!
HEY, EVERY-BODY!
HONAMI ...
...AND KONATSU !!

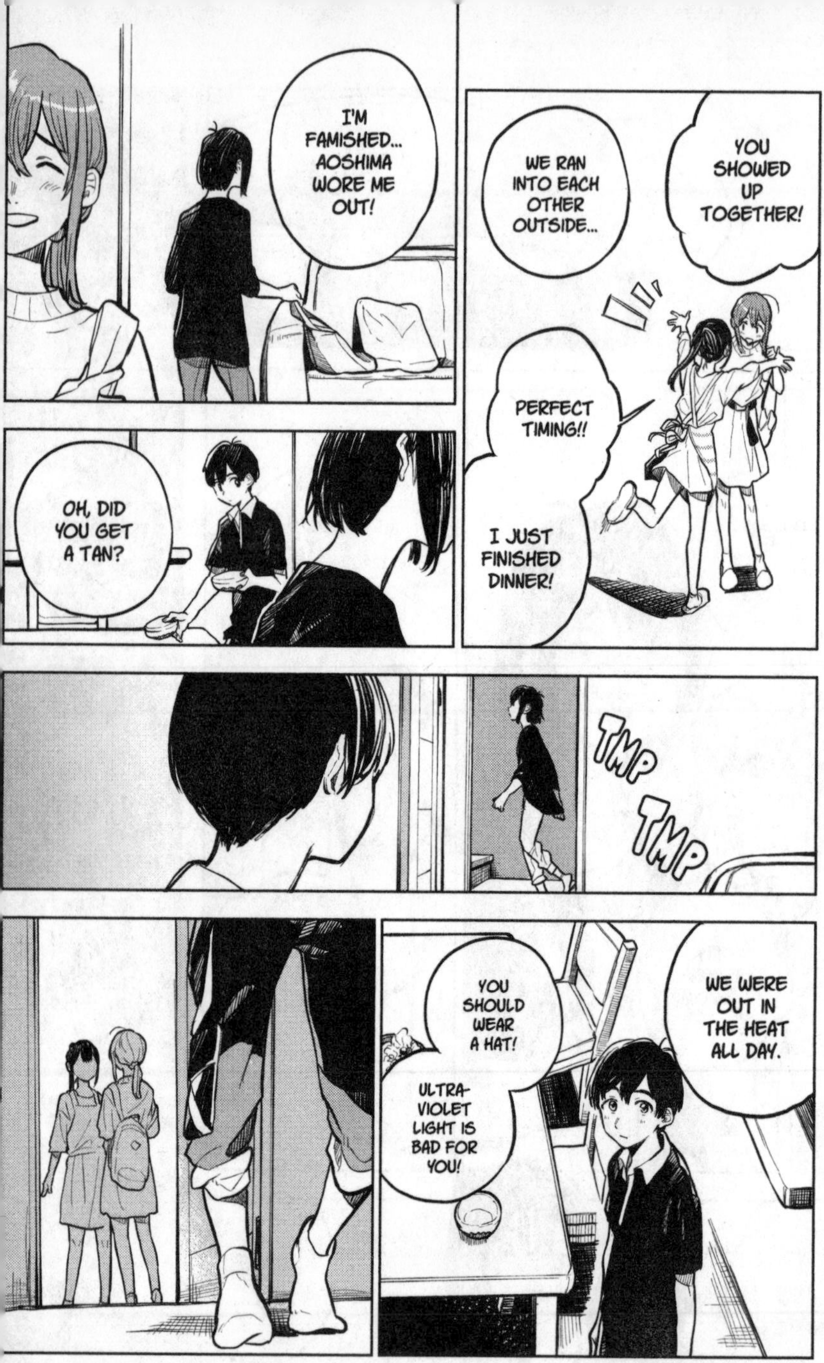
YOU SHOWED UP TOGETHER!
WE RAN INTO EACH OTHER OUTSIDE...
PERFECT TIMING!!
I JUST FINISHED DINNER!
I'M FAMISHED... AOSHIMA WORE ME OUT!
OH, DID YOU GET A TAN?
TMP
TMP
WE WERE OUT IN THE HEAT ALL DAY.
YOU SHOULD WEAR A HAT!
ULTRA-VIOLET LIGHT IS BAD FOR YOU!

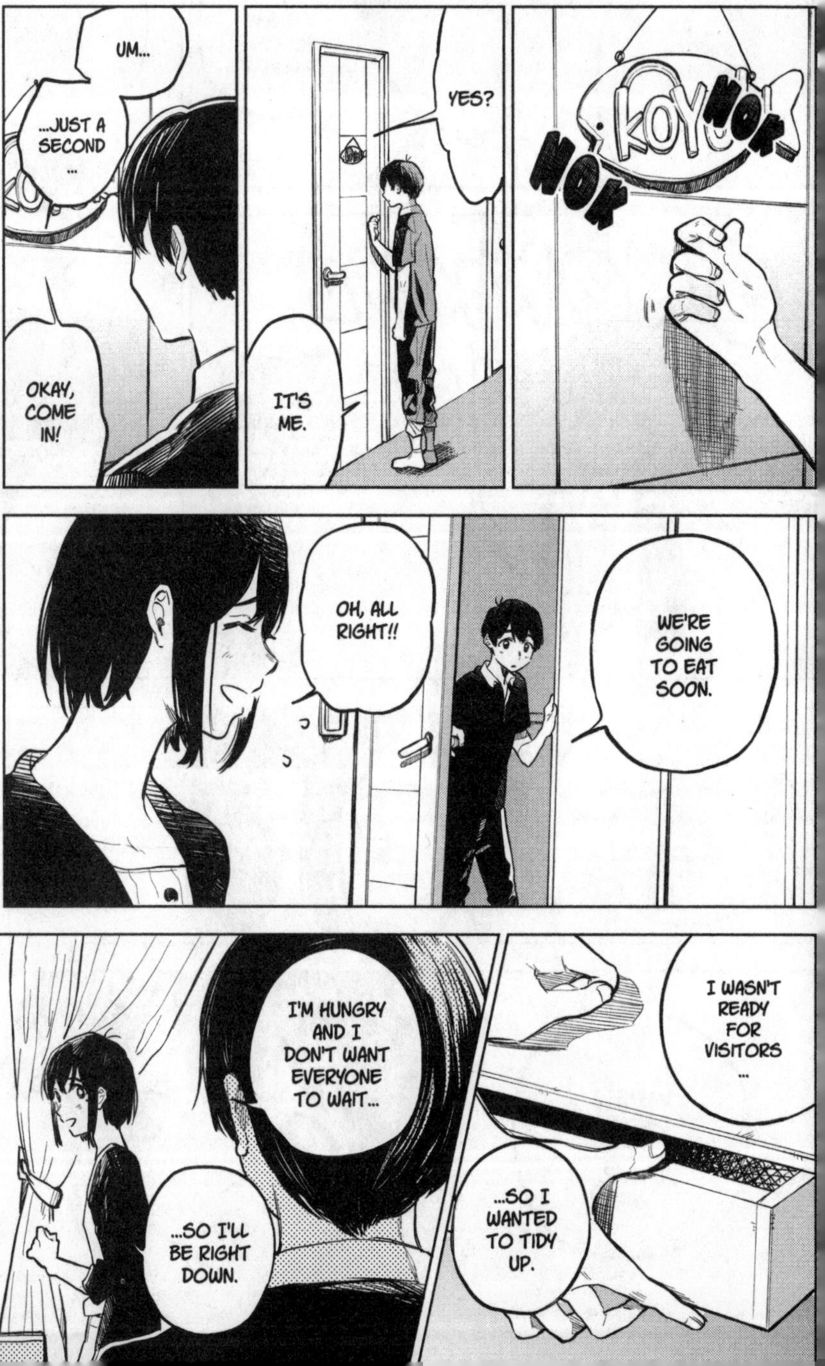
NOK
NOK
YES?
IT'S ME.
UM...
...JUST A SECOND ...
OKAY, COME IN!
WE'RE GOING TO EAT SOON.
OH, ALL RIGHT!!
I WASN'T READY FOR VISITORS ...
...SO I WANTED TO TIDY UP.
I'M HUNGRY AND I DON'T WANT EVERYONE TO WAIT...
...SO I'LL BE RIGHT DOWN.

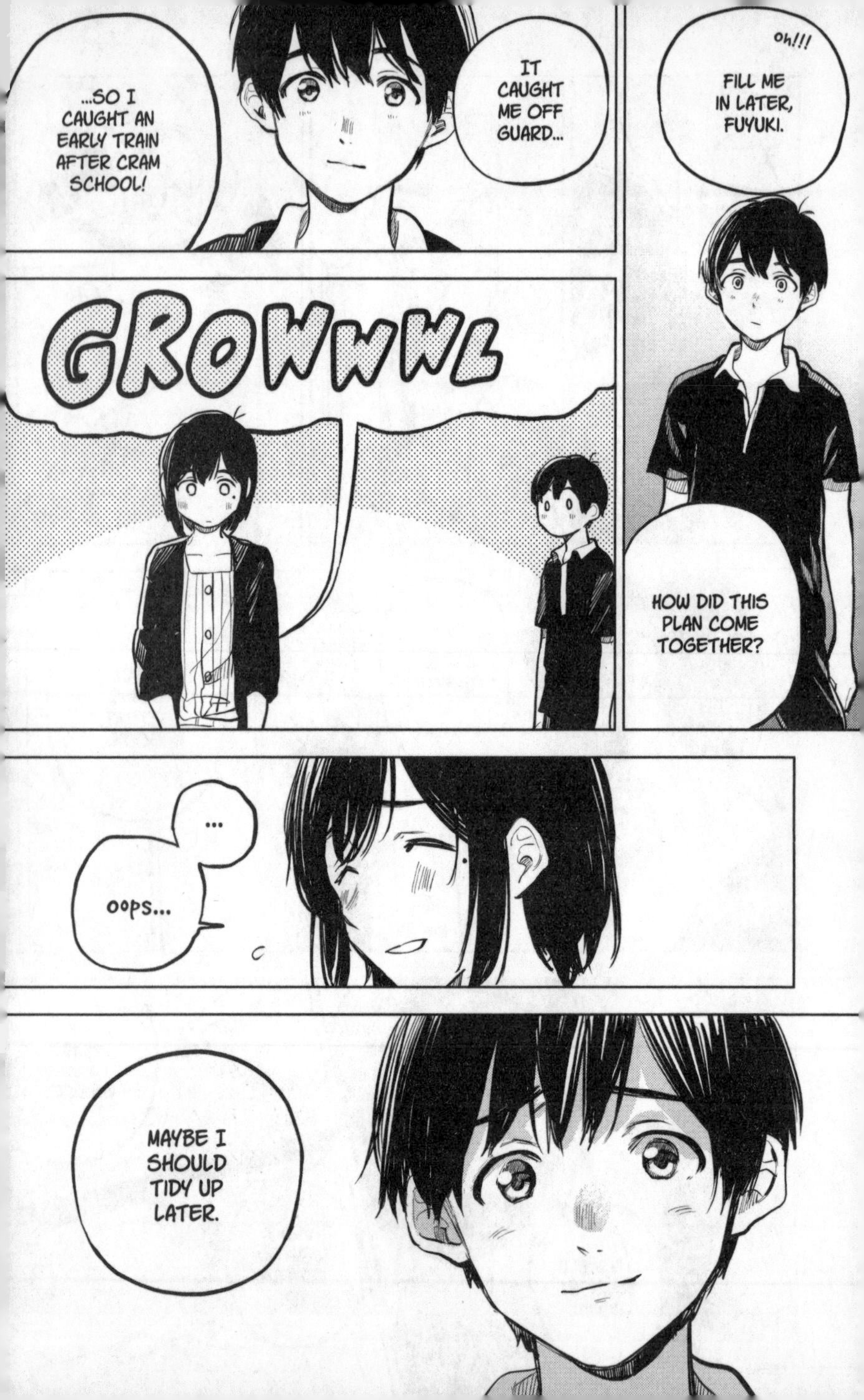

Oh!!!
FILL ME IN LATER, FUYUKI.
HOW DID THIS PLAN COME TOGETHER?
IT CAUGHT ME OFF GUARD...
...SO I CAUGHT AN EARLY TRAIN AFTER CRAM SCHOOL!
GROWWWL
...
oops...
MAYBE I SHOULD TIDY UP LATER.

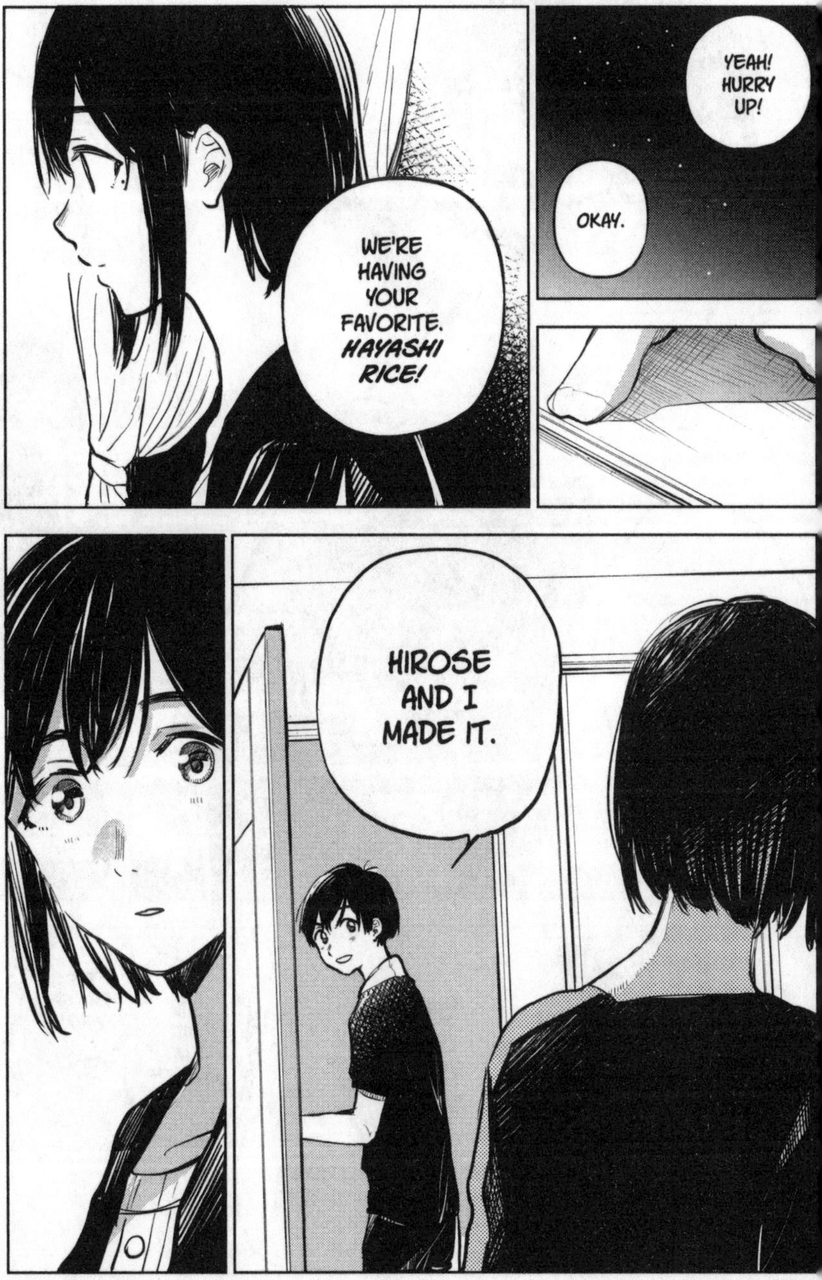
YEAH! HURRY UP!
OKAY.
WE'RE HAVING YOUR FAVORITE. *HAYASHI RICE!*
HIROSE AND I MADE IT.

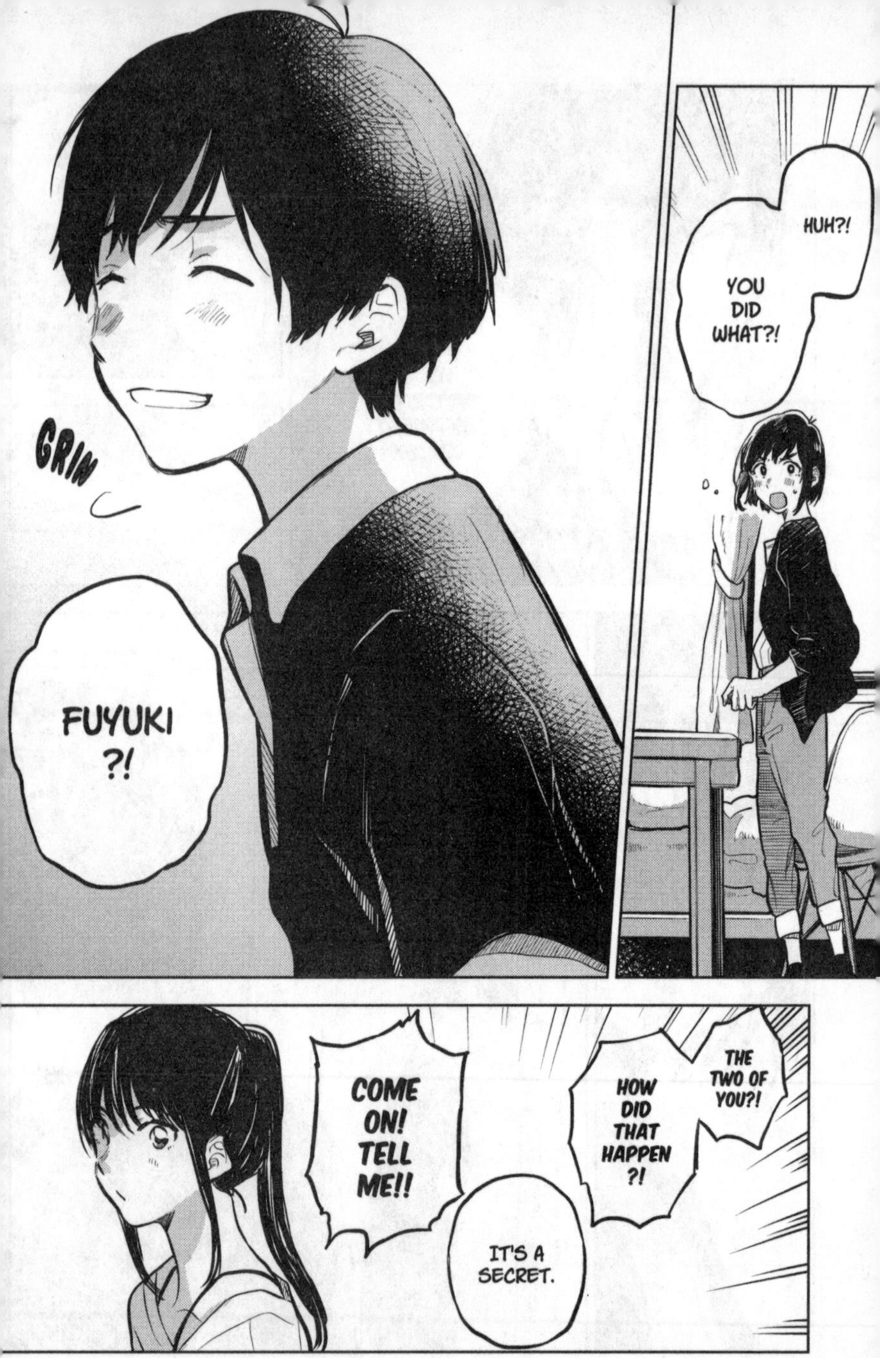
HUH?!
YOU DID WHAT?!
GRIN
FUYUKI ?!
THE TWO OF YOU?!
HOW DID THAT HAPPEN ?!
COME ON! TELL ME!!
IT'S A SECRET.

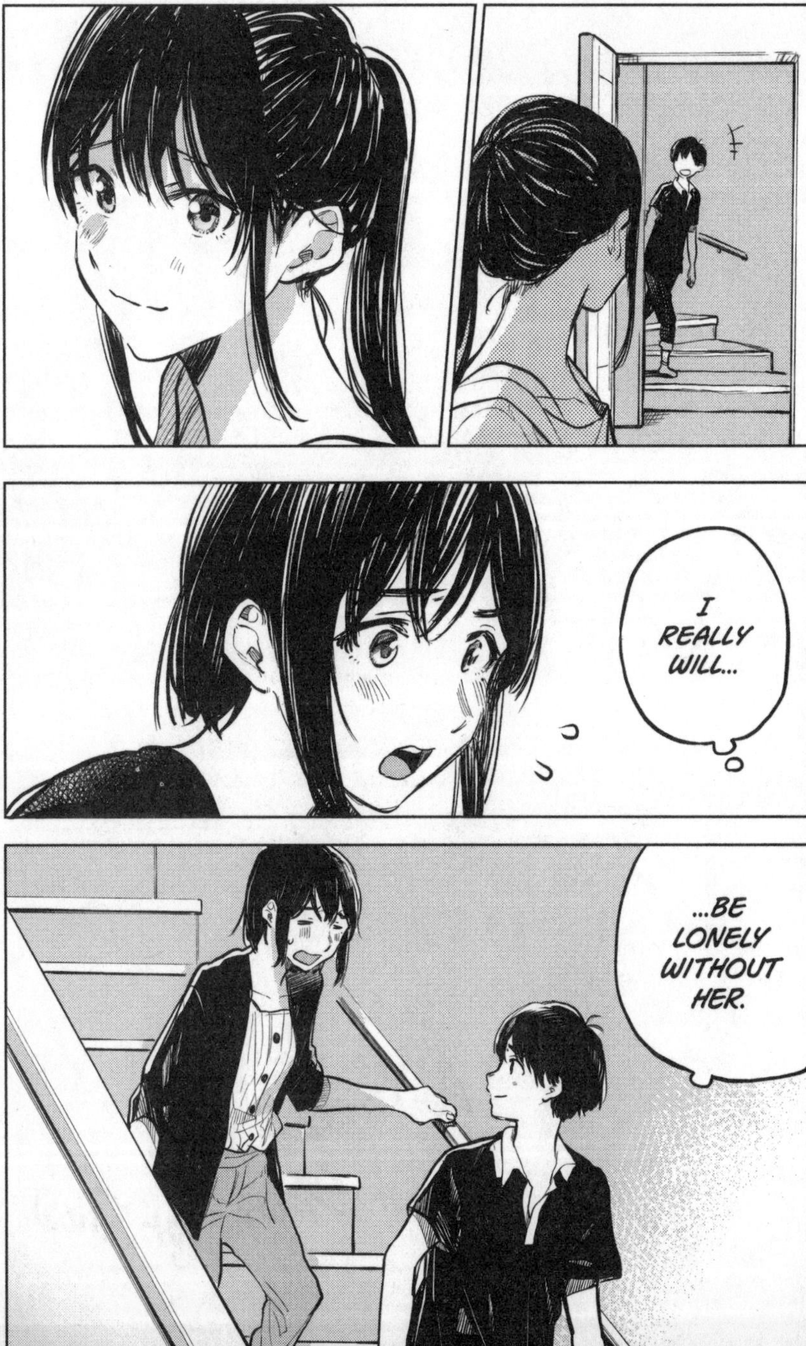
I REALLY WILL...
...BE LONELY WITHOUT HER.

A Tropical Fish
Yearns for Snow

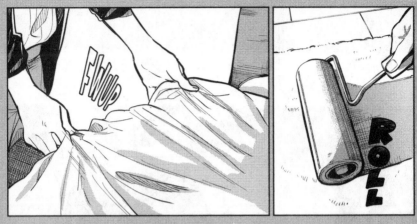

Tank 30:
Konatsu Amano Doesn't Get Attention

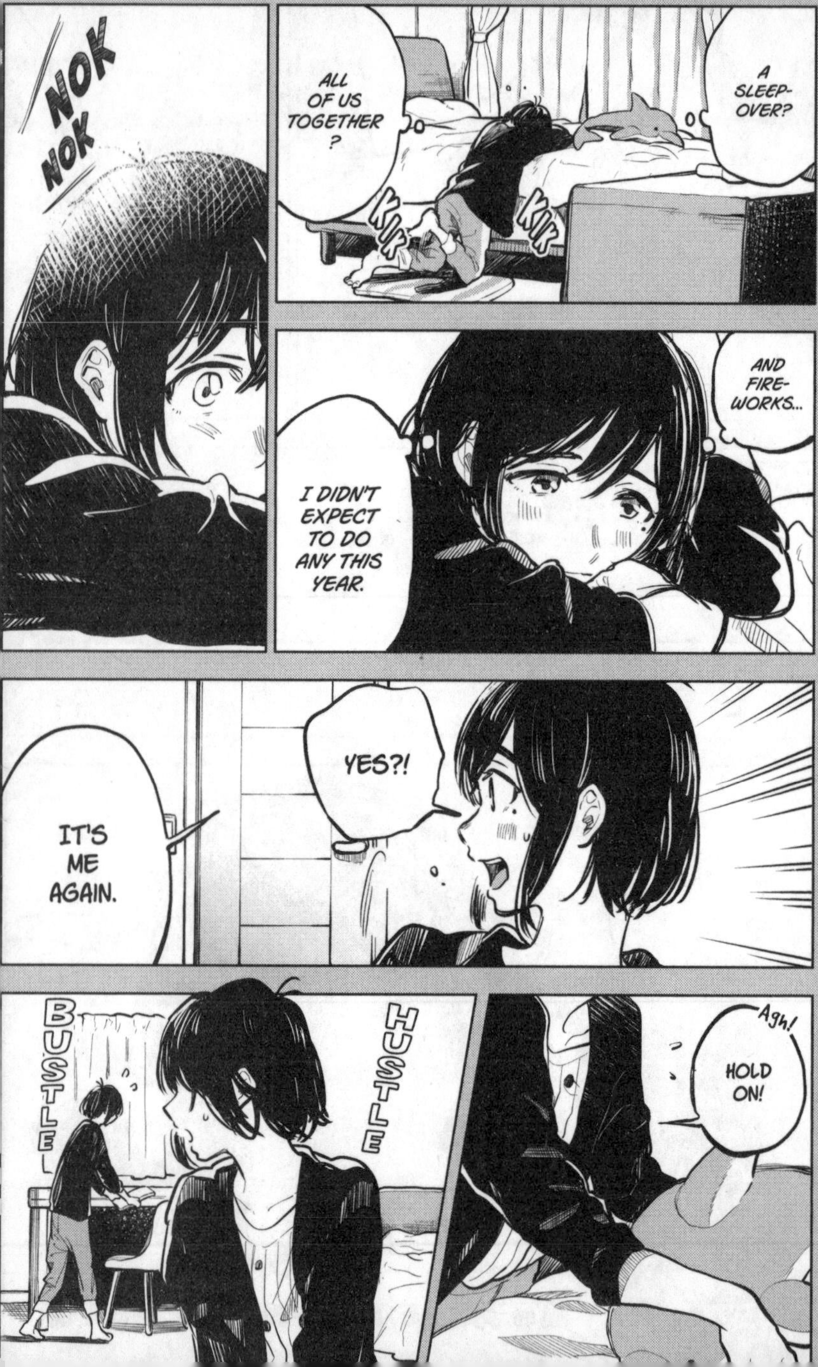
A SLEEP-OVER?
ALL OF US TOGETHER?
KIK KIK
AND FIRE-WORKS...
I DIDN'T EXPECT TO DO ANY THIS YEAR.
NOK NOK
YES?!
IT'S ME AGAIN.
Agh!
HOLD ON!
HUSTLE
BUSTLE

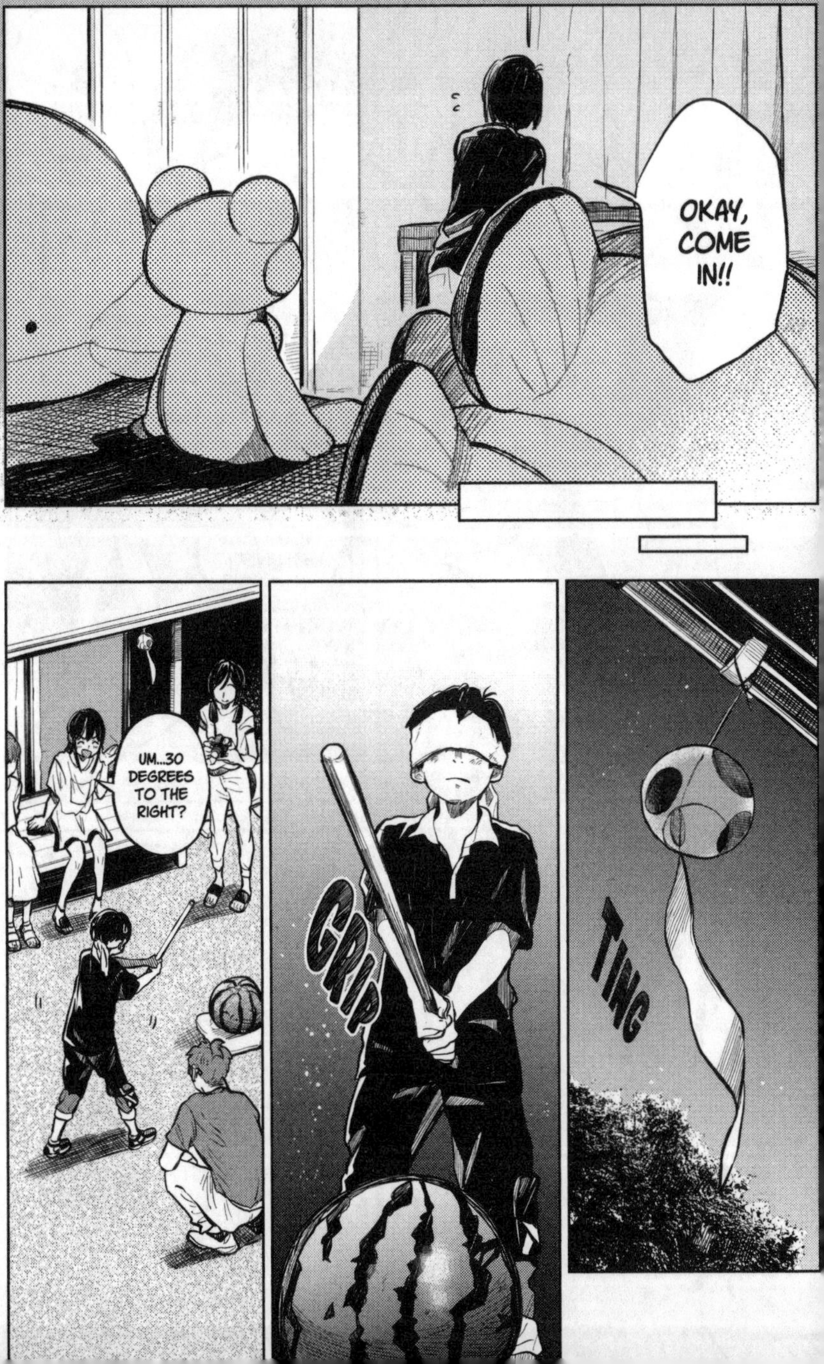
OKAY, COME IN!!
TING
GRIP
UM...30 DEGREES TO THE RIGHT?

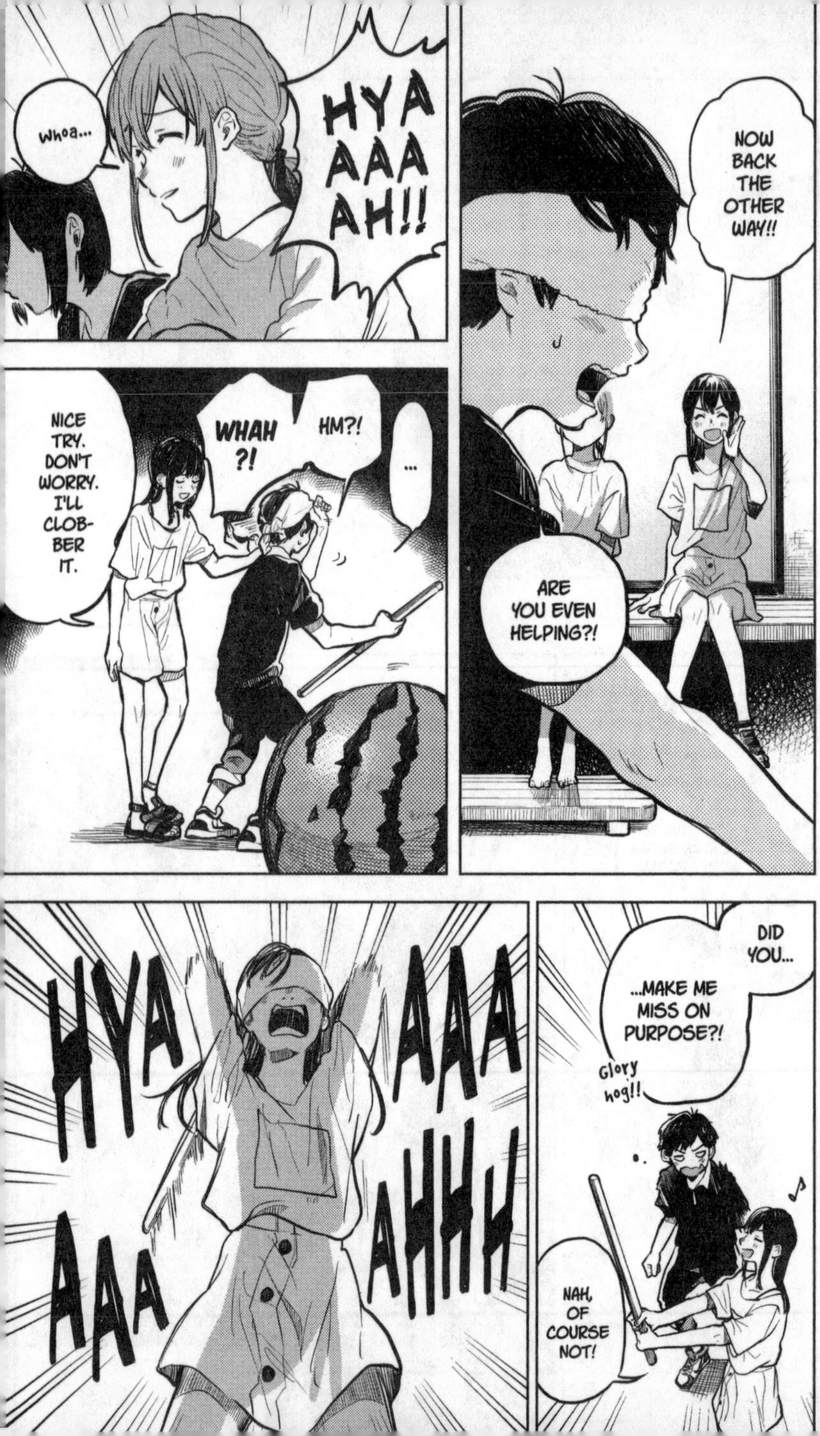

NOW BACK THE OTHER WAY!!
ARE YOU EVEN HELPING?!
HYAAAAAH!!
Whoa...
...
HM?!
WHAH?!
NICE TRY. DON'T WORRY. I'LL CLOBBER IT.
DID YOU...
...MAKE ME MISS ON PURPOSE?!
Glory hog!!
NAH, OF COURSE NOT!
HYA AAAAHHH
AAA

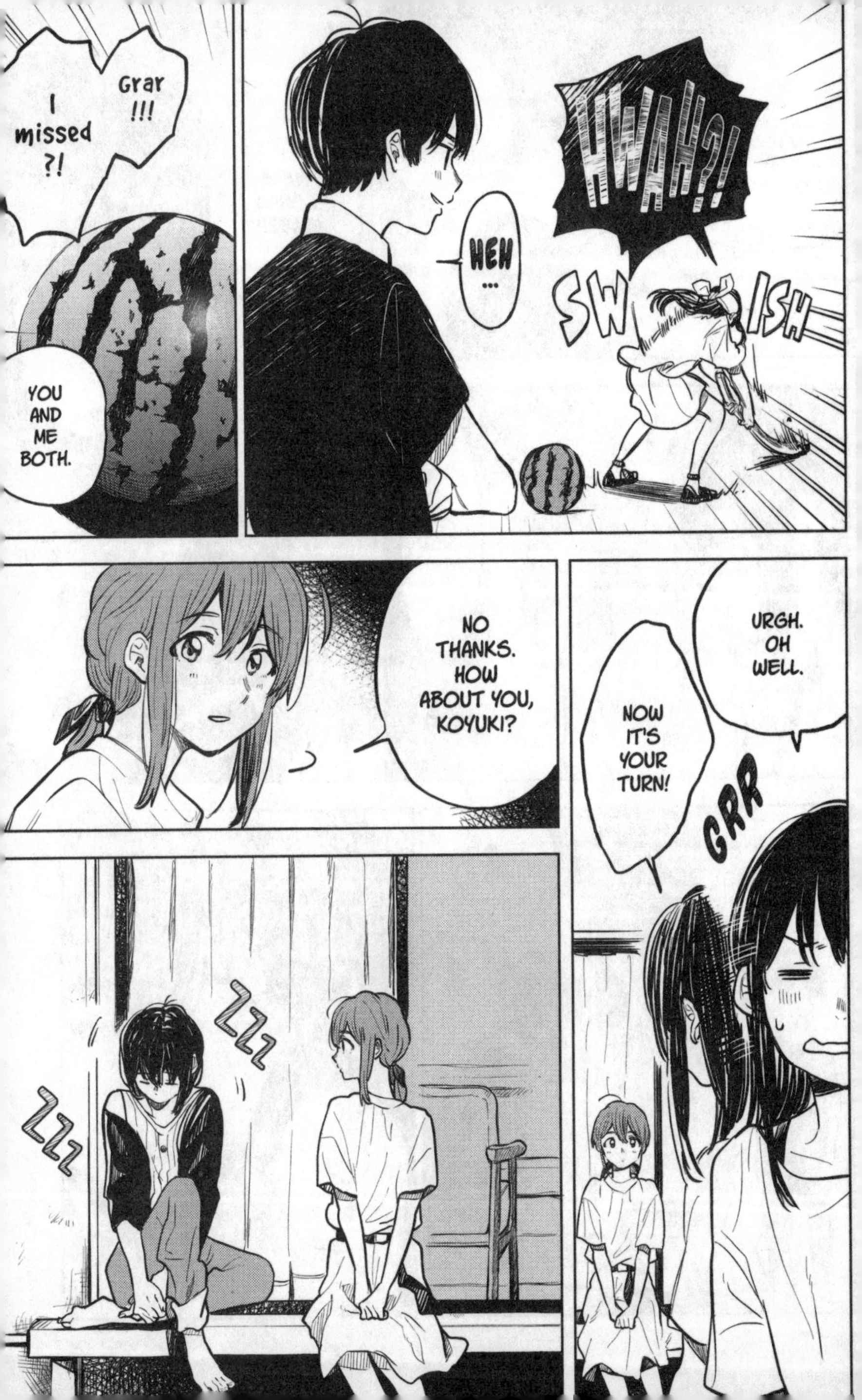
HWAH?!
SWISH
HEH...
Grar !!!
I missed ?!
YOU AND ME BOTH.
URGH. OH WELL.
NOW IT'S YOUR TURN!
GRR
NO THANKS. HOW ABOUT YOU, KOYUKI?
ZZZ
ZZZ

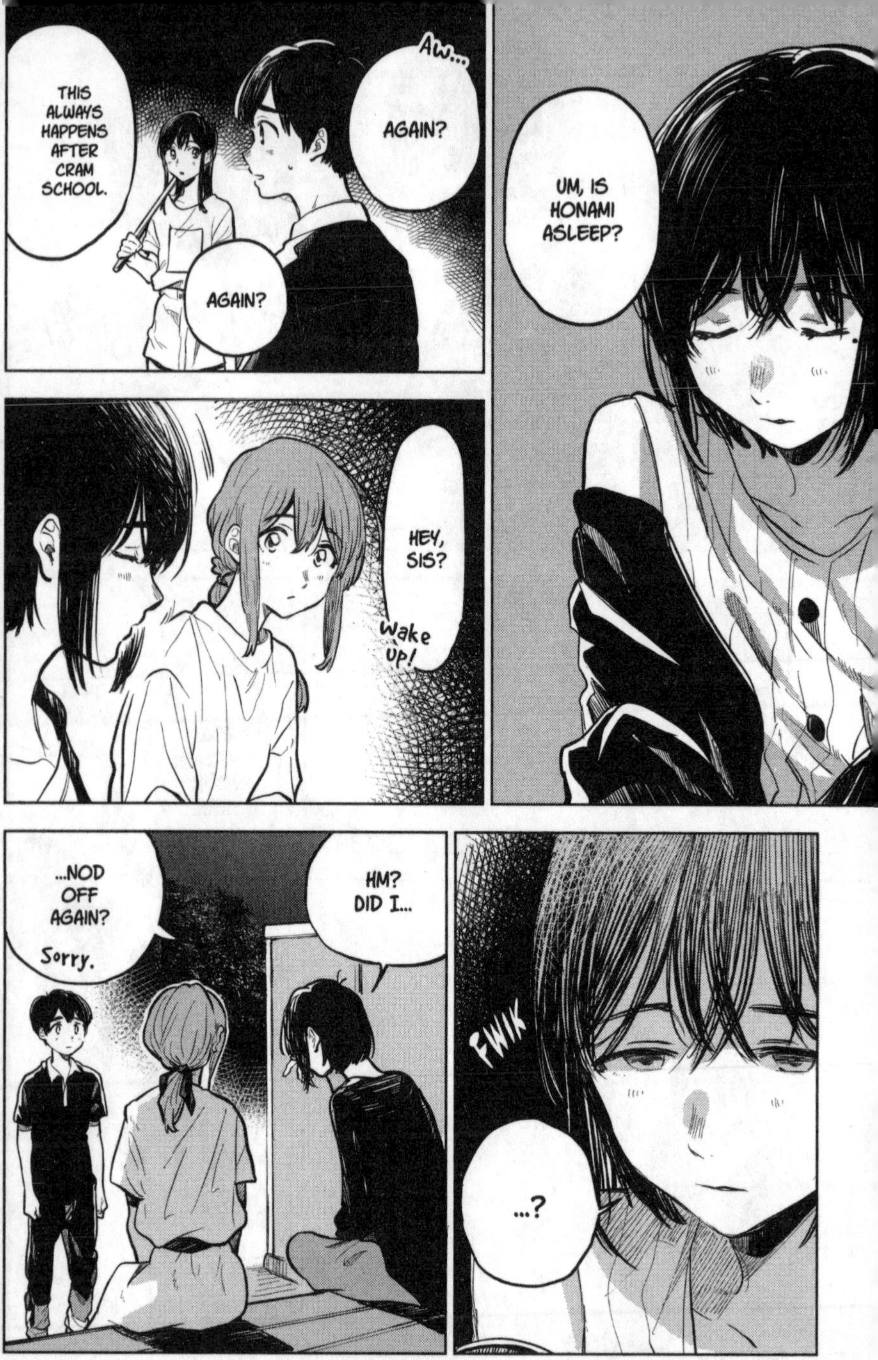
UM, IS HONAMI ASLEEP?
Aw...
AGAIN?
THIS ALWAYS HAPPENS AFTER CRAM SCHOOL.
AGAIN?
HEY, SIS?
Wake up!
FWIK
...?
HM? DID I...
...NOD OFF AGAIN?
Sorry.

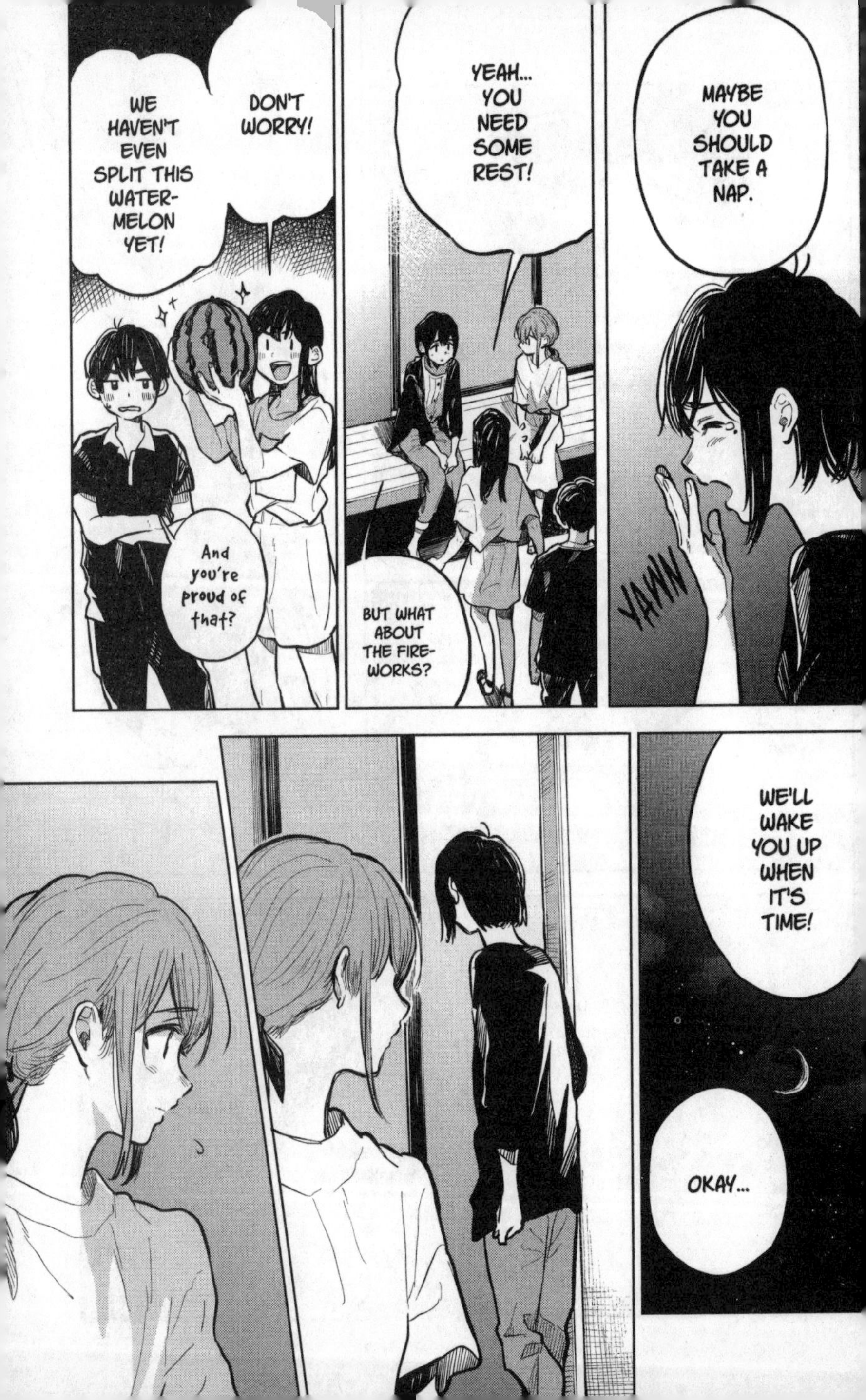
MAYBE YOU SHOULD TAKE A NAP.
YAWN
YEAH... YOU NEED SOME REST!
BUT WHAT ABOUT THE FIRE-WORKS?
DON'T WORRY!
WE HAVEN'T EVEN SPLIT THIS WATER-MELON YET!
And you're proud of that?
WE'LL WAKE YOU UP WHEN IT'S TIME!
OKAY...

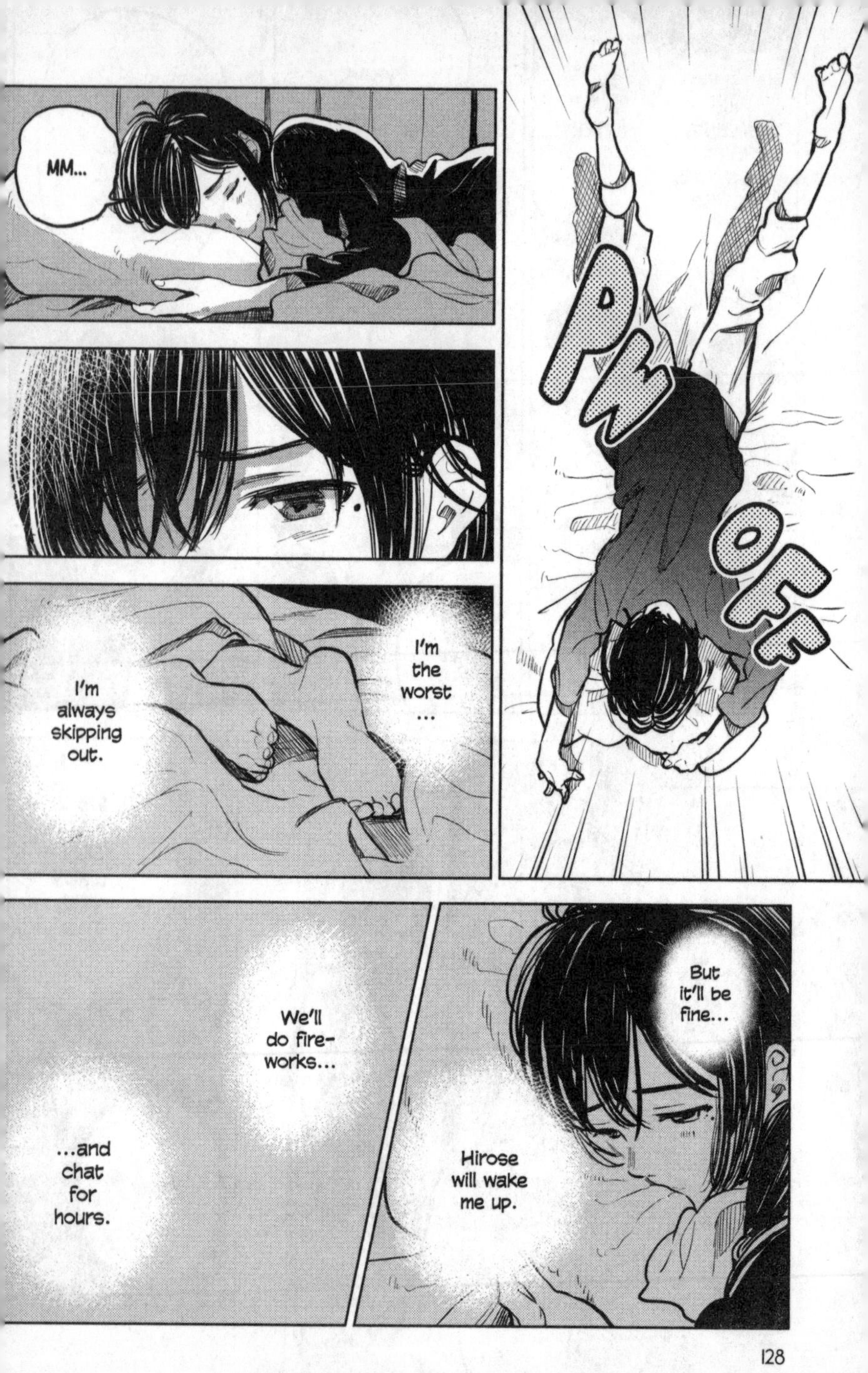
PWOFF
MM...
I'm the worst ...
I'm always skipping out.
But it'll be fine...
Hirose will wake me up.
We'll do fire-works...
...and chat for hours.

...DO A LOT TOGETHER.

WE CAN STILL...

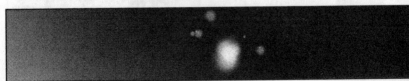

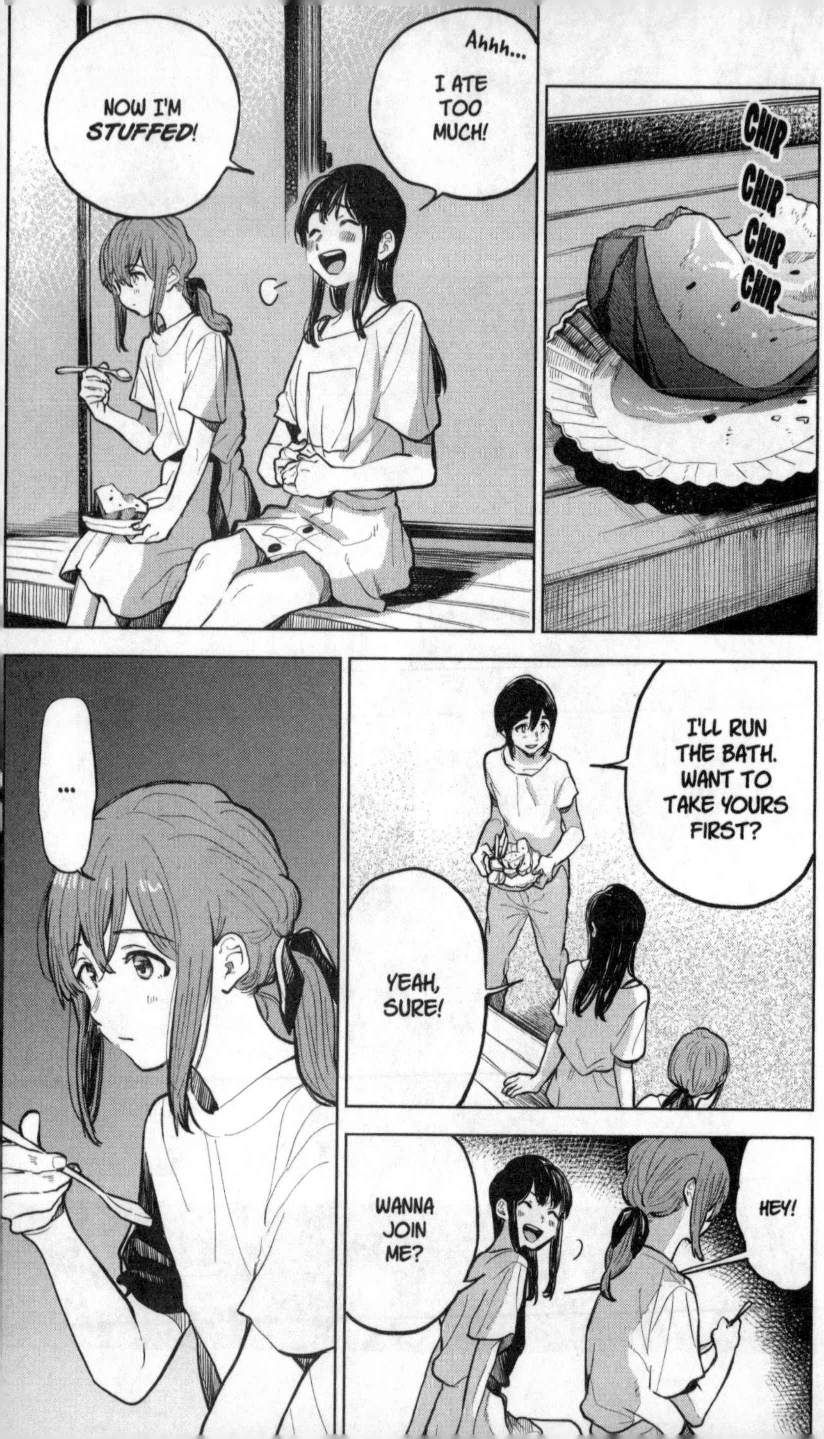
CHIR CHIR CHIR CHIR
Ahhh...
I ATE TOO MUCH!
NOW I'M *STUFFED!*
I'LL RUN THE BATH. WANT TO TAKE YOURS FIRST?
YEAH, SURE!
HEY!
WANNA JOIN ME?
...

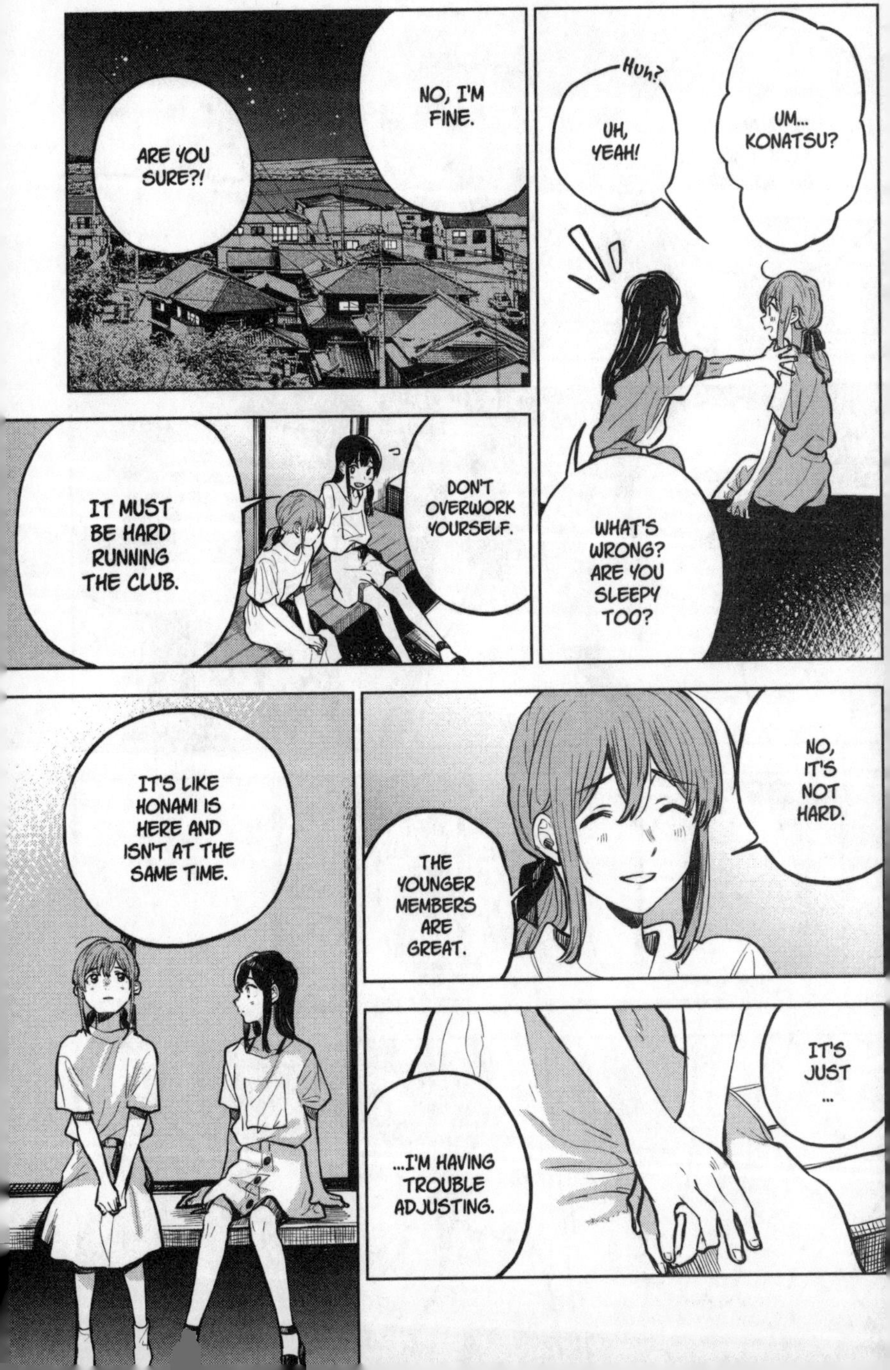
UM... KONATSU?
Huh?
UH, YEAH!
WHAT'S WRONG? ARE YOU SLEEPY TOO?
NO, I'M FINE.
ARE YOU SURE?!
DON'T OVERWORK YOURSELF.
IT MUST BE HARD RUNNING THE CLUB.
NO, IT'S NOT HARD.
THE YOUNGER MEMBERS ARE GREAT.
IT'S JUST ...
...I'M HAVING TROUBLE ADJUSTING.
IT'S LIKE HONAMI IS HERE AND ISN'T AT THE SAME TIME.

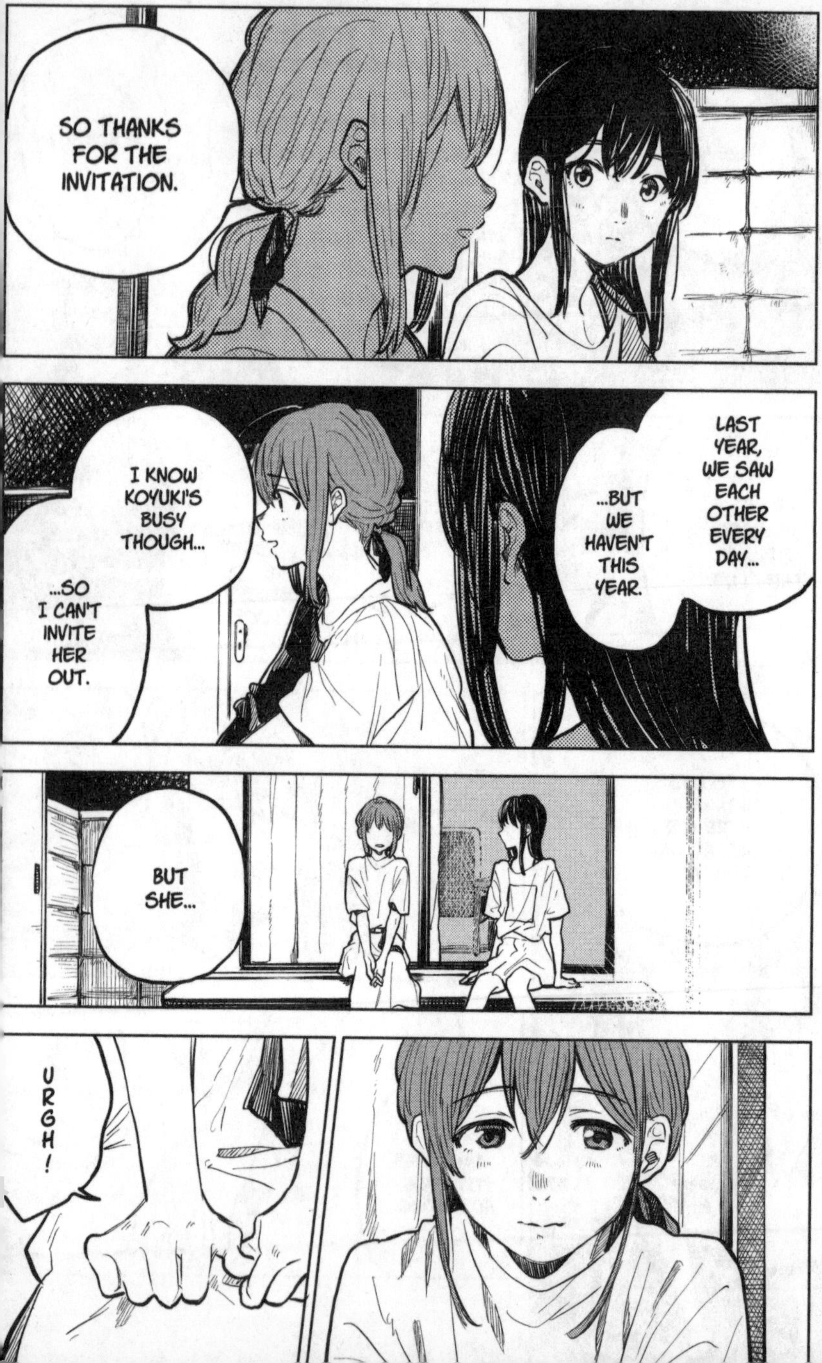
SO THANKS FOR THE INVITATION.
LAST YEAR, WE SAW EACH OTHER EVERY DAY...
...BUT WE HAVEN'T THIS YEAR.
I KNOW KOYUKI'S BUSY THOUGH...
...SO I CAN'T INVITE HER OUT.
BUT SHE...
URGH!

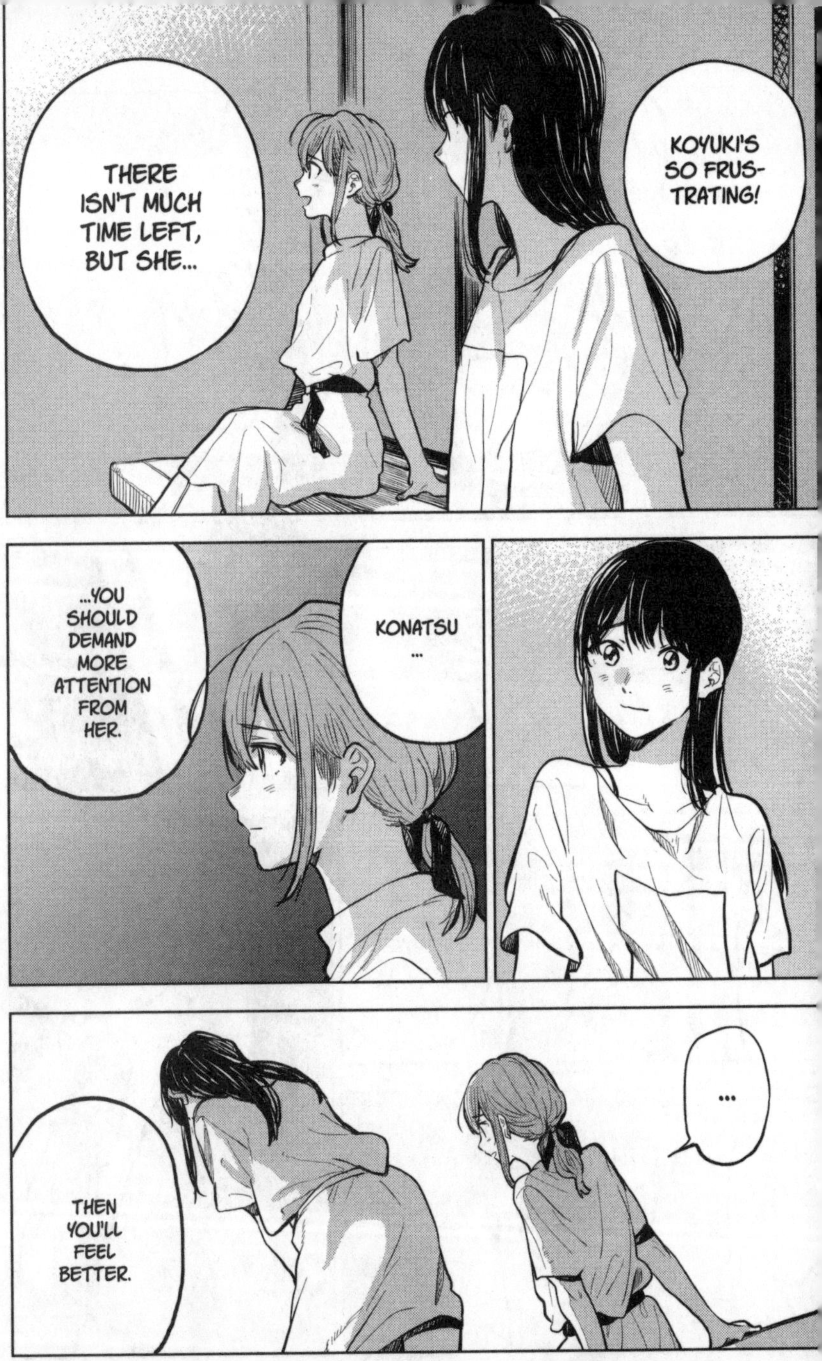
KOYUKI'S SO FRUS-TRATING!
THERE ISN'T MUCH TIME LEFT, BUT SHE...
KONATSU ...
...YOU SHOULD DEMAND MORE ATTENTION FROM HER.
...
THEN YOU'LL FEEL BETTER.

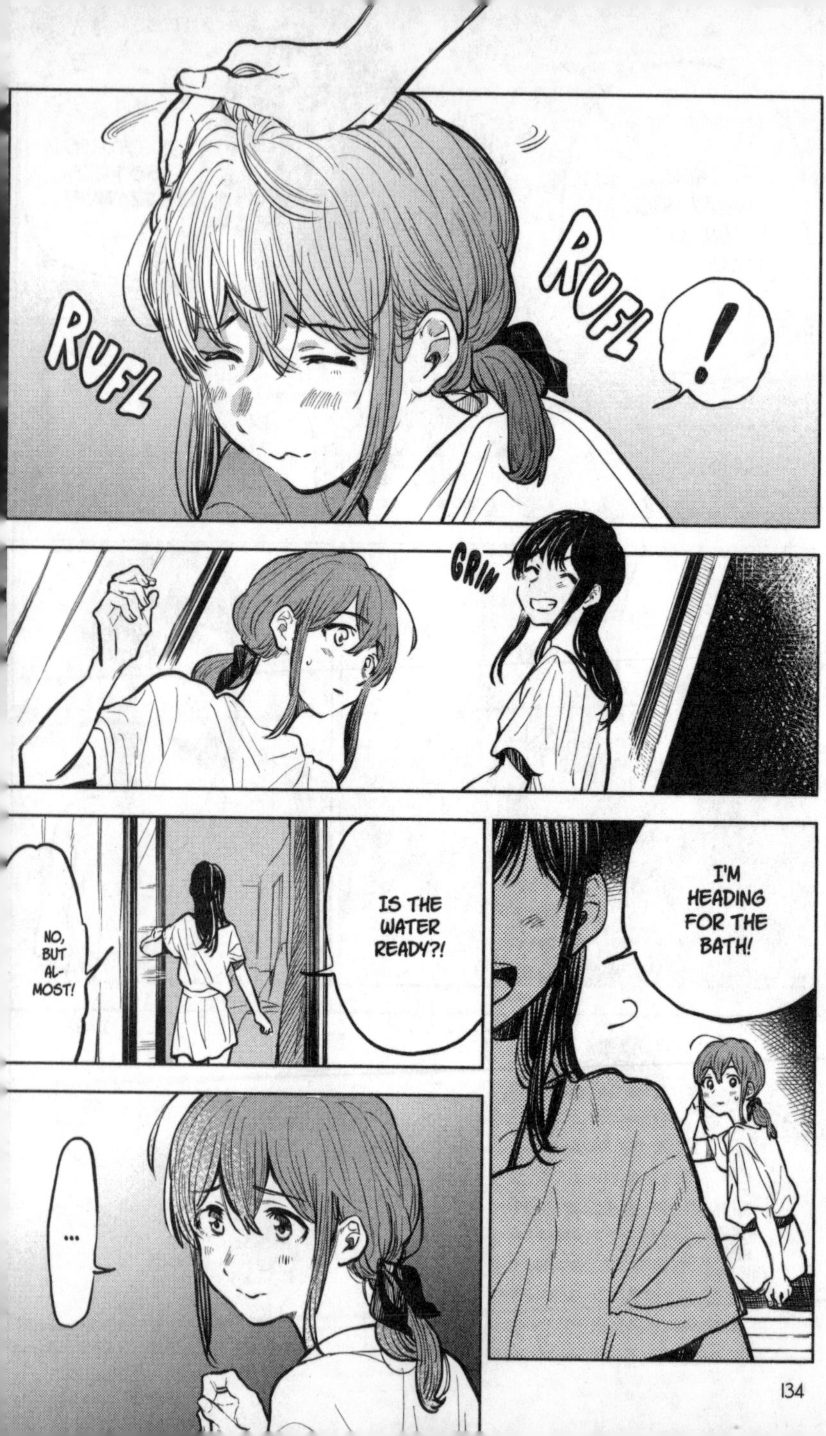
RUFL
!
RUFL
GRIN
I'M HEADING FOR THE BATH!
IS THE WATER READY?!
NO, BUT AL-MOST!
...

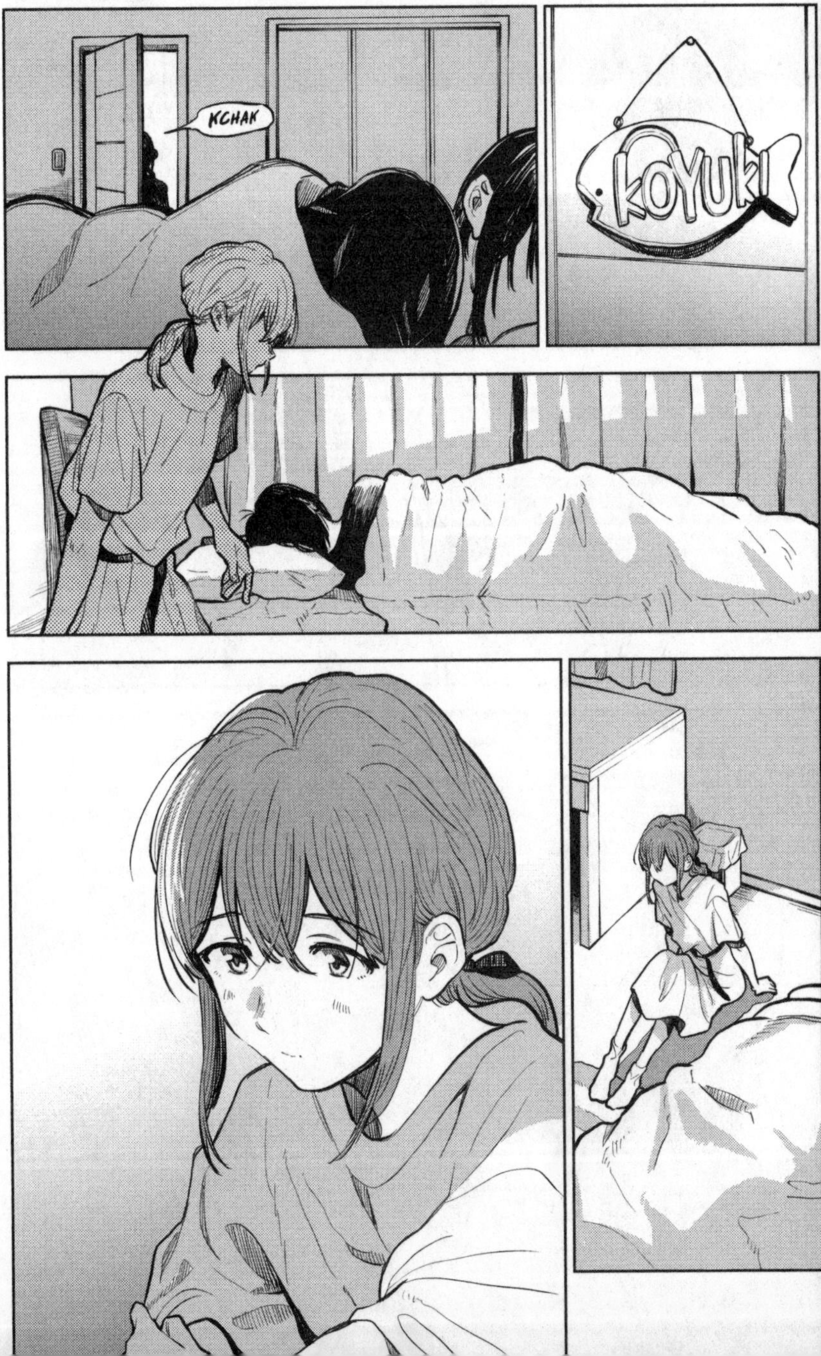
KOYUKI
KCHAK

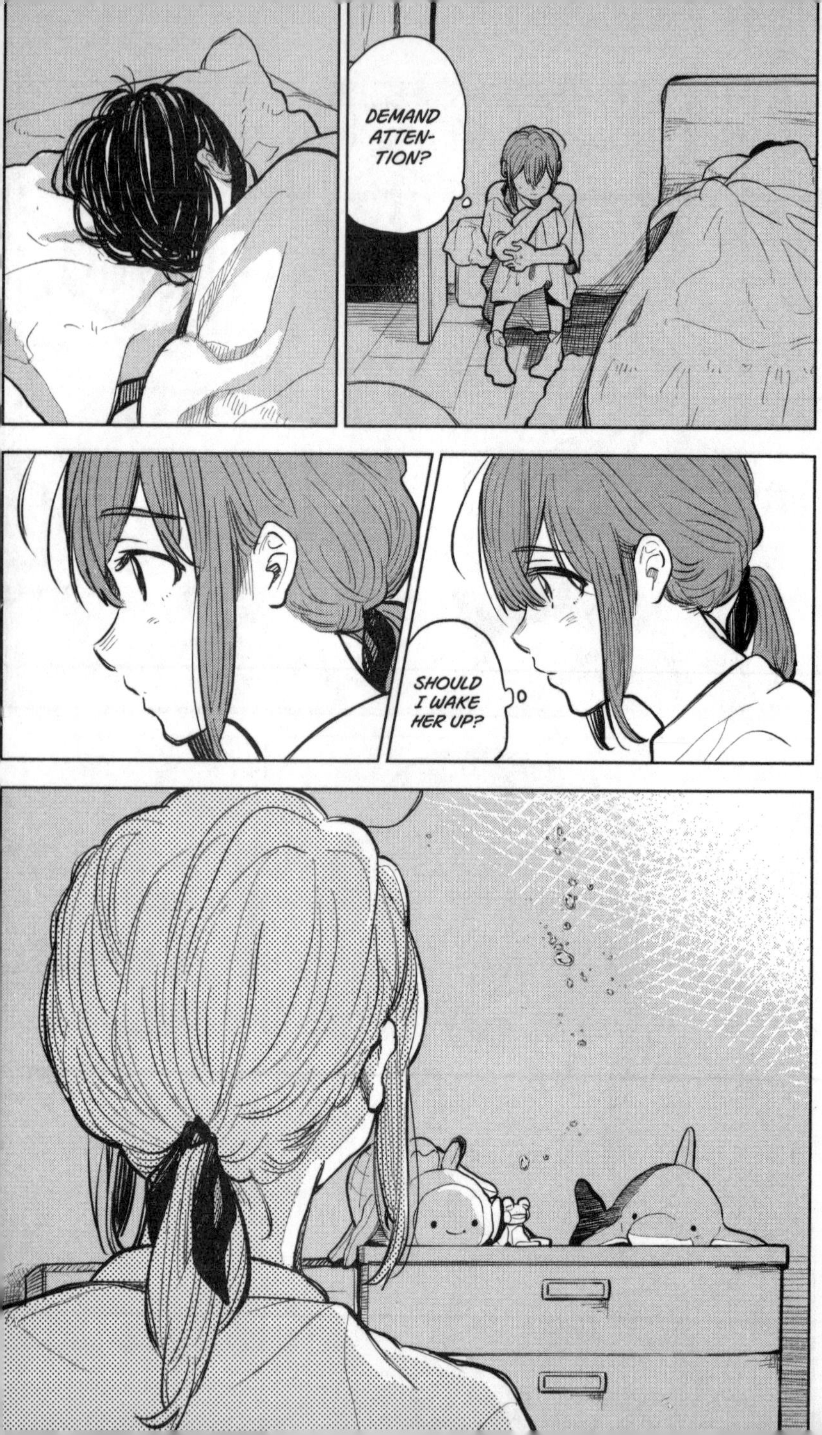
DEMAND ATTEN-TION?
SHOULD I WAKE HER UP?

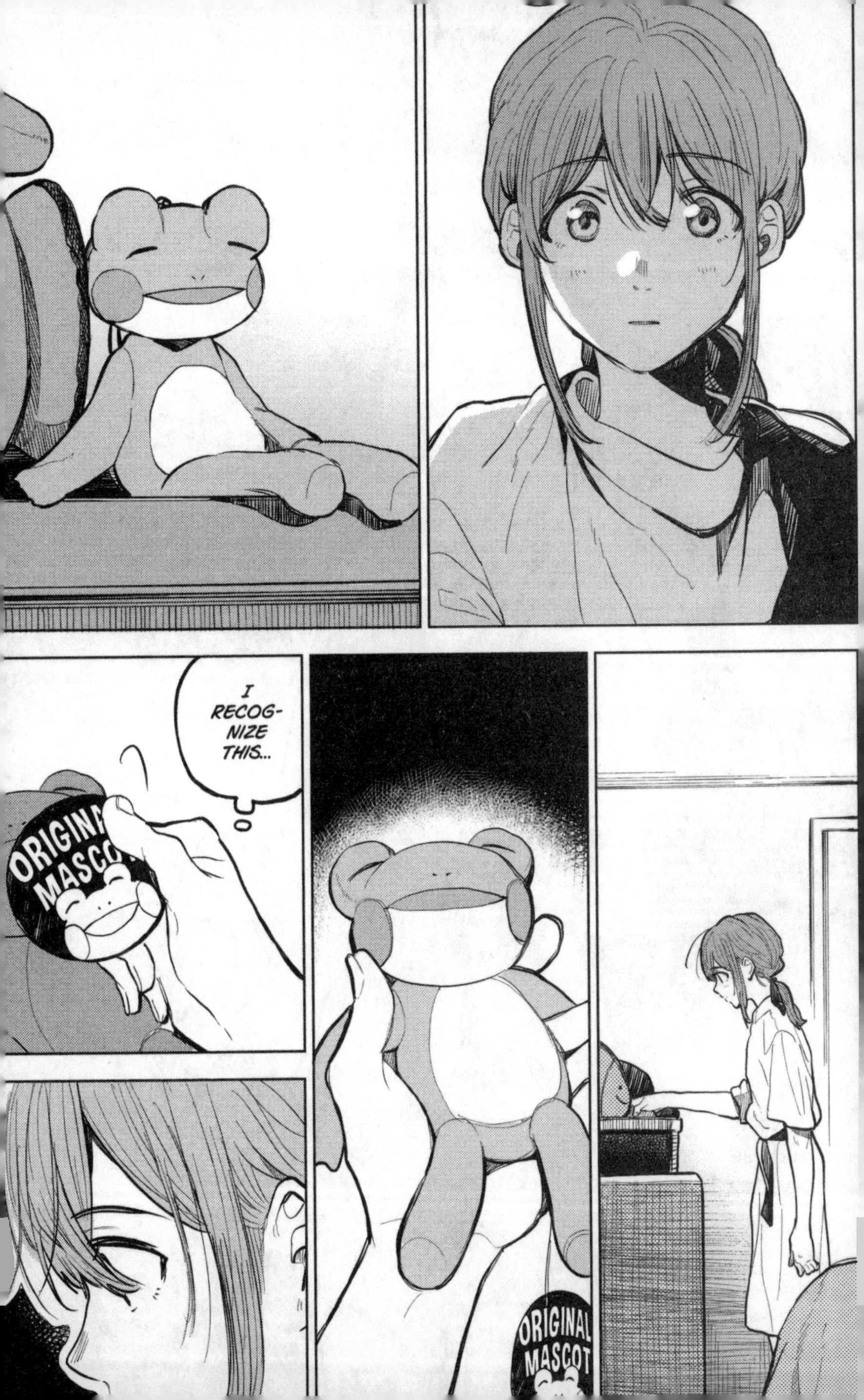
I RECOGNIZE THIS...
ORIGINAL MASCOT
ORIGINAL MASCOT

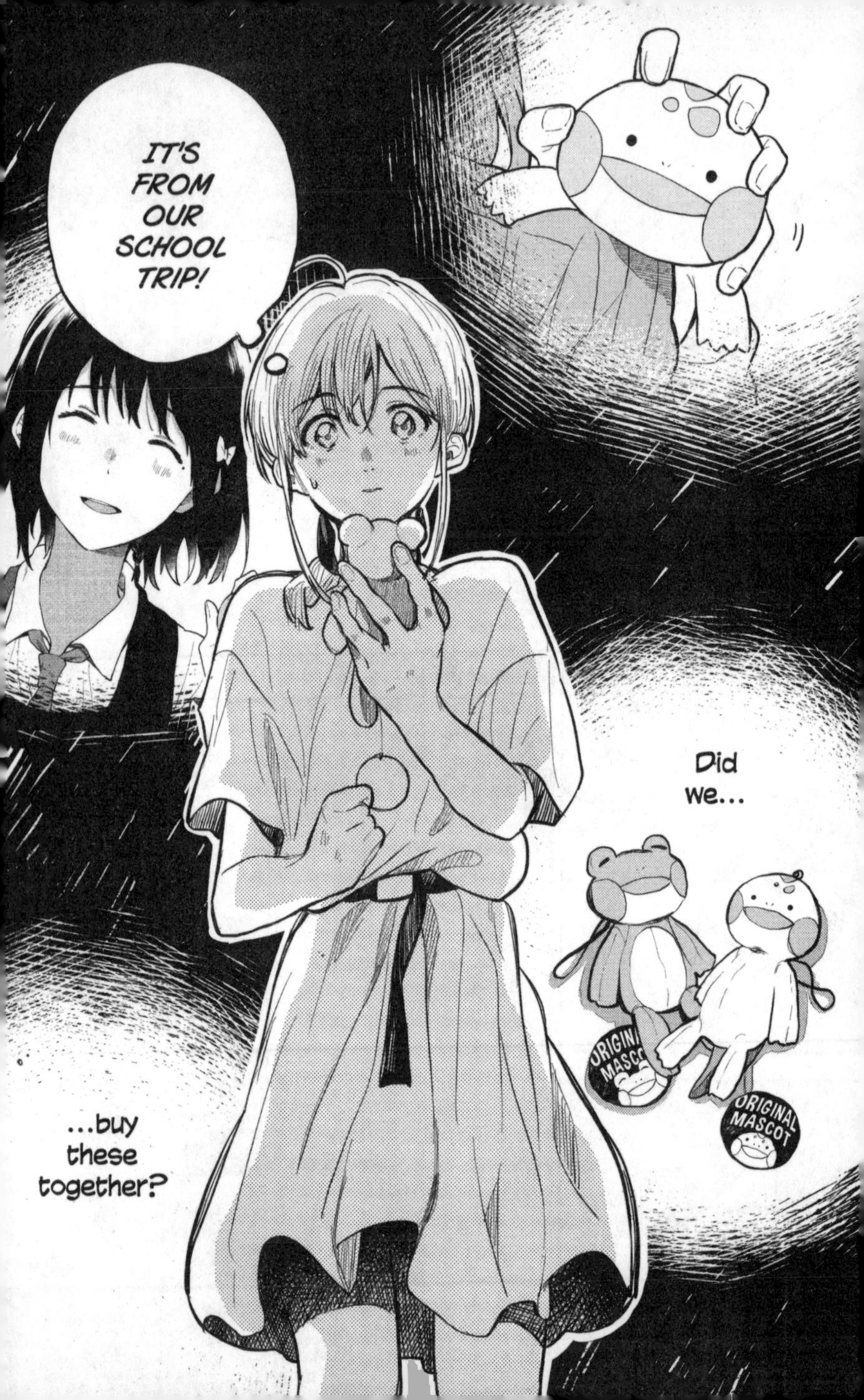
IT'S FROM OUR SCHOOL TRIP!
Did we...
ORIGINAL MASCOT
ORIGINAL MASCOT
...buy these together?

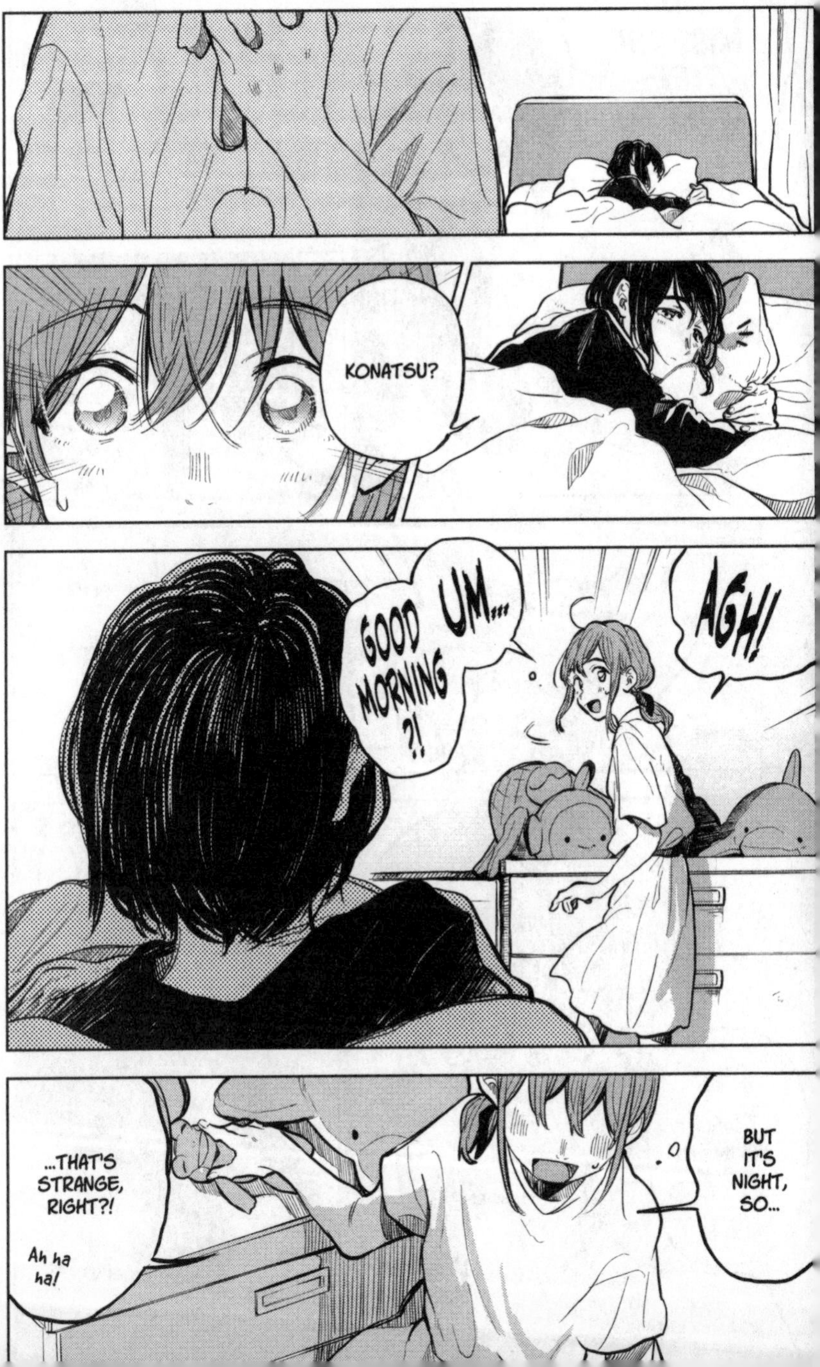
KONATSU?
AGH!
UM...
GOOD MORNING ?!
BUT IT'S NIGHT, SO...
...THAT'S STRANGE, RIGHT?!
Ah ha ha!

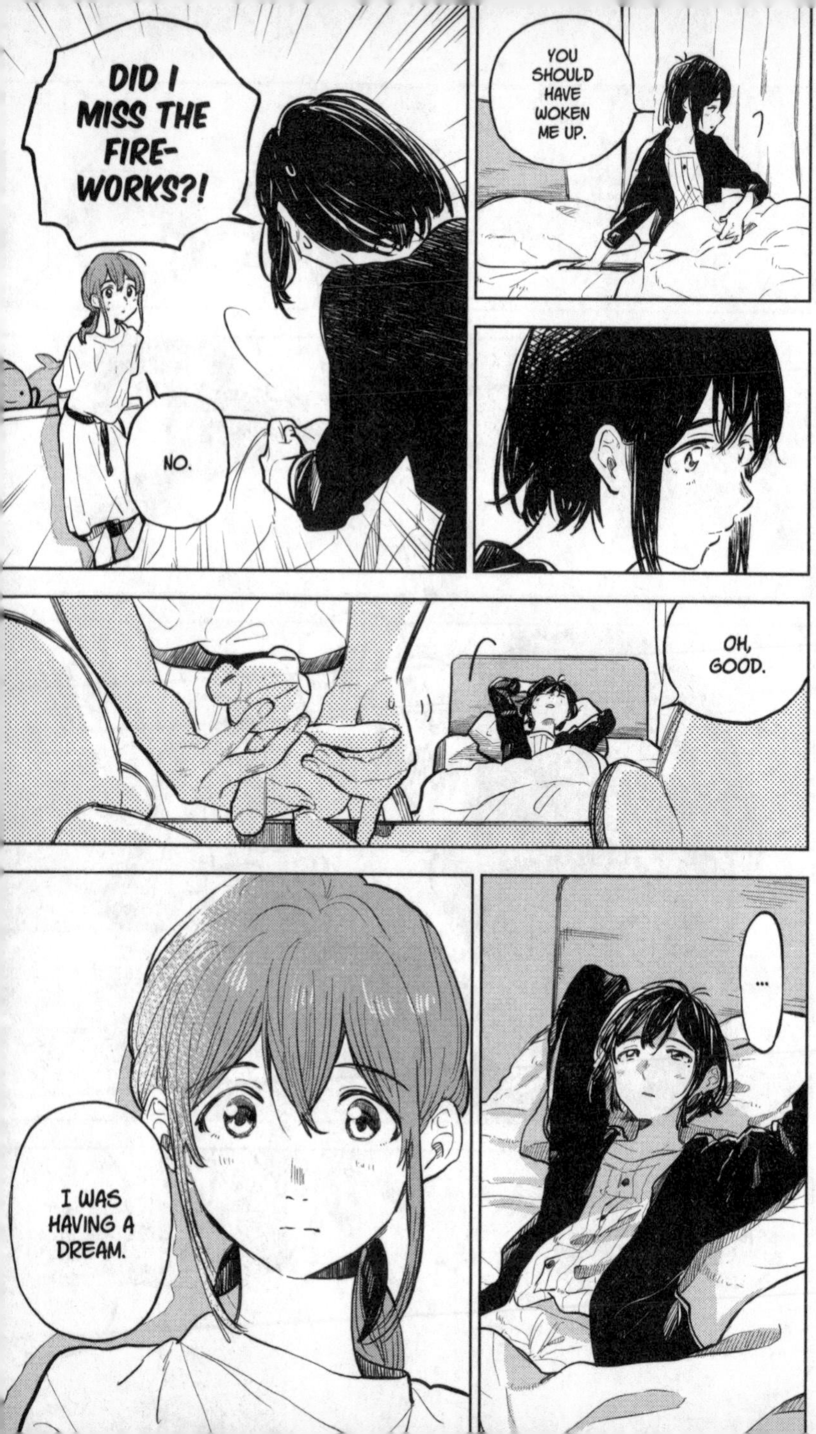
YOU SHOULD HAVE WOKEN ME UP.
DID I MISS THE FIRE-WORKS?!
NO.
OH, GOOD.
...
I WAS HAVING A DREAM.

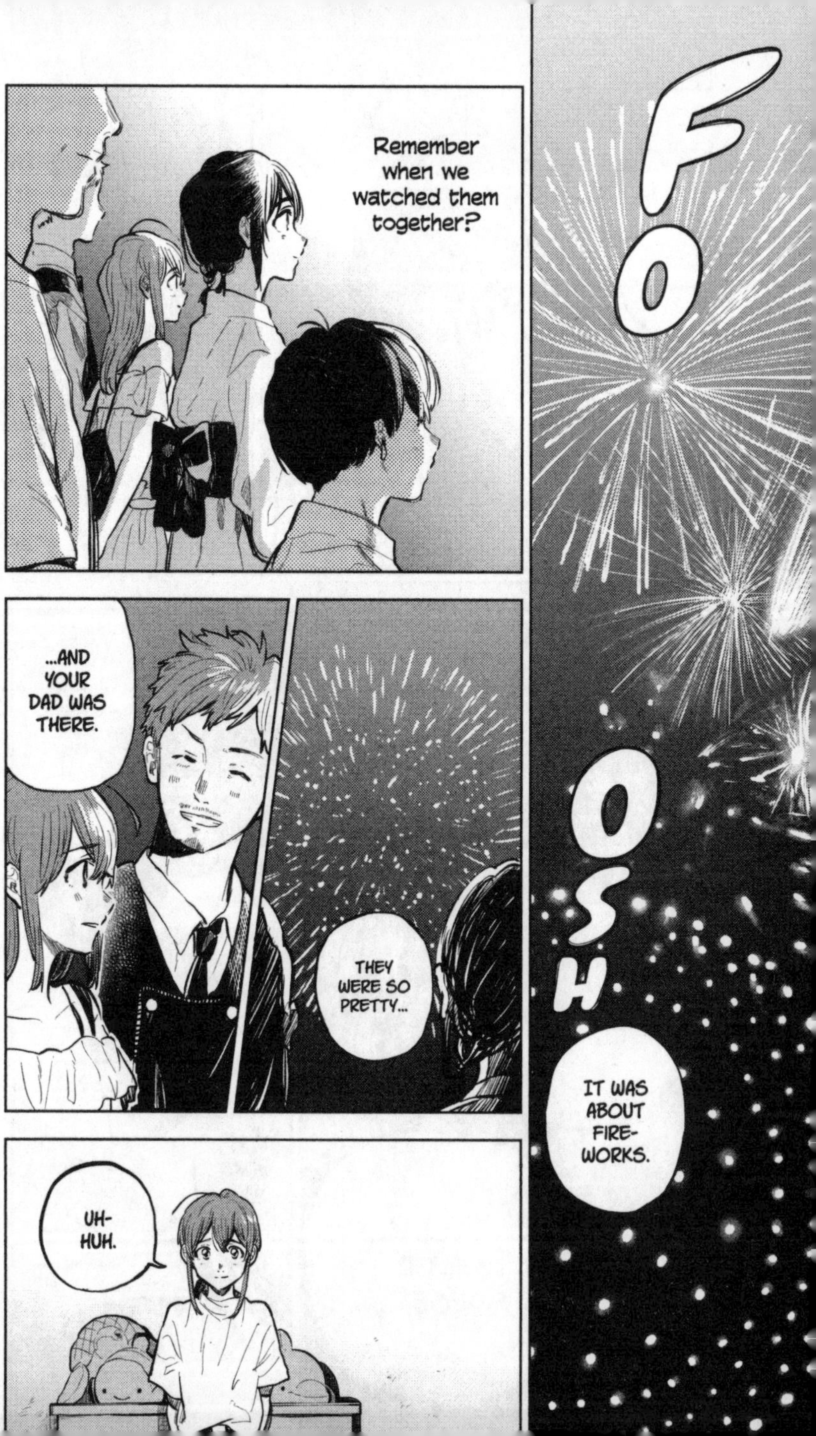
FOOSH
IT WAS ABOUT FIRE-WORKS.
Remember when we watched them together?
THEY WERE SO PRETTY...
...AND YOUR DAD WAS THERE.
UH-HUH.

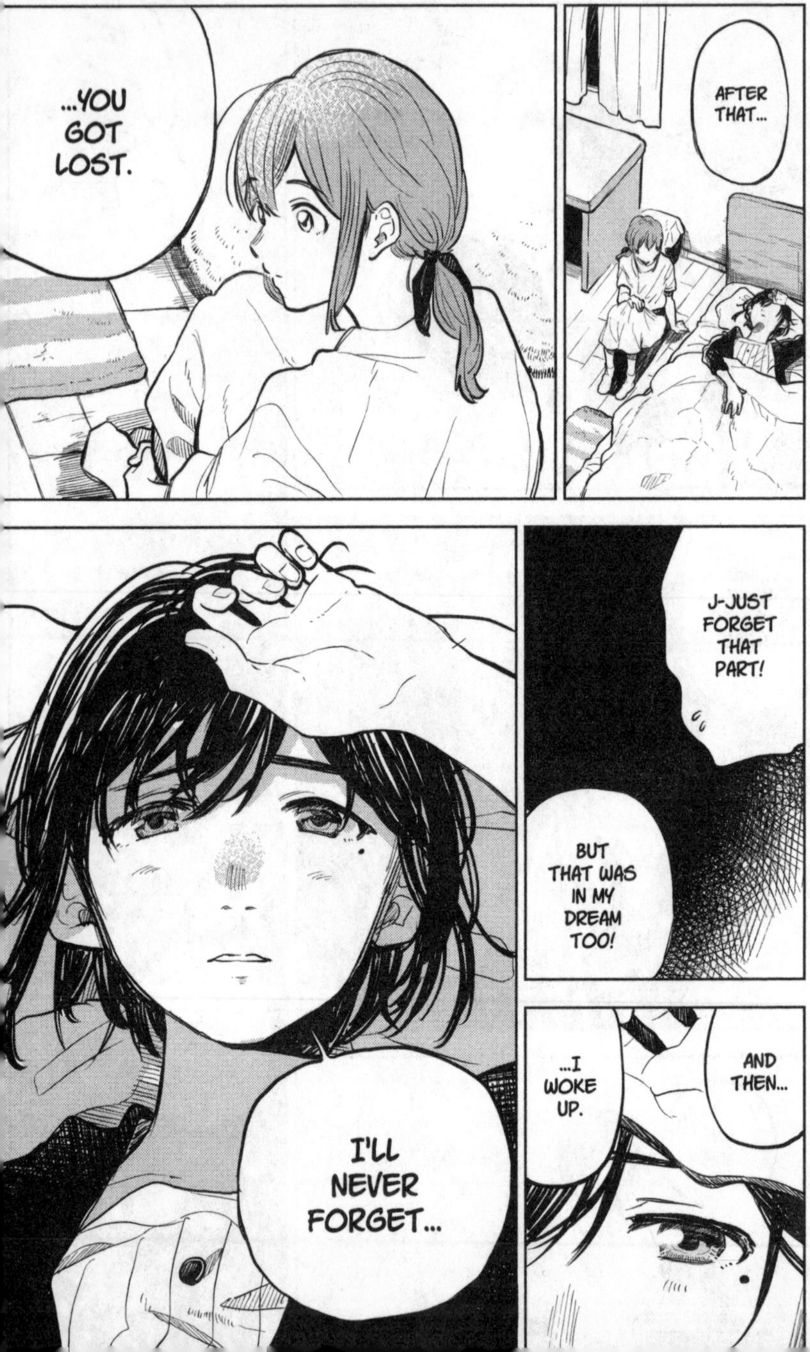
AFTER THAT...
...YOU GOT LOST.
J-JUST FORGET THAT PART!
BUT THAT WAS IN MY DREAM TOO!
AND THEN...
...I WOKE UP.
I'LL NEVER FORGET...

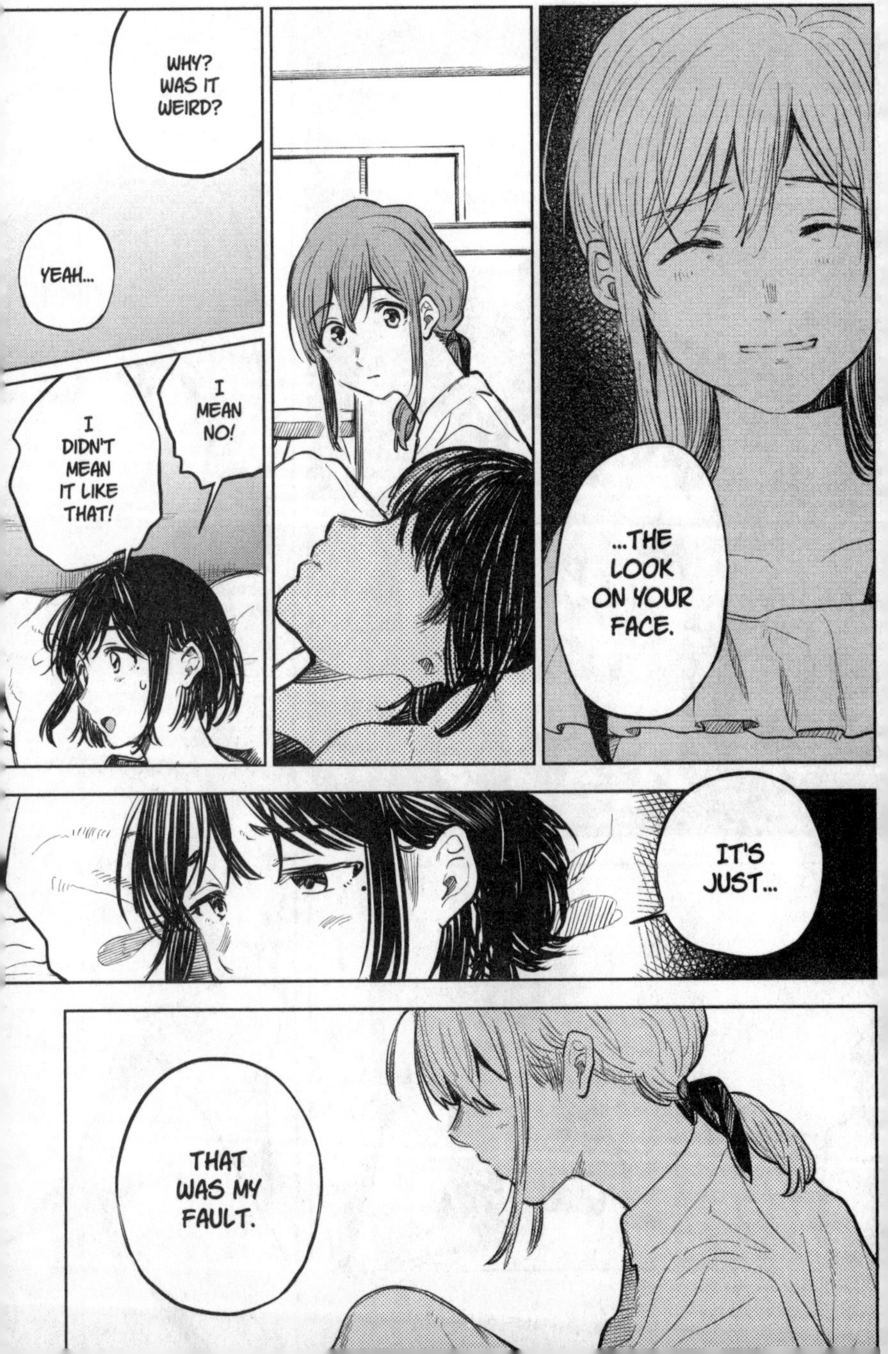
...THE LOOK ON YOUR FACE.
WHY? WAS IT WEIRD?
YEAH...
I MEAN NO!
I DIDN'T MEAN IT LIKE THAT!
IT'S JUST...
THAT WAS MY FAULT.

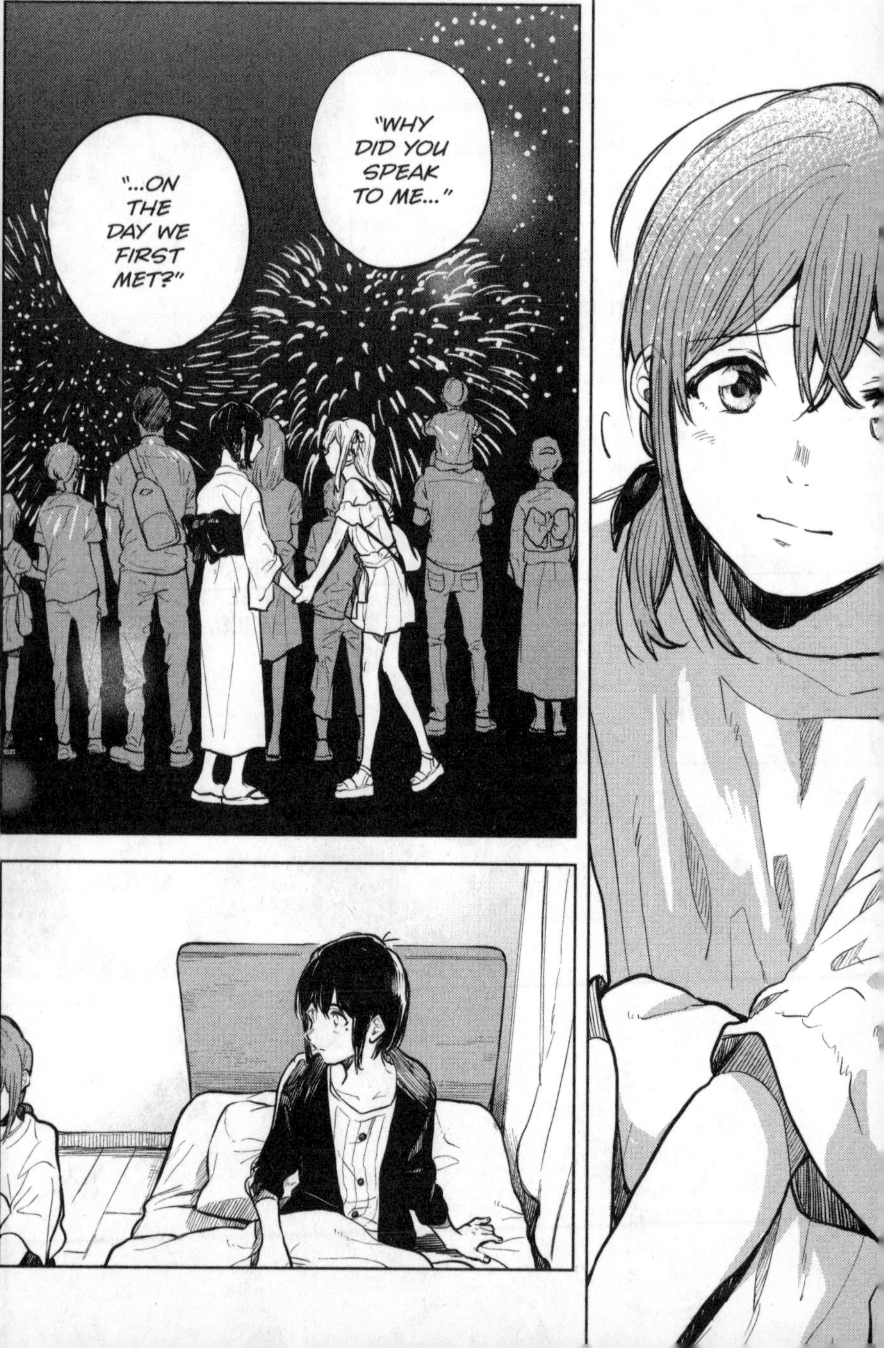
"WHY DID YOU SPEAK TO ME..."
"...ON THE DAY WE FIRST MET?"

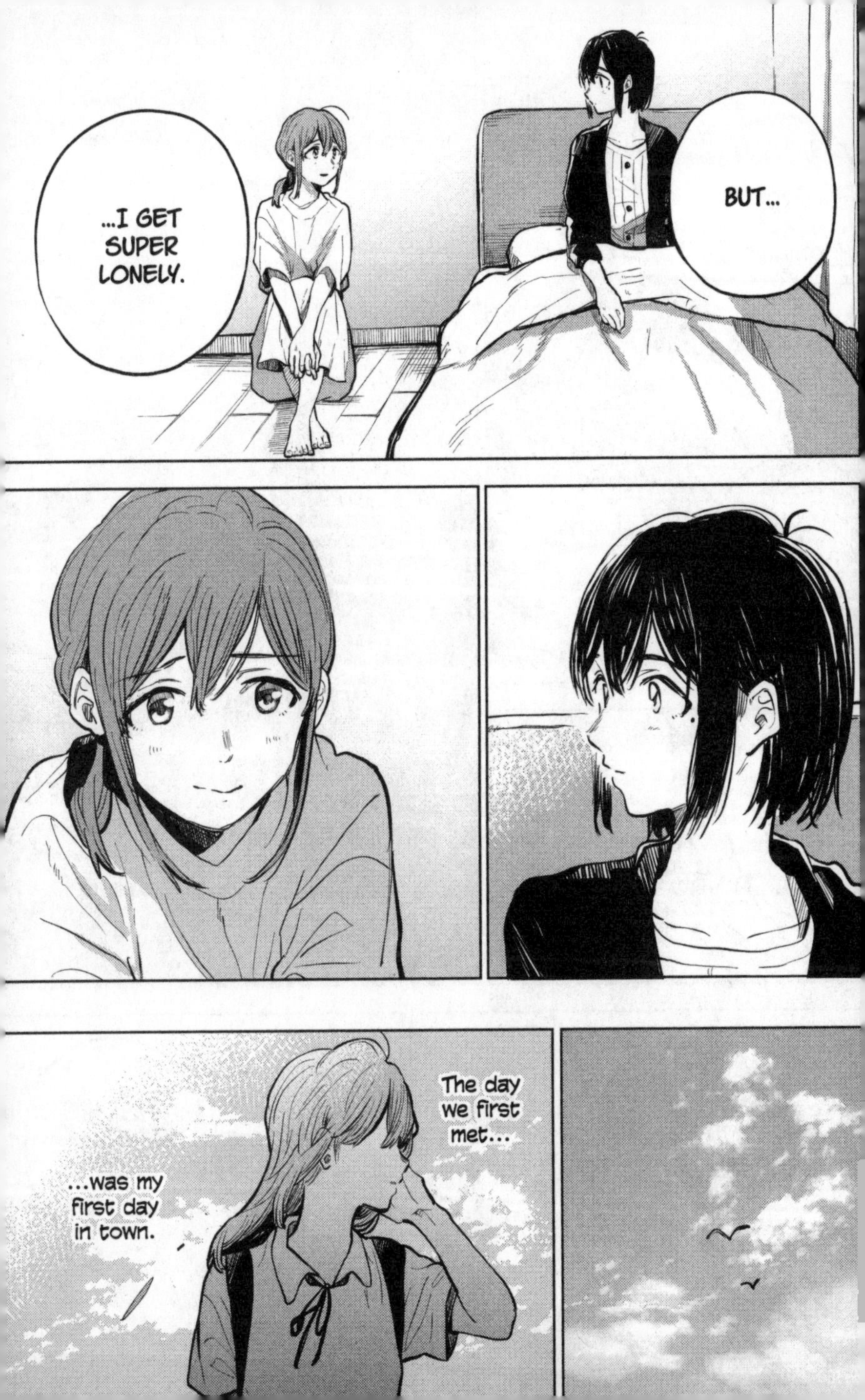
BUT...
...I GET SUPER LONELY.
The day we first met...
...was my first day in town.

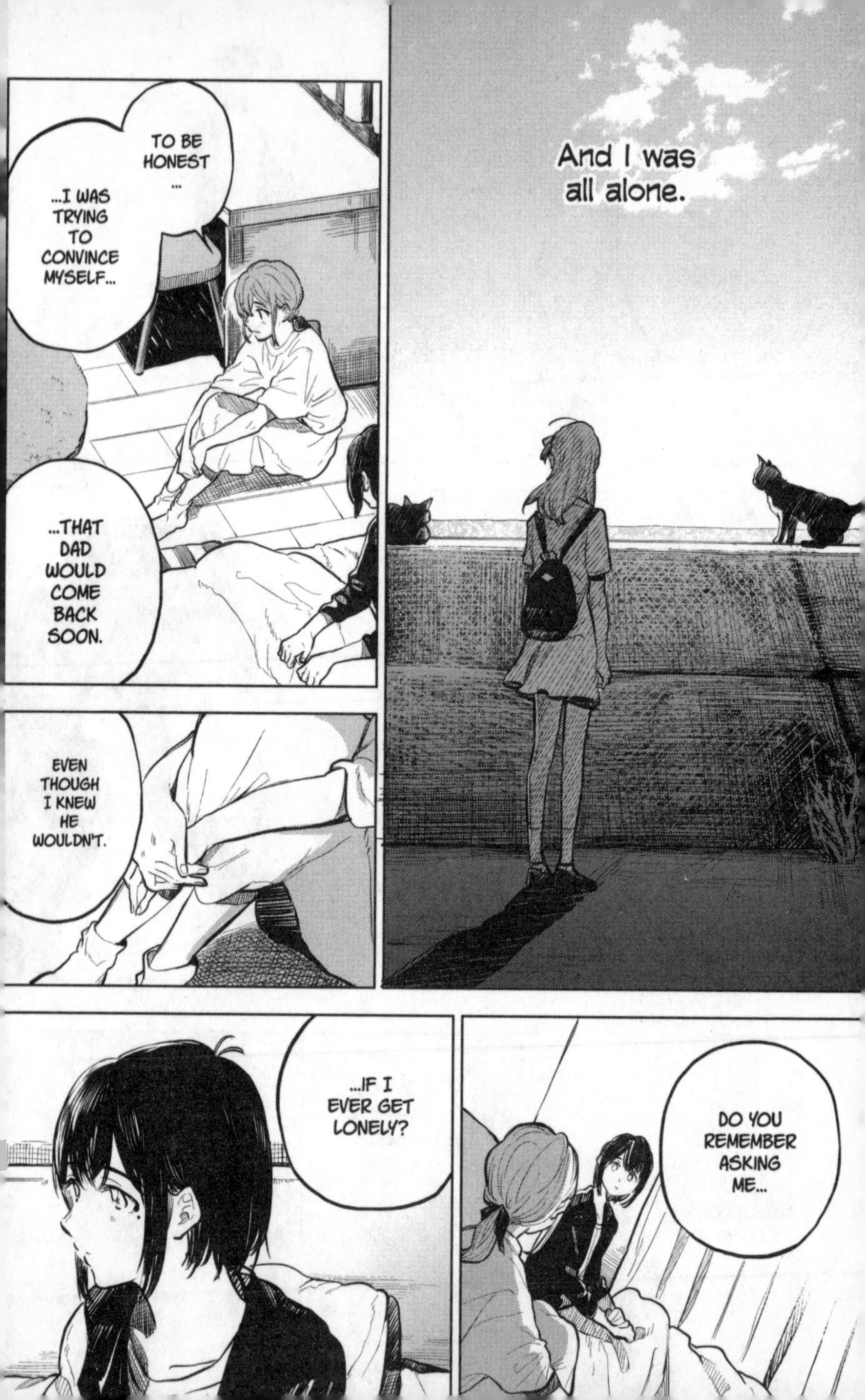
And I was all alone.
TO BE HONEST ...
...I WAS TRYING TO CONVINCE MYSELF...
...THAT DAD WOULD COME BACK SOON.
EVEN THOUGH I KNEW HE WOULDN'T.
DO YOU REMEMBER ASKING ME...
...IF I EVER GET LONELY?

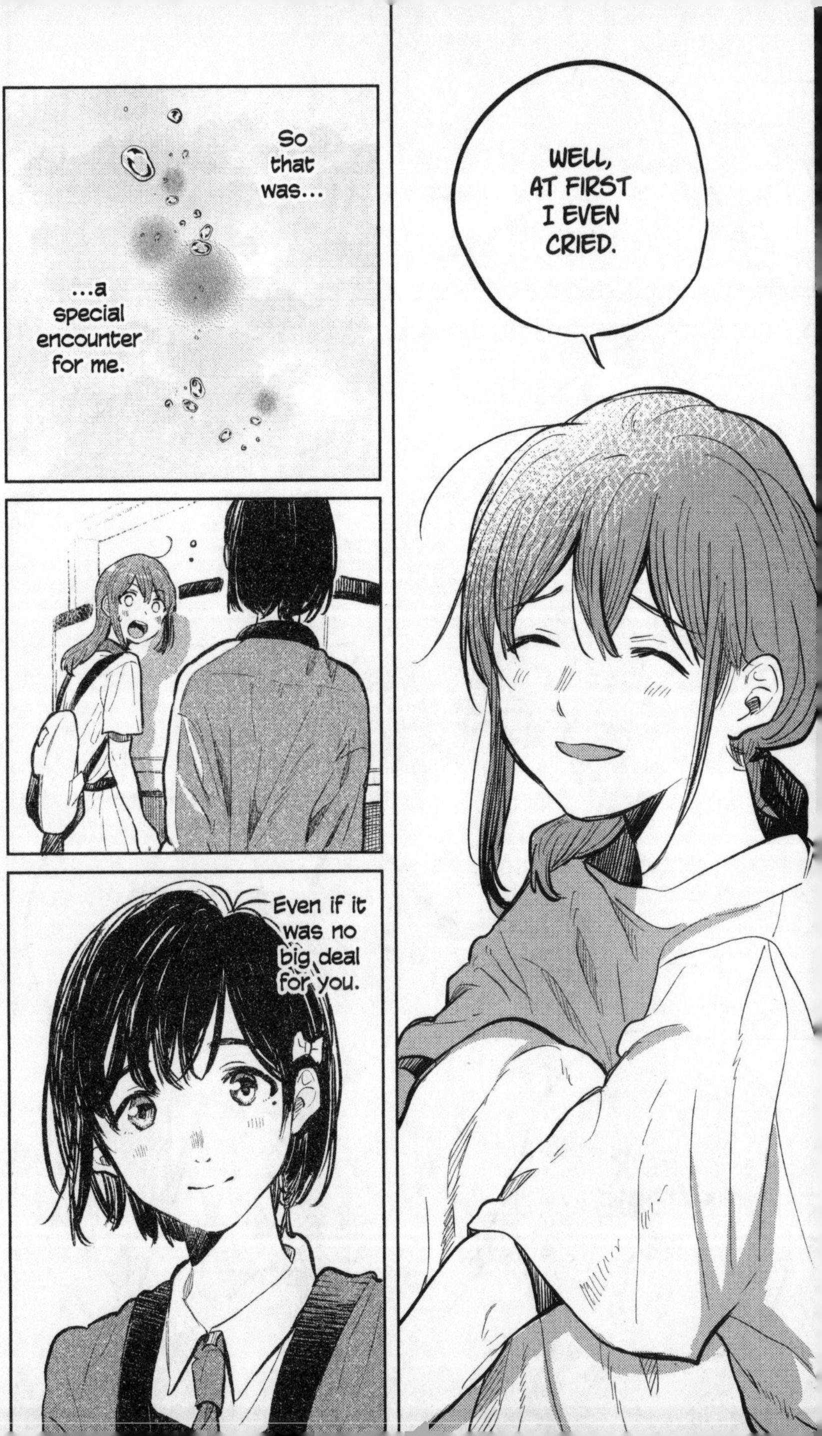
WELL, AT FIRST I EVEN CRIED.
So that was...
...a special encounter for me.
Even if it was no big deal for you.

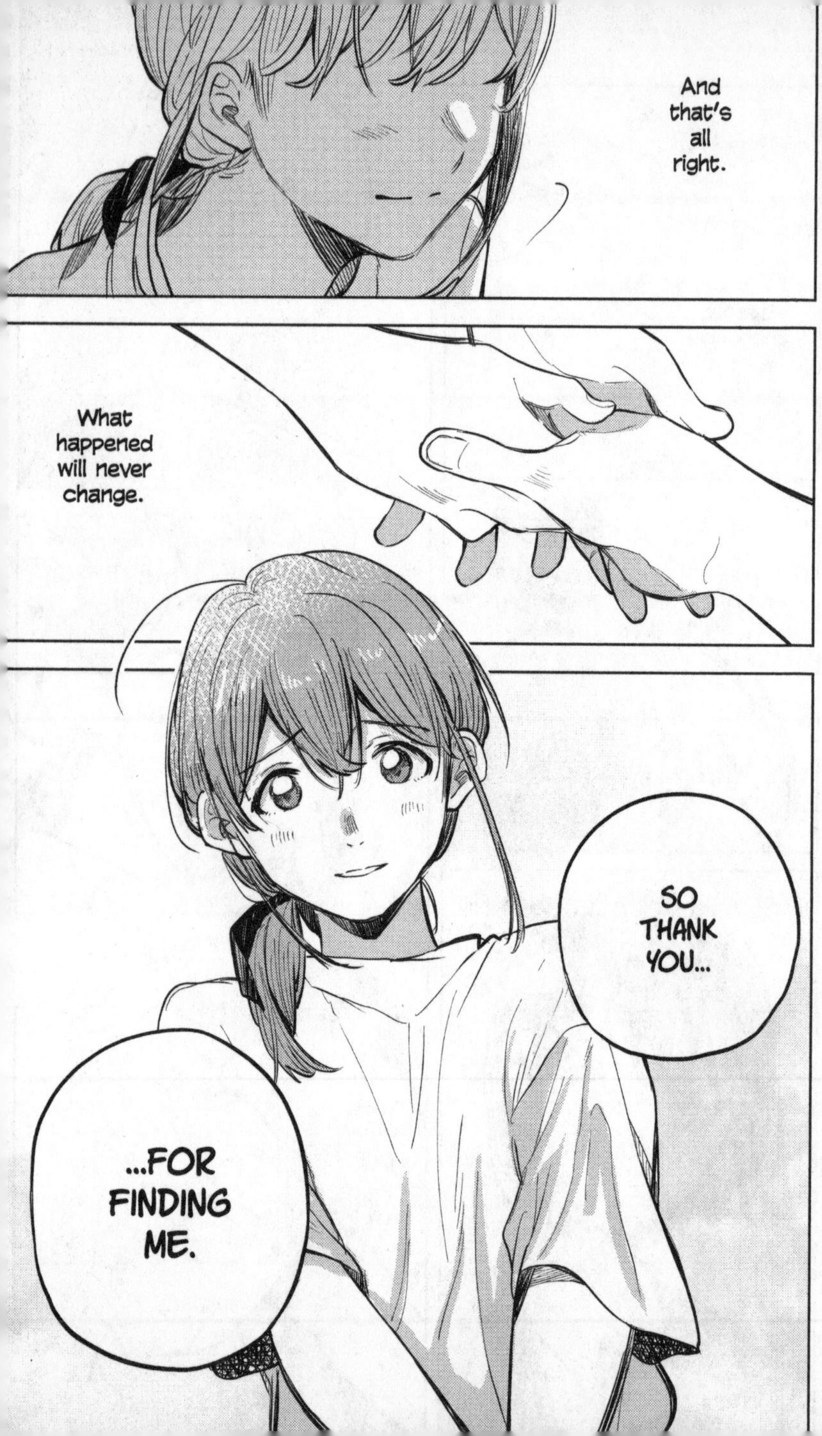
And that's all right.
What happened will never change.
SO THANK YOU...
...FOR FINDING ME.

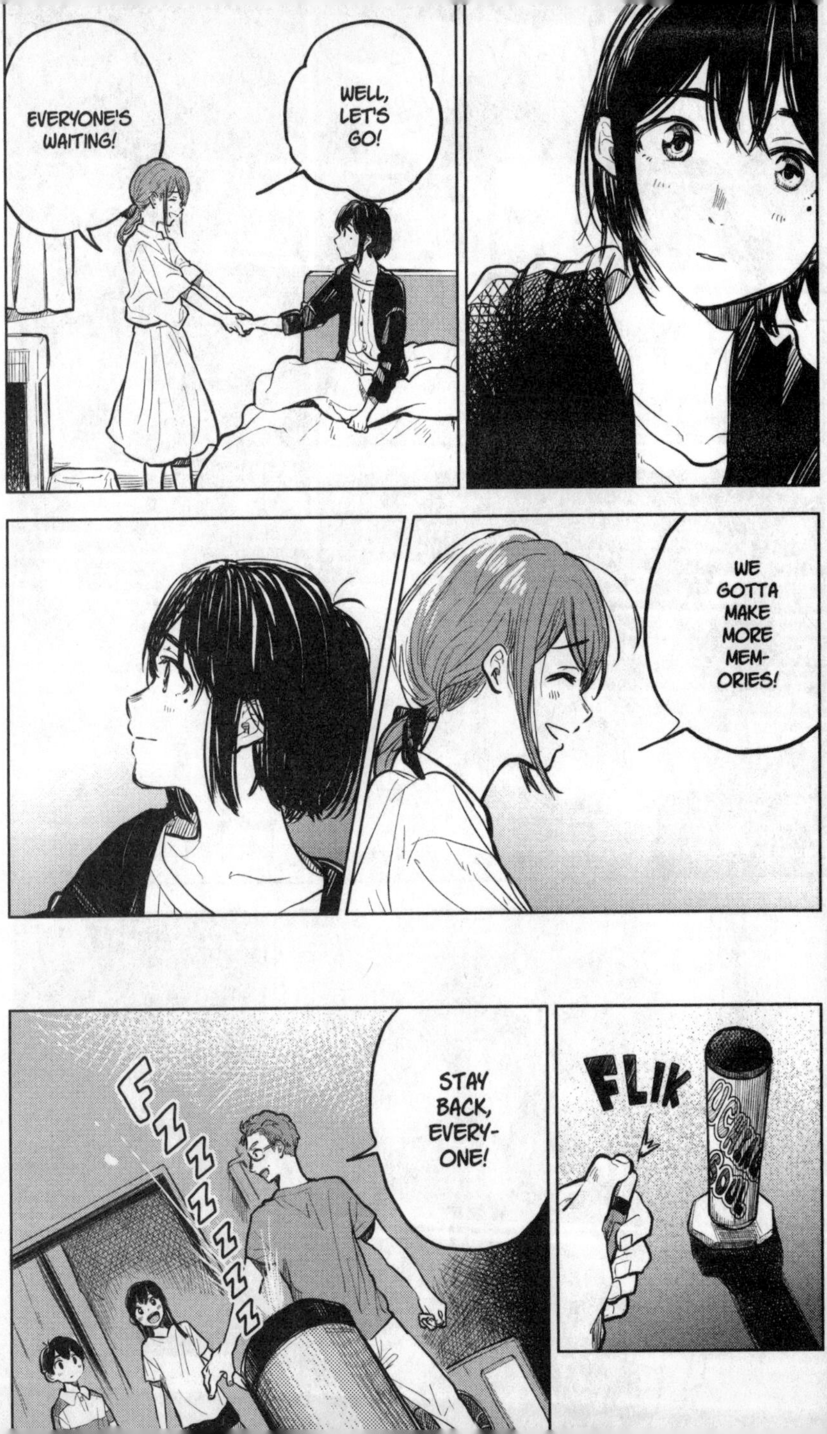
WELL, LET'S GO!
EVERYONE'S WAITING!
WE GOTTA MAKE MORE MEM-ORIES!
FLIK
STAY BACK, EVERY-ONE!
FZZZZZZ

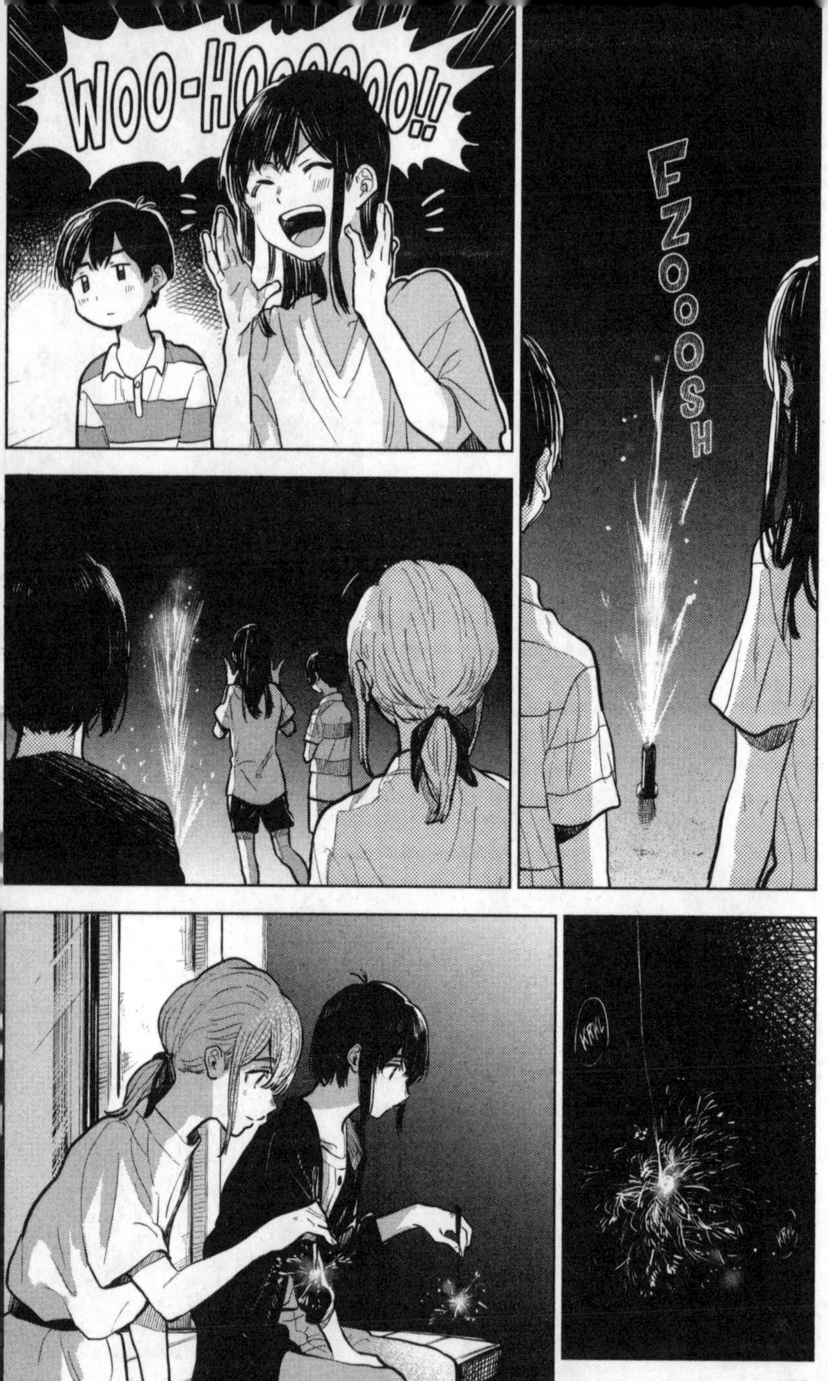
FZOOOOSH
WOO-HOOOOOO!!
KRKL
KRKL

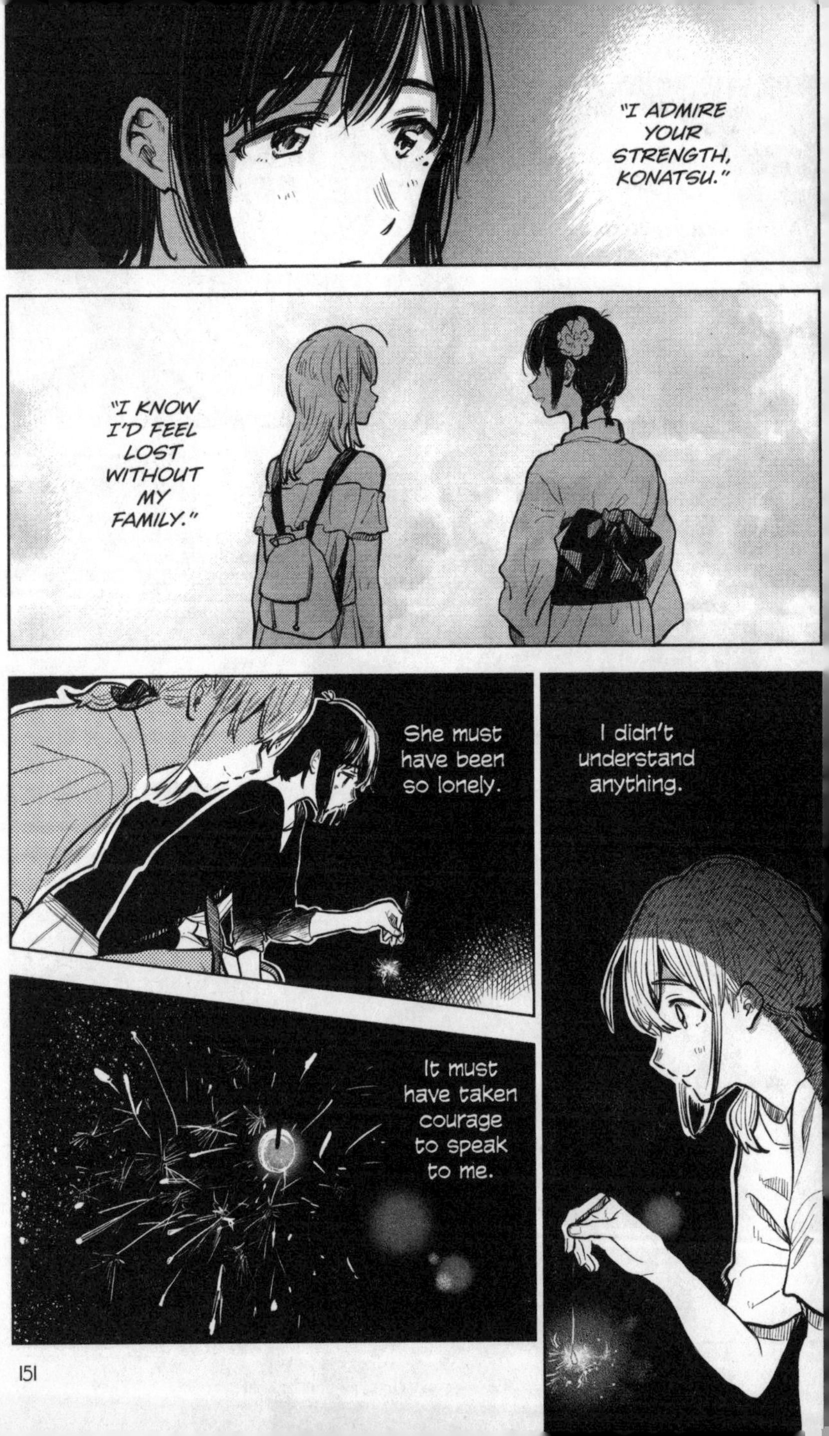
"I ADMIRE YOUR STRENGTH, KONATSU."
"I KNOW I'D FEEL LOST WITHOUT MY FAMILY."
I didn't understand anything.
She must have been so lonely.
It must have taken courage to speak to me.

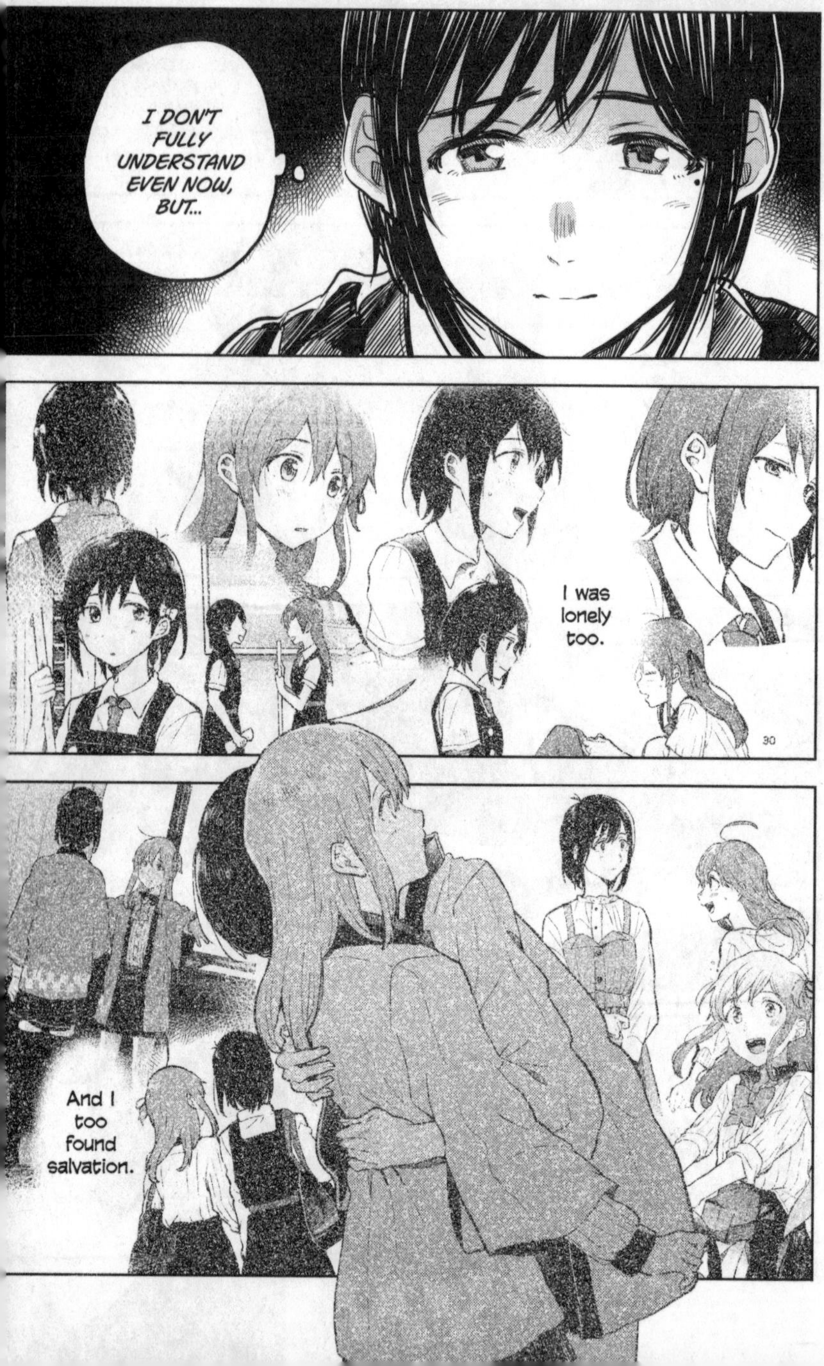
I DON'T FULLY UNDERSTAND EVEN NOW, BUT...
I was lonely too.
30
And I too found salvation.

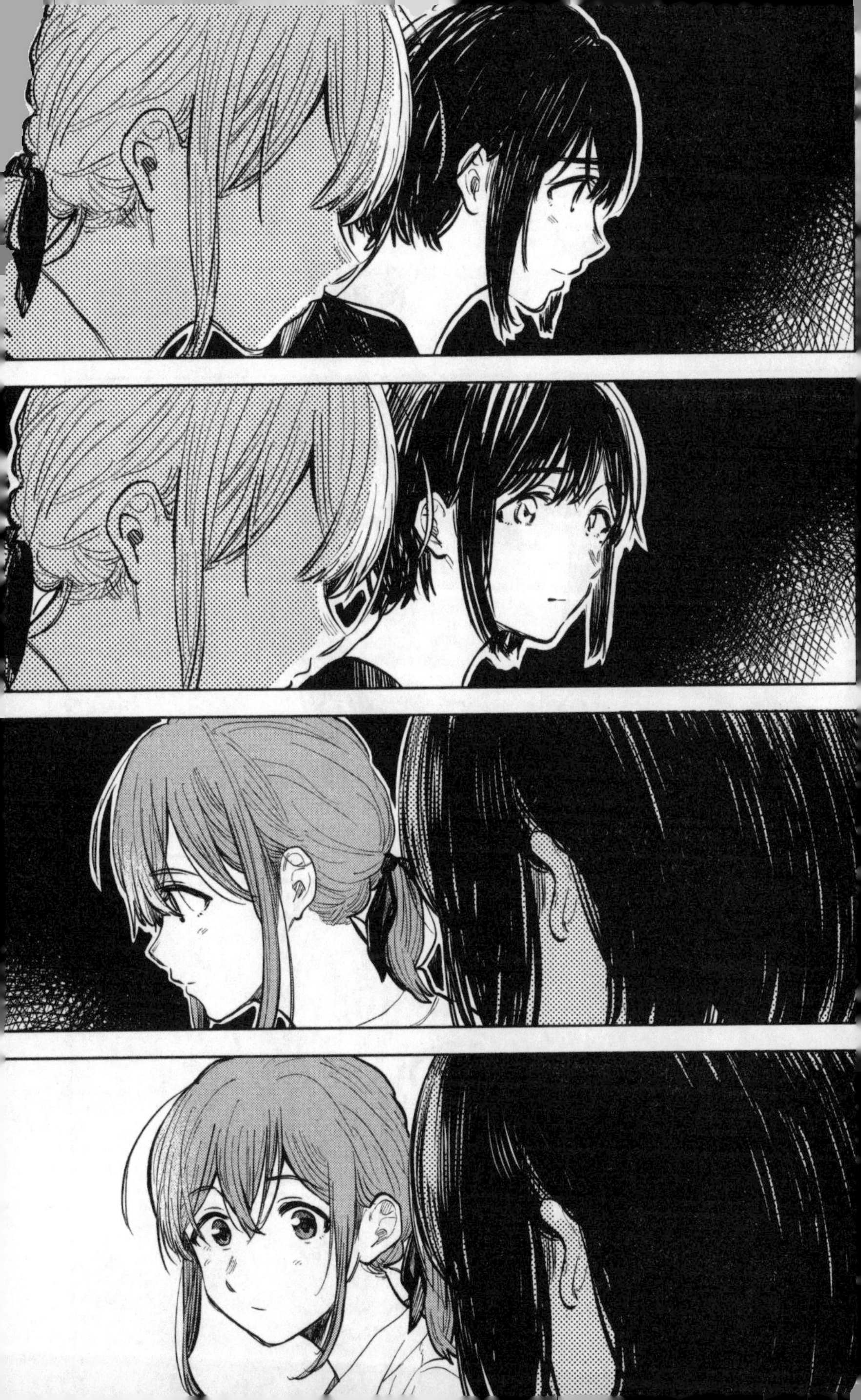

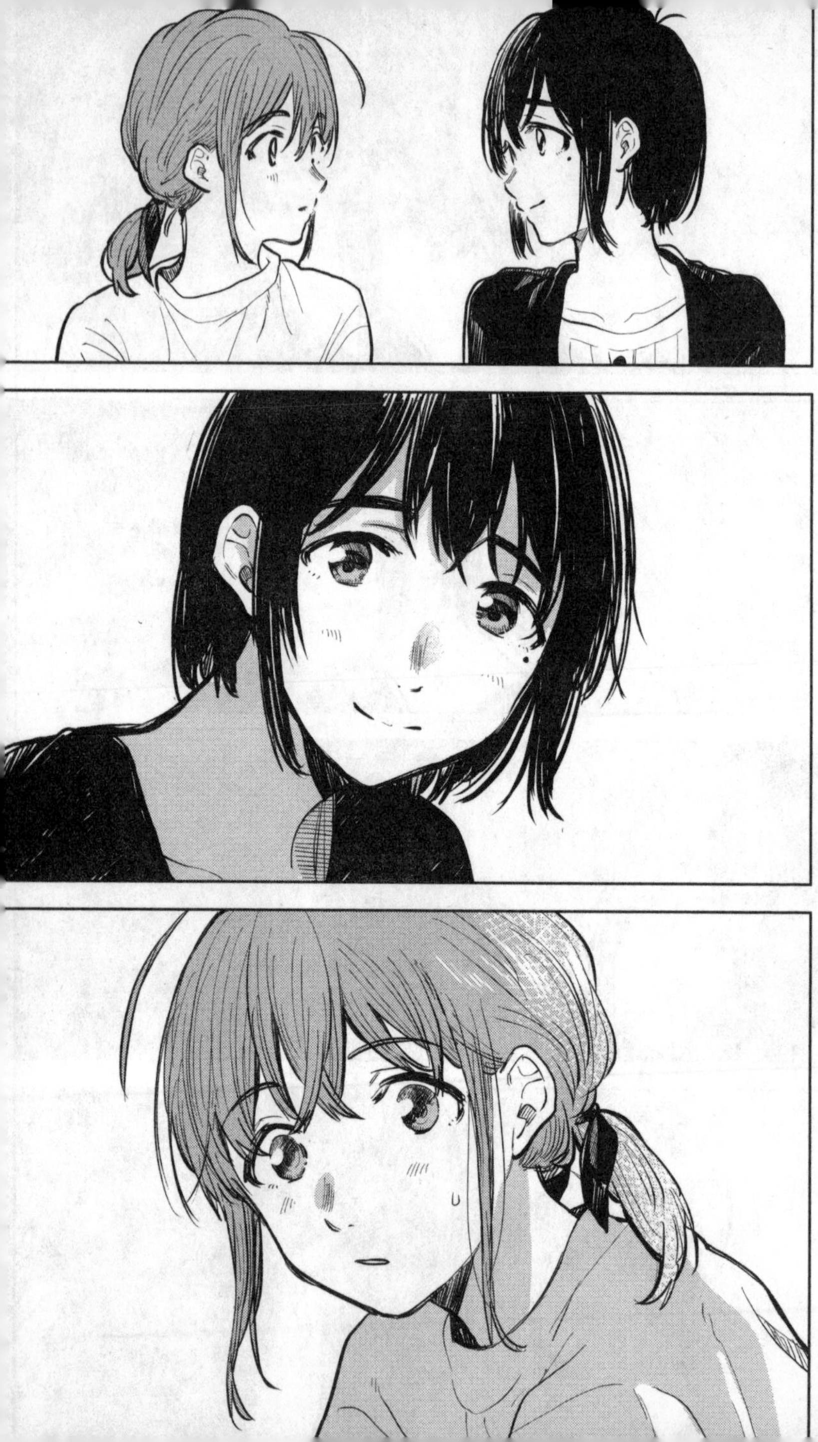

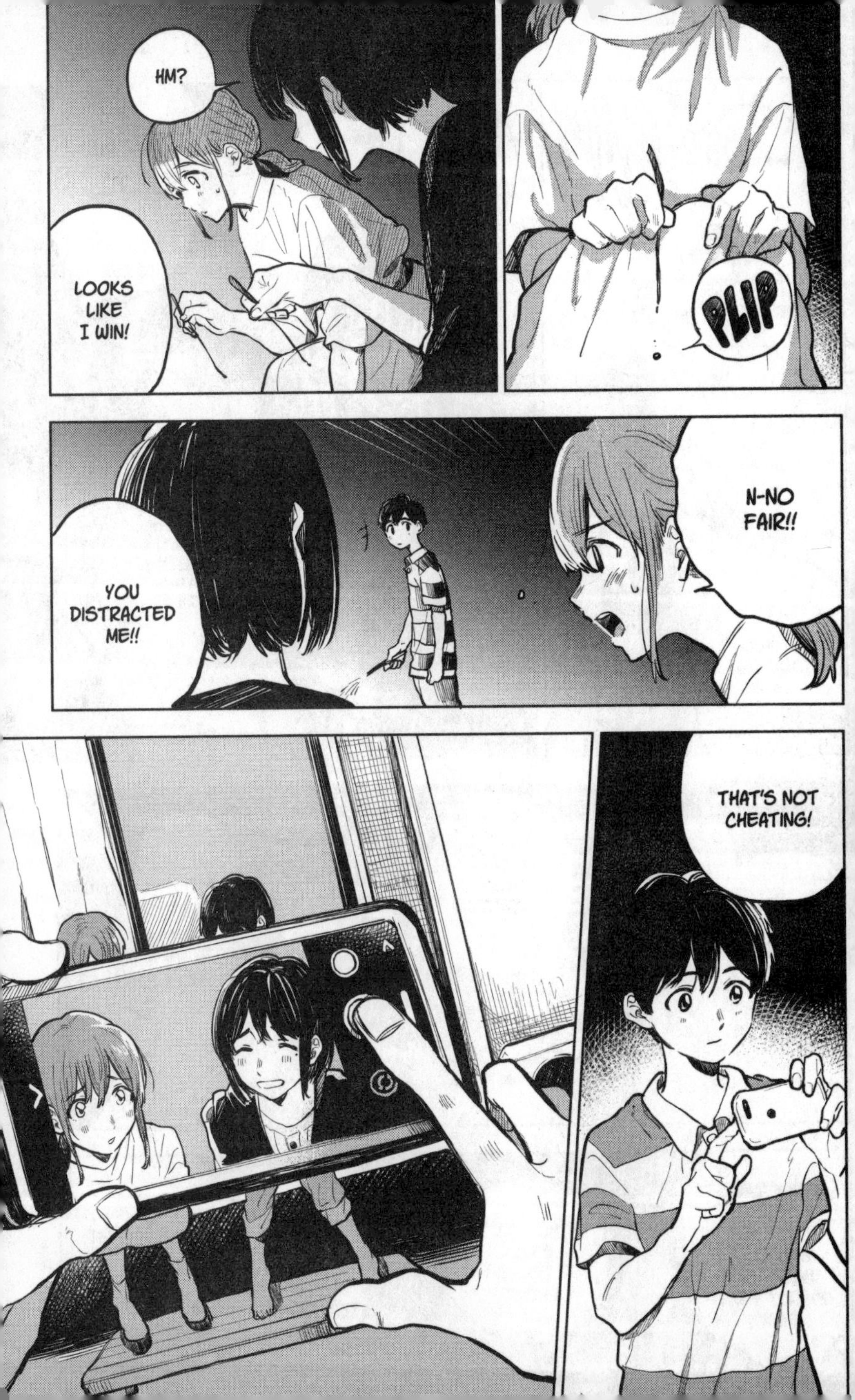
PLIP
HM?
LOOKS LIKE I WIN!
N-NO FAIR!!
YOU DISTRACTED ME!!
THAT'S NOT CHEATING!

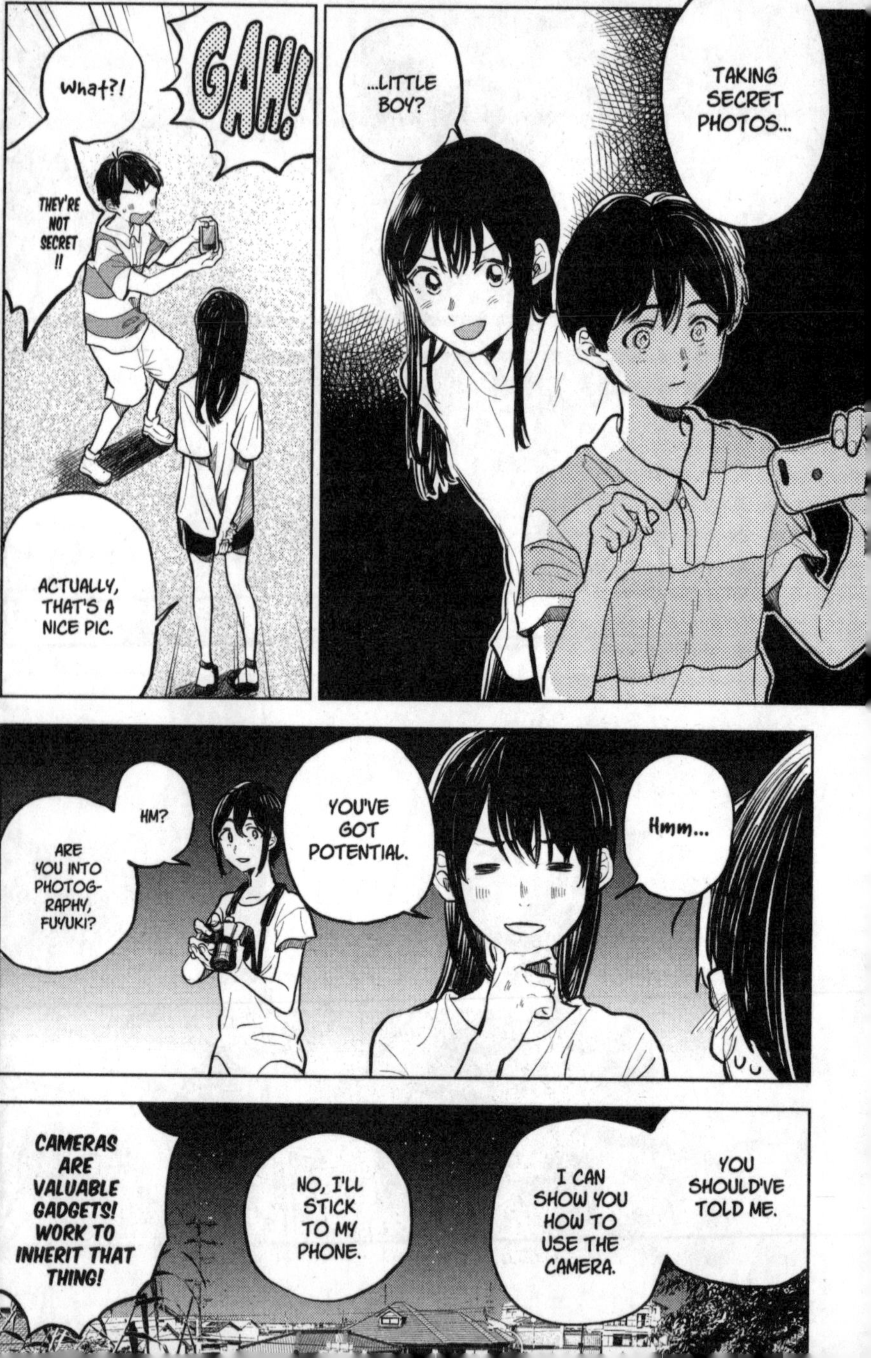
TAKING SECRET PHOTOS...
...LITTLE BOY?
GAH!
What?!
THEY'RE NOT SECRET !!
ACTUALLY, THAT'S A NICE PIC.
Hmm...
YOU'VE GOT POTENTIAL.
HM?
ARE YOU INTO PHOTOG-RAPHY, FUYUKI?
YOU SHOULD'VE TOLD ME.
I CAN SHOW YOU HOW TO USE THE CAMERA.
NO, I'LL STICK TO MY PHONE.
CAMERAS ARE VALUABLE GADGETS! WORK TO INHERIT THAT THING!

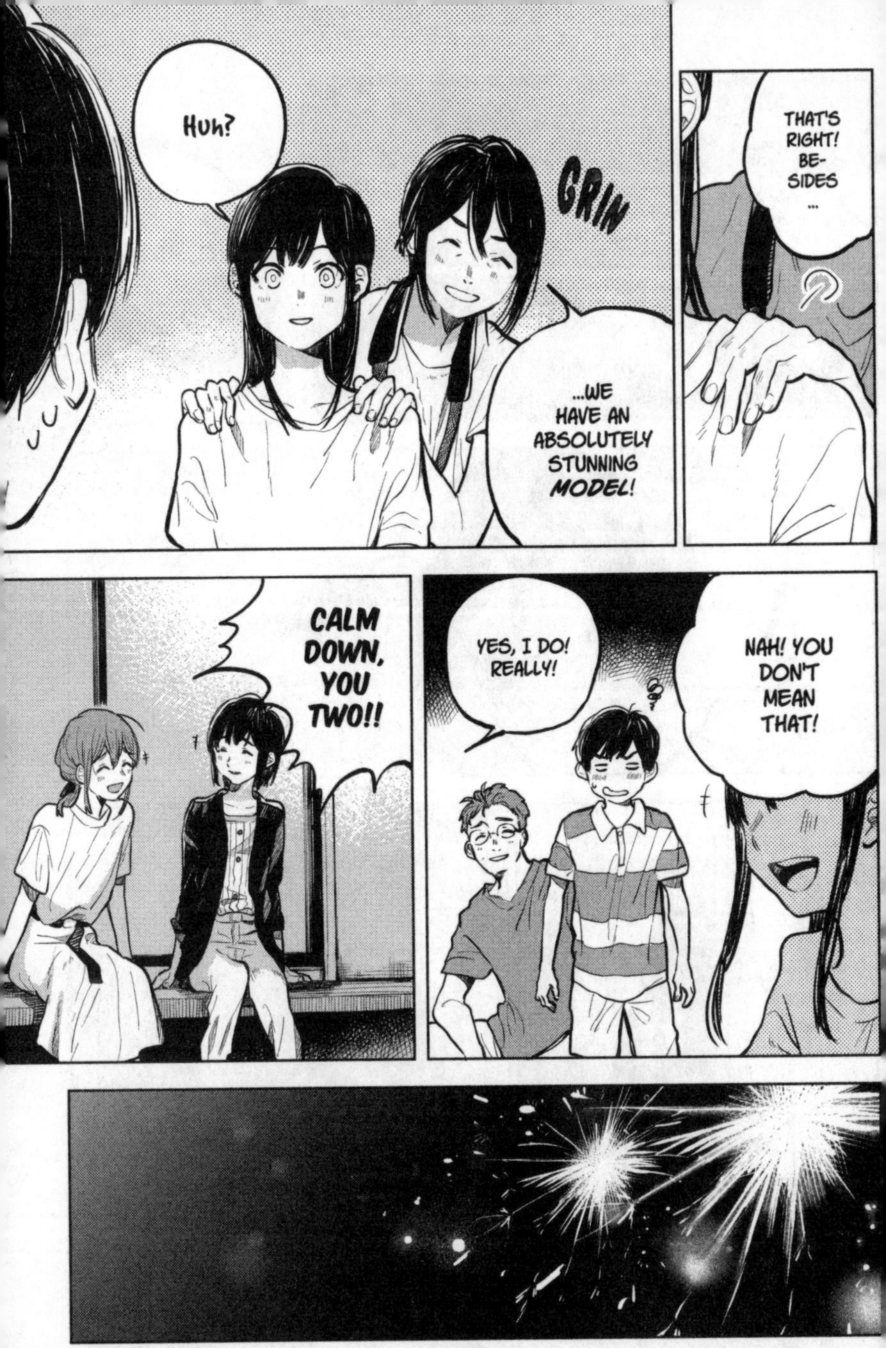
THAT'S RIGHT! BE-SIDES ...
GRIN
...WE HAVE AN ABSOLUTELY STUNNING MODEL!
Huh?
NAH! YOU DON'T MEAN THAT!
YES, I DO! REALLY!
CALM DOWN, YOU TWO!!

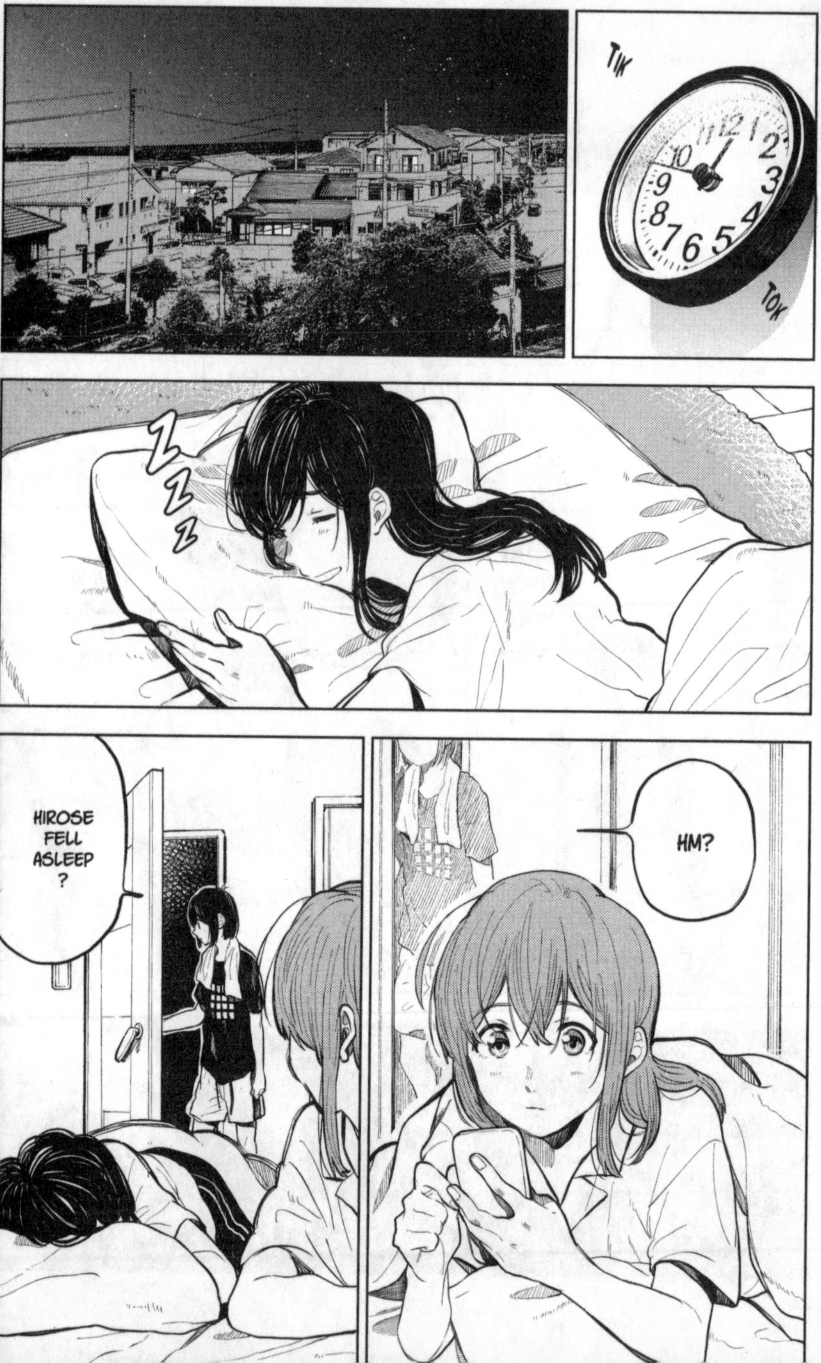
TIK
TOK
ZZZ
HM?
HIROSE FELL ASLEEP?

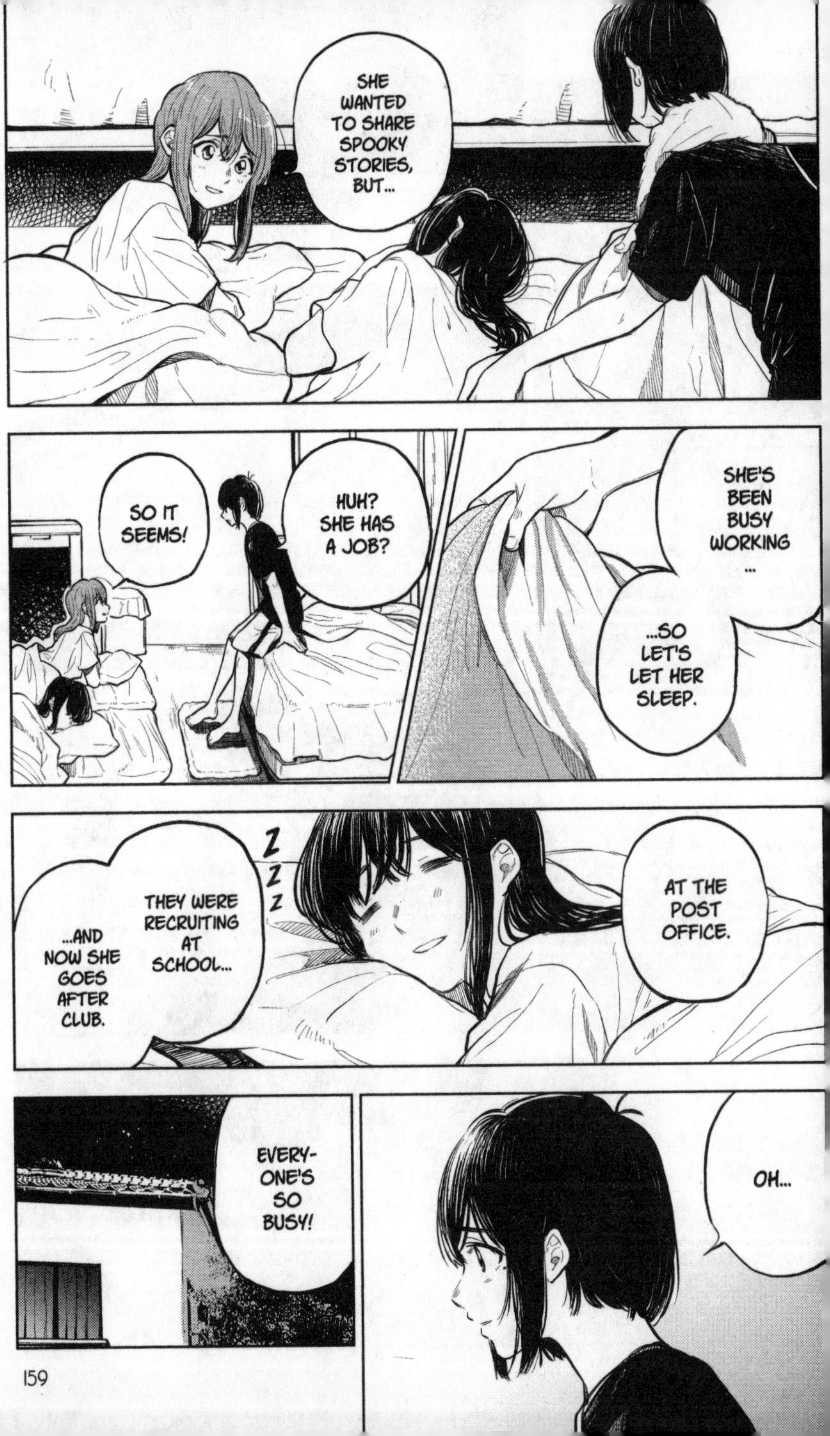
SHE WANTED TO SHARE SPOOKY STORIES, BUT...
SHE'S BEEN BUSY WORKING ...
...SO LET'S LET HER SLEEP.
HUH? SHE HAS A JOB?
SO IT SEEMS!
AT THE POST OFFICE.
Z Z Z
THEY WERE RECRUITING AT SCHOOL...
...AND NOW SHE GOES AFTER CLUB.
OH...
EVERY-ONE'S SO BUSY!

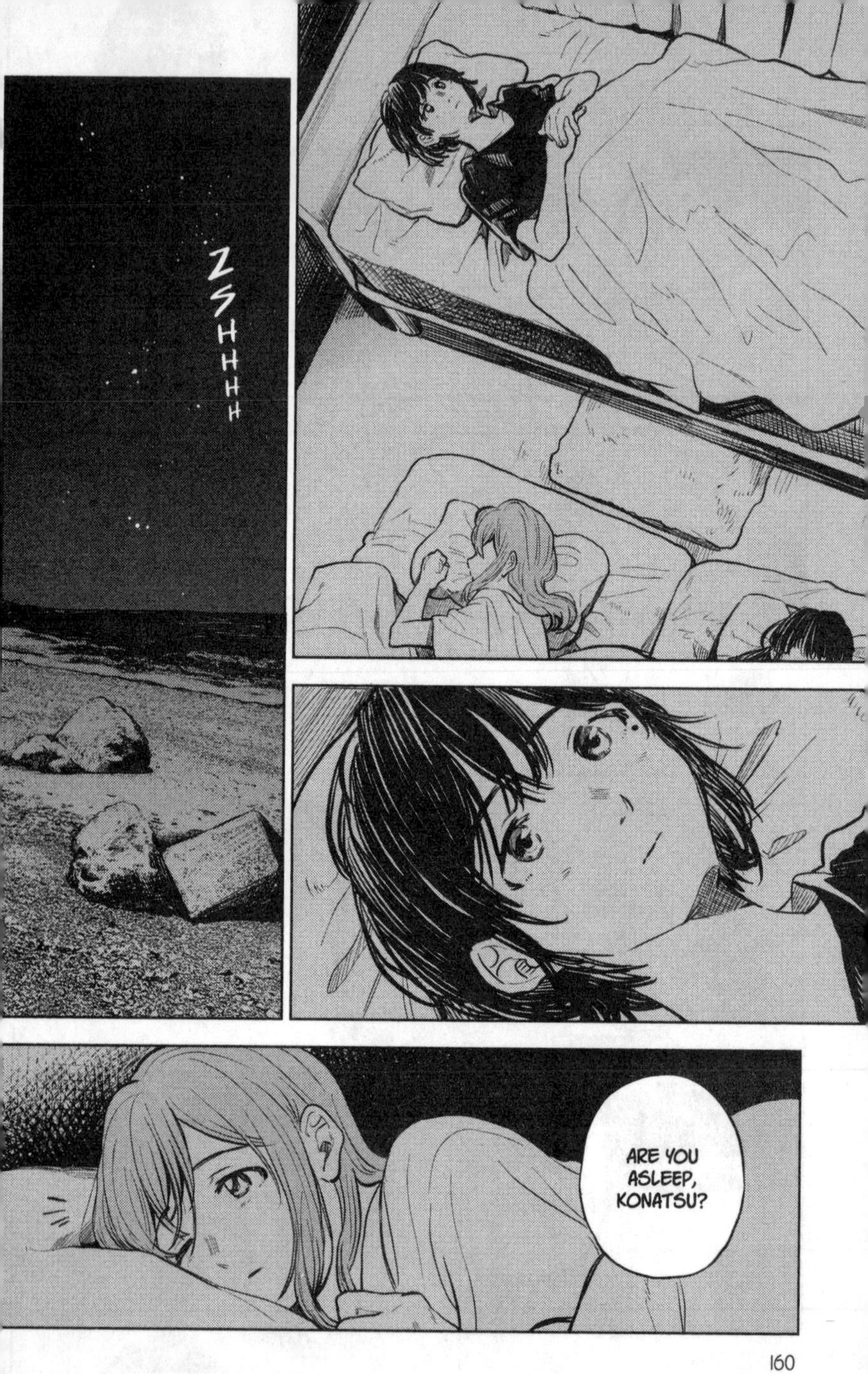
ZSHHHH
ARE YOU ASLEEP, KONATSU?

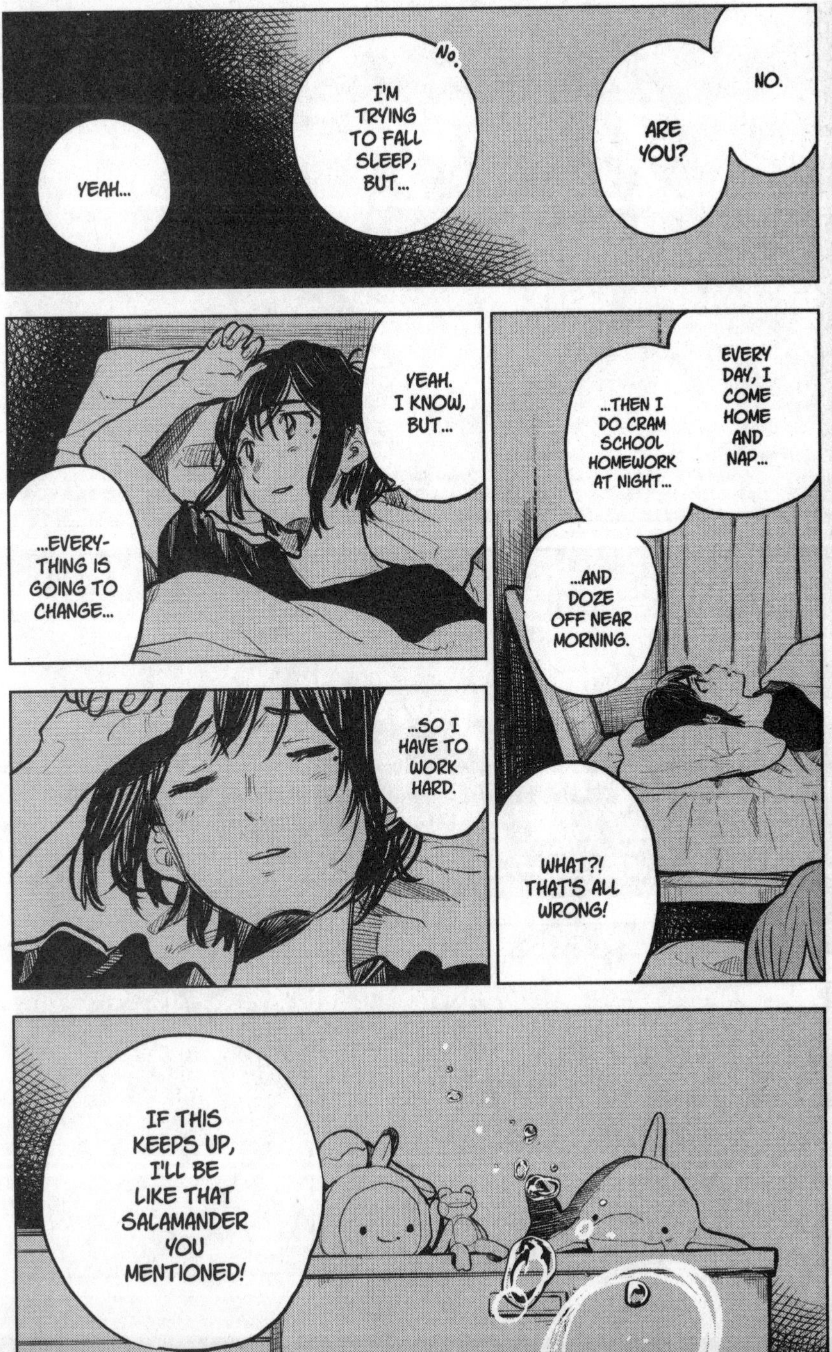
NO.
ARE YOU?
No.
I'M TRYING TO FALL SLEEP, BUT...
YEAH...
EVERY DAY, I COME HOME AND NAP...
...THEN I DO CRAM SCHOOL HOMEWORK AT NIGHT...
...AND DOZE OFF NEAR MORNING.
WHAT?! THAT'S ALL WRONG!
YEAH. I KNOW, BUT...
...EVERY-THING IS GOING TO CHANGE...
...SO I HAVE TO WORK HARD.
IF THIS KEEPS UP, I'LL BE LIKE THAT SALAMANDER YOU MENTIONED!

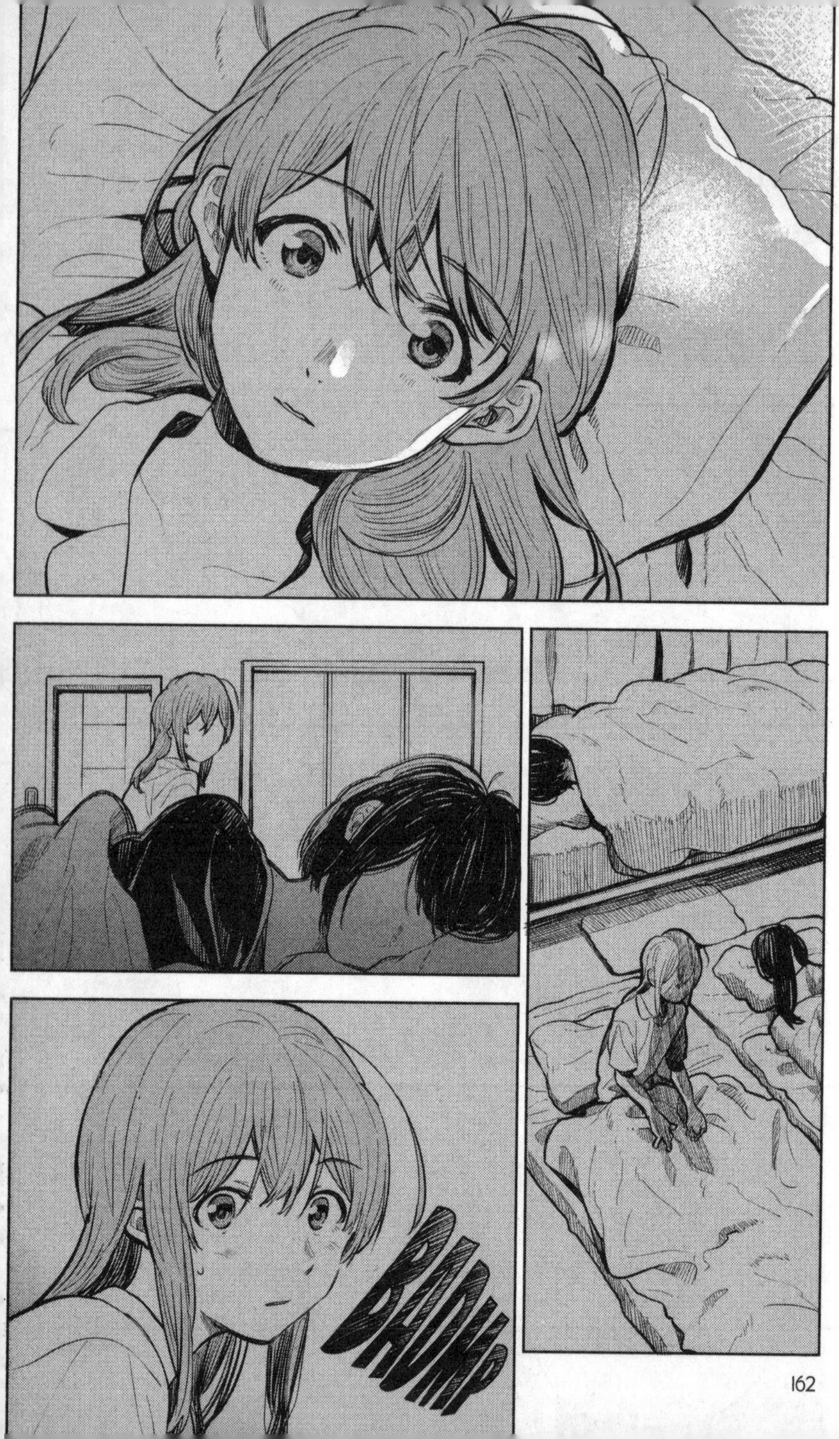
BADUMP

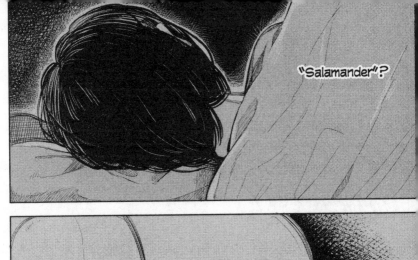

"Salamander"?

Oh right...
the
salamander!

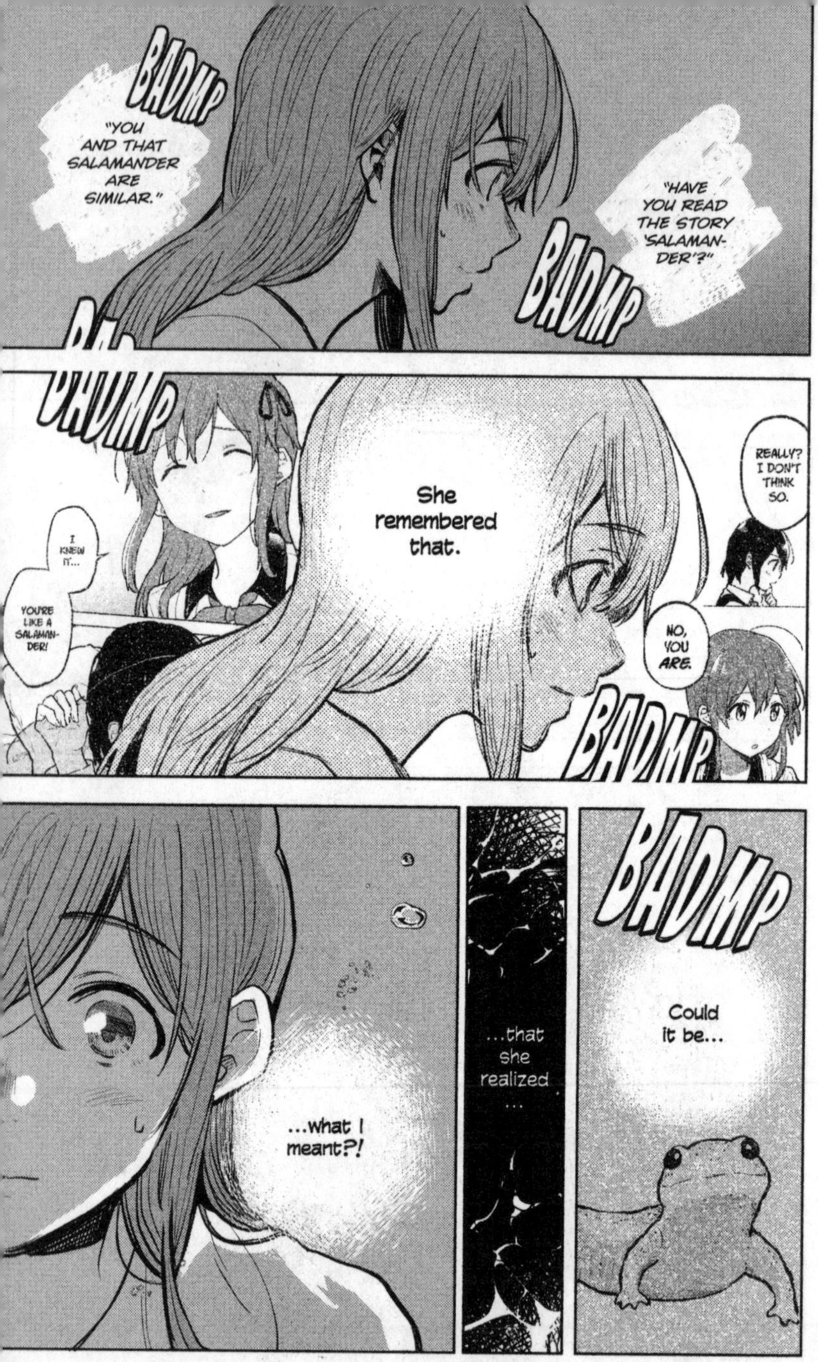
BADMP
"HAVE YOU READ THE STORY 'SALAMANDER'?"
BADMP
"YOU AND THAT SALAMANDER ARE SIMILAR."
BADMP
REALLY? I DON'T THINK SO.
NO, YOU ARE.
BADMP
She remembered that.
I KNEW IT...
YOU'RE LIKE A SALAMANDER!
BADMP
BADMP
Could it be...
...that she realized...
...what I meant?!

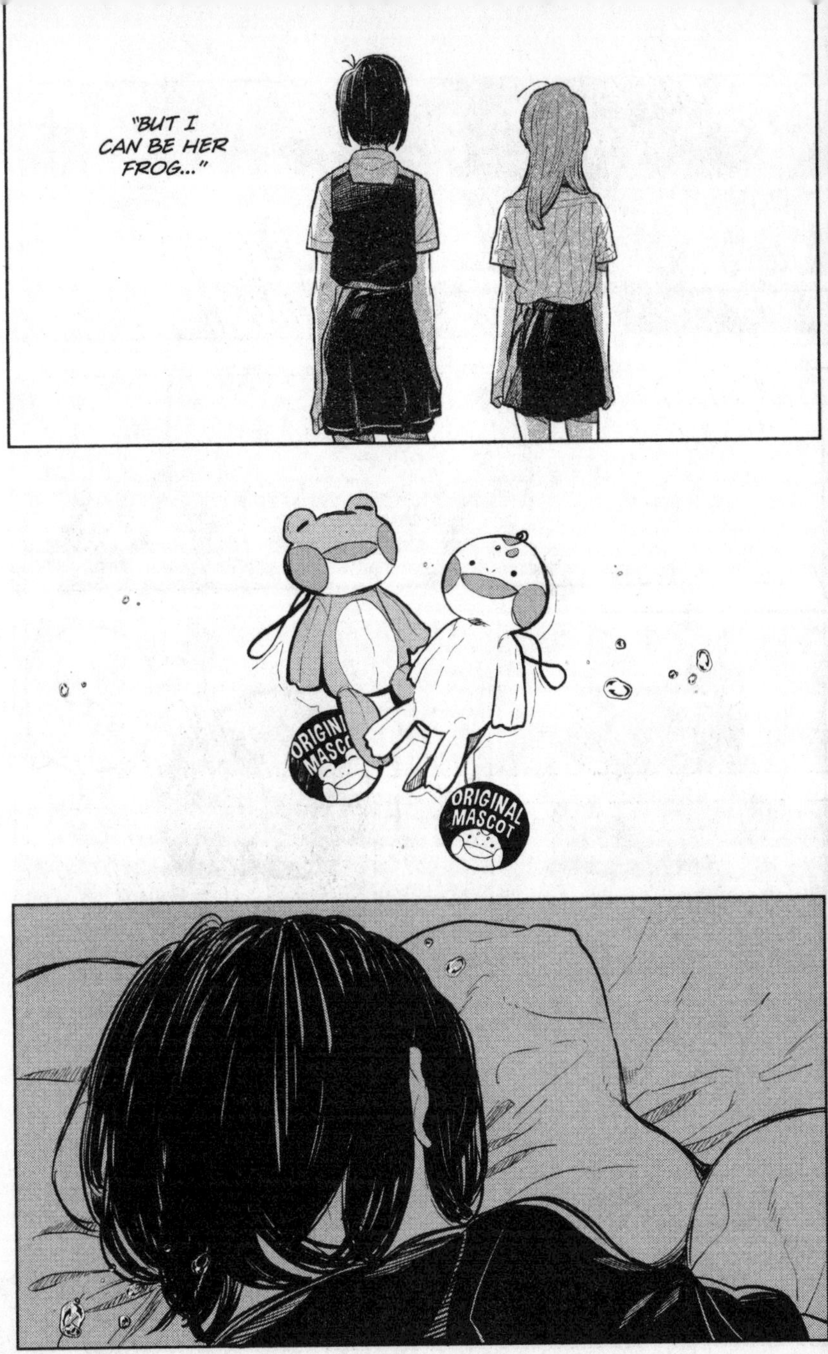
"BUT I CAN BE HER FROG..."
ORIGINAL MASCOT
ORIGINAL MASCOT

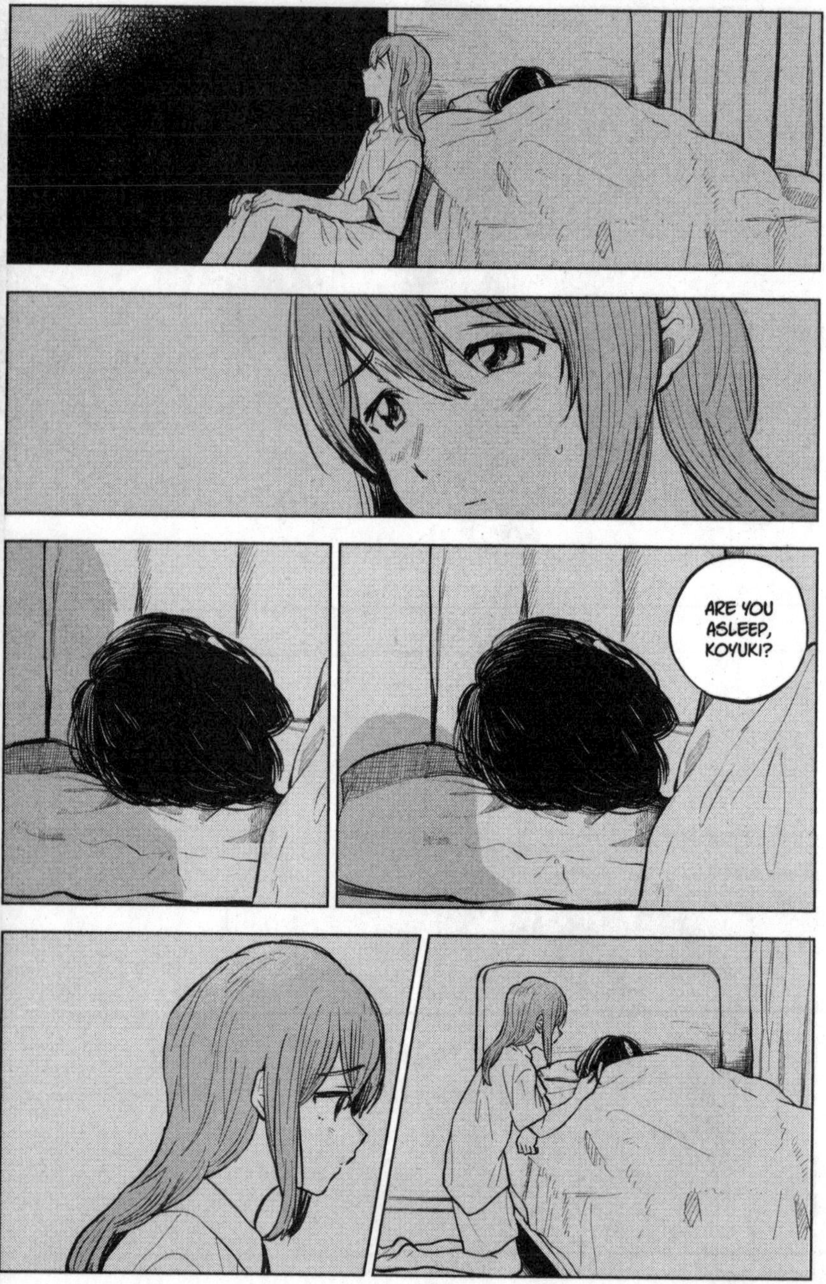
ARE YOU ASLEEP, KOYUKI?

Hey,
Koyuki?

There
are still
so many
things...

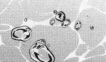

...I want
us to
talk
about.

I'm sure we will.

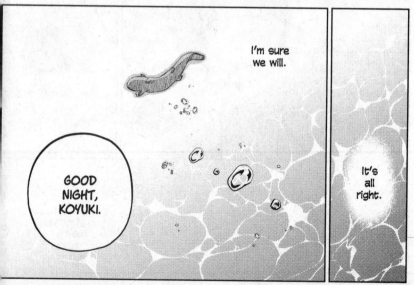

GOOD NIGHT, KOYUKI.

It's all right.

Continued in Volume 9!

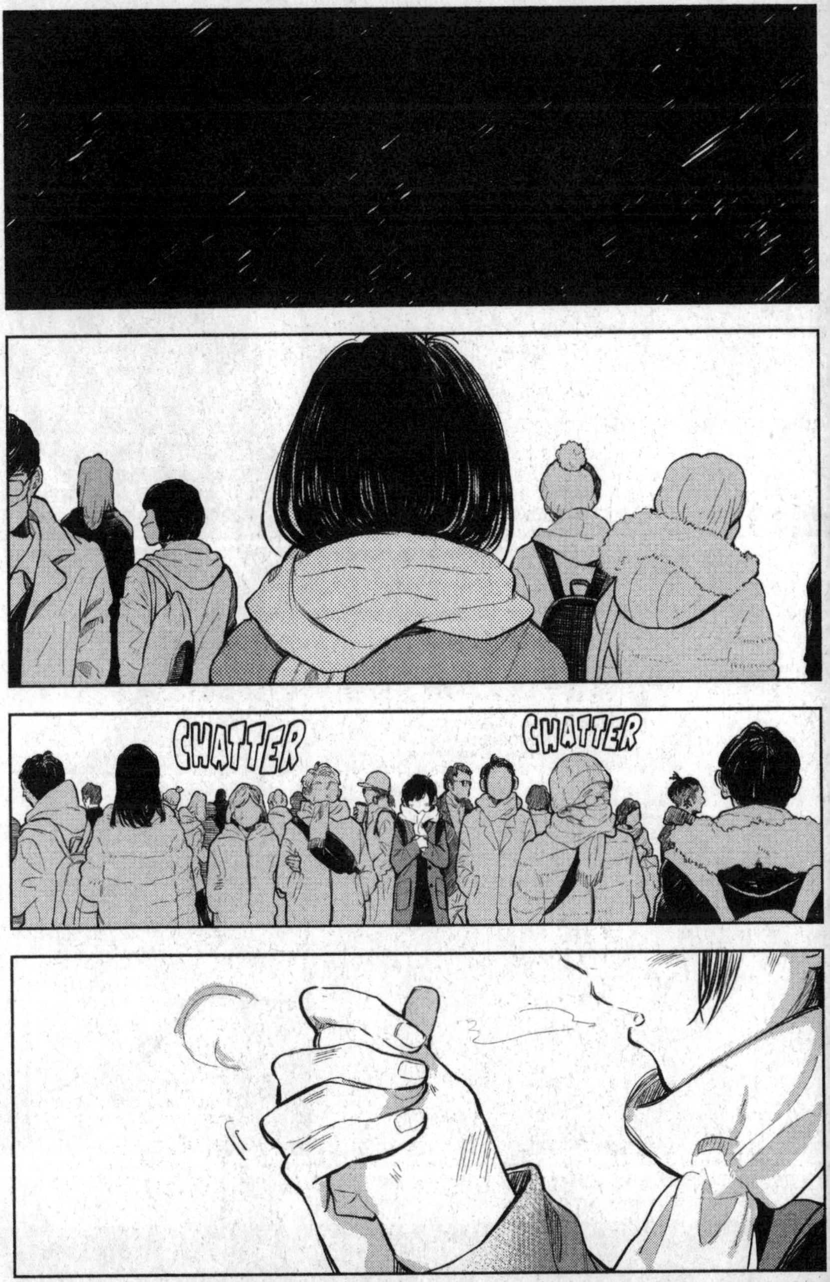
CHATTER
CHATTER

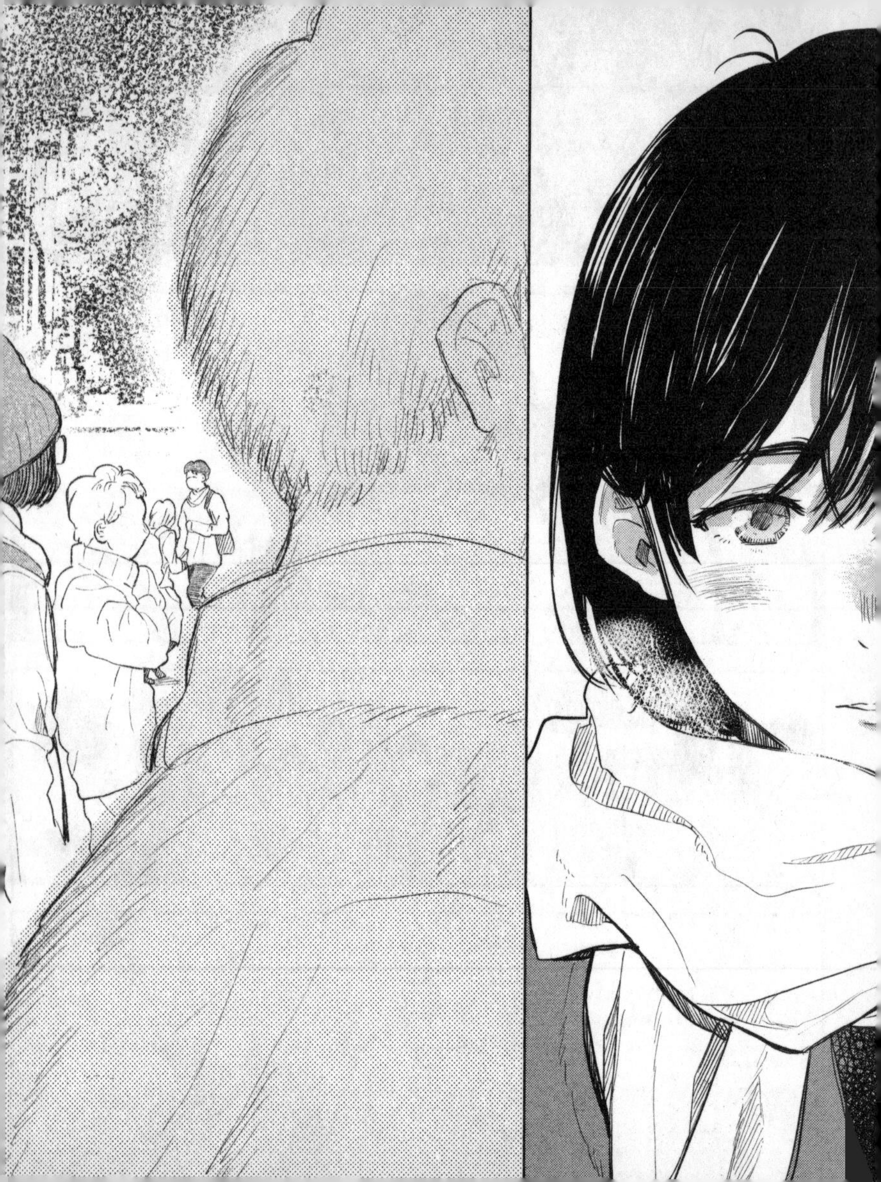

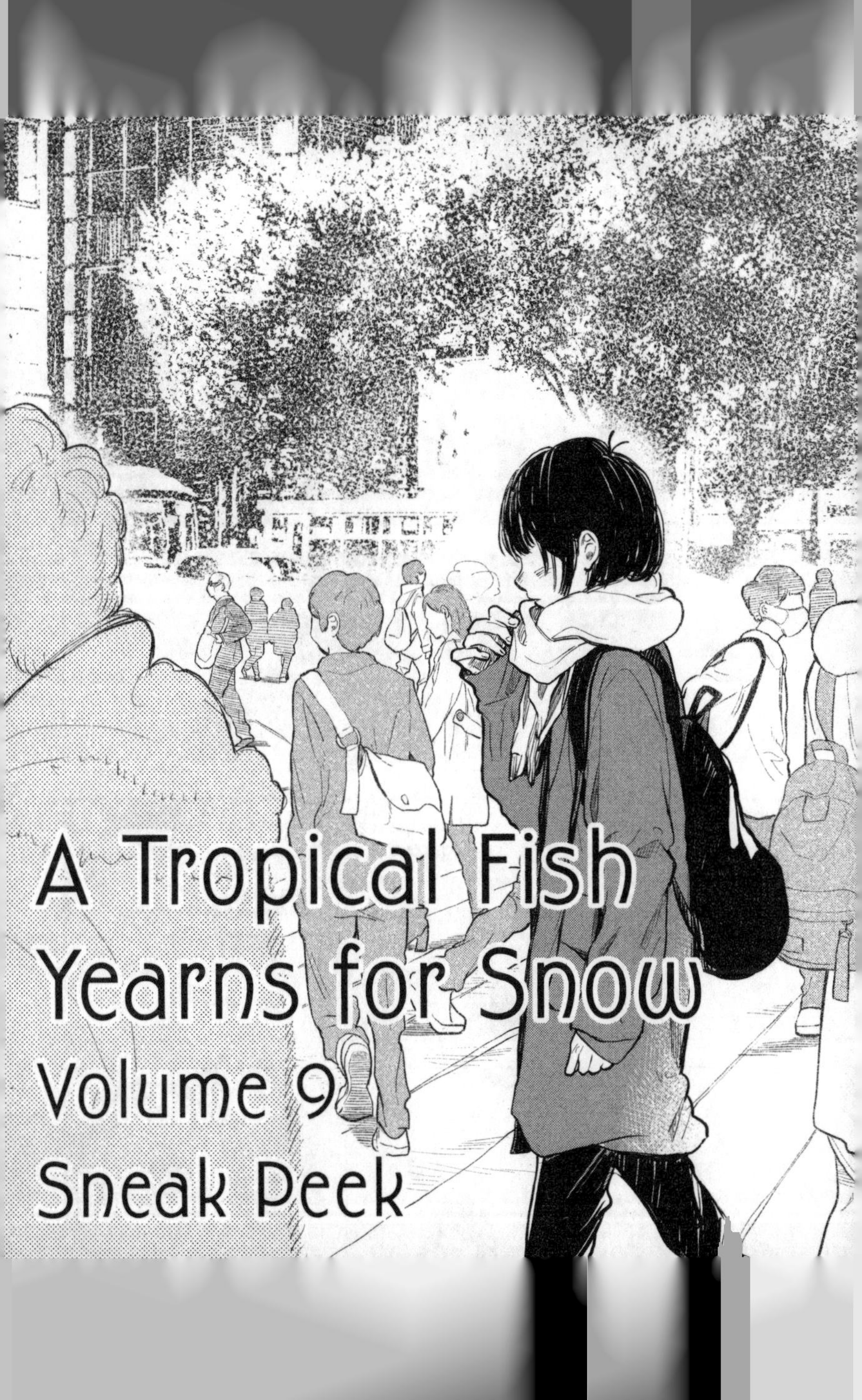
A Tropical Fish Yearns for Snow
Volume 9
Sneak Peek

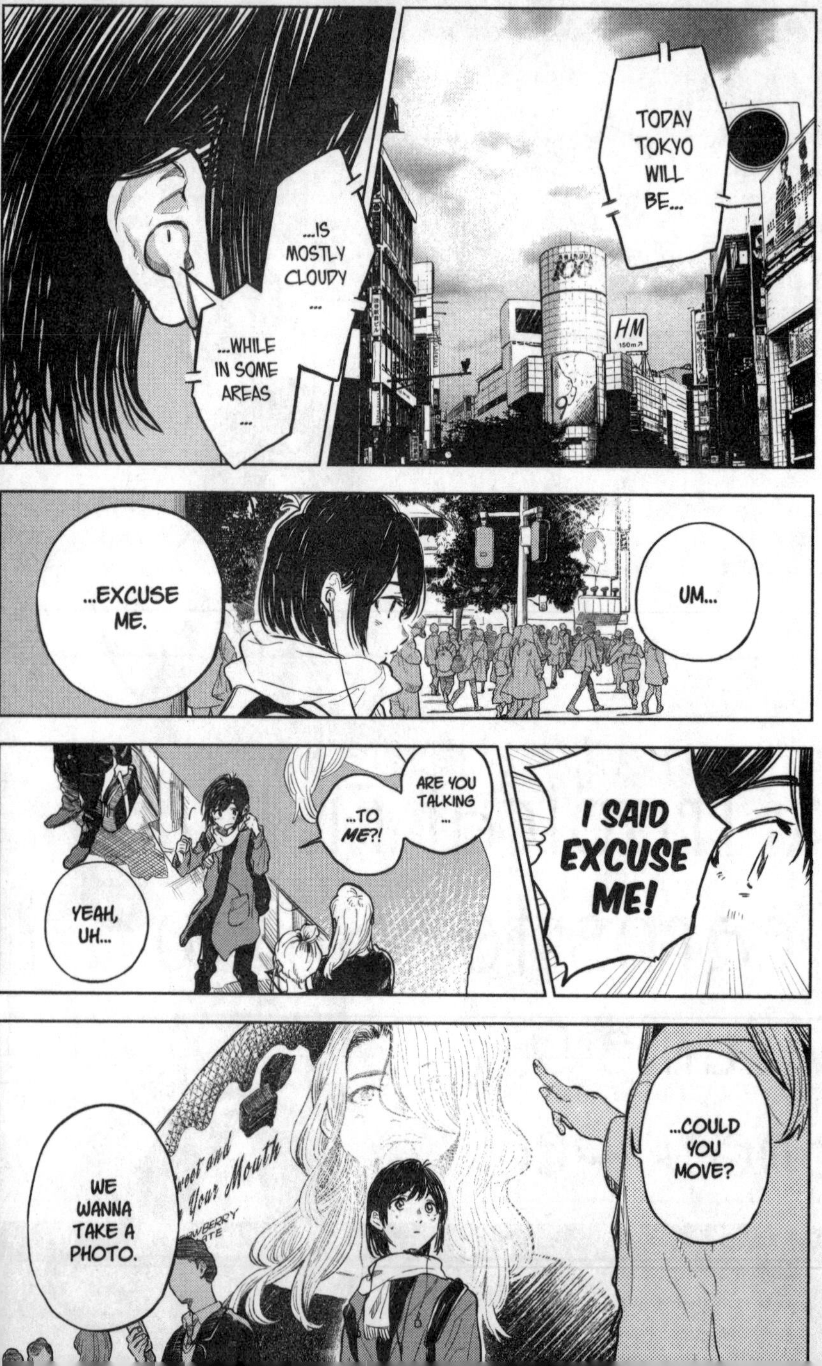
TODAY TOKYO WILL BE...
...IS MOSTLY CLOUDY ...
...WHILE IN SOME AREAS ...
UM...
...EXCUSE ME.
I SAID EXCUSE ME!
ARE YOU TALKING ...
...TO ME?!
YEAH, UH...
...COULD YOU MOVE?
WE WANNA TAKE A PHOTO.

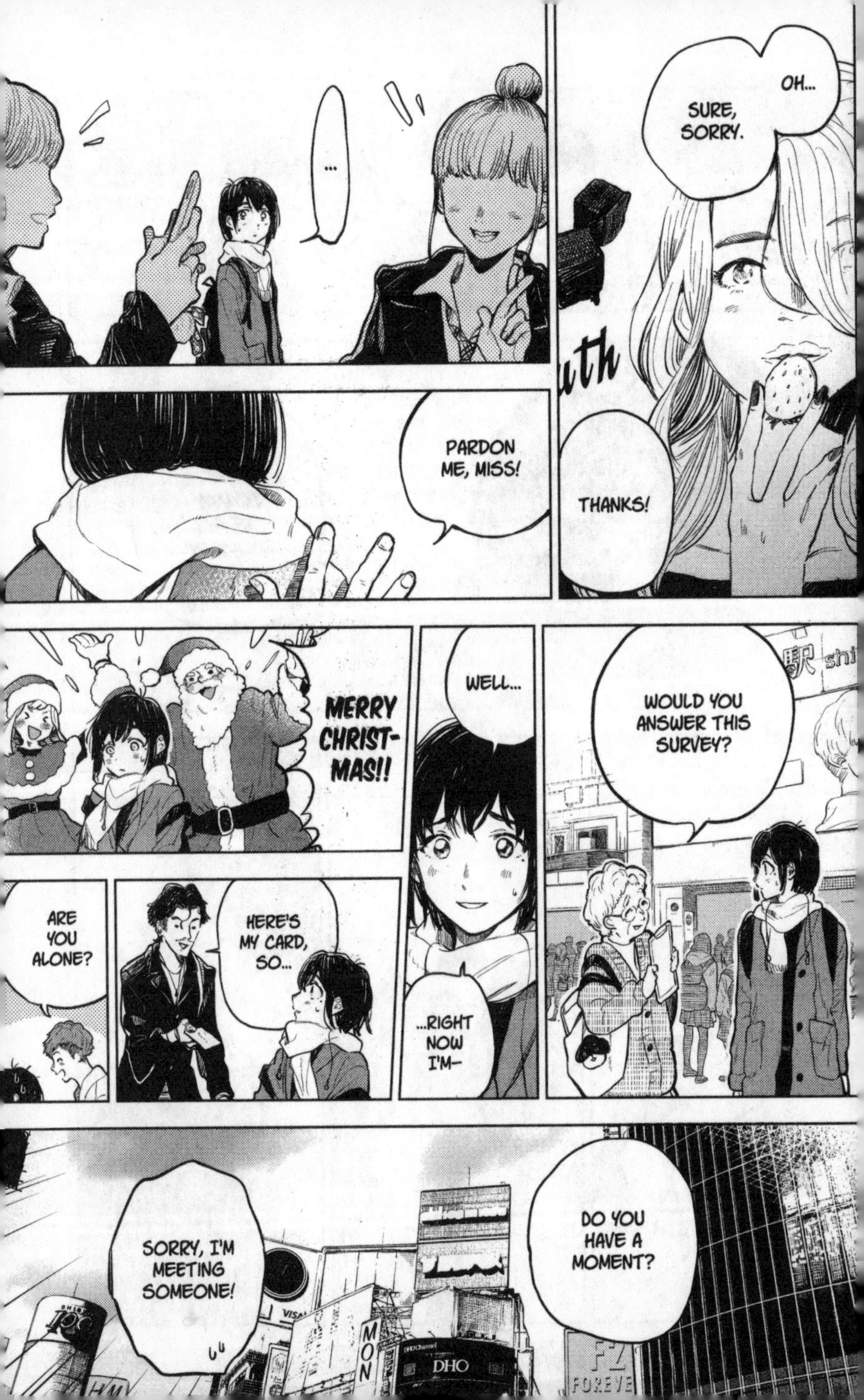
OH... SURE, SORRY.
THANKS!
...
PARDON ME, MISS!
WOULD YOU ANSWER THIS SURVEY?
WELL...
...RIGHT NOW I'M—
MERRY CHRISTMAS!!
HERE'S MY CARD, SO...
ARE YOU ALONE?
DO YOU HAVE A MOMENT?
SORRY, I'M MEETING SOMEONE!

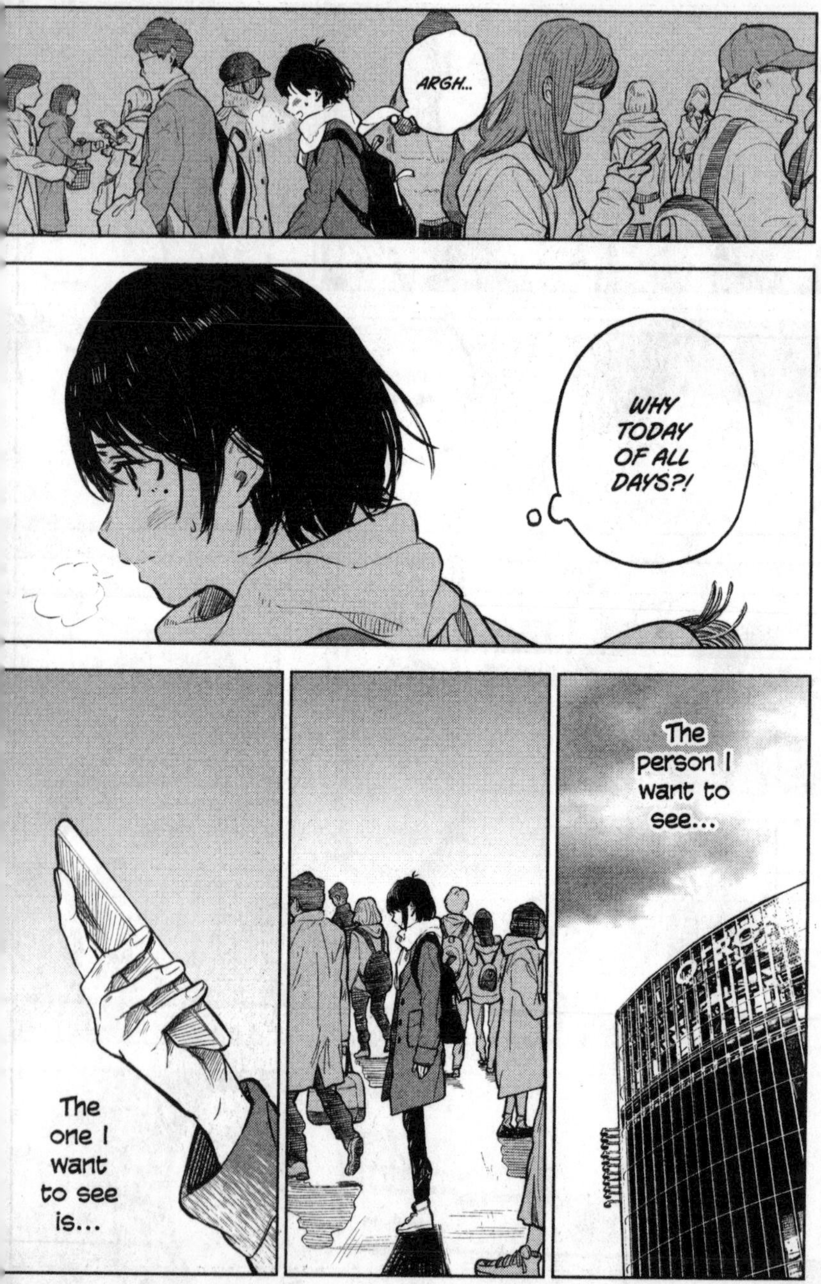
ARGH...
WHY TODAY OF ALL DAYS?!
The person I want to see...
The one I want to see is...

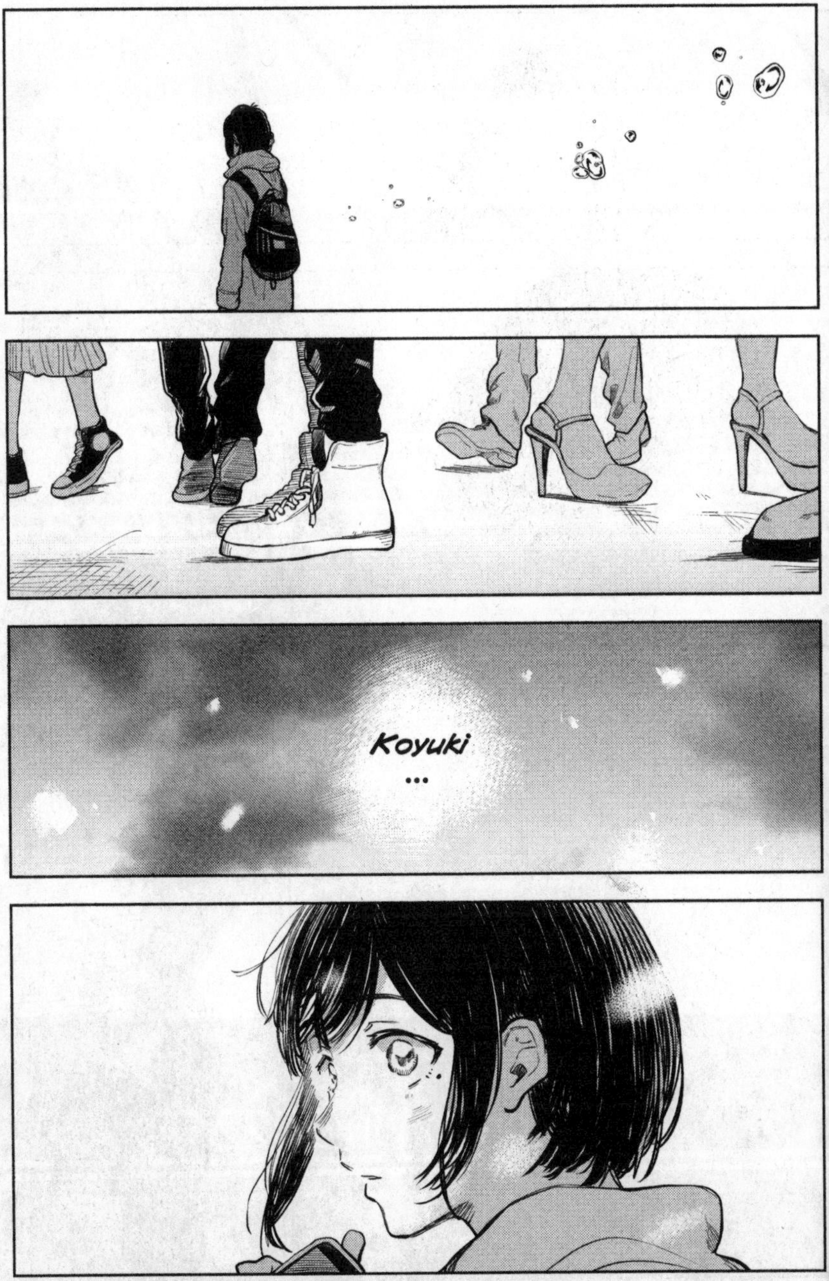
Koyuki
...

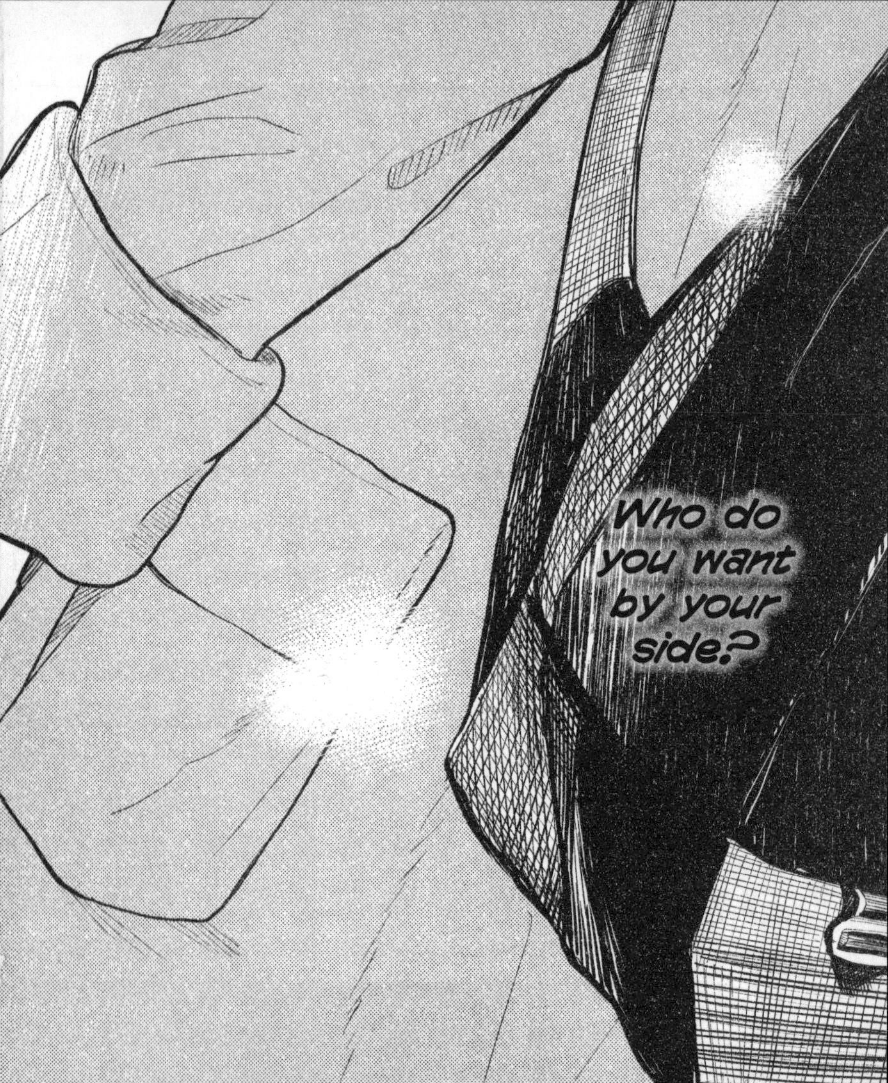
Who do you want by your side?

Coming in 2022

What do you call them?

A Tropical Fish Yearns for Snow
Final Volume

A TROPICAL FISH YEARNS FOR SNOW
Vol. 8
VIZ Media Edition

STORY AND ART BY
MAKOTO HAGINO

English Translation & Adaptation/John Werry
Touch-Up Art & Lettering/Eve Grandt
Design/Yukiko Whitley
Editor/Pancha Diaz

NETTAIGYO WA YUKI NI KOGARERU Vol. 8
©Makoto Hagino 2020
First published in Japan in 2020 by KADOKAWA CORPORATION, Tokyo.
English translation rights arranged with KADOKAWA CORPORATION, Tokyo.

Printed in Canada

Published by VIZ Media, LLC
P.O. Box 77010
San Francisco, CA 94107

10 9 8 7 6 5 4 3 2 1
First printing, December 2021

PARENTAL ADVISORY
A TROPICAL FISH YEARNS FOR SNOW is rated T
for Teen and is recommended for ages 13 and up.

viz.com

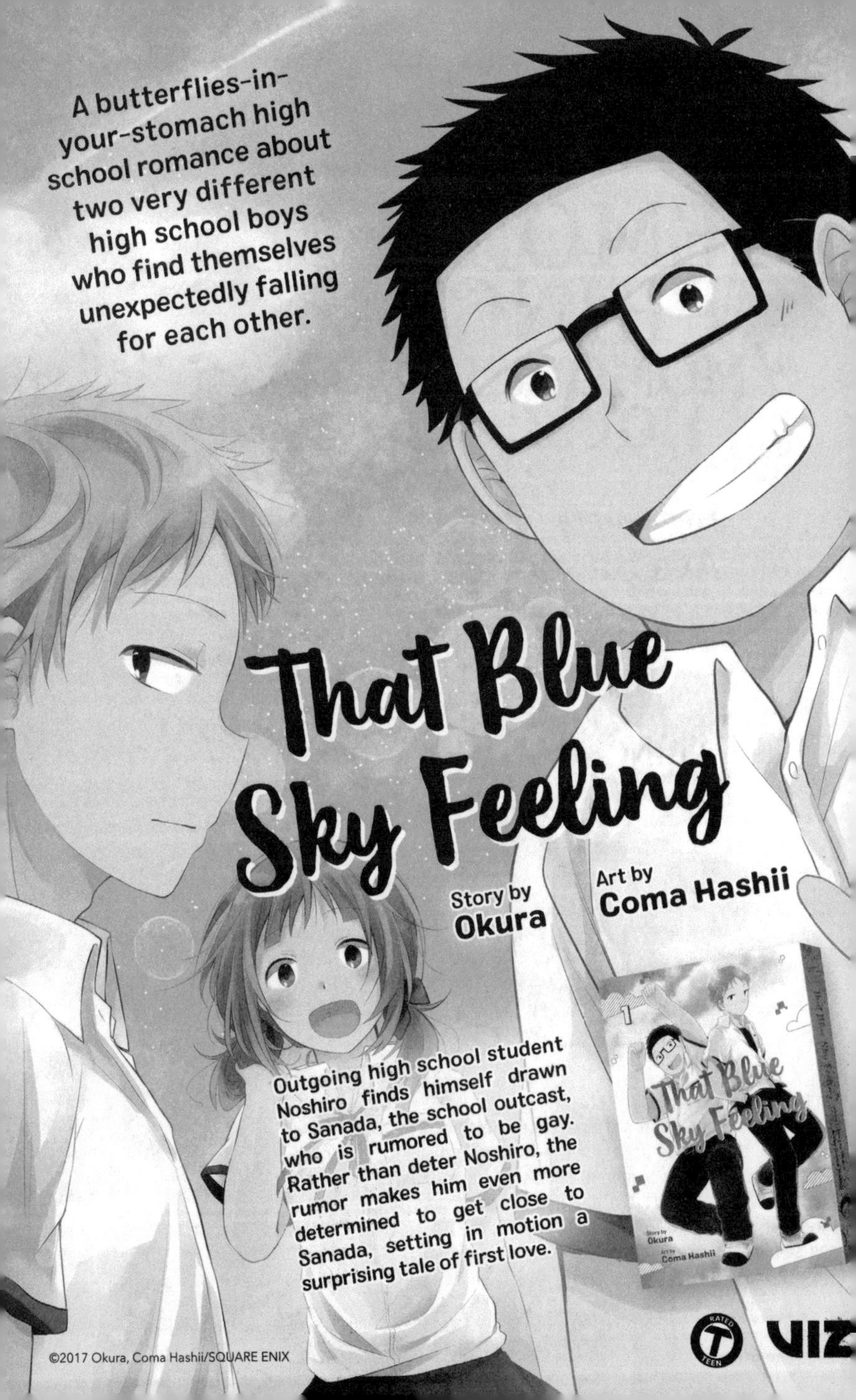
A butterflies-in-your-stomach high school romance about two very different high school boys who find themselves unexpectedly falling for each other.
That Blue Sky Feeling
Story by Okura
Art by Coma Hashii
Outgoing high school student Noshiro finds himself drawn to Sanada, the school outcast, who is rumored to be gay. Rather than deter Noshiro, the rumor makes him even more determined to get close to Sanada, setting in motion a surprising tale of first love.
That Blue Sky Feeling
1
Story by Okura
Art by Coma Hashii
RATED T TEEN
VIZ
©2017 Okura, Coma Hashii/SQUARE ENIX

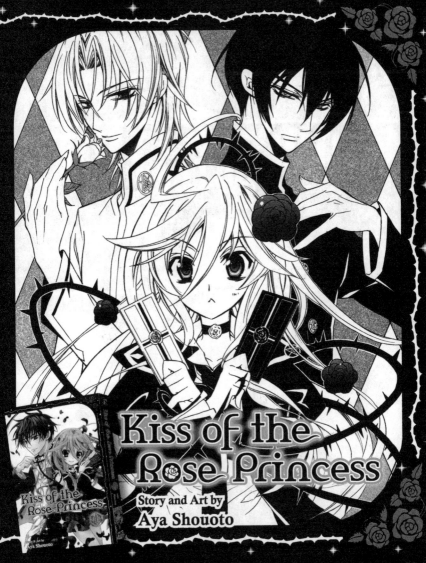

Kiss of the Rose Princess

Story and Art by Aya Shouoto

Anise Yamamoto has been told that if she ever removes the rose choker given to her by her father, a terrible punishment will befall her. Unfortunately she loses that choker when a bat-like being named Ninufa falls from the sky and hits her. Ninufa gives Anise four cards representing four knights whom she can summon with a kiss. But now that she has these gorgeous men at her beck and call, what exactly is her quest?!

"Bloody" Mary, a vampire with a death wish, has spent the past 400 years chasing down a modern-day exorcist named Maria who is thought to have inherited "The Blood of Maria" and is the only one who can kill Mary. To Mary's dismay, Maria doesn't know how to kill vampires. Desperate to die, Mary agrees to become Maria's bodyguard until Maria can find a way to kill him.

Bloody † Mary

Story and Art by
akaza samamiya

DAYTIME SHOOTING STAR

Story & Art by
Mika Yamamori

Small town girl Suzume moves to Tokyo and finds her heart caught between two men!

After arriving in Tokyo to live with her uncle, Suzume collapses in a nearby park when she remembers once seeing a shooting star during the day. A handsome stranger brings her to her new home and tells her they'll meet again. Suzume starts her first day at her new high school sitting next to a boy who blushes furious at her touch. And her homeroom teacher is no other than the handsome stranger!

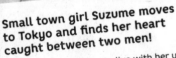

This is the last page.

A Tropical Fish Yearns for Snow **has been printed in the original Japanese format to preserve the orientation of the artwork.**

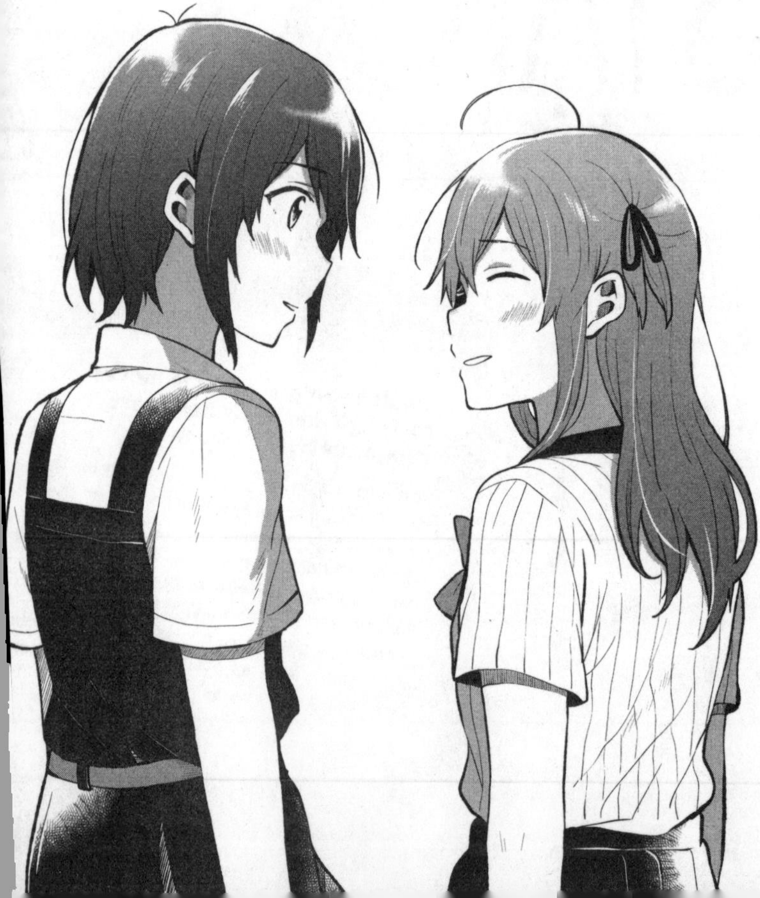